ACCA

C000157066

PAPER F9

FINANCIAL MANAGEMENT

BPP Learning Media is an **ACCA Approved Learning Partner – content** for the ACCA qualification. This means we work closely with the ACCA to ensure our products fully prepare you for your ACCA exams.

In this **ACCA examination team-reviewed** Practice and Revision Kit we:

- Discuss the **best strategies** for revising and taking your ACCA exams

- Ensure you are **well prepared** for your exam

- Provide you with **lots of great guidance** on tackling questions

- Provide you with **three** mock exams

- Provide the **ACCA examiner's answers** as well as our own for selected questions

Our **Passcard** and **i-Pass** products also support this paper.

FOR EXAMS TO JUNE 2015

BPP
LEARNING MEDIA

First edition 2007
Eighth edition April 2014

ISBN 9781 4727 1106 9
(previous ISBN 9781 4453 7999 9)

e-ISBN 9781 4727 1170 0

British Library Cataloguing-in-Publication Data
A catalogue record for this book
is available from the British Library

Published by

BPP Learning Media Ltd
BPP House, Aldine Place
London W12 8AA

www.bpp.com/learningmedia

Printed in the United Kingdom by

Polestar Wheatons
Hennock Road
Marsh Barton
Exeter
EX2 8RP

We are grateful to the Association of Chartered Certified
Accountants for permission to reproduce past
examination questions. The suggested solutions in the
practice answer bank have been prepared by BPP
Learning Media Ltd, except where otherwise stated.

Contents

Page

Finding questions
Question index v
Topic index ix

Helping you with your revision xi

Revising F9
Topics to revise xii
Question practice xii
Passing the F9 exam xiii
Exam formulae xvi
Exam information xix
Useful websites xx

Questions and answers
Questions 3
Answers 77

Exam practice

Mock exam 1
- Questions 221
- Plan of attack 231
- Answers 232

Mock exam 2
- Questions 249
- Plan of attack 259
- Answers 260

Mock exam 3 (Specimen paper)
- Questions 273
- Plan of attack 283
- Answers 284

ACCA examiner's answers
- Specimen paper 299

Mathematical tables and formulae 309

Review Form

A note about copyright

Dear Customer

What does the little © mean and why does it matter?

Your market-leading BPP books, course materials and e-learning materials do not write and update themselves. People write them: on their own behalf or as employees of an organisation that invests in this activity. Copyright law protects their livelihoods. It does so by creating rights over the use of the content.

Breach of copyright is a form of theft – as well as being a criminal offence in some jurisdictions, it is potentially a serious breach of professional ethics.

With current technology, things might seem a bit hazy but, basically, without the express permission of BPP Learning Media:

- Photocopying our materials is a breach of copyright

- Scanning, ripcasting or conversion of our digital materials into different file formats, uploading them to Facebook or emailing them to your friends is a breach of copyright

You can, of course, sell your books, in the form in which you have bought them – once you have finished with them. (Is this fair to your fellow students? We update for a reason.) Please note the e-products are sold on a single user licence basis: we do not supply 'unlock' codes to people who have bought them second-hand.

And what about outside the UK? BPP Learning Media strives to make our materials available at prices students can afford by local printing arrangements, pricing policies and partnerships which are clearly listed on our website. A tiny minority ignore this and indulge in criminal activity by illegally photocopying our material or supporting organisations that do. If they act illegally and unethically in one area, can you really trust them?

Question index

The headings in this checklist/index indicate the main topics of questions, but questions often cover several different topics.

The exam format is changing for the December 2014 paper. The format of old questions has been modified to reflect the new exam structure.

		Marks	Time allocation Mins	Page number Question	Answer
Part A: Financial management function					
1	MCQ bank – Financial management and financial objectives	20	36	3	77
2	MCQ bank – Financial management and financial objectives	10	18	5	78
3	ABC Co	10	18	6	78
4	Bark Co (12/11, amended)	10	18	6	79
Part B: Financial management environment					
5	MCQ bank – Financial management environment	10	18	7	80
6	MCQ bank – Financial management environment	10	18	8	81
7	MCQ bank – Financial management environment	10	18	9	82
8	Tagna (FMC, 6/03, amended)	10	18	10	82
9	Phoenix	10	18	10	83
Part C: Working capital management					
10	MCQ bank – Working capital	10	18	11	84
11	MCQ bank – Managing working capital	20	36	12	85
12	MCQ bank – Working capital finance	10	18	13	86
13	JIT	15	27	14	88
14	EOQ	10	18	15	89
15	Thorne Co (FMC, 12/05, amended)	15	27	15	90
16	Anjo Co	10	18	16	91
17	Joan Co	15	27	17	93
18	Special Gift Suppliers (FMC, 12/01, amended)	15	27	17	94
19	Ulnad Co (Specimen paper 2007, amended)	10	18	17	95
20	Danul Co (Specimen paper 2007, amended)	10	18	18	97
21	PKA Co (12/07, amended)	10	18	18	99
22	HGR Co (6/09, amended)	15	27	18	100
23	RGH Co (6/09, amended)	10	18	19	103
24	APX Co (12/09, amended)	15	27	19	104
25	ZSE Co (6/10, amended)	15	27	20	106
26	WQZ Co (12/10, amended)	15	27	21	108

	Marks	Time allocation Mins	Page number Question	Answer
27 Bold Co (12/11, amended)	10	18	21	109
28 Wobnig Co (6/12, amended)	15	27	22	110
29 ZPS Co (6/11, amended)	15	27	23	112
30 KXP Co (12/12, amended)	10	18	23	114
31 PXK Co (12/12, amended)	10	18	24	116
32 Gorwa (2) Co (12/08, amended)	10	18	24	117

Part D: Investment appraisal

	Marks	Time allocation Mins	Page number Question	Answer
33 MCQ bank – Investment decisions	20	36	25	119
34 MCQ bank – Investment appraisal using DCF	20	36	27	120
35 MCQ bank – Allowing for tax and inflation	20	36	29	122
36 MCQ bank – Project appraisal and risk	10	18	31	124
37 MCQ bank – Specific investment decisions	20	36	32	125
38 Calvic Co	15	27	34	127
39 Trecor Co (Specimen paper 2007, amended)	15	27	34	128
40 Corter Co (Specimen paper 2007, amended)	10	18	35	130
41 OKM Co (6/10, amended)	15	27	35	131
42 CJ Co (12/10, amended)	10	18	36	133
43 BRT Co (6/11, amended)	15	27	36	134
44 Umunat Co (FMC, 12/04, amended)	10	18	37	136
45 Tanumu Co (FMC, 12/04, amended)	15	27	37	137
46 Duo Co (12/07, amended)	15	27	38	139
47 SC Co (6/08, amended)	15	27	38	141
48 PV Co (6/09, amended)	15	27	39	143
49 AGD Co (FMC, 12/05, amended)	15	27	39	145
50 Leaminger Co (FMC, 12/02, amended)	15	27	40	147
51 ASOP Co (12/09, amended)	15	27	41	149
52 Capital rationing	10	18	41	151
53 Filtrex Co	15	27	42	152
54 Warden Co (12/11, amended)	15	27	42	154
55 Ridag Co (6/12, amended)	10	18	43	155
56 Gadir Co (6/12, amended)	15	27	43	157
57 BQK Co (12/12, amended)	15	27	44	158

		Marks	Time allocation Mins	Page number Question	Answer
Part E: Business finance					
58	MCQ bank – Sources of finance	10	18	45	160
59	MCQ bank – Dividend policy	10	18	46	160
60	MCQ bank – Gearing and capital structure	10	18	47	161
61	MCQ bank – The cost of capital	20	36	48	162
62	MCQ bank – Capital structure	20	36	50	164
63	Tirwen Co (FMC, 12/04, amended)	15	27	51	165
64	Food retailers 1	15	27	52	167
65	Food retailers 2	10	18	52	168
66	TFR Co (FMC, 6/07, amended)	15	27	52	169
67	Echo Co (12/07, amended)	10	18	53	171
68	Echo Beach Co (12/07, amended)	15	27	54	173
69	Nugfer Co (12/10, amended)	15	27	55	175
70	Nug Co (12/10, amended)	10	18	55	177
71	YNM Co (6/11, amended)	10	18	56	178
72	Bar Co (12/11, amended)	10	18	57	180
73	IML Co	15	27	57	181
74	Li Co	10	18	58	182
75	FAQ	15	27	58	184
76	Droxfol Co (Specimen paper 2007, amended)	15	27	59	185
77	Burse Co (6/08, amended)	10	18	60	188
78	Purse Co (6/08, amended)	15	27	60	190
79	DD Co (12/09, amended)	15	27	60	191
80	YGV Co (6/10, amended)	15	27	61	193
81	NN Co (12/10, amended)	10	18	62	195
82	NNN Co (12/10, amended)	10	18	62	196
83	AQR Co (6/11, amended)	15	27	63	197
84	Corhig Co (6/12, amended)	15	27	63	199
85	BKB Co (12/12, amended)	15	27	64	201
86	Zigto Co (6/12, amended)	10	18	65	203

BPP
LEARNING MEDIA

		Marks	Time allocation Mins	Page number Question	Page number Answer

Part F: Business valuations

		Marks	Time allocation Mins	Question	Answer
87	MCQ bank – Business valuations	20	36	66	204
88	MCQ bank – Market efficiency	10	18	68	205
89	Phobis Co (12/07, amended)	10	18	68	206
90	Close Co (12/11, amended)	10	18	68	207
91	Boluje Co (12/08, amended)	10	18	69	209

Part G: Risk management

		Marks	Time allocation Mins	Question	Answer
92	MCQ bank – Foreign currency risk	20	36	70	210
93	MCQ bank – Interest rate risk	10	18	71	211
94	ZPS Co (6/11, amended)	10	18	72	212
95	Gorwa Co (12/08, amended)	10	18	73	213
96	Ziggazigto Co (6/12, amended)	10	18	74	215

Mock exam 1

Mock exam 2

Mock exam 3 (Specimen paper)

Topic index

Listed below are the key Paper F9 syllabus topics and the numbers of the questions in this Kit covering those topics.

If you need to concentrate your practice and revision on certain topics or if you want to attempt all available questions that refer to a particular subject, you will find this index useful.

Syllabus topic	Question numbers
Asset replacement decisions	38, 56
Betas	73, 75
Business valuation	90, 91. Mock 2 Q5, Mock 3 Q2
Capital rationing	38, 50, 52, 53
CAPM	73, 75, 78, 84
Cash management	15, 19, 22, 28, 31, 52
Cash operating cycle	16, 27, Mock 1 Q1
Dividend policy	65, 67, 71, 79, 81, Mock 3 Q5
Exchange rate risk	94, 96, Mock 1 Q2, Mock 3 Q3
Financial intermediaries	9
Gearing	67, 69, 80
Interest rates	8, 70, 95, Mock 2 Q3
Inventory management	13, 14, 21, Mock 2 Q1
IRR	40, 46, 47, 48, Mock 3 Q4
Islamic finance	Mock 2 Q3
Leasing	49, 50, 51, 68, Mock 2 Q2
NPV	38, 41, 42, 43, 46, 47, 48, 51, 54, 55, 56, Mock 1 Q4, Mock 2 Q4
Objectives	4, 8
Overtrading	28, 32, 69
Payables management	29, 30, Mock 3 Q1
Payback	44, 48
Pecking order	91
Project-specific discount rate	75
Ratio analysis	3, 16, 28, 32, 63, 64, 66, 71, 80
Receivables management	17, 18, 19, 20, 26, 30, 31, Mock 1 Q1
Rights issue	63, 68, 72, Mock 1 Q3
Risk and uncertainty	23, 25, 44, 45
Sensitivity analysis	45, 54, 56
Shareholder wealth maximisation	48, 71
Sources of finance	65, 66, 68, 69, 86, Mock 2 Q2
Stock market efficiency	70, 89
Total shareholder return	3
Value for money	4, 8

Syllabus topic	Question numbers
WACC	74, 76, 77, 78, 80, 82, 83, 84, 85, Mock 1 Q5, Mock 2 Q5, Mock 3 Q5
Working capital financing	18, 20, 22, 24
Working capital management	17, 21, 25, 26, 27, 29, Mock 1 Q1, Mock 2 Q1, Mock 3 Q1

Helping you with your revision

As ACCA's **Approved Learning Partner – content**, BPP Learning Media gives you the **opportunity** to use **exam team reviewed** revision materials. By incorporating the examiner's comments and suggestions regarding syllabus coverage, the BPP Learning Media Practice and Revision Kit provides excellent, **ACCA-approved** support for your revision.

Tackling revision and the exam

Using feedback obtained from the ACCA exam team review:

* We look at the dos and don'ts of revising for, and taking, ACCA exams
* We focus on Paper F9; we discuss revising the syllabus, what to do (and what not to do) in the exam, how to approach different types of question and ways of obtaining easy marks

Selecting questions

We provide signposts to help you plan your revision.

* A full **question index**
* A **topic index** listing all the questions that cover key topics, so that you can locate the questions that provide practice on these topics, and see the different ways in which they might be examined

Making the most of question practice

At BPP Learning Media we realise that you need more than just questions and model answers to get the most from your question practice.

* Our **top tips** included for certain questions provide essential advice on tackling questions, presenting answers and the key points that answers need to include.
* We show you how you can pick up **easy marks** on some questions, as we know that picking up all readily available marks often can make the difference between passing and failing.
* We include **marking guides** to show you what the examiner rewards.
* We include **comments from the examiners** to show you where students struggled or performed well in the actual exam.
* We refer to the **2014 BPP Study Text** (for exams up to June 2015) for detailed coverage of the topics covered in questions.
* In a bank at the end of this Kit we include the **official ACCA answers** to the Specimen paper. Used in conjunction with our answers they provide an indication of all possible points that could be made, issues that could be covered and approaches to adopt.

Attempting mock exams

There are three mock exams that provide practice at coping with the pressures of the exam day. We strongly recommend that you attempt them under exam conditions. **Mock exams 1 and 2** reflect the question styles and syllabus coverage of the exam; **Mock exam 3** is the Specimen paper.

Revising F9

The exam consists of 20 multiple choice questions and 5 longer form questions, all of which are compulsory. No one section in the syllabus is more important than another so there are no short-cuts. You will have to be able to answer questions on the entire syllabus.

Question practice

You need to practise exam standard and exam style questions on a regular basis.

As you get closer to the exam, try to do complete questions to time so that you are able to work at an appropriate speed.

Make sure you practise written sections as well as the calculations.

Passing the F9 exam

Displaying the right qualities

The aim of Paper F9 is to develop the knowledge and skills expected of a finance manager in relation to investment, financing and dividend decisions.

You need to be able to communicate your understanding clearly in an exam context. Calculations and discussions are equally important so do not concentrate on the numbers and ignore the written parts.

You need to be able to:

- Discuss the role and purpose of the financial management function
- Assess and discuss the impact of the economic environment on financial management
- Discuss and apply working capital management techniques
- Carry out effective investment appraisal
- Identify and evaluate alternative sources of business finance
- Explain and calculate cost of capital and the factors that affect it
- Explain and apply risk management techniques in business

Avoiding weaknesses

- There is no choice in this paper, all questions have to be answered. You must therefore study the entire syllabus, there are no short-cuts.

- Ability to answer multiple choice questions improves with practice. Try to get as much practice with these questions as you can.

- The longer questions will be based on simple scenarios and answers must be focused and specific to the organisation.

- Answer plans for the longer questions will help you to focus on the requirements of the question and enable you to manage your time effectively – but there will not be much time.

- Answer all parts of the longer questions. Even if you cannot do all the calculation elements, you will still be able to gain marks in the discussion parts.

Using the reading time

You will have 15 minutes reading time for Paper F9. Here are some helpful tips on how best to utilise this time.

- Speed read through Section B on the question paper, jotting down any ideas that come to you about any of the questions.

- Decide the order which you're likely to tackle the questions (probably easiest questions first, most difficult questions last).

- Spend the remainder of the reading time starting on the multiple choice questions, noting answers down on your question booklet. They can be transferred to your answer booklet after time has finished.

- When you are allowed to start writing, transfer your multiple choice answers to your answer booklet and complete the remainder of Section A.

Choosing which questions to answer first

You can use the planning time in the exam to choose the order in which to attempt the questions for Section B. You may prefer to attempt the questions that you are more confident about first. However, make sure you watch the time carefully and do not spend too long on any one question.

Alternatively, you could answer the questions in strict order. This will force you to spend an equal time on each question but make sure you leave plenty of space if you decide to move on and finish a question later.

Tackling questions

With the multiple choice questions in Section A, there are several techniques that may help you, for example:

- A process of elimination – discount obviously incorrect answers to narrow down your options.

- Working with the options – sometimes it's quicker to test out the options given to see which one works, rather than working out the correct answer from first principles. For example, rather than calculating the Internal Rate of Return, you could discount the cash flows in the question at the rates given to you in the alternative answers and see which gives you a zero net present value. The one that does is the/an internal rate of return.

For Section B questions:

- Write a short plan for each question containing bullet points per mark and **use** it to write your answer when the writing time begins.

- If you get stuck, make an assumption, write it down and **move on**.

- Make sure your answers are **focused** and **specific** to the organisation in the question. Show clear workings for your calculations and write full sentences in your explanations.

- Never overrun on any question and once the time is up (1.8 minutes per mark), move on to the next.

Gaining the easy marks

Easy marks in this paper tend to fall into three categories.

Multiple choice questions

Some MCQs are easier than others. Answer those that you feel fairly confident about as quickly as you can. Come back later to those you find more difficult. This could be a way of making use of the time in the examination most efficiently and effectively.

Many MCQs will not involve calculations. Make sure that you understand the wording of 'written' MCQs before selecting your answer.

Calculations in Section B questions

The calculations within a question will get progressively harder and easy marks will be available in the easy stages. Set our your calculations clearly and show all your workings in a clear format. Use a proforma, for example in complex NPV questions and slot the simpler figures into the proforma straight away before you concentrate on the figures that need a lot of adjustment.

Discussions in Section B questions

A Section B question may separate discussion requirements from calculations, so that you do not need to do the calculations first in order to answer the discussion part. This means that you should be able to gain marks from making sensible, practical comments without having to complete the calculations.

Discussions that are focused on the specific organisation in the question will gain more marks than regurgitation of knowledge. Read the question carefully and more than once, to ensure you are actually answering the specific requirements.

Pick out key words such as 'describe', 'evaluate' and 'discuss'. These all mean something specific.

- 'Describe' means to communicate the key features of
- 'Evaluate' means to assess the value of
- 'Discuss' means to examine in detail by argument

Clearly label the points you make in discussions so that the marker can identify them all rather than getting lost in the detail.

Provide answers in the form requested. Use a report format if asked for and give recommendations if required.

Exam formulae

Set out below are the formulae which you will be given in the exam, and formulae which you should learn. If you are not sure what the symbols mean, or how the formulae are used, you should refer to the appropriate chapter in this Study Text

Exam formulae	Chapter in Study Text

Economic Order Quantity — 5

$$= \sqrt{\frac{2C_0D}{C_h}}$$

Miller-Orr Model — 6

Return point = Lower limit + (1/3 × spread)

$$\text{Spread} = 3 \left[\frac{\frac{3}{4} \times \text{transaction cost} \times \text{variance of cash flows}}{\text{interest rate}} \right]^{\frac{1}{3}}$$

The Capital Asset Pricing Model — 15

$$E(r_i) = R_f + \beta_i (E(r_m) - R_f)$$

The Asset Beta Formula — 16

$$\beta_a = \left[\frac{V_e}{(V_e + V_d(1-T))} \beta_e \right] + \left[\frac{V_d(1-T)}{(V_e + V_d(1-T))} \beta_d \right]$$

The Growth Model — 17

$$P_0 = \frac{D_0(1+g)}{(r_e - g)}$$

Gordon's Growth Approximation — 17

$$g = br_e$$

The weighted average cost of capital — 15

$$\text{WACC} = \left[\frac{V_e}{V_e + V_d} \right] k_e + \left[\frac{V_d}{V_e + V_d} \right] k_d (1-T)$$

The Fisher formula — 19

$$(1 + i) = (1 + r)(1 + h)$$

Purchasing Power Parity and Interest Rate Parity

$$S_1 = S_0 \times \frac{(1+h_c)}{(1+h_b)}$$ — 19

$$F_0 = S_0 \times \frac{(1+i_c)}{(1+i_b)}$$ — 19

Formulae to learn

Profitability ratios include:

$$ROCE = \frac{\text{Profit before interest and tax (PBIT)}}{\text{Capital employed}}$$

$$ROCE = \frac{PBIT}{\text{Revenue}} \times \frac{\text{Revenue}}{\text{Capital employed}}$$

$$ROCE = \text{Profit margin} \times \text{asset turnover}$$

Debt ratios include:

$$Gearing = \frac{\text{Debt}}{\text{Equity}} \text{ or } \frac{\text{Debt}}{\text{Debt} + \text{Equity}} \text{ (and either book values or market values can be used)}$$

$$Gearing = \frac{\text{Prior charge capital}}{\text{Equity capital (including reserves)}}$$

$$\text{Interest coverage} = \frac{PBIT}{\text{Interest}}$$

Liquidity ratios include:

Current ratio = Current assets : Current liabilities

Acid Test ratio = Current assets less inventory : Current liabilities

Shareholder investor ratios include:

$$\text{Dividend yield} = \frac{\text{Dividend per share}}{\text{Market price per share}} \times 100$$

$$\text{Earnings per share} = \frac{\text{Profits distributable to ordinary shareholders}}{\text{Number of ordinary shares issued}}$$

$$\text{Price earnings (P/E) ratio} = \frac{\text{Market price per share}}{\text{EPS}}$$

Accounts receivable days $= \dfrac{\text{Receivables}}{\text{(credit) sales}} \times 365 \text{ days}$

Inventory days

(a)　Finished goods $= \dfrac{\text{Finished goods}}{\text{Cost of sales}} \times 365 \text{ days}$

(b)　WIP $= \dfrac{\text{Average WIP}}{\text{Cost of sales}} \times 365 \text{ days}$

(c)　Raw material: $\dfrac{\text{Average raw material inventory}}{\text{Annual raw material purchases}} \times 365 \text{ days}$

Accounts payable period $\dfrac{\text{Payables}}{\text{Credit purchases (or cost of sales if purchases unavailable)}} \times 365 \text{ days}$

IRR $= a + \dfrac{NPV_a}{NPV_a - NPV_b} (b - a)$

Equivalent annual cost $= \dfrac{\text{PV of cost over one replacement cycle}}{\text{Annuity factor for the number of years in the cycle}}$

Cost of equity $= K_e = \dfrac{D_1}{P_0} + g$

Cost of debt $= K_d = \dfrac{i(1-T)}{P_0}$

Cost of preference shares $= K_{pref} = \dfrac{\text{Preference Dividend}}{\text{Market Value}_{(ex\,div)}} = \dfrac{d}{P_0}$

Profitability index $= \dfrac{\text{PV of cash flows (not including capital investment)}}{\text{Capital investment}}$

Exam information

The exam is a three-hour paper and the format is changing from (and including) the December 2014 exam to:

Section A: 20 multiple choice questions each worth 2 marks drawn from the whole syllabus.

Section B: 5 questions: 3 × 10 marks drawn from the whole syllabus.

2 × 15 marks drawn from the working capital management, investment appraisal and business finance sections of the syllabus. Note 'business finance' also includes the cost of capital.

All questions are compulsory. There will be a mixture of calculations and discussion and the examiner's aim is to cover as much of the syllabus as possible.

The **old** format was **four** compulsory 25 mark questions.

Additional information

The Study Guide provides more detailed guidance on the syllabus.

Useful websites

The websites below provide additional sources of information of relevance to your studies for *Financial Management*.

- www.accaglobal.com

    ACCA's website. The students' section of the website is invaluable for detailed information about the qualification, past issues of Student Accountant (including technical articles) and a free downloadable Student Planner App.

- www.bpp.com

    Our website provides information about BPP products and services, with a link to the ACCA website.

- www.ft.com

    This website provides information about current international business. You can search for information and articles on specific industry groups as well as individual companies. (**Note**: Subscription required)

- www.economist.com

    Here you can search for business information on a week-by-week basis, search articles by business subject and use the resources of the Economist Intelligence Unit to research sectors, companies or countries.

    (**Note**: Subscription required for some content)

- www.invweek.co.uk

    This site carries business news and articles on markets from Investment Week and International Investment.

- www.pwc.com

    The PricewaterhouseCoopers website includes UK Economic Outlook.

- www.cfo.com

    Good website for financial officers.

- www.bankofengland.co.uk

    This website is useful for sourcing Bank of England publications.

- www.yieldcurve.com

    A useful website for research and articles on such areas as interest rate derivatives.

Questions

FINANCIAL MANAGEMENT FUNCTION

Questions 1 to 4 cover Financial management function, the subject of Part A of the BPP Study Text for Paper F9.

1 MCQ bank – Financial management and financial objectives

36 mins

1.1 Which of the following are the 3 key areas covered by financial management decisions?

1 Investment
2 Cash flow
3 Finance
4 Dividend

A 1, 2 and 3
B 2, 3 and 4
C 1, 3 and 4
D 1, 2 and 4 **(2 marks)**

1.2 Which of the following does NOT form part of the objectives of a corporate governance best practice framework?

A Separation of chairperson and CEO roles
B Establishment of audit, nomination and remuneration committees
C Minimisation of risk
D Employment of non-executive directors **(2 marks)**

1.3 The following information relates to A Co for the last financial year.

Revenue $200 million

Asset turnover   10 times

Interest payable $1.5m

Interest cover ratio 5 times

What is the return on capital employed for A Co for the year?

A 37.5%
B 3.75%
C 7.5%
D 15% **(2 marks)**

1.4 A school decides to have larger classes and examination results suffer as a result. In terms of the 'value for money' framework, which one of the following statements is true?

A Economy has increased but efficiency has decreased
B Efficiency has increased but effectiveness has decreased
C Economy has increased but effectiveness has decreased
D Economy has increased, but efficiency and effectiveness have decreased **(2 marks)**

1.5 H Co's share price is $3.50 at the end of 20X1 and this includes a capital gain of $0.75 since the beginning of the period. A dividend of $0.25 has been declared for 20X1.

What is the shareholder return?

A 21.4%
B 23.6%
C 28.6%
D 36.4% **(2 marks)**

1.6 Stakeholders can be classified as internal, connected or external. Which of the following is an external stakeholder?

A   Shareholders
B   Customers
C   Bankers
D   Government   (2 marks)

1.7 A government body uses measures based upon the 'three Es' to the measure value for money generated by a publicly funded hospital. It considers the most important performance measure to be 'cost per successfully treated patient'.

Which of the three E's best describes the above measure?

A   Economy
B   Effectiveness
C   Efficiency
D   Externality   (2 marks)

1.8 In not-for-profit businesses and state-run entities, a value-for-money audit can be used to measure performance. It covers three key areas: economy, efficiency and effectiveness. Which of the following could be used to describe effectiveness in this context?

A   Avoiding waste of inputs
B   Achieving agreed targets
C   Achieving a given level of profit
D   Obtaining suitable quality inputs at the lowest price   (2 marks)

1.9 Which of the following statements are valid criticisms of return on capital employed (ROCE) as a performance measure?

1   It is misleading if used to compare departments with different levels of risk
2   It is misleading if used to compare departments with assets of different ages
3   Its use may discourage investment in new or replacement assets
4   The figures needed are not easily available

A   2 and 3 only
B   2 and 4 only
C   1 and 3 only
D   1, 2 and 3   (2 marks)

1.10 Which of the following statements are true?

1   Cash flow forecasting is primarily the responsibility of Financial Reporting
2   Whether to undertake a particular new project is a Financial Management decision

A   Both statements are true
B   Both statements are false
C   Statement 1 is true and statement 2 is false
D   Statement 2 is true and statement 1 is false   (2 marks)

(Total = 20 marks)

2 MCQ bank – Financial management and financial objectives

2.1 Last year ABC Co made profits before tax of $2,628,000 The tax amounted to $788,000.

ABC Co's share capital was $2,000,000 (2,000,000 shares of $1) and $4,000,000 6% preference shares

What was the earnings per share (EPS) for the year?

A   31c
B   80c
C   92c
D   119c   **(2 marks)**

2.2 The following statements relate to various functions within a business.

1   The financial management function makes decisions relating to finance
2   Management accounts incorporate non-monetary measures

Are the statements true or false?

A   Statement 1 is true and statement 2 is false
B   Both statements are true
C   Statement 1 is false and statement 2 is true
D   Both statements are false   **(2 marks)**

2.3 A company has recently declared a dividend of 12c per share. The share price is $3.72 cum div and earnings for the most recent year were 60c per share.

What is the P/E ratio?

A   0.17
B   6.00
C   6.20
D   6.60   **(2 marks)**

2.4 The following information relates to the ordinary shares of G Co.

Earnings per share   60c
Dividend cover   2.5
Published dividend yield   4.8%

What is the price of G Co's ordinary shares implied by the data above?

A   24c
B   115c
C   313c
D   500c   **(2 marks)**

2.5 Which of the following is most appropriate as an objective of a not-for-profit organisation?

A   To achieve long term growth in earnings
B   To maximise shareholder wealth
C   To make efficient use of resources
D   To minimise input costs   **(2 marks)**

                                                                    (Total = 10 marks)

3 ABC Co

Summary financial information for ABC Co is given below, covering the last two years.

	Current year	Previous year
STATEMENT OF PROFIT OR LOSS (EXTRACT)	$'000	$'000
Revenue	74,521	68,000
Cost of sales	28,256	25,772
Salaries and wages	20,027	19,562
Other costs	11,489	9,160
Profit before interest and tax	14,749	13,506
Interest	1,553	1,863
Tax	4,347	3,726
Profit after interest and tax	8,849	7,917
Dividends payable	4,800	3,100

	Current year	Previous year
STATEMENT OF FINANCIAL POSITION (EXTRACT)	$'000	$'000
Shareholders' funds	39,900	35,087
Long term debt	14,000	17,500
Other information		
Number of shares in issue ('000)	14,000	14,000
P/E ratio (average for year)		
ABC Co	14.0	13.0
Industry	15.2	15.0

Required

Using profitability, debt, and shareholders' investment ratios, discuss the performance of ABC Co over the last two years. **(10 marks)**

4 Bark Co (12/11, amended)

Compare and contrast the financial objectives of a stock exchange listed company and the financial objectives of a not-for-profit organisation such as a large charity. **(10 marks)**

FINANCIAL MANAGEMENT ENVIRONMENT

Questions 5 to 9 cover Financial management environment, the subject of Part B of the BPP Study Text for Paper F9.

5 MCQ bank – Financial management environment   18 mins

5.1 A government has adopted a contractionary fiscal policy.

How would this typically affect businesses?

A   Higher interest rates and higher inflation
B   Lower taxes and higher government subsidies
C   Higher taxes and lower government subsidies
D   Lower inflation and lower interest rates   (2 marks)

5.2 A government follows an expansionary monetary policy.

How would this typically affect businesses?

A   Higher demand from customers, lower interest rates on loans and increased availability of credit
B   A contraction in demand from customers, higher interest rates and less available credit
C   Lower taxes, higher demand from customers but less government subsidies/available contracts
D   Lower interest rates, lower exchange rates and higher tax rates   (2 marks)

5.3 As the economy booms and approaches the limits of productivity at a point in time, a manufacturing business would typically feel which one of the following effects?

A   Increased inflation (higher sales prices and higher costs), difficulty in finding suitable candidates to fill roles and higher interest rates

B   High export demand, increasing growth rates, high inflation and high interest rates

C   Reducing inflation, falling demand, reducing investment, increasing unemployment

D   Higher government spending, lower tax rates, high inflation and low unemployment   (2 marks)

5.4 If the US dollar weakens against the pound sterling, will UK exporters and importers suffer or benefit?

	UK exporters to US	*UK importers from US*
A	Benefit	Benefit
B	Suffer	Suffer
C	Benefit	Suffer
D	Suffer	Benefit

(2 marks)

5.5 Government macroeconomic objectives typically include which of the following?

1   Economic growth and high employment
2   Low inflation
3   Balance of payments stability
4   A guaranteed minimum income for all

A   1, 2 and 4 only
B   1, 3 and 4 only
C   1, 2 and 3 only
D   All the above   (2 marks)

(Total = 10 marks)

6 MCQ bank – Financial management environment   18 mins

6.1   Which of the following is NOT a function that financial intermediaries fulfil for customers and borrowers?

   A   Maturity transformation
   B   Fund aggregation
   C   Dividend creation
   D   Pooling of losses   **(2 marks)**

6.2   Which of the following are money market instruments?

   1   Certificate of deposit
   2   Corporate bond
   3   Commercial paper
   4   Treasury bill

   A   1, 2 and 4 only
   B   1 and 3 only
   C   1, 3 and 4 only
   D   1, 2, 3 and 4   **(2 marks)**

6.3   Which of the following statements about obtaining a full stock market listing is NOT correct?

   A   Compliance costs are likely to increase, but better public profile and access to funds benefit the business.

   B   All else being equal the value of the business is likely to be unaffected.

   C   It allows owners to realise their investment.

   D   It increases the liquidity of the shares for shareholders.   **(2 marks)**

6.4   AB plc, a company listed in UK and Australia, decides to issue unsecured US dollar bonds in Australia.

   What are these bonds referred to as?

   A   Junk bonds
   B   Commercial paper
   C   Eurobonds
   D   Intercontinental bills   **(2 marks)**

6.5   Rank the following from highest risk to lowest risk from the investor's perspective.

   1   Preference share
   2   Treasury bill
   3   Corporate bond
   4   Ordinary share

   A   1, 4, 3, 2
   B   1, 4, 2, 3
   C   4, 2, 1, 3
   D   4, 1, 3, 2   **(2 marks)**

                                                                                          (Total = 10 marks)

7   MCQ bank – Financial management environment   18 mins

7.1   The following statements relate to fiscal policy and demand management.

1   If a government spends more by borrowing more, it will raise demand in the economy
2   If demand in the economy is high then government borrowing will fall

Are the statements true or false?

A   Both statements are true
B   Both statements are false
C   Statement 1 is true and statement 2 is false
D   Statement 2 is true and statement 1 is false   (2 marks)

7.2   Which one of the following statements is incorrect?

A   Money markets are markets for long-term capital

B   Money markets are operated by banks and other financial institutions

C   Money market instruments include interest-bearing instruments, discount instruments and derivatives

D   Money market instruments are traded over the counter between institutional investors   (2 marks)

7.3   Which of the following organisations is most likely to benefit from a period of high price inflation?

A   An organisation which has a large number of long term payables

B   An exporter of goods to a country with relatively low inflation

C   A supplier of goods in a market where consumers are highly price sensitive and substitute imported goods are available

D   A large retailer with a high level of inventory on display and low rate of inventory turnover   (2 marks)

7.4   Which of the following are among the main goals of macroeconomic policy?

1   Encouraging economic growth
2   Low and stable inflation
3   Achievement of a balance between exports and imports
4   Encouraging an equitable distribution of income

A   1 and 2
B   1, 2 and 4
C   2, 3 and 4
D   1, 2 and 3   (2 marks)

7.5   If a government has a macro-economic policy objective of expanding the overall level of economic activity, which of the following measures would not be consistent with such an objective?

A   Increasing public expenditure
B   Lowering interest rates
C   Increasing the exchange rate
D   Decreasing taxation   (2 marks)

(Total = 10 marks)

8 Tagna (FMC, 6/03, amended)

18 mins

Tagna is a medium-sized company that manufactures luxury goods for several well-known chain stores. In real terms, the company has experienced only a small growth in turnover in recent years, but it has managed to maintain a constant, if low, level of reported profits by careful control of costs. It has paid a constant nominal (money terms) dividend for several years and its managing director has publicly stated that the primary objective of the company is to increase the wealth of shareholders. Tagna is financed as follows:

	$m
Overdraft	1.0
10 year fixed interest bank loan	2.0
Share capital and reserves	4.5
	7.5

Required

(a) On the assumption that the Central Bank makes a substantial interest rate increase, discuss the possible consequences for Tagna in the following areas:

    (i)   sales;
    (ii)   operating costs; and,
    (iii) earnings (profit after tax). **(6 marks)**

(b) Explain and compare the public sector objective of 'value for money' and the private sector objective of 'maximisation of shareholder wealth'. **(4 marks)**

(Total = 10 marks)

9 Phoenix

18 mins

(a) Explain what is meant by the 'risk/return trade-off'. **(4 marks)**

(b) A bank is an example of a financial intermediary. Explain the role of financial intermediaries and their usefulness to the private investor. **(6 marks)**

(Total = 10 marks)

WORKING CAPITAL MANAGEMENT

Questions 10 to 32 cover Working capital management, the subject of Part C of the BPP Study Text for Paper F9.

10 MCQ bank – Working capital

18 mins

10.1 The following has been calculated for BB Co:

Receivables days: 58

Inventory turnover: 10 times per annum

Payables days: 45

Non-current asset days: 36

What is the length of the cash operating cycle?

A   23 days
B   49.5 days
C   85.5 days
D   139.5 days   **(2 marks)**

10.2 D Co decides to offer a 2% early settlement discount that half of all customers take up. They pay in 1 month instead of the usual 2. D Co pays 10% per annum for its overdraft facility.

What impact will this have?

	Cash operating cycle	Reported profits
A	Reduce	Increase
B	Unaffected	Increase
C	Reduce	Reduce
D	Unaffected	Reduce

(2 marks)

10.3 WW Co has a current ratio of 2. Receivables are $3 million and current liabilities are $2 million.

What are inventory days if cost of sales is $10 million per annum?

A   36.5 days
B   91.25 days
C   14.6 days
D   243.3 days   **(2 marks)**

10.4 Which of the following best describes overtrading?

A   Selling more than you can manufacture and/or you hold in inventory.
B   Having too much working capital thus reducing profitability.
C   Selling stocks and shares outside the stock exchange opening hours.
D   Suffering liquidity issues as a result of growing too quickly.   **(2 marks)**

10.5 MM Co sells some inventory on credit for a profit.

All else being equal, what will happen to the quick and current ratio after this sale?

	Quick	Current
A	Increase	Decrease
B	No change	Increase
C	Increase	No change
D	Increase	Increase

(2 marks)

(Total = 10 marks)

11 MCQ bank – Managing working capital

11.1 TS Co has daily demand for ball bearings of 40 a day for each of the 250 working days (50 weeks) of the year. The ball bearings are purchased from a local supplier for $2 each. The cost of placing an order is $64 per order, regardless of the size of the order. The inventory holding costs, expressed as a percentage of inventory purchase price, is 25% per annum.

What is the economic order quantity?

A   101 ball bearings
B   253 ball bearings
C   1,600 ball bearings
D   2,262 ball bearings   (2 marks)

11.2 EE Co has calculated the following in relation to its inventories.

Buffer inventory level	50 units
Reorder size	250 items
Fixed order costs	$50 per order
Cost of holding onto one item pa	$1.25 p.a.
Annual demand	10,000 items
Purchase price	$2 per item

What are the total inventory related costs for a year (to the nearest whole $)?

A $2,219
B $22,219
C $20,894
D $20,219   (2 marks)

11.3 Which of the following is NOT generally a benefit of a 'just in time' approach?

A   Lower inventory levels
B   Better product customisation
C   Ease of production scheduling
D   Higher quality   (2 marks)

11.4 XYZ Co has annual credit sales of $20 million and accounts receivable of $4 million. Working capital is financed by an overdraft at 12% interest per year. Assume 365 days in a year.

What is the annual financial effect if management reduces the collection period to 60 days by offering an early settlement discount of 1% that all customers adopt?

A $85,479 benefit
B $114,521 cost
C $85,479 cost
D $285,479 benefit   (2 marks)

11.5 Which of the following services may be provided by a debt factor?

1   Bad debt insurance
2   Advancement of credit
3   Receivables ledger management
4   Management of debt collection processes

A   1, 2 and 4 only
B   1 and 4 only
C   1, 2 and 3 only
D   1, 2, 3 and 4   (2 marks)

11.6 Which of the following is least likely to be used in the management of foreign accounts receivable?

    A   Letters of credit
    B   Bills of exchange
    C   Invoice discounting
    D   Commercial paper   **(2 marks)**

11.7 ABC Co offers an early settlement discount of 2% to its customers if they pay cash instead of taking 60 days' credit.

What is the annualised percentage cost of this discount to ABC?

    A   12%
    B   13%
    C   6%
    D   18%   **(2 marks)**

11.8 Which of the following is NOT a drawback of the EOQ model?

    A   Assumes certain or zero lead times.
    B   Assumes certainty in demand.
    C   Assumes a small number of close suppliers.
    D   Ignores hidden costs such as the risk of obsolescence.   **(2 marks)**

11.9 Which of the following is NOT a potential hidden cost of increasing credit taken from suppliers?

    A   Damage to goodwill
    B   Early settlement discounts lost
    C   Business disruption
    D   Increased risk of bad debts   **(2 marks)**

11.10 Which of the following would be LEAST likely to arise from the introduction of a just-in-time inventory ordering system?

    A   Lower inventory holding costs
    B   Less risk of inventory shortages
    C   More frequent deliveries
    D   Increased dependence on suppliers   **(2 marks)**

                                        (Total = 20 marks)

12 MCQ bank – Working capital finance   **18 mins**

12.1 JP Co has budgeted that sales will be $300,100 in January 20X2, $501,500 in February, $150,000 in March and $320,500 in April. Half of sales will be credit sales. 80% of receivables are expected to pay in the month after sale, 15% in the second month after sale, while the remaining 5% are expected to be bad debts. Receivables who pay in the month after sale can claim a 4% early settlement discount.

What level of sales receipts should be shown in the cash budget for March 20X2 (to the nearest $)?

    A   290,084
    B   298,108
    C   580,168
    D   596,216   **(2 marks)**

12.2 WW Co is a subsidiary of BB Co. WW Co requires $10 million in finance to be easily spread over the coming year, which BB Ltd will supply. Research shows:

There is a standing bank fee of $200 for each drawdown.

The interest cost of holding cash (ie finance cost less deposit interest) is 6% pa.

How much should WW Co draw down at a time (to the nearest $'000)?

A $8,000
B $67,000
C $258,000
D $26,000   (2 marks)

12.3 The treasury department in TB Co has calculated, using the Miller-Orr model, that the lowest cash balance they should have is $1m, and the highest is $10m. If the cash balance goes above $10m they transfer the cash into money market securities.

Which of the following is/are true?

1   When the balance reaches $10m they would buy $6m of securities

2   When the cash balance falls to $1m they will sell $3m of securities

3   If the variance of daily cash flows increases the spread between upper and lower limit will be increased.

A 1 and 2 only
B 3 only
C 2 and 3 only
D 1, 2 and 3   (2 marks)

12.4 Which statement best reflects an aggressive working capital *finance* policy?

A   More short-term finance is used because it is cheaper although it is risky.
B   Investors are forced to accept lower rates of return.
C   More long-term finance is used as it is less risky.
D   Inventory levels are reduced.   (2 marks)

12.5 What are the 2 key risks for the borrower associated with short-term working capital finance?

A   Rate risk and renewal risk
B   Inflexibility and rate risk
C   Renewal risk and inflexibility
D   Maturity mismatch and renewal risk   (2 marks)

(Total = 10 marks)

13 JIT   27 mins

PS Co has an opportunity to engage in a just-in-time inventory delivery arrangement with its main customer, who normally takes 90 days to settle accounts with PS Co. The customer accounts for 20% of PS Co's annual turnover of $20 million. This involves borrowing $0.5m on overdraft to invest in dedicated handling and transport equipment. This would be depreciated over five years on a straight-line basis. The customer is uninterested in the early payment discount but would be prepared to settle after 60 days and to pay a premium of 5% over the present price in exchange for guarantees regarding product quality and delivery. PS Co judges the probability of failing to meet these guarantees in any one year at 5%. Failure would trigger a penalty payment of 10% of the value of total sales to this customer (including the premium). PS Co borrows from the bank at 13%.

Required

(a) Calculate the improvement in *profits before tax* to be expected in the first trading year after entering into the JIT arrangement. Comment on your results.   **(8 marks)**

(b) Suggest the benefits PS Co might expect to derive from a JIT agreement in addition to the benefits specified in the question.   **(7 marks)**

(Total = 15 marks)

14 EOQ

18 mins

SP Co purchases many hundreds of components each year from external suppliers for assembling into products. It uses 40,000 units pa of one particular component. It is considering converting its purchasing, delivery and inventory control of this item to a just-in-time system. This will raise the number of orders placed but lower the administrative and other costs of placing and receiving orders. If successful, this will provide the model for switching most of its inwards supplies on to this system. Details of actual and expected ordering and carrying costs are given in the table below.

	Actual	Proposed
Ordering cost per order (O)	$100	$25
Purchase cost per item (P)	$2.50	$2.50
Inventory holding cost (as a percentage of the purchase cost) (I)	20%	20%

To implement the new arrangements will require 'one-off' reorganisation costs estimated at $4,000 which will be treated as a revenue item for tax purposes. The rate of corporation tax is 30% and SP can obtain finance at 12%. The effective life span of the new system can be assumed to be eight years.

Required

(a) Determine the effect of the new system on the economic order quantity (EOQ).

(b) Determine whether the new system is worthwhile in financial terms, assuming that the EOQ is used under the existing system.

Note. EOQ is given by $EOQ = \sqrt{\dfrac{2C_0 D}{C_h}}$.   **(10 marks)**

15 Thorne Co (FMC, 12/05, amended)

27 mins

Thorne Co values, advertises and sells residential property on behalf of its customers. The company has been in business for only a short time and has prepared a cash budget for the first four months of 20X6.

Cash budget extract

	Jan $'000	Feb $'000	March $'000	April $'000
Receipts				
Fee on sale	54	63	99	164
Payments				
General	39.55	44.05	62.35	70.15
Tax liability				95.80
	39.55	44.05	62.35	165.95
Net cash flow	14.45	18.95	36.65	(1.95)
Balance b/fwd	(40.00)	(25.55)	(6.6)	30.05
Balance c/fwd	(25.55)	(6.6)	30.05	28.10

Required

(a) Discuss the factors to be considered by Thorne Co when planning ways to invest any cash surplus forecast by its cash budgets. **(5 marks)**

(b) Discuss the advantages and disadvantages to Thorne Co of using overdraft finance to fund any cash shortages forecast by its cash budgets. **(5 marks)**

(c) Explain how the Baumol model can be employed to reduce the costs of cash management and discuss whether the Baumol cash management model may be of assistance to Thorne Co for this purpose.

(5 marks)

(Total = 15 marks)

16 Anjo Co   18 mins

Extracts from the recent financial statements of Anjo Co are as follows:

STATEMENT OF PROFIT OR LOSS

	20X6	20X5
	$'000	$'000
Revenue	15,600	11,100
Cost of sales	9,300	6,600
Gross profit	6,300	4,500
Administration expenses	1,000	750
Profit before interest and tax	5,300	3,750
Interest	100	15
Profit before tax	5,200	3,735

STATEMENT OF FINANCIAL POSITION EXTRACTS

	20X6		20X5	
	$'000	$'000	$'000	$'000
Non-current assets		5,750		5,400
Current assets				
Inventories	3,000		1,300	
Receivables	3,800		1,850	
Cash	120		900	
		6,920		4,050
Total assets		12,670		9,450
Current liabilities				
Trade payables	2,870		1,600	
Overdraft	1,000		150	
		3,870		1,750

All sales were on credit. Anjo Co has no long-term debt. Credit purchases in each year were 95% of cost of sales. Current sector averages are as follows:

Inventory days: 90 days   Receivable days: 60 days   Payable days: 80 days

Required

(a) Calculate the following ratios for each year and comment on your findings.

   (i)   Inventory days
   (ii) Receivable days
   (iii) Payable days   **(6 marks)**

(b) Calculate the length of the cash operating cycle (working capital cycle) for each year and explain its significance. **(4 marks)**

(Total = 10 marks)

17 Joan Co

27 mins

(a) A factor has offered to take over receivables ledger administration and debt collection for Joan Co for an annual fee of 0.5% of credit sales. A condition of the offer is that the factor will advance Joan Co 80% of the face value of its receivables at an interest rate 1% above the current overdraft rate. Joan Co pays interest on its overdraft at an annual rate of 8%. The factor claims that it would reduce outstanding receivables by 30% and reduce administration expenses by 2% per year if its offer were accepted.

Other information:

Annual trade receivables	$3,800,000
Annual revenue	$15,600,000
Administration expenses	$1,000,000

Required

Evaluate whether the factor's offer is financially acceptable. **(8 marks)**

(b) Discuss the relationship between working capital management and business solvency, and explain the factors that influence the optimum cash level for a business. **(7 marks)**

(Total = 15 marks)

18 Special Gift Suppliers (FMC, 12/01, amended)

27 mins

Special Gift Suppliers Co is a wholesale distributor of a variety of imported goods to a range of retail outlets.

In looking to reduce the working capital funding requirement, the financial controller of Special Gift Suppliers is assessing the current credit control procedure and considering factoring credit sales.

As an adviser to Special Gift Suppliers Co, write a report to the financial controller that outlines:

(a) How a credit control department might function
(b) The benefits of factoring
(c) How the financing of working capital can be arranged in terms of short and long term sources of finance

In particular, make reference to:

(i) The financing of working capital or net current assets when short term sources of finance are exhausted
(ii) The distinction between fluctuating and permanent current assets. **(15 marks)**

19 Ulnad Co (Specimen paper 2007, amended)

18 mins

Ulnad Co has annual sales revenue of $6 million and all sales are on 30 days' credit, although customers on average take ten days more than this to pay. Contribution represents 60% of sales and the company currently has no bad debts. Accounts receivable are financed by an overdraft at an annual interest rate of 7%.

Ulnad Co plans to offer an early settlement discount of 1.5% for payment within 15 days and to extend the maximum credit offered to 60 days. The company expects that these changes will increase annual credit sales by 5%, while also leading to additional incremental costs equal to 0.5% of turnover. The discount is expected to be taken by 30% of customers, with the remaining customers taking an average of 60 days to pay.

Required

(a) Evaluate whether the proposed changes in credit policy will increase the profitability of Ulnad Co. **(5 marks)**

(b) Renpec Co, a subsidiary of Ulnad Co, has set a minimum cash account balance of $7,500. The average cost to the company of making deposits or selling investments is $18 per transaction and the standard deviation of its cash flows was $1,000 per day during the last year. The average interest rate on investments is 5.11%.

Determine the spread, the upper limit and the return point for the cash account of Renpec Co using the Miller-Orr model and explain the relevance of these values for the cash management of the company.

(5 marks)

(Total = 10 marks)

20 Danul Co (Specimen paper 2007, amended)

18 mins

(a) Identify and explain the key areas of accounts receivable management. **(5 marks)**

(b) Discuss the key factors to be considered when formulating a working capital funding policy. **(5 marks)**

(Total = 10 marks)

21 PKA Co (12/07, amended)

18 mins

PKA Co is a European company that sells goods solely within Europe. The recently-appointed financial manager of PKA Co has been investigating the working capital management of the company and has gathered the following information about the inventory policy.

Inventory management

The current policy is to order 100,000 units when the inventory level falls to 35,000 units. Forecast demand to meet production requirements during the next year is 625,000 units. The cost of placing and processing an order is €250, while the cost of holding a unit in stores is €0.50 per unit per year. Both costs are expected to be constant during the next year. Orders are received two weeks after being placed with the supplier. You should assume a 50-week year and that demand is constant throughout the year.

Required

(a) Identify the objectives of working capital management and discuss the conflict that may arise between them. **(3 marks)**

(b) Calculate the cost of the current ordering policy and determine the saving that could be made by using the economic order quantity model. **(7 marks)**

(Total = 10 marks)

22 HGR Co (6/09, amended)

27 mins

The following financial information relates to HGR Co.

Statement of financial position at the current date (extracts)

	$'000	$'000	$'000
Non-current assets			48,965
Current assets			
Inventory		8,160	
Accounts receivable		8,775	
			16,935
Total assets			65,900
Current liabilities			
Overdraft	3,800		
Accounts payable	10,200		
		14,000	

Cash flow forecasts from the current date are as follows:

	Month 1	Month 2	Month 3
Cash operating receipts ($'000)	4,220	4,350	3,808
Cash operating payments ($'000)	3,950	4,100	3,750
Six-monthly interest on traded bonds ($'000)		200	
Capital investment ($'000)			2,000

The finance director has completed a review of accounts receivable management and has proposed staff training and operating procedure improvements, which he believes will reduce accounts receivable days to the average sector value of 53 days. This reduction would take six months to achieve from the current date, with an equal reduction in each month. He has also proposed changes to inventory management methods, which he hopes will reduce inventory days by two days per month each month over a three-month period from the current date. He does not expect any change in the current level of accounts payable.

HGR Co has an overdraft limit of $4,000,000. Overdraft interest is payable at an annual rate of 6.17% per year, with payments being made each month based on the opening balance at the start of that month. Credit sales for the year to the current date were $49,275,000 and cost of sales was $37,230,000. These levels of credit sales and cost of sales are expected to be maintained in the coming year. Assume that there are 365 working days in each year.

Required

(a) Discuss the working capital financing strategy of HGR Co. **(5 marks)**

(b) For HGR Co calculate:

　(i)　The bank balance in three months' time
　(ii)　The bank balance in three months' time if the finance director's proposals are implemented

Comment on the forecast cash flow position of HGR Co and recommend a suitable course of action. **(10 marks)**

(Total = 15 marks)

23 RGH Co (6/09, amended) 18 mins

Discuss how risks arising from granting credit to foreign customers can be managed and reduced. **(10 marks)**

24 APX Co (12/09, amended) 27 mins

APX Co achieved a turnover of $16 million in the year that has just ended and expects turnover growth of 8.4% in the next year.

The financial statements of APX Co for the year that has just ended contain the following statement of financial position:

	$m	$m
Non-current assets		22.0
Current assets		
Inventory	2.4	
Trade receivables	2.2	
		4.6
Total assets		26.6
Equity finance:	$m	$m
Ordinary shares	5.0	
Reserves	7.5	
		12.5
Long-term bank loan		10.0
		22.5
Current liabilities		
Trade payables	1.9	
Overdraft	2.2	
		4.1
Total equity and liabilities		26.6

The long-term bank loan has a fixed annual interest rate of 8% per year. APX Co pays taxation at an annual rate of 30% per year.

The following accounting ratios have been forecast for the next year:

Gross profit margin:	30%
Operating profit margin:	20%
Dividend payout ratio:	50%
Inventory turnover period:	110 days
Trade receivables period:	65 days
Trade payables period:	75 days

Overdraft interest in the next year is forecast to be $140,000. No change is expected in the level of non-current assets and depreciation should be ignored.

Required

(a)   Prepare the following forecast financial statements for APX Co using the information provided:

(i)   A statement of profit or loss for the next year
(ii)   A statement of financial position at the end of the next year   **(9 marks)**

(b)   Analyse and discuss the working capital financing policy of APX Co.   **(6 marks)**

(Total = 15 marks)

25 ZSE Co (6/10, amended)   27 mins

ZSE Co is concerned about exceeding its overdraft limit of $2 million in the next two periods. It has been experiencing considerable volatility in cash flows in recent periods because of trading difficulties experienced by its customers, who have often settled their accounts after the agreed credit period of 60 days. ZSE has also experienced an increase in bad debts due to a small number of customers going into liquidation.

The company has prepared the following forecasts of net cash flows for the next two periods, together with their associated probabilities, in an attempt to anticipate liquidity and financing problems. These probabilities have been produced by a computer model which simulates a number of possible future economic scenarios. The computer model has been built with the aid of a firm of financial consultants.

Period 1 cash flow $'000	Probability	Period 2 cash flow $'000	Probability
8,000	10%	7,000	30%
4,000	60%	3,000	50%
(2,000)	30%	(9,000)	20%

ZSE Co expects to be overdrawn at the start of period 1 by $500,000.

Required

(a)   Calculate the following:

(i)   the expected value of the period 1 closing balance;
(ii)   the expected value of the period 2 closing balance;
(iii)   the probability of a negative cash balance at the end of period 2;
(iv)   the probability of exceeding the overdraft limit at the end of period 2.

Discuss whether the above analysis can assist the company in managing its cash flows.   **(10 marks)**

(b)   Discuss whether profitability or liquidity is the primary objective of working capital management.   **(5 marks)**

(Total = 15 marks)

26 WQZ Co (12/10, amended)

27 mins

WQZ Co is considering making the following changes in the area of receivables management:

WQZ Co could introduce an early settlement discount of 1% for customers who pay within 30 days and at the same time, through improved operational procedures, maintain a maximum average payment period of 60 days for credit customers who do not take the discount. It is expected that 25% of credit customers will take the discount if it were offered.

It is expected that administration and operating cost savings of $753,000 per year will be made after improving operational procedures and introducing the early settlement discount.

Credit sales of WQZ Co are currently $87.6 million per year and trade receivables are currently $18 million. Credit sales are not expected to change as a result of the changes in receivables management. The company has a cost of short-term finance of 5.5% per year.

Required

(a) Calculate and comment on whether the proposed changes in receivables management will be acceptable. Assuming that only 25% of customers take the early settlement discount, what is the maximum early settlement discount that could be offered? **(7 marks)**

(b) Discuss the factors that should be considered in formulating working capital policy on the management of trade receivables. **(8 marks)**

(Total = 15 marks)

27 Bold Co (12/11, amended)

18 mins

Extracts from the recent financial statements of Bold Co are given below.

	$'000
Turnover	21,300
Cost of sales	16,400
Gross profit	4,900

	$'000	$'000
Non-current assets		3,000
Current assets		
Inventory	4,500	
Trade receivables	3,500	
		8,000
Total assets		11,000
Equity		
Ordinary shares	1,000	
Reserves	1,000	
		2,000
Non-current liabilities		
Bonds		3,000
Current liabilities		
Trade payables	3,000	
Overdraft	3,000	
		6,000
		11,000

Required

(a) Explain the meaning of the term 'cash operating cycle' and discuss the relationship between the cash operating cycle and the level of investment in working capital. Your answer should include a discussion of relevant working capital policy and the nature of business operations. **(6 marks)**

(b) Calculate the cash operating cycle of Bold Co. (Ignore the factor's offer in this part of the question). **(4 marks)**

(Total = 10 marks)

28 Wobnig Co (6/12, amended) 27 mins

The following financial information relates to Wobnig Co.

	20X1	20X0
	$'000	$'000
Revenue	14,525	10,375
Cost of sales	10,458	6,640
Profit before interest and tax	4,067	3,735
Interest	355	292
Profit before tax	3,712	3,443
Taxation	1,485	1,278
Distributable profit	2,227	2,165

	20X1		20X0	
	$'000	$'000	$'000	$'000
Non-current assets		15,284		14,602
Current assets				
Inventory	2,149		1,092	
Trade receivables	3,200		1,734	
		5,349		2,826
Total assets		20,633		17,428
Equity				
Ordinary shares	8,000		8,000	
Reserves	4,268		3,541	
		12,268		11,541
Non-current liabilities				
7% Bonds		4,000		4,000
Current liabilities				
Trade payables	2,865		1,637	
Overdraft	1,500		250	
		4,365		1,887
Total equity and liabilities		20,633		17,428

Average ratios for the last two years for companies with similar business operations to Wobnig Co are as follows:

Current ratio	1.7 times
Quick ratio	1.1 times
Inventory days	55 days
Trade receivables days	60 days
Trade payables days	85 days
Sales revenue/net working capital	10 times

Required

(a)   Using suitable working capital ratios and analysis of the financial information provided, evaluate whether Wobnig Co can be described as overtrading (undercapitalised).   **(12 marks)**

(b)   Wobnig Co is considering using the Miller-Orr model to manage its cash flows. The minimum cash balance would be $200,000 and the spread is expected to be $75,000.

   Required

   Calculate the Miller-Orr model upper limit and return point, and explain how these would be used to manage the cash balances of Wobnig Co.   **(3 marks)**

   (Total = 15 marks)

29 ZPS Co (6/11, amended)   27 mins

ZPS Co places monthly orders with a supplier for 10,000 components that are used in its manufacturing processes. Annual demand is 120,000 components. The current terms are payment in full within 90 days, which ZPS Co meets, and the cost per component is $7.50. The cost of ordering is $200 per order, while the cost of holding components in inventory is $1.00 per component per year.

The supplier has offered either a discount of 0.5% for payment in full within 30 days, or a discount of 3.6% on orders of 30,000 or more components. If the bulk purchase discount is taken, the cost of holding components in inventory would increase to $2.20 per component per year due to the need for a larger storage facility.

Assume that there are 365 days in the year and that ZPS Co can borrow short-term at 4.5% per year.

Required

(a)   Discuss the factors that influence the formulation of working capital policy.   **(8 marks)**

(b)   Calculate if ZPS Co will benefit financially by accepting the offer of:

   (1)   The early settlement discount
   (2)   The bulk purchase discount   **(7 marks)**

   (Total = 15 marks)

30 KXP Co (12/12, amended)   18 mins

KXP Co is an e-business which trades solely over the internet. In the last year the company had sales of $15 million. All sales were on 30 days' credit to commercial customers.

Extracts from the company's most recent statement of financial position relating to working capital are as follows:

	$'000
Trade receivables	2,466
Trade payables	2,220
Overdraft	3,000

In order to encourage customers to pay on time, KXP Co proposes introducing an early settlement discount of 1% for payment within 30 days, while increasing its normal credit period to 45 days. It is expected that, on average, 50% of customers will take the discount and pay within 30 days, 30% of customers will pay after 45 days, and 20% of customers will not change their current paying behaviour.

KXP Co currently orders 15,000 units per month of Product Z, demand for which is constant. There is only one supplier of Product Z and the cost of Product Z purchases over the last year was $540,000. The supplier has offered a 2% discount for orders of Product Z of 30,000 units or more. Each order costs KXP Co $150 to place and the holding cost is 24 cents per unit per year. KXP Co has an overdraft facility charging interest of 6% per year.

Required

(a) Calculate the net benefit or cost of the proposed changes in trade receivables policy and comment on your findings. **(5 marks)**

(b) Calculate whether the bulk purchase discount offered by the supplier is financially acceptable and comment on the assumptions made by your calculation. **(5 marks)**

(Total = 10 marks)

31 PXK Co (12/12, amended)   18 mins

(a) Identify and discuss the factors to be considered in determining the optimum level of cash to be held by a company. **(5 marks)**

(b) Discuss the factors to be considered in formulating a trade receivables management policy. **(5 marks)**

(Total = 10 marks)

32 Gorwa (2) Co (12/08, amended)   18 mins

The following financial information related to Gorwa Co:

	20X7	20X6
	$'000	$'000
Sales (all on credit)	37,400	26,720
Cost of sales	34,408	23,781
Operating profit	2,992	2,939
Finance costs (interest payments)	355	274
Profit before taxation	2,637	2,665

	20X7		20X6	
	$'000	$'000	$'000	$'000
Non-current assets		13,632		12,750
Current assets				
Inventory	4,600		2,400	
Trade receivables	4,600		2,200	
		9,200		4,600
Total assets		22,832		17,350
Capital and reserves				
Share capital		6,000		6,000
Reserves		6,432		5,325
		12,432		11,325
Non-current liabilities				
8% Bonds		2,425		2,425
Current liabilities				
Trade payables	4,750		2,000	
Overdraft	3,225		1,600	
		7,975		3,600
Total equity and liabilities		22,832		17,350

The average variable overdraft interest rate in each year was 5%. The 8% bonds are redeemable in ten years' time.

Required

Use the above financial information to discuss, with supporting calculations, whether or not Gorwa Co is overtrading. **(10 marks)**

Questions 33 to 57 cover Investment appraisal, the subject of Part D of the BPP Study Text for Paper F9.

33 MCQ bank – Investment decisions   36 mins

The following information relates to questions 33.1 and 33.2.

NW Co is considering investing $46,000 in a new delivery lorry that will last for four years, after which time it will be sold for $7,000. Depreciation is charged on a straight-line basis. Forecast operating profits/(losses) to be generated by the machine are as follows.

Year	$
1	16,500
2	23,500
3	13,500
4	(1,500)

33.1 What is the return on capital employed (ROCE) for the lorry (using the average investment method)?

A 70%
B 28%
C 49%
D 36%   **(2 marks)**

33.2 Assuming operational cash flows arise evenly over the year, what is the payback period for this investment (to the nearest month)?

A 1 year 7 months
B 2 years 7 months
C 1 year 5 months
D 3 years 2 months   **(2 marks)**

33.3 Which of the following are benefits of the return on capital employed method of investment appraisal?

1 It considers the whole project

2 It is cash flow based

3 It is a percentage which, being meaningful to non-finance professionals, helps communicate the benefits of investment decisions.

A 1, 2 and 3
B 1 and 3 only
C 1, and 2 only
D 2 and 3 only   **(2 marks)**

33.4 SW Co has a barrel of chemicals in its warehouse that it purchased for a project a while ago at a cost of $1,000. It would cost $400 for a professional disposal company to collect the barrel and dispose of it safely. However, the chemicals could be used in a potential project which is currently being assessed.

What is the relevant cost of using the chemicals in a new project proposal?

A $1,000 cost
B $400 benefit
C $400 cost
D Zero   **(2 marks)**

33.5 A new project being considered by BLW Co would require 1,000 hours of skilled labour. The current workforce is already fully employed but more workers can be hired in at a cost of $20 per hour. The current workers are paid $15 per hour on a project that earns a contribution of $10 per hour.

What is the relevant cost of labour to be included in the project appraisal?

A $10,000
B $15,000
C $20,000
D $25,000   (2 marks)

33.6 LW Co has a half empty factory on which it pays $5,000 pa. If it takes on a new project, it will have to move to a new bigger factory costing $17,000 pa and it could rent the old factory out for $3,000 pa until the end of the current lease.

What is the rental cost to be included in the project appraisal?

A $14,000
B $17,000
C $9,000
D $19,000   (2 marks)

33.7 Which of the following is a drawback of the payback period method of investment appraisal?

A   It is cash flow based
B   It considers the time value of money
C   It doesn't measure the potential impact on shareholder wealth
D   It is profit based   (2 marks)

33.8 Which stage is missing or in the wrong order from the investment decision making process below?

1   Origination of ideas
2   Financial analysis
3   Acceptance, implementation, monitoring and review

A   Project screening should follow after stage 1
B   Project screening should follow after stage 2
C   Raising finance should be before stage 1
D   Implementation should follow stage 1   (2 marks)

33.9 EE Co is considering investing in a new 40-year project which will require an initial investment of $50,000 (with zero scrap value) and has a payback period of 20 years.

What is the return on capital employed (using the average investment method)?

A   2.5%
B   10%
C   7.5%
D   5%   (2 marks)

33.10 An accountant is paid $30,000 per annum and spends two weeks one month working on appraising project Alpha.

Why should the accountant NOT charge half his salary to the project?

A   Because his salary is sunk
B   Because his salary is not incremental
C   Because his salary is not a cash flow
D   Because his salary is an opportunity cost   (2 marks)

(Total = 20 marks)

34 MCQ bank – Investment appraisal using DCF   36 mins

34.1 An investor has a cost of capital of 10%. He is due to receive a 5 year annuity starting in 3 year's time of $7,000 per annum.

What amount lump sum would you need to offer today to make him indifferent between the annuity and your offer?

A $26,537
B $19,936
C $16,667
D $21,924   (2 marks)

34.2 A newspaper reader has won first prize in a national competition and they have a choice as to how they take the prize:

1   They can take $90,000 per annum indefinitely starting in 3 years' time (and bequeath this right to their children and so on); or

2   They can take a lump sum of $910,000 in 1 year's time

Assuming a cost of capital of 10%, which would you advise and why?

A   Statement 1 because $90,000 pa indefinitely is an infinite amount of money compared to a one-off payment.

B   Statement 1 because it is worth more in present value terms.

C   Statement 2 because it is worth more in present value terms.

D   Statement 2 because the lump sum has the flexibility to be invested and earn a larger return than $90,000 pa   (2 marks)

The following information relates to questions 34.3 and 34.4.

JCW Co is appraising an opportunity to invest in some new machinery that has the following cash flows.

Initial investment	$40,000
Net cash inflows for 5 years in advance	$12,000 per annum
Decommissioning costs after 5 years	$15,000

34.3 At a cost of capital of 10% what is the net present value of this project (to the nearest $100)?

A   Negative $3,800
B   Positive $14,800
C   Positive $700
D   Negative $11,275   (2 marks)

34.4 What is the internal rate of return of the project (to the nearest whole %)?

A   12
B   10
C   14
D   9   (2 marks)

34.5 Four mutually exclusive projects have been appraised using net present value (NPV), internal rate of return (IRR), return on capital employed (ROCE) and payback period (PP).

Which should be chosen?

	NPV	IRR	ROCE	PP
A Project A	$1m	40%	34%	4 years
B Project B	$1.1m	24%	35%	2.5 years
C Project C	$0.9m	18%	25%	3 years
D Project D	$1.5m	12%	18%	7 years

(2 marks)

34.6 Which of the following are advantages of the internal rate of return (IRR) approach to investment appraisal?

1 Clear decision rule
2 Takes into account the time value of money
3 Assumes funds are re-invested at the IRR
4 Considers the whole project

A 1, 2 and 4 only
B 2, 3 and 4 only
C 2 and 4 only
D 1, 2 and 3 only

(2 marks)

34.7 A project has an initial outflow followed by years of inflows.

What would be the effect on net present value and the internal rate of return of an increase in the cost of capital?

	NPV	IRR
A	Decrease	Decrease
B	Increase	Decrease
C	Decrease	No change
D	Increase	No change

(2 marks)

34.8 A lease agreement has a net present value of $26,496 at a rate of 8%. The lease involves an immediate down payment of $10,000 followed by four equal annual payments.

What is the amount of the annual payment?

A $11,020
B $4,981
C $11,513
D $14,039

(2 marks)

34.9 Which of the following statements about net present value (NPV) and internal rate of return (IRR) are accurate?

A Two NPV calculations are needed to estimate the IRR using linear interpolation.

B The graphical approach to IRR is only an estimate; linear interpolation using the formula is required for a precise answer.

C The IRR is unique.

D An IRR graph with NPV on the 'Y' axis and discount rate on the 'X' axis will have a negative slope.

(2 marks)

34.10 Peter plans to buy a holiday villa in five years time for cash. He estimates the cost will be $1.5m. He plans to set aside the same amount of funds each year for 5 years starting immediately earning a rate of 10% interest per annum compound.

To the nearest $100, how much does he need to set aside each year?

A $223,400
B $245,600
C $359,800
D $395,600

(2 marks)

(Total = 20 marks)

35 MCQ bank – Allowing for tax and inflation   36 mins

35.1 SW Co has a 31 December year end and pays corporation tax at a rate of 30%, 12 months after the end of the year to which the cash flows relate. It can claim tax allowable depreciation at a rate of 25% reducing balance. It pays $1m for a machine on 31 December 20X4. SW Co's cost of capital is 10%.

What is the present value on 31 December 20X4 of the benefit of the first portion of tax allowable depreciation?

A $250,000
B $227,250
C $68,175
D $75,000

(2 marks)

35.2 A company receives a perpetuity of $20,000 per annum in arrears, and pays 30% corporation tax 12 months after the end of the year to which the cash flows relate.

At a cost of capital of 10%, what is the after tax present value?

A $140,000
B $145,454
C $144,000
D $127,274

(2 marks)

35.3 A project has the following projected cash inflows.

Year 1   100,000

Year 2   125,000

Year 3   105,000

Working capital is required to be in place at the start of each year equal to 10% of the cash inflow for that year. The cost of capital is 10%.

What is the present value of the working capital?

A $ Nil
B $(30,036)
C $(2,735)
D $33,000

(2 marks)

35.4 AW Co needs to have $100,000 working capital in place immediately for the start of a 2 year project. The amount will stay constant in real terms. Inflation is running at 10% per annum, and AW Co's money cost of capital is 12%.

What is the present value of the cash flows relating to working capital?

A $(21,060)
B $(20,300)
C $(108,730)
D $(4,090)

(2 marks)

35.5 NCW Co is considering investing $10,000 immediately in a 1 year project with the following cash flows.

Income $100,000

Expenses $35,000

The cash flows will arise at the end of the year. The above are stated in current terms. Income is subject to 10% inflation, expenses will not vary. The real cost of capital is 8% and general inflation is 2%.

Using the money cost of capital to the nearest whole %, what is the net present value of the project?

A $68,175
B $60,190
C $58,175
D $78,175 (2 marks)

35.6 AM Co will receive a perpetuity starting in 2 years' time of $10,000 per annum, increasing by the rate of inflation (which is 2%).

What is the present value of this perpetuity assuming a money cost of capital of 10.2%?

A $90,910
B $125,000
C $115,740
D $74,403 (2 marks)

35.7 FW Co is expecting a net of tax receipt of $10,000 (in real terms) in 1 year's time.

If FW Co expects inflation to increase, what impact will this have on the present value of that receipt?

A Nil
B Reduce
C Increase
D Cannot say (2 marks)

35.8 Shadowline Co has a money cost of capital of 10%. If inflation is 4%, what is Shadowline Co's real cost of capital?

A 6%
B 5.8%
C 14%
D 14.4% (2 marks)

35.9 Juicy Co is considering investing in a new industrial juicer for use on a new contract. It will cost $150,000 and will last 2 years. Juicy Co pays corporation tax at 30% (as the cash flows occur) and, due to the health benefits of juicing, the machine attracts 100% tax allowable depreciation immediately.

Given a cost of capital of 10%, what is the minimum value of the pre-tax contract revenue receivable in 2 years to recover the net cost of the juicer?

A $150,000
B $105,000
C $127,050
D $181,500 (2 marks)

35.10 Which of the following are true about the 'inflation' figure that is included in the money cost of capital?

A It is historic and specific to the business.
B It is historic general inflation suffered by the investors.
C It is expected and specific to the business.
D It is expected general inflation suffered by the investors. (2 marks)

(Total = 20 marks)

36 MCQ bank – Project appraisal and risk

18 mins

36.1   Which of the following are true in respect of using expected values in net present value calculations?

1   Appropriate for one-off events
2   Hides risk
3   Probably won't actually occur
4   Eliminates uncertainty

A   1, 2 and 3 only
B   3 and 4 only
C   2 and 3 only
D   1, 2 and 4   **(2 marks)**

36.2   Sales volumes are expected to be either 20,000 units with 60% probability or they are expected to be 25,000 units. Price will either be $10 (0.3 probability) or else $15. Margins are expected to be 30% or 40% of sales with an even chance of each.

What is the expected total cost?

A $103,950
B $193,050
C $297,000
D $105,000   **(2 marks)**

36.3   SAC Co has a cost of capital of 8% and is appraising project Gamma. It has the following cash flows.

T0   Investment   100,000

T1-5   Net cash inflow   40,000

What is the adjusted payback period for this project?

A   2.5 years
B   Just under 3 years
C   2 years
D   Just over 4 years   **(2 marks)**

36.4   A project has the following cash flows.

T0   Outflow $110,000

T1-4   Inflow $40,000

At the company's cost of capital of 10% the NPV of the project is $16,800.

Applying sensitivity analysis to the cost of capital, what percentage change in the cost of capital would cause the project NPV to fall to zero.?

A   70%
B   17%
C   5%
D   41%   **(2 marks)**

36.5   What is the main advantage of using simulations to assist in investment appraisal?

A   A clear decision rule
B   More than one variable can change at a time
C   Statistically more accurate than other methods
D   Being diagrammatic it is easier to understand   **(2 marks)**
                                                                                                   (Total = 10 marks)

37 MCQ bank – Specific investment decisions

37.1 PD Co is deciding whether to replace its delivery vans every year or every other year. The initial cost of a van is $20,000. Maintenance costs would be nil in the first year, and $5,000 at the end of the second year. Second-hand value would fall from $10,000 to $8,000 if it held on to the van for two years instead of just one. PD Co's cost of capital is 10%.

How often should PD Co replace their vans, and what is the annual equivalent cost ('EAC') of that option?

	Replace every	EAC ($)
A	1	10,910
B	1	12,002
C	2	10,093
D	2	8,761

(2 marks)

37.2 Which of the following relate to finance leases as opposed to operating leases?

1   Maintained and insured by the lessor
2   Asset appears on statement of financial position of lessee
3   Equipment leased for a shorter period than its expected useful life

A   2 only
B   1 and 2 only
C   2 and 3 only
D   1 and 3 only

(2 marks)

37.3 AB Co is considering either leasing an asset or borrowing to buy it, and is attempting to analyse the options by calculating the net present value of each. When comparing the two, AB Co is uncertain whether they should include interest payments in their option to 'borrow and buy' as it is a future, incremental cash flow associated with that option. They are also uncertain which discount rate to use in the net present value calculation for the lease option.

How should AB Co treat the interest payments and what discount rate should they use?

	Include Interest?	Discount rate
A	Yes	After tax cost of the loan if they borrow and buy
B	Yes	AB Co's weighted average cost of capital
C	No	After tax cost of the loan if they borrow and buy
D	No	AB Co's weighted after cost of capital

(2 marks)

37.4 Which of the following is always true about capital rationing?

1   A soft constraint is flexible
2   Projects being divisible is an unrealistic assumption

	Statement 1	Statement 2
A	True	True
B	True	False
C	False	True
D	False	False

(2 marks)

The following information relates to questions 37.5 and 37.6.

NB Co is faced with an immediate capital constraint of $100 million available to invest.

It is considering investing in 4 divisible projects:

$m	Initial cost	NPV
Project 1	40	4
Project 2	30	5
Project 3	50	6
Project 4	60	5

37.5 What is the NPV generated from the optimum investment programme?

A $11 million
B $13 million
C $9 million
D $15 million

(2 marks)

37.6 What is the NPV generated from the optimum investment programme if the projects were indivisible?

A $11 million
B $13 million
C $6 million
D $12 million

(2 marks)

37.7 Which of the following is potentially a benefit to the lessee if they lease as opposed to buy?

A Avoiding tax exhaustion
B Attracting lease customers that may not have been otherwise possible
C Exploiting a low cost of capital
D Potential future scrap proceeds

(2 marks)

37.8 A professional kitchen is attempting to choose between gas and electricity for its main heat source. Once a choice is made, the kitchen intends to keep to that source indefinitely. Each gas oven has a net present value (NPV) of $50,000 over its useful life of 5 years. Each electric oven has an NPV of $68,000 over its useful life of 7 years. The cost of capital is 8%.

Which should the kitchen choose and why?

A Gas because its average NPV per year is higher than electric
B Electric because its NPV is higher than gas
C Electric because its equivalent annual benefit is higher
D Electric because it lasts longer than gas

(2 marks)

37.9 Which of the following are typically benefits of a shorter replacement cycle?

1 Higher scrap value
2 Better company image and efficiency
3 Lower annual depreciation
4 Less time to benefit from owning the asset

A 1 and 2 only
B 1 and 3 only
C 1, 2 and 4 only
D 2, 3 and 4 only

(2 marks)

37.10 Which of the following are potentially practical ways of attempting to deal with a capital constraint?

1 Lease
2 Joint venture
3 Delay one or more of the projects

A 1 and 3 only
B 2 and 3 only
C 1 and 2 only
D 1, 2 and 3

(2 marks)
(Total = 20 marks)

38 Calvic Co

Cavic Co services custom cars and provides its clients with a courtesy car while servicing is taking place. It has a fleet of 10 courtesy cars which it plans to replace in the near future. Each new courtesy car will cost $15,000. The trade-in value of each new car declines over time as follows:

Age of courtesy car (years)	1	2	3
Trade-in value ($/car)	11,250	9,000	6,200

Servicing and parts will cost $1,000 per courtesy car in the first year and this cost is expected to increase by 40% per year as each vehicle grows older. Cleaning the interior and exterior of each courtesy car to keep it up to the standard required by Cavic's clients will cost $500 per car in the first year and this cost is expected to increase by 25% per year.

Cavic Co has a cost of capital of 10%. Ignore taxation and inflation.

Required

(a) Using the equivalent annual cost method, calculate whether Cavic Co should replace its fleet after one year, two years, or three years. **(10 marks)**

(b) Discuss the causes of capital rationing for investment purposes. **(5 marks)**

(Total = 15 marks)

39 Trecor Co (Specimen paper 2007, amended)

Trecor Co plans to buy a new machine to meet expected demand for a new product, Product T. This machine will cost $250,000 and last for four years, at the end of which time it will be sold for $5,000. Trecor Co expects demand for Product T to be as follows:

Year	*1*	*2*	*3*	*4*
Demand (units)	35,000	40,000	50,000	25,000

The selling price for Product T is expected to be $12.00 per unit and the variable cost of production is expected to be $7.80 per unit. Incremental annual fixed production overheads of $25,000 per year will be incurred. Selling price and costs are all in current price terms.

Selling price and costs are expected to increase as follows:

	Increase
Selling price of Product T:	3% per year
Variable cost of production:	4% per year
Fixed production overheads:	6% per year

Other information

Trecor Co has a real cost of capital of 5.7% and pays tax at an annual rate of 30% one year in arrears. It can claim tax allowable depreciation on a 25% reducing balance basis. General inflation is expected to be 5% per year.

Required

Calculate the net present value of buying the new machine and comment on your findings (work to the nearest $1,000). **(15 marks)**

40 Corter Co (Specimen paper 2007, amended)   18 mins

Corter Co plans to buy a machine costing $250,000 which will last for four years and then be sold for $5,000.

Net cash flows before tax are expected to be as follows.

	T_1	T_2	T_3	T_4
Net cash flow $	122,000	143,000	187,000	78,000

Corter Co has a target return on capital employed of 20%. Depreciation is charged on a straight-line basis over the life of an asset.

(a)   Calculate the before-tax return on capital employed (accounting rate of return) based on the average investment and comment on your findings.   **(5 marks)**

(b)   Discuss the strengths and weaknesses of internal rate of return in appraising capital investments. **(5 marks)**

(Total = 10 marks)

41 OKM Co (6/10, amended)   27 mins

The following draft appraisal of a proposed investment project has been prepared for the finance director of OKM Co by a trainee accountant. The project is consistent with the current business operations of OKM Co.

Year	1	2	3	4	5
Sales (units/yr)	250,000	400,000	500,000	250,000	
	$000	$000	$000	$000	$000
Contribution	1,330	2,128	2,660	1,330	
Fixed costs	(530)	(562)	(596)	(631)	
Depreciation	(438)	(438)	(437)	(437)	
Interest payments	(200)	(200)	(200)	(200)	
Taxable profit	162	928	1,427	62	
Taxation	(49)	(278)	(428)	(19)	
Profit after tax	162	879	1,149	(366)	(19)
Scrap value				250	
After–tax cash flows	162	879	1,149	(116)	(19)
Discount at 10%	0.909	0.826	0.751	0.683	0.621
Present values	147	726	863	(79)	(12)

Net present value = 1,645,000 − 2,000,000 = ($355,000) so reject the project.

The following information was included with the draft investment appraisal:

(1)   The initial investment is $2 million

(2)   Selling price: $12/unit (current price terms), selling price inflation is 5% per year

(3)   Variable cost: $7/unit (current price terms), variable cost inflation is 4% per year

(4)   Fixed overhead costs: $500,000/year (current price terms), fixed cost inflation is 6% per year

(5) $200,000/year of the fixed costs are development costs that have already been incurred and are being recovered by an annual charge to the project

(6)   Investment financing is by a $2 million loan at a fixed interest rate of 10% per year

(7)   OKM Co can claim 25% reducing balance tax allowable depreciation on this investment and pays taxation one year in arrears at a rate of 30% per year

(8)   The scrap value of machinery at the end of the four-year project is $250,000

(9)   The real weighted average cost of capital of OKM Co is 7% per year

(10)   The general rate of inflation is expected to be 4.7% per year

Required

(a)   Identify and comment on any errors in the investment appraisal prepared by the trainee accountant.

(5 marks)

(b)   Prepare a revised calculation of the net present value of the proposed investment project and comment on the project's acceptability.

(10 marks)

(Total = 15 marks)

42 CJ Co (12/10, amended)   18 mins

CJ Co is considering an investment project, as follows.

Project A

This project is an expansion of existing business costing $3.5 million, payable at the start of the project, which will increase annual sales by 750,000 units. Information on unit selling price and costs is as follows:

Selling price: $2.00 per unit (current price terms)

Selling costs: $0.04 per unit (current price terms)

Variable costs: $0.80 per unit (current price terms)

Selling price inflation and selling cost inflation are expected to be 5% per year and variable cost inflation is expected to be 4% per year. Additional initial investment in working capital of $250,000 will also be needed and this is expected to increase in line with general inflation.

Other information

CJ Co has a nominal weighted average after-tax cost of capital of 10% and pays profit tax one year in arrears at an annual rate of 30%. The company can claim tax-allowable depreciation on a 25% reducing balance basis on the initial investment.

General rate of inflation: 4.5% per year

Required

Calculate the net present value of Project A and advise on its acceptability if the project were to be appraised using this method.

(10 marks)

43 BRT Co (6/11, amended)   27 mins

BRT Co has developed a new confectionery line that can be sold for $5.00 per box and that is expected to have continuing popularity for many years. The Finance Director has proposed that investment in the new product should be evaluated over a four-year time-horizon, even though sales would continue after the fourth year, on the grounds that cash flows after four years are too uncertain to be included in the evaluation. The variable and fixed costs (both in current price terms) will depend on sales volume, as follows.

Sales volume (boxes)	less than 1 million	1–1.9 million	2–2.9 million	3–3.9 million
Variable cost ($ per box)	2.80	3.00	3.00	3.05
Total fixed costs ($)	1 million	1.8 million	2.8 million	3.8 million

Forecast sales volumes are as follows.

Year	1	2	3	4
Demand (boxes)	0.7 million	1.6 million	2.1 million	3.0 million

The production equipment for the new confectionery line would cost $2 million and an additional initial investment of $750,000 would be needed for working capital. Tax-allowable depreciation on a 25% reducing balance basis could be claimed on the cost of equipment. Profit tax of 30% per year will be payable one year in arrears. A balancing allowance would be claimed in the fourth year of operation.

The average general level of inflation is expected to be 3% per year and selling price, variable costs, fixed costs and working capital would all experience inflation of this level. BRT Co uses a nominal after-tax cost of capital of 12% to appraise new investment projects.

Required

Assuming that production only lasts for four years, calculate the net present value of investing in the new product using a nominal terms approach and advise on its financial acceptability (work to the nearest $1,000). **(15 marks)**

44 Umunat Co (FMC, 12/04, amended)   18 mins

Umunat Co is considering investing $50,000 in a new machine with an expected life of five years. The machine will have no scrap value at the end of five years. It is expected that 20,000 units will be sold each year at a selling price of $3.00 per unit. Variable production costs are expected to be $1.65 per unit, while incremental fixed costs, mainly the wages of a maintenance engineer, are expected to be $10,000 per year. Umunat Co uses a discount rate of 12% for investment appraisal purposes and expects investment projects to recover their initial investment within two years.

Required

(a)   Explain why risk and uncertainty should be considered in the investment appraisal process.   **(5 marks)**
(b)   Calculate and comment on the payback period of the project   **(5 marks)**

(Total = 10 marks)

45 Tanumu Co (FMC, 12/04, amended)   27 mins

Tanumu Co is considering investing $50,000 in a new machine with an expected life of five years. The machine will have no scrap value at the end of five years. It is expected that 20,000 units will be sold each year at a selling price of $3.00 per unit. Variable production costs are expected to be $1.65 per unit, while incremental fixed costs, mainly the wages of a maintenance engineer, are expected to be $10,000 per year. Tanumu Co uses a discount rate of 12% for investment appraisal purposes and expects investment projects to recover their initial investment within two years.

Required

(a)   Evaluate the sensitivity of the project's net present value to a change in the following project variables:

   (i)   sales volume;
   (ii)   sales price;
   (iii)   variable cost;

   and discuss the use of sensitivity analysis as a way of evaluating project risk.   **(10 marks)**

(b)   Upon further investigation it is found that there is a significant chance that the expected sales volume of 20,000 units per year will not be achieved. The sales manager of Umunat Co suggests that sales volumes could depend on expected economic states that could be assigned the following probabilities:

Economic state	Poor	Normal	Good
Probability	0.3	0.6	0.1
Annual sales volume (units)	17,500	20,000	22,500

   Calculate and comment on the expected net present value of the project.   **(5 marks)**

(Total = 15 marks)

46 Duo Co (12/07, amended)

27 mins

Duo Co needs to increase production capacity to meet increasing demand for an existing product, 'Quago', which is used in food processing. A new machine, with a useful life of four years and a maximum output of 600,000 kg of Quago per year, could be bought for $800,000, payable immediately. The scrap value of the machine after four years would be $30,000. Forecast demand and production of Quago over the next four years is as follows:

Year	1	2	3	4
Demand (kg)	1.4 million	1.5 million	1.6 million	1.7 million

Existing production capacity for Quago is limited to one million kilograms per year and the new machine would only be used for demand additional to this.

The current selling price of Quago is $8.00 per kilogram and the variable cost of materials is $5.00 per kilogram. Other variable costs of production are $1.90 per kilogram. Fixed costs of production associated with the new machine would be $240,000 in the first year of production, increasing by $20,000 per year in each subsequent year of operation.

Duo Co pays tax one year in arrears at an annual rate of 30% and can claim tax-allowable depreciation on a 25% reducing balance basis. A balancing allowance is claimed in the final year of operation.

Duo Co uses its after-tax weighted average cost of capital when appraising investment projects. It has a cost of equity of 11% and a before-tax cost of debt of 8.6%. The long-term finance of the company, on a market-value basis, consists of 80% equity and 20% debt.

Required

(a)   Calculate the net present value of buying the new machine and advise on the acceptability of the proposed purchase (work to the nearest $1,000).   **(12 marks)**

(b)   The NPV of buying the new machine is ($16,000) at a cost of capital of 15%.

Calculate the internal rate of return of buying the new machine and advise on the acceptability of the proposed purchase (work to the nearest $1,000).   **(3 marks)**

(Total = 15 marks)

47 SC Co (6/08, amended)

27 mins

SC Co is evaluating the purchase of a new machine to produce product P, which has a short product life-cycle due to rapidly changing technology. The machine is expected to cost $1 million. Production and sales of product P are forecast to be as follows:

Year	1	2	3	4
Production and sales (units/year)	35,000	53,000	75,000	36,000

The selling price of product P (in current price terms) will be $20 per unit, while the variable cost of the product (in current price terms) will be $12 per unit. Selling price inflation is expected to be 4% per year and variable cost inflation is expected to be 5% per year. No increase in existing fixed costs is expected since SC Co has spare capacity in both space and labour terms.

Producing and selling product P will call for increased investment in working capital. Analysis of historical levels of working capital within SC Co indicates that at the start of each year, investment in working capital for product P will need to be 7% of sales revenue for that year.

SC Co pays tax of 30% per year in the year in which the taxable profit occurs. Liability to tax is reduced by tax allowable depreciation on machinery, which SC Co can claim on a straight-line basis over the four-year life of the proposed investment. The new machine is expected to have no scrap value at the end of the four-year period.

SC Co uses a nominal (money terms) after-tax cost of capital of 12% for investment appraisal purposes.

Required

(a) Calculate the net present value of the proposed investment in product P. **(12 marks)**

(b) Calculate the internal rate of return of the proposed investment in product P. **(3 marks)**

(Total = 15 marks)

48 PV Co (6/09, amended) 27 mins

PV Co is evaluating an investment proposal to manufacture Product W33, which has performed well in test marketing trials conducted recently by the company's research and development division. The following information relating to this investment proposal has now been prepared.

Initial investment	$2 million
Selling price (current price terms)	$20 per unit
Expected selling price inflation	3% per year
Variable operating costs (current price terms)	$8 per unit
Fixed operating costs (current price terms)	$170,000 per year
Expected operating cost inflation	4% per year

The research and development division has prepared the following demand forecast as a result of its test marketing trials. The forecast reflects expected technological change and its effect on the anticipated life-cycle of Product W33.

Year	1	2	3	4
Demand (units)	60,000	70,000	120,000	45,000

It is expected that all units of Product W33 produced will be sold, in line with the company's policy of keeping no inventory of finished goods. No terminal value or machinery scrap value is expected at the end of four years, when production of Product W33 is planned to end. For investment appraisal purposes, PV Co uses a nominal (money) discount rate of 10% per year and a target return on capital employed of 30% per year. Ignore taxation.

Required

(a) Calculate the following values for the investment proposal:

(i)   net present value;
(ii)   internal rate of return;
(iii) return on capital employed (accounting rate of return) based on average investment; and
(iv) discounted payback period. **(10 marks)**

(b) Discuss your findings in each section of (b) above and advise whether the investment proposal is financially acceptable. **(5 marks)**

(Total = 15 marks)

49 AGD Co (FMC, 12/05, amended) 27 mins

AGD Co is a profitable company which is considering the purchase of a machine costing $320,000. If purchased, AGD Co would incur annual maintenance costs of $25,000. The machine would be used for three years and at the end of this period would be sold for $50,000. Alternatively, the machine could be obtained under an operating lease for an annual lease rental of $120,000 per year, payable in advance.

AGD Co can claim tax allowable depreciation on a 25% reducing balance basis. The company pays tax on profits at an annual rate of 30% and all tax liabilities are paid one year in arrears. AGD Co has an accounting year that ends on 31 December. If the machine is purchased, payment will be made in January of the first year of operation. If leased, annual lease rentals will be paid in January of each year of operation.

Required

(a) Using an after-tax borrowing rate of 7%, evaluate whether AGD Co should purchase or lease the new machine. **(10 marks)**

(b) The after-tax borrowing rate of 7% was used in the evaluation because a bank had offered to lend AGD Co $320,000 for a period of five years at a before-tax rate of 10% per year with interest payable every six months.

   Required

   (i) Calculate the annual percentage rate (APR) implied by the bank's offer to lend at 10% per year with interest payable every six months. **(2 marks)**

   (ii) Calculate the amount to be repaid at the end of each six-month period if the offered loan is to be repaid in equal instalments. **(3 marks)**

   (Total = 15 marks)

50 Leaminger Co (FMC, 12/02, amended)   27 mins

Leaminger Co has decided it must replace its major turbine machine on 31 December 20X2. The machine is essential to the operations of the company. The company is, however, considering whether to purchase the machine outright or to use lease financing.

Purchasing the machine outright

The machine is expected to cost $360,000 if it is purchased outright, payable on 31 December 20X2. After four years the company expects new technology to make the machine redundant and it will be sold on 31 December 20X6 generating proceeds of $20,000. Tax allowable depreciation is available on the cost of the machine at the rate of 25% per annum reducing balance. A full year's allowance is given in the year of acquisition but no tax allowable depreciation is available in the year of disposal. The difference between the proceeds and the tax written down value in the year of disposal is allowable or chargeable for tax as appropriate.

Leasing

The company has approached its bank with a view to arranging a lease to finance the machine acquisition. The bank has offered two options with respect to leasing which are as follows:

	Finance lease	Operating lease
Contract length (years)	4	4
Annual rental	$135,000	$140,000
First rent payable	31 December 20X3	31 December 20X2

General

For both the purchasing and the finance lease option, maintenance costs of $15,000 per year are payable at the end of each year. All lease rentals (for both finance and operating options) can be assumed to be allowable for tax purposes in full in the year of payment. Assume that tax is payable one year after the end of the accounting year in which the transaction occurs. For the operating lease only, contracts are renewable annually at the discretion of either party. Leaminger Co has adequate taxable profits to relieve all its costs. The rate of tax on profits can be assumed to be 30%. The company's accounting year-end is 31 December. The company's annual after tax cost of capital is 10%.

Required

(a)   Calculate the present value at 31 December 20X2, using the after tax cost of capital, for

      (i)   purchasing the machine outright;
      (ii)   using the finance lease to acquire the machine; and
      (iii)   using the operating lease to acquire the machine.

      Recommend the optimal method.   **(10 marks)**

(b)   Assume now that the company is facing capital rationing up until 30 December 20X3 when it expects to make a share issue. During this time the most marginal investment project, which is perfectly divisible, requires an outlay of $500,000 and would generate a net present value of $100,000. Investment in the turbine would reduce funds available for this project. Investments cannot be delayed.

      Calculate the revised net present values of the three options for the turbine given capital rationing. Advise whether your recommendation in (a) would change.   **(5 marks)**

      (Total = 15 marks)

51 ASOP Co (12/09, amended)   27 mins

ASOP Co is considering an investment in new technology that will reduce operating costs through increasing energy efficiency and decreasing pollution. The new technology will cost $1 million and have a four-year life, at the end of which it will have a scrap value of $100,000.

A licence fee of $104,000 is payable at the end of the first year. This licence fee will increase by 4% per year in each subsequent year.

The new technology is expected to reduce operating costs by $5.80 per unit in current price terms. This reduction in operating costs is before taking account of expected inflation of 5% per year.

Forecast production volumes over the life of the new technology are expected to be as follows:

Year	1	2	3	4
Production (units per year)	60,000	75,000	95,000	80,000

If ASOP Co bought the new technology, it would finance the purchase through a four-year loan paying interest at an annual before-tax rate of 8.6% per year.

Alternatively, ASOP Co could lease the new technology. The company would pay four annual lease rentals of $380,000 per year, payable in advance at the start of each year. The annual lease rentals include the cost of the licence fee.

If ASOP Co buys the new technology it can claim tax allowable depreciation on the investment on a 25% reducing balance basis. The company pays taxation one year in arrears at an annual rate of 30%. ASOP Co has an after-tax weighted average cost of capital of 11% per year.

Required

(a)   Based on financing cash flows only, calculate and determine whether ASOP Co should lease or buy the new technology.   **(10 marks)**

(b)   Using a nominal terms approach, calculate the net present value of buying the new technology and advise whether ASOP Co should undertake the proposed investment.   **(5 marks)**

      (Total = 15 marks)

52 Capital rationing   18 mins

(a)   Explain how cash shortages can restrict the investment opportunities of a business.   **(5 marks)**

(b)   Distinguish between 'hard' and 'soft' capital rationing, explaining why a company may deliberately choose to restrict its capital expenditure.   **(5 marks)**

      (Total = 10 marks)

53 Filtrex Co

(a) Filtrex Co is a medium-sized, all equity-financed, unquoted company which specialises in the development and production of water- and air-filtering devices to reduce the emission of effluents. Its small but ingenious R & D team has recently made a technological breakthrough which has revealed a number of attractive investment opportunities. It has applied for patents to protect its rights in all these areas. However, it lacks the financial resources required to exploit all of these projects, whose required outlays and post-tax NPVs are listed in the table below. Filtrex's managers consider that delaying any of these projects would seriously undermine their profitability, as competitors bring forward their own new developments. All projects are thought to have a similar degree of risk.

Project	Required outlay	NPV
	$	$
A	150,000	65,000
B	120,000	50,000
C	200,000	80,000
D	80,000	30,000
E	400,000	120,000

The NPVs have been calculated using as a discount rate the 18% post-tax rate of return which Filtrex requires for risky R & D ventures. The maximum amount available for this type of investment is $400,000, corresponding to Filtrex's present cash balances, built up over several years' profitable trading. Projects A and C are mutually exclusive and no project can be sub-divided. Any unused capital will either remain invested in short-term deposits or used to purchase marketable securities, both of which offer a return well below 18% post-tax.

Required

(i) Advise Filtrex Co, using suitable supporting calculations, which combination of projects should be undertaken in the best interests of shareholders; and

(ii) Suggest what further information might be obtained to assist a fuller analysis. **(9 marks)**

(b) Explain how, apart from delaying projects, Filtrex Co could manage to exploit more of these opportunities.

(6 marks)

(Total = 15 marks)

54 Warden Co (12/11, amended)

Warden Co plans to buy a new machine. The cost of the machine, payable immediately, is $800,000 and the machine has an expected life of five years. Additional investment in working capital of $90,000 will be required at the start of the first year of operation. At the end of five years, the machine will be sold for scrap, with the scrap value expected to be 5% of the initial purchase cost of the machine. The machine will not be replaced.

Production and sales from the new machine are expected to be 100,000 units per year. Each unit can be sold for $16 per unit and will incur variable costs of $11 per unit. Incremental fixed costs arising from the operation of the machine will be $160,000 per year.

Warden Co has an after-tax cost of capital of 11% which it uses as a discount rate in investment appraisal. The company pays profit tax one year in arrears at an annual rate of 30% per year. Tax allowable depreciation and inflation should be ignored.

Required

(a) Calculate the net present value of investing in the new machine and advise whether the investment is financially acceptable. **(7 marks)**

(b) (i) Explain briefly the meaning of the term 'sensitivity analysis' in the context of investment appraisal.

(2 marks)

(ii) Calculate the sensitivity of the investment in the new machine to a change in selling price and to a change in discount rate, and comment on your findings. **(6 marks)**

(Total = 15 marks)

55 Ridag Co (6/12, amended)

18 mins

Ridag Co is a project called Project 1.

Project 1

This is an investment in new machinery to produce a recently-developed product. The cost of the machinery, which is payable immediately, is $1.5 million, and the scrap value of the machinery at the end of four years is expected to be $100,000. Tax-allowable depreciation can be claimed on this investment on a 25% reducing balance basis. Information on future returns from the investment has been forecast to be as follows:

Year	1	2	3	4
Sales volume (units/year)	50,000	95,000	140,000	75,000
Selling price ($/unit)	25.00	24.00	23.00	23.00
Variable cost ($/unit)	10.00	11.00	12.00	12.50
Fixed costs ($/unit)	105,000	115,000	125,000	125,000

This information must be adjusted to allow for selling price inflation of 4% per year and variable cost inflation of 2.5% per year. Fixed costs, which are wholly attributable to the project, have already been adjusted for inflation. Ridag Co pays profit tax of 30% per year one year in arrears.

Other information

Ridag Co has a nominal before-tax weighted average cost of capital of 12% and a nominal after-tax weighted average cost of capital of 7%.

Required

Calculate the net present value of Project 1 and comment on whether this project is financially acceptable.

(10 marks)

56 Gadir Co (6/12, amended)

27 mins

Gadir Co plans to replace an existing machine and must choose between two machines. Machine 1 has an initial cost of $200,000 and will have a scrap value of $25,000 after four years. Machine 2 has an initial cost of $225,000 and will have a scrap value of $50,000 after three years. Annual maintenance costs of the two machines are as follows:

Year	1	2	3	4
Machine 1 ($/year)	25,000	29,000	32,000	35,000
Machine 2 ($/year)	15,000	20,000	25,000	

Where relevant, all information relating to Project 2 has already been adjusted to include expected future inflation. Taxation and tax allowable depreciation must be ignored in relation to Machine 1 and Machine 2.

Other information

Gadir Co has a nominal before-tax weighted average cost of capital of 12% and a nominal after-tax weighted average cost of capital of 7%.

Required

(a) Calculate the equivalent annual costs of Machine 1 and Machine 2, and discuss which machine should be purchased. **(7 marks)**

(b) Critically discuss the use of sensitivity analysis and probability analysis as ways of including risk in the investment appraisal process, referring in your answer to the relative effectiveness of each period. **(8 marks)**

(Total = 15 marks)

57 BQK Co (12/12, amended)

BQK Co, a house-building company, plans to build 100 houses on a development site over the next four years. The purchase cost of the development site is $4,000,000, payable at the start of the first year of construction. Two types of house will be built, with annual sales of each house expected to be as follows:

Year	1	2	3	4
Number of small houses sold:	15	20	15	5
Number of large houses sold:	7	8	15	15

Houses are built in the year of sale. Each customer finances the purchase of a home by taking out a long-term personal loan from their bank. Financial information relating to each type of house is as follows:

	Small house	Large house
Selling price:	$200,000	$350,000
Variable cost of construction:	$100,000	$200,000

Selling prices and variable cost of construction are in current price terms, before allowing for selling price inflation of 3% per year and variable cost of construction inflation of 4.5% per year.

Fixed infrastructure costs of $1,500,000 per year in current price terms would be incurred. These would not relate to any specific house, but would be for the provision of new roads, gardens, drainage and utilities. Infrastructure cost inflation is expected to be 2% per year.

BQK Co pays profit tax one year in arrears at an annual rate of 30%. The company can claim tax allowable depreciation on the purchase cost of the development site on a straight-line basis over the four years of construction.

BQK Co has a real after-tax cost of capital of 9% per year and a nominal after-tax cost of capital of 12% per year.

Required

Calculate the net present value of the proposed investment and comment on its financial acceptability. Work to the nearest $1,000. **(15 marks)**

58 MCQ bank – Sources of finance   18 mins

58.1   Which of the following is not a benefit, to the borrower, of an overdraft as opposed to a short-term loan?

A   Flexible repayment schedule
B   Only charged for the amount drawn down
C   Easy to arrange
D   Lower interest rates   (2 marks)

58.2   According to the creditor hierarchy, list the following from high risk to low risk:

1   Ordinary share capital
2   Preference share capital
3   Trade payables
4   Bank loan with fixed and floating charges

A   1,2,3,4
B   1,3,2,4
C   4,3,2,1
D   4,2,3,1   (2 marks)

58.3   Alpha is a listed company with a share price of $2 per share. It announces a 1-for-4 rights issue at $1.60 per share.

What is the theoretical ex-rights price?

A $2.40
B $1.80
C $1.68
D $1.92   (2 marks)

58.4   Which one of the following is issued at a discount to its redemption value and pays its holder no interest during its life?

A   A deep discount bond
B   A gilt-edged security
C   An unsecured loan note
D   A zero coupon bond   (2 marks)

58.5   Which of the following describes a sukuk?

A   A bond in Islamic finance where the lender owns the underlying asset and shares in the risks and rewards of ownership.

B   Equity in Islamic finance where profits are shared according to a pre agreed contract – dividends are not paid as such.

C   Trade credit in Islamic finance where a pre agreed mark up is agreed in advance for the convenience of paying later.

D   A lease in Islamic finance where the lessor retains ownership and the risk and rewards of ownership of the underlying asset.   (2 marks)

(Total = 10 marks)

59 MCQ bank – Dividend policy

18 mins

59.1 Which of the following are assumptions for Modigliani and Miller's dividend irrelevance theory?

1 Perfect capital markets
2 No taxes or tax preferences
3 No transaction costs
4 No inflation

A 1,2,3 only
B 1,2,4 only
C 2,3,4 only
D 1,2,3,4   (2 marks)

59.2 Which of the below best describes the signalling effect of dividend policy/announcements?

A The current dividend policy signals future dividend patterns.

B A dividend that is different to investor expectations signals information about the business to the investors.

C It flags reported financial results to follow.

D It indicates cash flow health or otherwise.   (2 marks)

59.3 In Modigliani & Miller's Dividend Irrelevance theory, the process of 'manufacturing dividends' refers to which of the following?

A Dividends from manufacturing businesses.
B Investors selling some shares to realise some capital gain.
C Creative accounting to allow dividends to be paid.
D Investing plans designed to create regular returns to shareholders.   (2 marks)

59.4 What does an enhanced scrip dividend mean?

A In addition to the scrip dividend cash is also paid
B Bonus shares are paid in return for accepting a delay
C More than $1 worth of shares is offered as an alternative to every $1 cash dividend to be paid
D A higher scrip dividend is offered to a limited shareholder group.   (2 marks)

59.5 Three companies (A, B and C) have the following dividend payments history:

Company	20X1	20X2	20X3
A – Dividend	100	110	121
A - Earnings	200	200	201
B – Dividend	50	150	25
B – Earnings	100	300	50
C – Dividend	nil	300	nil
C - Earnings	400	350	500

Which best describes their apparent dividend policies?

	A	B	C
A	Constant growth	Constant pay-out	Residual
B	Constant pay-out	Constant growth	Residual
C	High pay-out	Residual	Random
D	Constant growth	Residual	Random

(2 marks)

(Total = 10 marks)

60 MCQ bank – Gearing and capital structure

60.1 A summary of HM Co's recent statement of profit or loss is given below:

	$'000
Turnover	10,123
Cost of sales	(7,222)
Gross profit	2,901
Expenses	(999)
Profit before interest and tax	1,902
Interest	(1,000)
Tax	(271)
Profit after interest and tax	631

70% of cost of sales and 10% of expenses are variable costs.

What is HM Co's operational gearing?

A   7.87
B   0.71
C   2.61
D   0.40   **(2 marks)**

60.2 The following is an extract of ELW's statement of financial position.

	$million	$million
Total assets		1,000
$1 Ordinary share capital	100	
Retained earnings	400	
Total equity	500	
Loan notes	500	
		1,000

The ordinary shares are currently quoted at $5.50, and loan notes are trading at $125 per $100 nominal.

What is ELW's financial gearing ratio (debt/debt+equity) using market values?

A   40%
B   56%
C   57%
D   53%   **(2 marks)**

60.3 Who suffers financial risk as financial gearing increases, and why?

A   Lenders because they are less likely to be repaid.
B   Lenders because there are fewer assets to offer as security.
C   Shareholders as their returns are lower.
D   Shareholders as their dividends become more variable.   **(2 marks)**

60.4 AB Co has an interest cover greater than one and gearing (debt/debt + equity) of 50%.

What will be the impact on interest cover and gearing of issuing shares to repay half the debt?

	Interest cover	Gearing
A	Rise	Rise
B	Rise	Fall
C	Fall	Rise
D	Fall	Fall

(2 marks)

60.5 All else being equal, a poor set of results and lower dividends that aren't as bad as shareholders were expecting would probably have the following impact:

	P/E ratio	Dividend yield
A	Increase	Increase
B	Increase	Decrease
C	Decrease	Increase
D	Decrease	Decrease

(2 marks)

(Total = 10 marks)

61 MCQ bank – The cost of capital

36 mins

61.1 GG Co has a cost of equity of 25%. It has 4 million shares in issue, and has had for many years.

Its dividend payments in the years 20X9 to 20Y3 were as follows.

End of year	Dividends
	$'000
20X9	220
20Y0	257
20Y1	310
20Y2	356
20Y3	423

Dividends are expected to continue to grow at the same average rate into the future.

According to the dividend valuation model, what should be the share price at the start of 20Y4?

A $0.96
B $1.10
C $1.47
D $1.73

(2 marks)

61.2 IPA Co is about to pay a $0.50 dividend on each ordinary share. Its earnings per share was $1.50.

Net assets per share is $6. Current share price is $4.50 per share.

What is the cost of equity?

A 31%
B 30%
C 22%
D 21%

(2 marks)

61.3 Which of the following best describes systematic risk?

A The chance that automated processes may fail
B The risk associated with investing in equity
C The diversifiable risk associated with investing in equity
D The residual risk associated with investing in a well-diversified portfolio.

(2 marks)

61.4 A share in MS Co has an equity beta of 1.3. MS Co's debt beta is 0.1. It has a gearing ratio of 20% (debt:equity). The market premium is 8% and the risk free rate is 3%. MS Co pays 30% corporation tax.

What is the cost of equity for MS Co?

A 8.4%
B 12.2%
C 13.4%
D 9.5%

(2 marks)

61.5 HB Co has in issue 10% irredeemable loan notes, currently traded at 95% cum-interest.

If the tax rate changes from 30% to 20% for the company, the cost of irredeemable debt:

A   Increases to 9.4%
B   Increases to 8.4%
C   Decreases to 9.4%
D   Decreases to 8.4%   (2 marks)

61.6 BRW Co has 10% redeemable loan notes in issue trading at $90. The loan notes are redeemable at a 10% premium in 5 years time, or convertible at that point into 20 ordinary shares. The current share price is $2.50 and is expected to grow at 10% per annum for the foreseeable future. BRW Co pays 30% corporation tax.

What is the best estimate of the cost of these loan notes?

A   9.8%
B   7.9%
C   11.5%
D   15.2%   (2 marks)

61.7 IDO Co has a capital structure as follows:

	£m
10m $0.50 ordinary shares	5
Reserves	20
13% Irredeemable loan notes	7
	32

The ordinary shares are currently quoted at $3.00, and the loan notes at $90. IDO Co has a cost of equity of 12% and pays corporation tax at a rate of 30%.

What is IDO Co's weighted average cost of capital?

A   10.4%
B   11.1%
C   11.7%
D   11.8%   (2 marks)

61.8 Which of the following are assumed if a company's current weighted average cost of capital ('WACC') is to be used to appraise a potential project?

1   Capital structure will remain unchanged for the duration of the project
2   The business risk of the project is the same as the current business operations
3   The project is relatively small in size

A   1 and 2 only
B   2 and 3 only
C   1 and 3 only
D   1, 2 and 3   (2 marks)

61.9 Which of the following assumptions is not required when using the capital asset pricing model to estimate the cost of equity for project appraisal?

A   Efficient capital markets
B   Well diversified investors
C   Future periods are consistent with the present
D   Companies are well diversified   (2 marks)

61.10 An 8% irredeemable $0.50 preference share is being traded for $0.30 cum-div currently in a company that pays corporation tax at a rate of 30%.

What is the cost of capital for these preference shares?

A   10.8%
B   15.4%
C   26.7%
D   18.7%   (2 marks)
                                                                        (Total = 20 marks)

62 MCQ bank – Capital structure

36 mins

62.1 A Co's gearing is 1:1 Debt:equity. The industry average is 1:5. A Co are looking to raise finance for investment in a new project and they are wondering whether to raise debt or equity.

According to the traditional view:

A   They should take on debt finance as to do so will save tax.
B   They should take on equity finance as their gearing is probably beyond optimal.
C   It doesn't matter as it won't affect the returns the projects generate.
D   More information is needed before a decision can be made.

(2 marks)

62.2 **Why do Modigliani-Miller (with tax) assume increased gearing will reduce the weighted average cost of capital ('WACC')?**

A   Debt is cheaper than equity
B   Interest payments are tax deductible
C   Reduced levels of expensive equity capital will reduce the WACC
D   Financial risk is not pronounced at moderate borrowing levels

(2 marks)

62.3 SD Co increased its gearing and its weighted average cost of capital reduced.

Which of the following theories might explain this?

1   Modigliani-Miller (with tax)
2   The traditional view
3   Pecking order theory
4   Modigliani-Miller (no tax)

A   1, 2 and 3 only
B   1 and 4 only
C   1 and 2 only
D   2 and 4 only

(2 marks)

62.4 Director A believes there is an optimal balance of debt:equity whereas director B doesn't believe the gearing decision affects the value of the business.

Which theories are the directors subscribing to?

	Director A	Director B
A	MM (with tax)	MM (no tax)
B	traditional view	MM (no tax)
C	traditional view	MM (with tax)
D	MM (no tax)	traditional view

(2 marks)

62.5 **Pecking order theory suggests finance should be raised in which order?**

A   Internal funds, rights issue, debt
B   Internal funds, debt, new equity
C   Debt, internal funds, new equity
D   Rights issue, internal funds, debt

(2 marks)

The following information relates to questions 62.6 and 62.7.

TR Co has a gearing level of 1:3 debt: equity. TR is considering diversifying into a new market. B Co is already operating in the new market. B Co has an equity beta of 1.05 and a gearing level of 1:4 Debt:equity. Both companies pay 30% corporation tax.

62.6 **What is the asset beta relevant to TR for the new market?**

A   0.89
B   0.84
C   0.28
D   0.75

(2 marks)

62.7 The risk free rate is 4% and the market premium is 4%.

What is TR Co's cost of equity for assessing the decision to diversify into the new market?

A   4%
B   7.6%
C   8.4%
D   6.3%   (2 marks)

62.8 **Why is an asset beta generally lower than an equity beta?**

A   An equity beta also includes an element of financial risk
B   Returns from assets are tax deductible.
C   Asset betas contain less business risk
D   Capital markets are generally more efficient than business operations.   (2 marks)

62.9 **When should a project-specific cost of capital be used for investment appraisal?**

A   If new finance is required before the project can go ahead.
B   If the project is small.
C   If the project is different from current operations.
D   If the project is the same as current operations.   (2 marks)

62.10 **What does tax exhaustion mean?**

A   All avenues have been explored to minimise corporation tax.
B   As deductions have reduced tax payable to zero, further deductions won't save tax.
C   Non current assets have a zero tax written down value.
D   Tax liabilities have been completely discharged.   (2 marks)
                                                                       (Total = 20 marks)

63 Tirwen Co (FMC, 12/04,amended)   27 mins

Tirwen Co is a medium-sized manufacturing company which is considering a 1 for 5 rights issue at a 15% discount to the current market price of $4.00 per share. Issue costs are expected to be $220,000 and these costs will be paid out of the funds raised. It is proposed that the rights issue funds raised will be used to redeem some of the existing loan stock at nominal value. Financial information relating to Tirwen Co is as follows:

Current statement of financial position

	$'000	$'000
Non-current assets		6,550
Current assets		
Inventory	2,000	
Receivables	1,500	
Cash	300	
		3,800
Total assets		10,350
Ordinary shares (nominal value 50c)		2,000
Reserves		1,500
12% loan notes 2X12		4,500
Current liabilities		
Trade payables	1,100	
Overdraft	1,250	
		2,350
Total equity and liabilities		10,350

Other information:

Price/earnings ratio of Tirwen Co:	15.24
Overdraft interest rate:	7%
Tax rate:	30%
Sector averages: debt/equity ratio (book value):	100%
interest cover:	6 times

Required

(a)   Ignoring issue costs and any use that may be made of the funds raised by the rights issue, calculate:

    (i)   the theoretical ex rights price per share;

    (ii)   the value of rights per existing share. **(3 marks)**

(b)   What alternative actions are open to the owner of 1,000 shares in Tirwen Co as regards the rights issue? Determine the effect of each of these actions on the wealth of the investor. **(6 marks)**

(c)   Calculate the current earnings per share and the revised earnings per share if the rights issue funds are used to redeem some of the existing loan notes. **(6 marks)**

(Total = 15 marks)

64 Food retailers 1

27 mins

Food Retailers: Ordinary Shares, Key Stock Market Statistics

		Share price (cents)		Dividend	P/E
Company	Current	52 week high	52 week low	Yield (%)	ratio
Ply	63	112	54	1.8	14.2
Axis	291	317	187	2.1	13.0
Spin	187	201	151	2.3	21.1

Required

(a)   Illustrating your answer by use of data in the table above, define and explain the term P/E ratio, and comment on the way it may be used by an investor to appraise a possible share purchase. **(7 marks)**

(b)   Using data in the above table, calculate the dividend cover for Spin and Axis, and explain the meaning and significance of the measure from the point of view of equity investors. **(8 marks)**

(Total = 15 marks)

65 Food retailers 2

18 mins

(a)   Under what circumstances might a company be tempted to pay dividends which are in excess of earnings, and what are the dangers associated with such an approach?

You should ignore tax in answering this question. **(6 marks)**

(b)   The directors of Axis Co are currently considering whether to raise finance by means of a bond issue or an issue of preference shares.

Describe the reasons why the directors might choose to issue bonds rather than preference shares to raise the required finance. **(4 marks)**

(Total = 10 marks)

66 TFR Co (FMC, 6/07, amended)

27 mins

TFR Co is a small, profitable, owner-managed company which is seeking finance for a planned expansion. A local bank has indicated that it may be prepared to offer a loan of $100,000 at a fixed annual rate of 9%. TFR Co would repay $25,000 of the capital each year for the next four years. Annual interest would be calculated on the opening balance at the start of each year. Current financial information on TFR Co is as follows:

Current turnover	$210,000
Net profit margin	20%
Annual taxation rate	25%
Average overdraft	$20,000
Average interest on overdraft	10% per year
Dividend payout ratio	50%
Shareholders funds	$200,000
Market value of non-current assets	$180,000

As a result of the expansion, turnover would increase by $45,000 per year for each of the next four years, while net profit margin would remain unchanged. No tax allowable depreciation would arise from investment of the amount borrowed.

TFR Co currently has no other debt than the existing and continuing overdraft and has no cash or near-cash investments. The non-current assets consist largely of the building from which the company conducts its business. The current dividend payout ratio has been maintained for several years.

Required

(a)   Assuming that TFR is granted the loan, calculate the following ratios for TFR Co for each of the next four years.

     (i)   interest cover
     (ii)   medium to long-term debt/equity ratio
     (iii)   return on equity
     (iv)   return on capital employed   **(10 marks)**

(b)   Discuss the difficulties commonly faced by small firms such as TFR Co when seeking additional finance.

     (5 marks)

     (Total = 15 marks)

67 Echo Co (12/07, amended)   18 mins

The following financial information relates to Echo Co:

Statement of profit or loss information for the last year

	$m
Profit before interest and tax	12
Interest	3
Profit before tax	9
Income tax expense	3
Profit for the period	6
Dividends	2
Retained profit for the period	4

Statement of financial position information as at the end of the last year

	$m	$m
Ordinary shares, nominal value 50c	5	
Retained earnings	15	
Total equity		20
8% loan notes, redeemable in three years' time		30
Total equity and non-current liabilities		50

Average data on companies similar to Echo Co:

Interest coverage ratio	8 times
Long-term debt/equity (book value basis)	80%

The board of Echo Co is considering two proposals that have been made by its finance director. Each proposal is independent of any other proposal.

Proposal A

The current dividend per share should be increased by 20% in order to make the company more attractive to equity investors.

Proposal B

A bond issue should be made in order to raise $15 million of new debt capital. Although there are no investment opportunities currently available, the cash raised would be invested on a short-term basis until a suitable investment opportunity arose. The loan notes would pay interest at a rate of 10% per year and be redeemable in eight years' time at nominal value.

Required

(a) Analyse and discuss Proposal A. **(5 marks)**
(b) Evaluate and discuss Proposal B. **(5 marks)**

(Total = 10 marks)

68 Echo Beach Co (12/07, amended) 27 mins

The following financial information relates to Echo Beach Co:

Statement of profit or loss information for the last year

	$m
Profit before interest and tax	12
Interest	3
Profit before tax	9
Income tax expense	3
Profit for the period	6
Dividends	2
Retained profit for the period	4

Statement of financial position information as at the end of the last year

	$m	$m
Ordinary shares, nominal value 50c	5	
Retained earnings	15	
Total equity		20
8% loan notes, redeemable in three years' time		30
Total equity and non-current liabilities		50

Average data on companies similar to Echo Beach Co:

Interest coverage ratio	8 times
Long-term debt/equity (book value basis)	80%

The board of Echo Beach Co is considering a proposal made by its finance director.

Proposal

A 1 for 4 rights issue should be made at a 20% discount to the current share price of $2.30 per share in order to reduce gearing and the financial risk of the company.

Required

(a) Calculate the theoretical ex rights price per share and the amount of finance that would be raised under the proposal. Evaluate and discuss the proposal to use these funds to reduce gearing and financial risk.

(8 marks)

(b) Discuss the attractions of operating leasing as a source of finance. **(7 marks)**

(Total = 15 marks)

69 Nugfer Co (12/10, amended)

27 mins

The following financial position statement as at 30 November 20X0 refers to Nugfer Co, a stock exchange-listed company, which wishes to raise $200m in cash in order to acquire a competitor.

	$m	$m	$m
Assets			
Non-current assets			300
Current assets			211
Total assets			511
Equity and liabilities			
Share capital		100	
Retained earnings		121	
Total equity			221
Non-current liabilities			
Long-term borrowings		100	
Current liabilities			
Trade payables	30		
Short-term borrowings	160		
Total current liabilities		190	
Total liabilities			290
Total equity and liabilities			511

The recent performance of Nugfer Co in profitability terms is as follows:

Year ending 30 November	20W7	20W8	20W9	20X0
	$m	$m	$m	$m
Revenue	122.6	127.3	156.6	189.3
Operating profit	41.7	43.3	50.1	56.7
Finance charges (interest)	6.0	6.2	12.5	18.8
Profit before tax	35.7	37.1	37.6	37.9
Profit after tax	25.0	26.0	26.3	26.5

Notes:

(1) The long-term borrowings are 6% bonds that are repayable in 20X2

(2) The short-term borrowings consist of an overdraft at an annual interest rate of 8%

(3) The current assets do not include any cash deposits

(4) Nugfer Co has not paid any dividends in the last four years

(5) The number of ordinary shares issued by the company has not changed in recent years

(6) The target company has no debt finance and its forecast profit before interest and tax for 20X1 is $28 million

Required

Evaluate suitable methods of raising the $200 million required by Nugfer Co, supporting your evaluation with both analysis and critical discussion. **(15 marks)**

70 Nug Co (12/10, amended)

18 mins

(a) Briefly explain the factors that will influence the rate of interest charged on a new issue of bonds. **(4 marks)**

(b) Identify and describe the three forms of efficiency that may be found in a capital market. **(6 marks)**

(Total = 10 marks)

71 YNM Co (6/11, amended)

The following financial information relates to YNM Co, which has a cost of equity of 12%. Assume that it is now 31 March 20X8 and that the ordinary share price of YNM Co is $4.17 per share. YNM Co has been experiencing trading difficulties due to a continuing depressed level of economic activity.

Statement of profit or loss information for recent years ending 31 March

	20X6	20X7	20X8
	$m	$m	$m
Profit before interest and tax	29.3	26.6	25.3
Finance charges (interest)	4.8	5.3	5.5
Profit before tax	24.5	21.3	19.8
Taxation expense	7.3	6.4	5.9
Profit for the period	17.2	14.9	13.9

Statement of financial position information as at 31 March 20X8

	$m	$m
Ordinary shares, nominal value $1	19.0	
Retained earnings	88.5	
Total equity		107.5
8% bonds, redeemable in two years' time		50.0
Total equity and non-current liabilities		157.5

Note: the statement of financial position takes no account of any dividend to be paid. The ordinary share capital of YNM Co has not changed during the period under consideration and the 8% bonds were issued in 20W6.

Dividend and share price information

	20X5	20X6	20X7
Total cash dividend paid ($m)		9.5	9.5
Share price at end of year ($/share)	5.94	5.10	4.59

Average data on companies similar to YNM Co:

Interest coverage ratio   10 times

Long-term debt/equity (book value basis)   40%

Financial objective of YNM Co

YNM Co has a declared objective of maximising shareholder wealth.

Dividend decision

YNM Co is considering two alternative dividend choices for the year ending 31 March 20X8:

(1)   To pay the same total cash dividend as in 20X7
(2)   To pay no dividend at all for the year ending 31 March 20X8

Financing decision

YNM Co is also considering raising $50 million of new debt finance to support existing business operations.

Required

Analyse and discuss the recent financial performance and the current financial position of YNM Co, commenting on:

(a)   achievement of the objective of maximising shareholder wealth;
(b)   the two dividend choices;
(c)   the proposal to raise $50 million of new debt finance.   **(10 marks)**

72 Bar Co (12/11, amended)

Bar Co is a stock exchange listed company that is concerned by its current level of debt finance. It plans to make a rights issue and to use the funds raised to pay off some of its debt. The rights issue will be at a 20% discount to its current ex-dividend share price of $7.50 per share and Bar Co plans to raise $90 million. Bar Co believes that paying off some of its debt will not affect its price/earnings ratio, which is expected to remain constant.

Statement of profit or loss information

	$m
Turnover	472
Cost of sales	423
Profit before interest and tax	49
Interest	10
Profit before tax	39
Tax	12
Profit after tax	27

Statement of financial position information

	$m
Equity	
Ordinary shares ($1 nominal)	60
	80
	140
Long-term liabilities	
8% bonds ($100 nominal)	125
	265

The 8% bonds are currently trading at $112.50 per $100 bond and bondholders have agreed that they will allow Bar Co to buy back the bonds at this market value. Bar Co pays tax at a rate of 30% per year

Required

(a) Calculate the theoretical ex rights price per share of Bar Co following the rights issue. **(3 marks)**

(b) Calculate and discuss whether using the cash raised by the rights issue to buy back bonds is likely to be financially acceptable to the shareholders of Bar Co, commenting in your answer on the belief that the current price/earnings ratio will remain constant. **(7 marks)**

(Total = 10 marks)

73 IML Co

IML Co is an all equity financed listed company. It develops customised software for clients which are mainly large civil engineering companies. Nearly all its shares are held by financial institutions.

IML Co's chairman has been dissatisfied with the company's performance for some time. Some directors were also concerned about the way in which the company is perceived by financial markets. In response, the company recently appointed a new finance director who advocated using the capital asset pricing model as a means of evaluating risk and interpreting the stock market's reaction to the company.

The following initial information was put forward by the finance director for two rival companies operating in the same industry:

	Equity Beta
AZT Co	0.7
BOR Co	1.4

The *finance director* notes that the risk-free rate is 5% each year and the expected rate of return on the market portfolio is 15% each year.

The *chairman* set out his concerns at a meeting of the board of directors: 'I fail to understand these calculations. AZT Co operates largely in overseas markets with all the risk which that involves, yet you seem to be arguing that it is a lower risk company than BOR Co, whose income is mainly derived from long-term contracts in our domestic building industry. I am very concerned that we can take too much notice of the stock market. Take last year for instance, we had to announce a loss and the share price went up.'

Required

(a)   Calculate, using the capital asset pricing model, the required rate of return on equity of:

    (i)   AZT Co
    (ii)   BOR Co   **(4 marks)**

(b)   Calculate the equity beta of IML Co, assuming its required annual rate of return on equity is 17% and the stock market uses the capital asset pricing model to calculate the equity beta, and explain the significance of the beta factor.   **(5 marks)**

(c)   Explain the assumptions and limitations of the capital asset pricing model.   **(6 marks)**

          (Total = 15 marks)

74 Li Co   18 mins

The following is an extract from the statement of financial position of Li Co at 31 December 20X9.

	$'000
Ordinary shares of 50c each	5,200
Reserves	4,850
9% preference shares of $1 each	4,500
14% loan notes	5,000
Total long-term funds	19,550

The ordinary shares are quoted at 80c. Assume the market estimate of the next ordinary dividend is 4c, growing thereafter at 12% per annum indefinitely. The preference shares which are irredeemable are quoted at 72c and the loan notes are quoted at nominal value. Tax on profits is 33%.

Required

(a)   Use the relevant data above to calculate the company's weighted average cost of capital (WACC), ie the return required by the providers of the three types of capital, using the respective market values as weighting factors.   **(5 marks)**

(b)   Assume that the loan notes have recently been issued specifically to fund the company's expansion programme under which a number of projects are being considered. It has been suggested at a project appraisal meeting that because these projects are to be financed by the loan notes, the cutoff rate for project acceptance should be the after-tax interest rate on the loan notes rather than the WACC. Discuss this suggestion.   **(5 marks)**

          (Total = 10 marks)

75 FAQ   27 mins

FAQ is a profitable, listed manufacturing company, which is considering a project to diversify into the manufacture of computer equipment. This would involve spending $220 million on a new production plant.

It is expected that FAQ will continue to be financed by 60% debt and 40% equity. The debt consists of 10% loan notes, redeemable at nominal value after 10 years with a current market value of $90. Any new debt is expected to have the same cost of capital.

FAQ pays tax at a rate of 30% and its ordinary shares are currently trading at 453c. The equity beta of FAQ is estimated to be 1.21. The systematic risk of debt may be assumed to be zero. The risk free rate is 6.75% and market return 12.5%.

The estimated equity beta of the main competitor in the same industry as the new proposed plant is 1.4, and the competitor's capital gearing is 35% equity and 65% debt by book values.

Required

(a)   Calculate the after-tax cost of debt of FAQ's loan notes.   **(3 marks)**

(b)   Calculate a project-specific discount rate for the proposed investment.   **(6 marks)**

(c)   Discuss the problems that may be encountered in applying this discount rate to the proposed investment.

                                                                                                      (6 marks)

                                                                                          (Total = 15 marks)

76 Droxfol Co (Specimen paper 2007, amended)   27 mins

Current financial information on Droxfol Co is as follows.

Statement of profit or loss information for the last year

		$000
Profit before interest and tax		7,000
Interest		(500)
Profit before tax		6,500
Tax		(1,950)
Profit for the period		4,550

Statement of financial position for the last year	$000	$000
Non-current assets		20,000
Current assets		20,000
Total assets		40,000
Equity and liabilities		
Ordinary shares, nominal value $1	5,000	
Retained earnings	22,500	
Total equity		27,500
10% loan notes	5,000	
9% preference shares, nominal value $1	2,500	
Total non-current liabilities		7,500
Current liabilities		5,000
Total equity and liabilities		40,000

The current ex div ordinary share price is $4.50 per share. An ordinary dividend of 35 cents per share has just been paid and dividends are expected to increase by 4% per year for the foreseeable future. The current ex div preference share price is 76.2 cents. The loan notes are secured on the existing non-current assets of Droxfol Co and are redeemable at nominal value in eight years' time. They have a current ex interest market price of $105 per $100 loan note. Droxfol Co pays tax on profits at an annual rate of 30%.

Required

(a)   Calculate the current weighted average cost of capital of Droxfol Co.   **(9 marks)**

(b)   Discuss whether financial management theory suggests that Droxfol Co can reduce its weighted average cost of capital to a minimum level.   **(6 marks)**

                                                                                          (Total = 15 marks)

77 Burse Co (6/08, amended)

18 mins

Burse Co wishes to calculate its weighted average cost of capital and the following information relates to the company at the current time:

Number of ordinary shares	20 million
Book value of 7% convertible debt	$29 million
Book value of 8% bank loan	$2 million
Market price of ordinary shares	$5.50 per share
Market value of convertible debt	$107.11 per $100 bond
Equity beta of Burse Co	1.2
Risk-free rate of return	4.7%
Equity risk premium	6.5%
Rate of taxation	30%

Burse Co expects share prices to rise in the future at an average rate of 6% per year. The convertible debt can be redeemed at nominal value in eight years' time, or converted in six years' time into 15 shares of Burse Co per $100 bond.

Required

Calculate the market value weighted average cost of capital of Burse Co. State clearly any assumptions that you make. **(10 marks)**

78 Purse Co (6/08, amended)

27 mins

(a) Discuss the circumstances under which the weighted average cost of capital can be used in investment appraisal. **(7 marks)**

(a) Discuss whether the dividend growth model or the capital asset pricing model offers the better estimate of the cost of equity of a company. **(8 marks)**

(Total = 15 marks)

79 DD Co (12/09, amended)

27 mins

DD Co has a dividend payout ratio of 40% and has maintained this payout ratio for several years. The current dividend per share of the company is 50c per share and it expects that its next dividend per share, payable in one year's time, will be 52c per share.

The capital structure of the company is as follows:

	$m	$m
Equity		
Ordinary shares (nominal value $1 per share)	25	
Reserves	35	
		60
Debt		
Bond A (nominal value $100)	20	
Bond B (nominal value $100)	10	
		30
		90

Bond A will be redeemed at nominal value in ten years' time and pays annual interest of 9%. The current ex interest market price of the bond is $95.08.

Bond B will be redeemed at nominal value in four years' time and pays annual interest of 8%. The cost of debt of this bond is 7.82% per year. The current ex interest market price of the bond is $102.01.

Bond A and Bond B were issued at the same time.

DD Co has an equity beta of 1.2. The risk-free rate of return is 4% per year and the average return on the market of 11% per year. Ignore taxation.

Required

(a)   Calculate the cost of debt of Bond A.   **(3 marks)**

(b)   Discuss the reasons why different bonds of the same company might have different costs of debt.

                                                                                                                (6 marks)

(c)   Discuss whether a change in dividend policy will affect the share price of DD Co.   **(6 marks)**

                                                                                                        (Total = 15 marks)

80 YGV Co (6/10, amended)   27 mins

YGV Co is a listed company selling computer software. Its profit before interest and tax has fallen from $5 million to $1 million in the last year and its current financial position is as follows:

	$000	$000
Non-current assets		
Property, plant and equipment	3,000	
Intangible assets	8,500	11,500
Current assets		
Inventory	4,100	
Trade receivables	11,100	15,200
Total assets		26,700
Equity		
Ordinary shares	10,000	
Reserves	7,000	17,000
Current liabilities		
Trade payables	5,200	
Overdraft	4,500	9,700
Total equity and liabilities		26,700

YGV Co has been advised by its bank that the current overdraft limit of $4.5 million will be reduced to $500,000 in two months' time. The finance director of YGV Co has been unable to find another bank willing to offer alternative overdraft facilities and is planning to issue bonds on the stock market in order to finance the reduction of the overdraft. The bonds would be issued at their nominal value of $100 per bond and would pay interest of 9% per year, payable at the end of each year. The bonds would be redeemable at a 10% premium to their nominal value after 10 years. The finance director hopes to raise $4 million from the bond issue.

The ordinary shares of YGV Co have a nominal value of $1.00 per share and a current market value of $4.10 per share. The cost of equity of YGV Co is 12% per year and the current interest rate on the overdraft is 5% per year. Taxation is at an annual rate of 30%.

Other financial information:

Average gearing of sector (debt/equity, market value basis):   10%

Average interest coverage ratio of sector: 8 times

Required

(a)   Calculate the after–tax cost of debt of the 9% bonds.   **(5 marks)**

(b)   Calculate and comment on the effect of the bond issue on the weighted average cost of capital of YGV Co, clearly stating any assumptions that you make.   **(6 marks)**

(c)   Calculate the effect of using the bond issue to finance the reduction in the overdraft on:

        (i)   the interest coverage ratio;
        (ii)   gearing.   **(4 marks)**

                                                                                                        (Total = 15 marks)

81 NN Co (12/10, amended)

18 mins

Discuss the factors to be considered in formulating the dividend policy of a stock-exchange listed company.

(10 marks)

82 NNN Co (12/10, amended)

18 mins

	$m	$m	$m
Assets			
Non-current assets			101
Current assets			
Inventory		11	
Trade receivables		21	
Cash		10	
			42
Total assets			143
Equity and liabilities			
Ordinary share capital		50	
Preference share capital		25	
Retained earnings		19	
Total equity			94
Non-current liabilities			
Long-term borrowings		20	
Current liabilities			
Trade payables	22		
Other payables	7		
Total current liabilities		29	
Total liabilities			49
Total equity and liabilities			143

The ordinary shares of the company have a nominal value of 50 cents per share and an ex div market value of $8.30 per share.

The long-term borrowings of NNN Co consist of 7% bonds that are redeemable in six years' time at their nominal value of $100 per bond. The current ex interest market price of the bonds is $103.50.

The preference shares of NNN Co have a nominal value of 50 cents per share and pay an annual dividend of 8%. The ex div market value of the preference shares is 67 cents per share.

NNN Co pay profit tax at an annual rate of 25% per year

Required

(a) Calculate the after-tax cost of debt of NNN Co. **(4 marks)**
(b) Calculate the weighted average after-tax cost of capital of NNN Co. **(6 marks)**

(Total = 10 marks)

83 AQR Co (6/11, amended)

27 mins

The finance director of AQR Co has heard that the market value of the company will increase if the weighted average cost of capital of the company is decreased. The company, which is listed on a stock exchange, has 100 million shares in issue and the current ex div ordinary share price is $2.50 per share. AQR Co also has in issue bonds with a book value of $60 million and their current ex interest market price is $104 per $100 bond. The current after-tax cost of debt of AQR Co is 7% and the tax rate is 30%.

The recent dividends per share of the company are as follows.

Year	20X0	20X1	20X2	20X3	20X4
Dividend per share (cents)	19.38	20.20	20.41	21.02	21.80

The finance director proposes to decrease the weighted average cost of capital of AQR Co, and hence increase its market value, by issuing $40 million of bonds at their nominal value of $100 per bond. These bonds would pay annual interest of 8% before tax and would be redeemed at a 5% premium to par after 10 years.

Required

(a)   Calculate the market value after-tax weighted average cost of capital of AQR Co in the following circumstances:

   (i)   before the new issue of bonds takes place;
   (ii)   after the new issue of bonds takes place.

   Comment on your findings.   **(10 marks)**

(b)   Identify and discuss briefly the factors that influence the market value of traded bonds.   **(5 marks)**

(Total = 15 marks)

84 Corhig Co (6/12, amended)

27 mins

Corhig Co is a company that is listed on a major stock exchange. The company has struggled to maintain profitability in the last two years due to poor economic conditions in its home country and as a consequence it has decided not to pay a dividend in the current year. However, there are now clear signs of economic recovery and Corhig Co is optimistic that payment of dividends can be resumed in the future. Forecast financial information relating to the company is as follows:

Year	1	2	3
Earnings ($000)	3,000	3,600	4,300
Dividends ($000)	nil	500	1,000

The company is optimistic that earnings and dividends will increase after Year 3 at a constant annual rate of 3% per year.

Corhig Co currently has a before-tax cost of debt of 5% per year and an equity beta of 1·6. On a market value basis, the company is currently financed 75% by equity and 25% by debt.

During the course of the last two years the company acted to reduce its gearing and was able to redeem a large amount of debt. Since there are now clear signs of economic recovery, Corhig Co plans to raise further debt in order to modernise some of its non-current assets and to support the expected growth in earnings. This additional debt would mean that the capital structure of the company would change and it would be financed 60% by equity and 40% by debt on a market value basis. The before-tax cost of debt of Corhig Co would increase to 6% per year and the equity beta of Corhig Co would increase to 2.

The risk-free rate of return is 4% per year and the equity risk premium is 5% per year. In order to stimulate economic activity the government has reduced profit tax rate for all large companies to 20% per year.

The current average price/earnings ratio of listed companies similar to Corhig Co is 5 times.

Required

(a) Estimate the value of Corhig Co using the price/earnings ratio method and discuss the usefulness of the
     variables that you have used.   **(4 marks)**

(b) Calculate the current cost of equity of Corhig Co and, using this value, calculate the value of the company
     using the dividend valuation model.   **(6 marks)**

(c) Calculate the current weighted average after-tax cost of capital of Corhig Co and the weighted average after-
     tax cost of capital following the new debt issue, and comment on the difference between the two values.
                                                                                            (5 marks)

                                                                                   (Total = 15 marks)

85 BKB Co (12/12, amended)   27 mins

The statement of financial position of BKB Co provides the following information:

	$m	$m
Equity finance		
Ordinary shares ($1 nominal value)	25	
Reserves	15	40
Non-current liabilities		
7% Convertible bonds ($100 nominal value)	20	
5% Preference shares ($1 nominal value)	10	30
Current liabilities		
Trade payables	10	
Overdraft	15	25
Total liabilities		95

BKB Co has an equity beta of 1.2 and the ex-dividend market value of the company's equity is $125 million. The ex-
interest market value of the convertible bonds is $21 million and the ex-dividend market value of the preference
shares is $6.25 million.

The convertible bonds of BKB Co have a conversion ratio of 19 ordinary shares per bond. The conversion date and
redemption date are both on the same date in five years' time. The current ordinary share price of BKB Co is
expected to increase by 4% per year for the foreseeable future.

The overdraft has a variable interest rate which is currently 6% per year and BKB Co expects this to increase in the
near future. The overdraft has not changed in size over the last financial year, although one year ago the overdraft
interest rate was 4% per year. The company's bank will not allow the overdraft to increase from its current level.

The equity risk premium is 5% per year and the risk-free rate of return is 4% per year. BKB Co pays profit tax at an
annual rate of 30% per year.

Required

(a) Calculate the market value after-tax weighted average cost of capital of BKB Co, explaining clearly any
     assumptions you make.   **(11 marks)**

(b) Discuss why market value weighted average cost of capital is preferred to book value weighted average cost
     of capital when making investment decisions.   **(4 marks)**

                                                                                   (Total = 15 marks)

86 Zigto Co (6/12, amended)

18 mins

Zigto Co is a medium-sized company whose ordinary shares are all owned by the members of one family.

Required

Discuss the factors that Zigto Co should consider when choosing a source of debt finance and the factors that may be considered by providers of finance in deciding how much to lend to the company. **(10 marks)**

BUSINESS VALUATIONS

Questions 87 to 91 cover Business valuations, the subject of Part F of the BPP Study Text for Paper F9.

87 MCQ bank – Business valuations

36 mins

87.1 **Which of the following best describes the replacement value of a business?**

    A   Value if sold off piece-meal
    B   Value to replace assets with new
    C   Cost of setting up an equivalent venture
    D   Net present value of current operations   **(2 marks)**

87.2 The following is a summary of Monkton Co's statement of financial position:

	£m
Non-current assets	5
Net current assets	3
	8
Financed by:	
$1 Ordinary shares	1
Reserves	5
Loan notes	2
	8

Non-current assets include machinery which cost $10 million which was purchased 7 years ago and has a useful life of 10 years. Monkton Co uses straight-line depreciation. These assets were recently professionally valued at $1 million.

What is the value per share using the realisable value basis of valuation?

    A $1
    B $2
    C $4
    D $6   **(2 marks)**

87.3 ELW Co recently paid a dividend of $0.50 a share. This is $0.10 more than 3 years ago. Shareholders have a required rate of return of 10%.

Using the dividend valuation model and assuming recent dividend growth is expected to continue, what is the current value of a share?

    A $23.41
    B $5
    C $38.48
    D $10.48   **(2 marks)**

87.4 **Which of the following need to be assumed when using the dividend valuation formula to estimate a share value?**

    1   The recent dividend, 'D_0', is typical ie doesn't vary significantly from historical trends
    2   Growth will be constant
    3   The cost of equity will remain constant
    4   A majority shareholding is being purchased

    A   1, 2 and 3 only
    B   3 and 4 only
    C   1 and 2 only
    D   1, 2, 3 and 4   **(2 marks)**

87.5 A Co is considering purchasing B Co. Both are listed companies. Recent information:

	A Co	B Co
Earnings	$4m	$2m
P/E ratio	21	16

A Co believes that if they were to purchase B Co the combined group would have earnings of $6.5 million (after synergies) and a P/E ratio of 19.

What is the maximum A Co should pay for B Co?

A $32 million
B $39.5 million
C $22.4 million
D $28 million

(2 marks)

87.6 DD Co's P/E ratio is 12. Its competitor's earnings yield is 10%.

When comparing DD Co to its competitor, which of the following is correct?

	Earnings yield	P/E ratio
A	Higher	Higher
B	Higher	Lower
C	Lower	Higher
D	Lower	Lower

(2 marks)

87.7 A 9% redeemable loan note in ATV Co is due to mature in 3 years time at a premium of 15%, or convertible into 25 ordinary shares at that point. The current share price is $4, expected to grow at 10% per annum. ATV pays corporation tax at a rate of 30%.

What is the current market value of the loan note if loan note holders require a 10% return?

A $108.75
B $115.63
C $102.03
D $122.34

(2 marks)

87.8 **Which of the following best defines the market capitalisation for a company's shares?**

A   When a company is listed ie goes 'public'
B   When a company issues new shares and thus increases its capital
C   Current share price
D   Share price x number of shares in issue

(2 marks)

87.9 HAL Co is considering purchasing SO Co and has produced the following valuations:

		$m
1	Historical cost adjusted for general inflation	3
2	Economic value – Net present value of projects	6
3	Piecemeal net realisable value	4
4	Cost of setting up an equivalent business	5

What is the maximum HAL Co should pay based on the above?

A $3 million
B $6 million
C $5 million
D $4 million

(2 marks)

87.10 NCW Co is considering acquiring the ordinary share capital of CEW Co. CEW has for years generated an annual cash inflow of $10 million. For a one off investment of $6m in new machinery, earnings can be increased by $2m per annum. NCW has a cost of capital of 10%.

What is the value of CEW Co?

A $114m
B $120m
C $100m
D $94m

(2 marks)
(Total = 20 marks)

88 MCQ bank – Market efficiency

18 mins

88.1 WC Co announces that it decided yesterday to invest in a new project with a huge positive net present value. Share price doubled yesterday.

What does this appear to be evidence of?

A   A semi-strong form efficient market
B   A strong form efficient market
C   Technical analysis
D   A weak form efficient market   **(2 marks)**

88.2 John doesn't believe there is any value to be had in reading the first edition of the newspaper to help formulate an investment strategy for his share portfolio.

How efficient does John believe the capital markets are?

A   Weak form efficient
B   Strong form efficient
C   Semi-strong form efficient
D   Semi-strong or strong form efficient   **(2 marks)**

88.3 Sarah decides to plot past share price movements to help spot patterns and create an investment strategy.

What does Sarah believe the stock market is?

A   Completely inefficient
B   Weak form efficient
C   Semi-strong form efficient
D   Strong form efficient   **(2 marks)**

88.4 **Which of the following is evidence that stock markets are semi-strong form efficient?**

A   Repeating patterns appear to exist.
B   Attempting to trade on consistently repeating patterns is unlikely to work.
C   The majority of share price reaction to new news occurs when it is announced.
D   Share price reaction occurs before announcements are made public.   **(2 marks)**

88.5 **Are the following statements true or false?**

1   Fundamental analysis values shares according to the expected future cash flows and risk of a business.

2   Technical analysis values a share based on past share price movements and patterns.

A   1 is true, 2 is true
B   1 is true, 2 is false
C   1 is false, 2 is true
D   1 is false, 2 is false   **(2 marks)**
    (Total = 10 marks)

89 Phobis Co (12/07, amended)

18 mins

Distinguish between weak form, semi-strong form and strong form stock market efficiency, and discuss the significance to a listed company if the stock market on which its shares are traded is shown to be semi-strong form efficient.   **(10 marks)**

90 Close Co (12/11, amended)

18 mins

Recent financial information relating to Close Co, a stock market listed company, is as follows.

	$m
Profit after tax (earnings)	66.6
Dividends	40.0

Statement of financial position information:

	$m	$m
Non-current assets		595
Current assets		125
Total assets		720
Current liabilities		70
Equity		
Ordinary shares ($1 nominal)	80	
Reserves	410	
		490
Non-current liabilities		
6% Bank loan	40	
8% Bonds ($100 nominal)	120	
		160
		720

Financial analysts have forecast that the dividends of Close Co will grow in the future at a rate of 4% per year. This is slightly less than the forecast growth rate of the profit after tax (earnings) of the company, which is 5% per year. The finance director of Close Co thinks that, considering the risk associated with expected earnings growth, an earnings yield of 11% per year can be used for valuation purposes.

Close Co has a cost of equity of 10% per year and a before-tax cost of debt of 7% per year. The 8% bonds will be redeemed at nominal value in six years' time. Close Co pays tax at an annual rate of 30% per year and the ex-dividend share price of the company is $8.50 per share.

Required

(a)   Calculate the value of Close Co using the following methods:

    (i)   net asset value method;
    (ii)   dividend growth model;
    (iii)   earnings yield method.   **(5 marks)**

(b)   Discuss the weaknesses of the dividend growth model as a way of valuing a company and its shares.

          (5 marks)

          (Total = 10 marks)

91   Boluje Co (12/08, amended)   18 mins

Three years ago Boluje Co built a factory in its home country costing $3.2 million. To finance the construction of the factory, Boluje Co issued peso-denominated bonds in a foreign country whose currency is the peso. Interest rates at the time in the foreign country were historically low. The foreign bond issue raised 16 million pesos and the exchange rate at the time was 5.00 pesos = $1.

Each foreign bond has a nominal value of 500 pesos and pays interest in pesos at the end of each year of 6.1%. The bonds will be redeemed in five years' time at nominal value. The current cost of debt of peso-denominated bonds of similar risk is 7%.

Required

(a)   Briefly explain the reasons why a company may choose to finance a new investment by an issue of debt finance.   **(6 marks)**

(b)   Calculate the current total market value (in pesos) of the foreign bonds used to finance the building of the new factory.   **(4 marks)**

          (Total = 10 marks)

RISK MANAGEMENT

Questions 92 to 96 cover Risk Management, the subject of Part G of the BPP Study Text for Paper F9.

92 MCQ bank – Foreign currency risk   36 mins

92.1 Exporters Co is concerned that the cash received from overseas sales will not be as expected due to exchange rate movements.

What type of risk is this?

A   Translation risk
B   Economic risk
C   Rate risk
D   Transaction risk   **(2 marks)**

92.2 The current euro / US dollar exchange rate is €1 : $2. ABC Co, a Eurozone company, makes a $1,000 sale to a US customer on credit. By the time the customer pays, the Euro has strengthened by 20%.

What will the Euro receipt be?

A   €416.67
B   €2,400
C   €600
D   €400   **(2 marks)**

92.3 The current spot rate for the Dollar /Euro is $/€ 2.0000 +/- 0.003. The dollar is quoted at a 0.2c premium for the forward rate.

What will a $2,000 receipt be translated to at the forward rate?

A   €4,002
B   €999.5
C   €998
D   €4,008   **(2 marks)**

92.4 **Which is true of forward contracts?**

1   They fix the rate for a future transaction.
2   They are a binding contract.
3   They are flexible once agreed.
4   They are traded openly.

A   1, 2 and 4 only
B   1, 2, 3 and 4
C   1 and 2 only
D   2 only   **(2 marks)**

92.5 A US company owes a European company €3.5m due to be paid in 3 months' time. The spot exchange rate is $1.96 - $2 : €1 currently. Annual interest rates in the two locations are as follows:

	Borrowing	Deposit
US	8%	3%
Europe	5%	1%

What will be the equivalent US $ value of the payment using a money market hedge?

A $6,965,432
B $6,979,750
C $7,485,149
D $7,122,195   **(2 marks)**

92.6 In comparison to forward contracts, which of the following are true in the relation to futures contracts?

1   They are more expensive.
2   They are only available in a small amount of currencies.
3   They are less flexible.
4   They are probably an imprecise match for the underlying transaction.

A   1, 2 and 4 only
B   2 and 4 only
C   1 and 3 only
D   1, 2, 3 and 4   **(2 marks)**

92.7 A company based in Farland (with the Splot as its currency) is expecting its US customer to pay $1,000,000 in 3 month's time and wants to hedge this transaction using currency options.

What is the option they require?

1   A Splot put option purchased in America
2   A US dollar put option purchased in Farland
3   A Splot call option purchased in America
4   A US dollar call option purchased in Farland.

A   2 or 3 only
B   2 only
C   1 or 4 only
D   4 only   **(2 marks)**

92.8 The current spot rate for the US$ to the European € is $2: €1. Annual interest rates in the two countries are 8% in the US, and 4% in Europe.

What is the 3 months forward rate (to 4 decimal places) likely to be?

A $1.9804: €1
B $2.0198: €1
C $1.9259: €1
D $2.0769: €1   **(2 marks)**

92.9 What does purchasing power parity refers to?

A   A situation where two businesses have equal available funds to spend.
B   Inflation in different locations is the same.
C   Prices are the same to different customers in an economy.
D   Exchange rate movements will absorb inflation differences.   **(2 marks)**

92.10 If a country's currency strengthens, what effect will it have on its exporters and importers?

	Exporters	Importers
A	Better off	Better off
B	Better off	Worse off
C	Worse off	Better off
D	Worse off	Worse off

(2 marks)
(Total = 20 marks)

93   MCQ bank – Interest rate risk   18 mins

93.1 Which is the best definition of basis risk?

A   Interest rates on deposits and on loans are revised at different times.
B   Interest rates on deposits and loans move by different amounts.
C   Interest rates move.
D   The bank base rate might move with a knock on effect to other interest rates.   **(2 marks)**

93.2   **If a business benefits from gap exposure what does this mean?**

   A   The timing of interest rate movements on deposits and loans means it has made a profit
   B   The timing of interest rate movements on deposits and loans means it has made a loss
   C   The interest rates reduce between deciding a loan is needed and signing for that loan.
   D   The inefficiencies between two markets means arbitrage gains are possible.   **(2 marks)**

93.3   **Which of the following explain the shape and movement of a yield curve?**

   1   Expectations theory
   2   Liquidity preference theory
   3   Market segmentation theory

   A   1 and 2 only
   B   2 and 3 only
   C   1 and 3 only
   D   1, 2 and 3 only   **(2 marks)**

93.4   Interest rates are currently 5%. ADB Co needs a $4 million six month loan in 3 months' time and buys a 3-9 Forward Rate Agreement (FRA) at 8%. When ADB Co signs the loan they agree to a rate of 7%.

   What is the payment or receipt ADB Co will make or receive under the FRA?

   A   ADB pays the bank $40,000
   B   ADB pays the bank $20,000
   C   ADB receives $40,000 from the bank
   D   ADB received $20,000 from the bank ·   **(2 marks)**

93.5   **Which of the following is true of exchange traded interest rate options?**

   1   They maintain access to upside risk whilst limiting the downside to the premium.
   2   They can be sold if not needed.
   3   They are expensive.
   4   They are tailored to an investor's needs.

   A   1 and 2 only
   B   1 and 3 only
   C   2, 3 and 4 only
   D   1, 2 and 3 only   **(2 marks)**
   (Total = 10 marks)

94   ZPS Co (6/11, amended)   18 mins

ZPS Co, whose home currency is the dollar, took out a fixed-interest peso bank loan several years ago when peso interest rates were relatively cheap compared to dollar interest rates. Economic difficulties have now increased peso interest rates while dollar interest rates have remained relatively stable. ZPS Co must pay interest of 5,000,000 pesos in six months' time. The following information is available.

	Per $
Spot rate: pesos	12.500 – pesos 12.582
Six-month forward rate: pesos	12.805 – pesos 12.889

Interest rates that can be used by ZPS Co:

	Borrow	Deposit
Peso interest rates:	10.0% per year	7.5% per year
Dollar interest rates:	4.5% per year	3.5% per year

Required

(a) Explain briefly the relationships between;

 (i) exchange rates and interest rates;
 (ii) exchange rates and inflation rates. **(5 marks)**

(b) Calculate whether a forward market hedge or a money market hedge should be used to hedge the interest payment of 5 million pesos in six months' time. Assume that ZPS Co would need to borrow any cash it uses in hedging exchange rate risk. **(5 marks)**

(Total = 10 marks)

95 Gorwa Co (12/08, amended) 18 mins

The following financial information related to Gorwa Co:

	20X7	20X6
	$'000	$'000
Sales (all on credit)	37,400	26,720
Cost of sales	34,408	23,781
Operating profit	2,992	2,939
Finance costs (interest payments)	355	274
Profit before taxation	2,637	2,665

	20X7		20X6	
	$'000	$'000	$000	$'000
Non-current assets		13,632		12,750
Current assets				
Inventory	4,600		2,400	
Trade receivables	4,600		2,200	
		9,200		4,600
Total assets		22,832		17,350
Capital and reserves				
Share capital		6,000		6,000
Reserves		6,432		5,325
		12,432		11,325
Non-current liabilities				
8% Bonds		2,425		2,425
Current liabilities				
Trade payables	4,750		2,000	
Overdraft	3,225		1,600	
		7,975		3,600
Total equity and liabilities		22,832		17,350

The average variable overdraft interest rate in each year was 5%. The 8% bonds are redeemable in ten years' time.

A factor has offered to take over the administration of trade receivables on a non-recourse basis for an annual fee of 3% of credit sales. The factor will maintain a trade receivables collection period of 30 days and Gorwa Co will save$100,000 per year in administration costs and $350,000 per year in bad debts. A condition of the factoring agreement is that the factor would advance 80% of the face value of receivables at an annual interest rate of 7%.

Required

Discuss, with supporting calculations, the possible effects on Gorwa Co of an increase in interest rates and advise the company of steps it can take to protect itself against interest rate risk. **(10 marks)**

96 Ziggazigto Co (6/12, amended)

Ziggazigto Co is a medium-sized company whose ordinary shares are all owned by the members of one family. It has recently begun exporting to a European country and expects to receive €500,000 in six months' time. The company plans to take action to hedge the exchange rate risk arising from its European exports.

Ziggazigto Co could put cash on deposit in the European country at an annual interest rate of 3% per year, and borrow at 5% per year. The company could put cash on deposit in its home country at an annual interest rate of 4% per year, and borrow at 6% per year. Inflation in the European country is 3% per year, while inflation in the home country of Ziggazigto Co is 4.5% per year.

The following exchange rates are currently available to Ziggazigto Co:

Current spot exchange rate	2.000 euro per $
Six-month forward exchange rate	1.990 euro per $
One-year forward exchange rate	1.981 euro per $

Required

(a) Calculate whether a forward exchange contract or a money market hedge would be financially preferred by Ziggazigto Co to hedge its future euro receipt. **(5 marks)**

(b) Calculate the one-year expected (future) spot rate predicted by purchasing power parity theory and explain briefly the relationship between the expected (future) spot rate and the current forward exchange rate.

(5 marks)

(Total = 10 marks)

Answers

1 MCQ bank – Financial management and financial objectives

1.1 **C** Although cash flow is vitally important, managing and maximising cash flow is achieved by the other 3 interlinking decisions.

Syllabus area A2(b)

1.2 **C** Corporate governance best practice aims to *manage* risk to desired and controlled levels, not to minimise risk. Running a business implies taking calculated risks in anticipation of a commensurate return.

Syllabus area A3(e)(ii)

1.3 **A** ROCE = Profit before interest and tax/Capital employed

As interest cover = 5 times, and interest payable = $1.5m, Profit before interest and tax = 5×1.5 = $7.5m

Asset turnover = Turnover/Capital employed. Turnover = $14m so Capital employed = 200/10 = $20m

Therefore ROCE = 7.5 / 20 = 0.375 = 37.5%

Syllabus area A3(d)(i)

1.4 **B** Economy is the cost of inputs (for example teacher salaries.) This is not mentioned in the question.

Efficiency is the ratio of inputs to outputs. Each teacher (input) is now teaching more students, so efficiency has increased.

Effectiveness is the quality of outputs. The output in this example is exam results, which have suffered hence effectiveness is reduced.

Syllabus area A4(c)

1.5 **D**
Shareholder return $= (P_1 - P_0 + D_1) / P_0$.
∴ shareholder return $= (0.75 + 0.25) / (3.50 - 0.75)$
$= 36.4\%$

Syllabus area A3(d)(ii)

1.6 **D** Government

Shareholders, customers and bankers are all connected stakeholders.

Syllabus area A3(a)

1.7 **C** Efficiency. Efficiency measures relate the resources used to the output produced.

Syllabus area A4(c)

1.8 **B** Effectiveness can only be measured in terms of achieved performance. Economy consists of minimising costs, for example, by obtaining suitable inputs at the lowest price. Efficiency, in the narrow sense used here, consists of achieving the greatest output per unit of input: avoiding waste of inputs would contribute to this. Achieving a given level of profit is a measure of overall efficiency.

Syllabus area A4(b)

1.9 **D** 1, 2 and 3. The figures needed to calculate ROCE are easily available from the financial accounting records.

Syllabus area A3(d)

1.10 **D** The Financial Management function is responsible for making decisions relating to investment (statement 2) but will also have primary responsibility for cash flow forecasting (statement 1). Financial Reporting control cash flow reporting but not forecasting

Syllabus area A1(a)

2 MCQ bank – Financial management and financial objectives

2.1 **B** 80c

	$
Profit before tax	2,628,000
Less tax	788,000
Profit after tax	1,840,000
Less preference dividend (6% × 4,000,000)	240,000
Earnings attributable to ordinary shareholders	1,600,000
Number of ordinary shares	2,000,000
EPS = 1,600,000 / 2,000,000 =	80c

Syllabus area A3(d)(i)

2.2 **B** Both statements are true.

Syllabus area A1(b)

2.3 **B** P/E ratio = $\dfrac{\text{MV ex div}}{\text{EPS}} = \dfrac{\$3.60}{60c} = 6$

MV ex div = 3.72 -0.12 = 3.60. The ex div price is used because it reflects the underlying value of the share after the dividend has been paid.

Syllabus area A3(d)

2.4 **D** *Step 1* Calculate the dividend amount using dividend cover

Dividend cover = EPS / Dividend per share

∴ Dividend per share = EPS / Dividend cover

∴ Dividend per share = 60 / 2.5 = 24c

Step 2 Calculate the market price of share using dividend yield

Dividend yield = Dividend per share / Market price per share

∴ Market price per share = Dividend per share / Dividend yield

∴ Market price per share = 24 / 0.048 = 500c

Syllabus area A3(d)

2.5 **C** Not-for-profit organisations have objectives generally concerned with efficient use of resources in the light of specific targets. Controlling input costs will be important (economy) but *minimising* input costs would be likely to affect quality.

Syllabus area A4(a)

3 ABC Co

Text references. Performance analysis is covered in Chapter 1 (although the gearing ratio and interest cover are covered in Chapter 14).

Top tips. Don't be tempted to calculate endless ratios and not leave enough time for the discussion. This type of analysis is an essential skill for the F9 exam so make sure you are happy with the technique.

Ratio analysis

	Current year	Previous year
Profitability		
ROCE (PBIT/Long-term capital)	14,749/(39,900 + 14,000) = 27.4%	13,506/(35,087 + 17,500) = 25.7%
Net profit margin	14,749/74,521 = 0.198 = 19.8%	13,506/68,000 = 0.199 = 19.9%
Debt		
Gearing (Debt/Equity)	14,000/39,900 = 35.1%	17,500/35,087 = 49.9%
Interest coverage (PBIT/Interest)	14,749/1,553 = 9.5	13,506/1,863 = 7.2
Shareholders' investment		
EPS	8,849/14,000 = $0.63	7,917/14,000 = $0.57
Share price (P/E × EPS)	14.0 × 0.63 = $8.82	13.0 × 0.57 = $7.41
Dividend per share	4,800/14,000 = $0.34	3,100/14,000 = $0.22
Dividend yield (DPS/Share price)	0.34/8.82 = 3.85%	0.22/7.41 = 2.97%

The performance of ABC Co

A shareholder of ABC Co would probably be reasonably pleased with their performance over these two years.

Growth of income

The company has grown in terms of turnover and profits. **Revenue** has grown by 9.6% ((74,521 – 68,000)/68,000 × 100%) and **return on capital employed** has increased from 25.7% to 27.4%. There may be some concern over the 25.4% increase ((11,489 – 9,160)/9,160 × 100%) in **other costs** and more information would be needed to determine if this is a one-off increase or a worrying long-term trend. The net profit margin is almost unchanged, showing that the increase in ROCE is due to an increase in asset turnover. **Salaries and wages** have only increased by 2.4% ((20,027 – 19,562)/19,562 × 100%) so employees may be less pleased with the situation. Employee discontent could create problems for the business in future.

Gearing

The financial risk that the shareholders are exposed to does not appear to be a problem area as **gearing** has decreased from 49.9% to 35.1% and **interest cover** is more than sufficient. The company may want to consider increasing gearing to invest in suitable projects and generate further growth.

Shareholder return

The **shareholders' investment ratios** all indicate that shareholders' wealth has increased. The **share price** has increased by 19% ((8.82 – 7.41)/7.41 × 100%). The **total shareholder return** is $(P_1 - P_0 + D_1)/P_0 = (8.82 - 7.41 + 0.34)/7.41 = 23.6\%$. This is probably sufficient to satisfy shareholders. The **P/E ratio** reflects the market's appraisal of the share's future prospects and this has improved. It is still lower than the industry average which suggests that more growth could be achieved.

4 Bark Co

Text references. Objectives in Chapter 1.

Top tips. Don't waste time considering non-financial objectives. Ensure that you highlight where there is common ground between the two types of organisation and not just the differences. Also note that for 10 marks you will be expected to write a reasonably lengthy answer. Make sure you are able to explain what an organisation's financial objectives may be.

Easy marks. The easy marks are for discussing maximising shareholder wealth and value for money as these issues should pop straight into your head.

	Marks
Maximising shareholder wealth	2-3
Maximising cash income	2-3
Controlling spending with budgets	2-3
Value for money	2-3
Other relevant discussion	2-3
Maximum	10

Maximising the wealth of shareholders is often seen as the main financial objective for a stock exchange listed company. This is often replaced by an objective to maximise the share price as this would represent the maximum capital gain in a period. To meet the need for dividends, it is recognised that share prices are seen as the sum of the present value of future dividends.

Maximising the share price is equivalent to maximising the market value of the equity of the company. This is because the market value of equity (also known as market capitalisation) is equal to the number of shares multiplied by the market share price. To maximise the market value of equity, a company should maximise its net corporate cash income and the expected growth in the income, while also minimising the cost of capital. As a result, many listed companies have the maximisation of net cash income as an important financial objective.

A not-for-profit (NFP) organisation, such as a charity, provides services to the public which require cash income. As a result, maximising cash income is also an important financial objective for NFP organisations. A large charity will want to raise funds to be able to meet its objectives, which will be non-financial in nature.

Both types of organisation need to have control over the use of cash in a financial period and to do so they will both make use of budgets. Another common key financial objective, therefore, is to keep spending levels within budget.

Value for money (VFM) is often given as an important objective for NFP organisations. This refers to focusing on the three Es (economy, efficiency and effectiveness). Economy is often seen as relevant to inputs – sourcing resources as economically as possible. Efficiency is seen as relevant to processes – the efficient employment of resources in an organisation. Effectiveness is usually seen as relevant to outputs – using resources effectively in order to achieve the objectives of the organisation.

When phrased as above, it can be seen that a listed company will also seek to achieve VFM. The difference between the two types of organisation comes from the emphasis. The listed company has a profit motive and therefore VFM is related to performance measures that monitor outputs, such as maximising the company share price. A NFP organisation struggles to measure its outputs in quantitative terms and so it will have performance measures that focus on inputs, such as minimising the input cost to maintain a given output level.

Both types of organisation may use the same accounting ratios to measure performance against financial objectives. For example return on capital employed may be used to monitor performance against a target by a listed company or a NFP organisation. The target levels, however are likely to be significantly different.

From a comparison of financial objectives of listed companies and NFP organisations, there is more common ground that may have originally been expected, given the apparent differences in the nature of the organisations.

5 MCQ bank – Financial management environment

5.1 **C** Fiscal policy is the balance of government taxation and spending. A contractionary fiscal policy implies a government budget surplus – the government is reducing demand by withdrawing higher amounts from the economy by way of higher taxation and/or spending less. 'B' would be the result of an expansionary fiscal policy. 'A' may happen as a result of an expansionary policy as an economy 'booms.' 'D' may happen following a contractionary fiscal policy, although lower inflation and interest rates are only a secondary effect. As an economy enters recession inflationary pressure may decrease and interest rates may be reduced to encourage borrowing. However as these are not directly due to fiscal policy, C is the more direct and immediate impact.

Syllabus area B1(c)

5.2 **A** Monetary policy manages demand by influencing the supply of money (including the availability of credit) and interest rates. An expansionary policy implies low interest rates to encourage borrowing and investment, and to discourage saving. It also implies an increased availability of credit to encourage spending and the stimulation of demand in an economy. Tax rates are a tool of fiscal policy hence C and D are incorrect. B would be the result of a contractionary monetary policy.

Syllabus area B1(c)

5.3 **A** As an economy approaches its peak, inflation increases because price increases 'soak up' high demand as productivity peaks. Unemployment is low so businesses struggle to fill vacancies. B is incorrect – export demand is affected by foreign demand not domestic, and growth rates are unlikely to be increasing as the economy reaches its peak - they will decrease. C describes a recession. D is incorrect because as an economy peaks a contractionary fiscal policy is likely to be employed implying lower government spending and higher taxation.

Syllabus area B1(c)

5.4 **D** A weakening dollar implies, for example, an exchange rate that moves from, say, $1:£1 to $2:£1. A UK exporter will therefore receive less £ sterling for their $ revenue. However a UK company importing from the US will benefit by way of a lower £ cost for any given $ price they need to pay for their imports.

Syllabus area B1(b)

5.5 **C** Option 4 is more likely to be a social policy objective as opposed to a macroeconomic objective.

Syllabus area B1(a)

6 MCQ bank – Financial management environment

6.1 **C** Dividend creation benefits the intermediaries' investors, not their customers/borrowers.

Syllabus area B2(b)

6.2 **C** Money markets focus on short-term financial instruments. A corporate bond is a long-term source of finance, hence is a capital market instrument. Certificates of deposit and commercial paper are short-term private sector lending/borrowing. A treasury bill is short-term government borrowing.

Syllabus area B3(c)

6.3 **B** Increased regulation and transparency reduce the actual and perceived risk from the point of view of shareholders, making the shares more attractive and hence more valuable. In addition listed company shares are naturally more liquid than an equivalent unlisted company, again adding to their value. The process of listing is therefore likely to create value.

Syllabus area B2(c)

6.4 **C** Eurobonds by definition are bonds issued in a currency other than the domestic currency of the country of issue. The prefix 'Euro' does not refer to the continent Europe or the European currency the 'Euro.'

Syllabus area B2(d)

6.5 **D** Ordinary shares are riskiest as all other investors are preferential to ordinary shareholders. Preference shares are riskier than corporate bonds as preference shares are paid after corporate bonds – bonds imply a contractual right to receive a pre-defined level of return. Treasury bills are short-term government borrowing hence are the lowest risk of all.

Syllabus area B2(d)

7 MCQ bank – Financial management environment

7.1   A   Both statements are true. If a government spends more, for example, on public services such as hospitals, without raising more money in taxation, it will increase expenditure in the economy and raise demand. Although the second statement appears to contradict the first, it is also true. After the government has kick-started demand (as in statement 1) then it should be able to repay the borrowing it has taken on as tax receipts rise due to higher economic activity.

Syllabus area B1(c)

7.2   A   Money markets are markets for short-term capital, not long-term capital.

Syllabus area B3(c)

7.3   A   Rationale: Debts lose 'real' value with inflation: a company that owes a lot of money would effectively pay less (in real terms) over time. The other organisations would suffer because: inflation would make exports relatively expensive and imports relatively cheap; business might be lost due to price rises; and the cost of implementing price changes would be high.

Syllabus area B1(d)

7.4   D   Rationale: The four main objectives of macroeconomic policy relate to economic growth, stable inflation, unemployment and the balance of payments (balance between exports and imports). Equitable income distribution of income is a social / political issue.

Syllabus area B1(a)

7.5   C   Rationale: Increasing the exchange rate will increase the price of exported goods and lower the price of imported goods, this is likely to lead to a fall in domestic economic activity. Increasing public expenditure should increase the level of consumer demand. Decreasing taxation has the opposite effect. Lowering interest rates should stimulate investment (by companies) and consumer expenditure, even if only after a time lag.

Syllabus area B1(b)

8 Tagna

Text references. The financial management environment is covered in Chapter 2.

Top tips. You should answer this well provided you read the question and are guided by what the examiner wants. In part (a) the question requires a specific discussion on the three areas outlined. In part (b), an explanation of the terms used is requires as well as a comparison between the two.

Easy marks. Any written element provided you know what you are writing about.

Examiner's comments. Many answers to part (a) lacked depth of discussion but were generally on the right track. One common error was to confuse financing costs with operating costs. Most answers to part (b) correctly defined and discussed the concepts of economy, efficiency and effectiveness (input, process and output), and were able to provide good answers on maximising shareholder wealth. Even good answers failed to recognise that a company in the private sector may pursue 'value for money' and 'shareholder wealth maximisation' at the same time.

Marking scheme

			Marks
(a)	Up to 2 marks for each detailed consequence		6
(b)	Value for money	2	
	Maximisation of shareholder wealth	2	
			4
			10

(a) (i)   If interest rates increase significantly, it is likely to have an adverse impact on Tagna's sales. As it sells luxury goods, it could be expected that these would be the first to be sacrificed by consumers if they are feeling 'the pinch' in other areas (such as mortgage payments) and their disposable income is reduced. The cost of consumer credit might also be pushed up to dampen spending, further denting consumer confidence and the willingness to spend money on luxury items.

(ii) Interest rates may also push up input costs such as materials and labour, although this would probably not be seen as quickly as an effect of higher interest rates upon sales, as the effect of the rise would have to make itself felt throughout the economy. Wages could go up as a result of inflation, but this will be countered by the effect of the interest rate increase on consumer demand.

(iii) Profit after tax will fall as a result of the interest rate increase, both for the reasons outlined above but also because the cost of servicing Tagna's overdraft will increase. With a fall in sales, increased operating costs and increased interest charges, there is likely to be a significant fall in earnings. As Tagna's profits have been low, this could represent a real threat to future profitability and dividend payments.

(b) Public sector organisations are generally set up with a prime objective which is not related to making profits. These organisations exist to pursue non-financial aims, such as providing a service to the community. However, there will be financial constraints which limit what any such organisation can do. A not-for-profit organisation **needs finance** to pay for its operations, and the major financial constraint is the amount of funds that it can obtain. Having obtained funds, a not-for-profit organisation should seek to get **value for money** from use of the funds:

(i)   **Economy**: not spending $2 when the same thing can be bought for $1
(ii) **Efficiency**: getting the best use out of what money is spent on
(iii) **Effectiveness**: spending funds so as to achieve the organisation's objectives

Since managing government (for example) is different from managing a company, a different framework is needed for **planning and control**. This is achieved by:

- setting **objectives** for each
- **careful planning** of public expenditure proposals
- emphasis on getting **value for money**

A private sector organisation has as its primary objective the making of sufficient profits to provide a satisfactory return for its owners and to keep the business operating.

So, it is job of senior management to **maximise the market value** of the company. Specifically, the main financial objective of a company should be to maximise the wealth of its ordinary shareholders. Within this context, the financial manager seeks to ensure that investments earn a **return**, for the benefit of shareholders. Part of this job will involve attracting funds from the market, such as new investors, but as with public sector organisations it is also important that the operations of the company are run economically and efficiently.

9 Phoenix

Text references. Risk-return trade off and financial intermediation are covered in Chapter 3.

Top tips. This question is fairly straightforward as you don't need to apply your knowledge to a given scenario. In (b), note who are classified as financial intermediaries. They are not the same as independent financial advisers.

(a) **The risk/return trade-off**

There is a **trade-off** between **risk and return**. Investors in riskier assets expect to be compensated for the risk. In the case of ordinary shares, investors hope to achieve their return in the form of an increase in the share price (a capital gain) as well as from dividends. In general, the **higher the risk** of the security, the **more important is the capital gain** component of the expected yield.

In the same way, **higher-risk borrowers** must **pay higher yields** on their borrowing to compensate lenders for the greater risk involved. Banks will assess the creditworthiness of the borrower and set a rate of interest on its loan at a certain mark-up above its base rate. The higher the risk, the higher the interest rate.

(b)   **The role of financial intermediaries**

A financial intermediary is an institution that links lenders with borrowers, by obtaining deposits from lenders and then re-lending them to borrowers. In the UK, the intermediaries include:

- Commercial banks
- Building societies
- Insurance companies
- Unit trust companies
- Finance houses
- National Savings Bank
- Pension funds
- Investment trust companies

Benefits of financial intermediation

(i)   **Reduction of risk through pooling**

Since financial intermediaries lend to a large number of individuals and organisations, any losses suffered through default by borrowers or through capital losses are effectively pooled and borne as costs by the intermediary. Provided that the intermediary is itself financially sound, the lender should not run the risk of losing his investment. Bad debts are borne by the financial intermediary in its re-lending operation.

(ii)   **Maturity transformation**

An example of this is the building society, which allows depositors to have immediate access to their savings while lending to mortgage holders for 25 years. The intermediary takes advantage of the continual turnover of cash between borrowers and investors to achieve this.

(iii)   **Convenience**

They provide a simple way for the lender to invest, without them having personally to find a suitable borrower directly. All the investor has to decide is for how long the money is to be deposited and what sort of return is required; all they then have to do is to choose an appropriate intermediary and form of deposit.

(iv)   **Regulation**

There is a comprehensive system of regulation in place in the financial markets that is aimed at protecting the investor against negligence or malpractice.

(v)   **Information**

Intermediaries can offer a wide range of specialist expert advice on the various investment opportunities that is not directly available to the private investor.

Financial intermediaries therefore have many benefits to offer the private investor, both in terms of general information and the investments available.

10 MCQ bank – Working capital

10.1   **B**   The length of the cash operating cycle is receivables days plus inventory days less payables days.

Inventory days = 365 days/10 = 36.5 days.

Therefore the length of the cash operating cycle is: 58 days + 36.5 days − 45 days = 49.5 days

Non-current assets are not relevant as they are not part of working capital.

Syllabus area C3(a)

10.2 C Receivables paying sooner will reduce receivables days and hence reduce the length of the cash operating cycle. The cost of the discount (approximately 2% per month as they pay a month earlier than usual) outweighs the interest saved on the overdraft (at 10% per annum this is less than 1% per month) hence the net effect will be reduced profit.

Syllabus area C2(d)

10.3 A Current ratio = current assets / current liabilities = 2

Here   = ($3m + inventory) / $2m = 2

So inventory = $1m

If cost of sales is $10m then inventory days = (1/10) × 365 = 36.5 days

Syllabus area C3(a)

10.4 D Overtrading often occurs with young, successful, fast growing businesses. Cash being received from sales made a while ago (which were relatively low if the business is growing quickly) is insufficient to finance current production levels if growth is excessive. The result is a strain on cash flows, even if the business is technically profitable. Option B describes over-capitalisation.

Syllabus area C3(a)

10.5 D The quick ratio = Current assets (less inventories)/Current liabilities.

If some inventory is sold on credit, all else being equal receivables (current assets) will increase, so the quick ratio will increase.

The current ratio = Current assets/Current liabilities. Inventory and receivables are both current assets. However as the inventory is sold at a profit, the increase in receivables will be more than the decrease in inventory, the net effect being an increase in current assets, hence the current ratio will increase.

Syllabus area C2(b)(i)

11 MCQ bank – Managing working capital

11.1 C Annual demand = 40 × 250 = 10,000 ball bearings = D

Order cost = $64 = C_o

Holding cost per year per unit = 25% of $2 = $0.50 = C_h

$$EOQ = \sqrt{\frac{2C_oD}{C_h}}$$

$$= \sqrt{\frac{2 \times 64 \times 10,000}{0.5}}$$

$$= 1,600 \text{ ball bearings}$$

Syllabus area C2(c)

11.2 B Total cost = Annual purchase costs + annual ordering cost + annual holding cost.

Annual purchase cost = 10,000 units × $2 = $20,000

Annual ordering cost = number of orders × cost per order = (10,000/250) × $50 = $2,000

Annual holding cost = Average inventory level × cost to hold per unit per annum

= [(250/2) + 50] × $1.25 = $218.75

Total cost = $20,000 + $2,000 + $218.75 = $22,218.75 = $22,219 (to nearest $).

Syllabus area C2(c)

11.3 **C** Manufacturing to order makes production scheduling inherently difficult as production levels are more difficult to plan for.

Syllabus area C2(c)

11.4 **B** The current collection period is $4/20 \times 365 = 73$ days

Therefore a reduction to 60 days would be a reduction of 13 days

Hence $13/365 \times \$20m = \$712,329$ reduction in receivables.

Finance cost saving $= \$712,329 \times 12\% = \$85,479$

Cost of discount $= 1\% \times \$20$ million $= \$200,000$ per annum

Net cost $= \$200,000 - \$85,479 = \$114,521$

Syllabus area C2(d)

11.5 **D** Bad debt insurance is provided by a non-recourse factoring arrangement. Factors also provide administrative services such as managing the receivables ledger and the collection procedures. Factors can also lend money using the receivables ledger as security so they are also a potential source of finance.

Syllabus area C2(d)

11.6 **D** Commercial paper is a source of finance and not directly applicable to the management of foreign debts.

Syllabus area C2(d)

11.7 **B** The annual cost is

$$\left\{ \left[\left(\frac{100}{100-d} \right)^{\frac{365}{t}} \right] -1 \right\} \%$$

where d = discount % and t = the reduction in payment period.

In this case, d= 2%, t=60 days hence the annual cost = $[100/(100-2)]^{365/60}-1 = 0.13$ or 13% per annum.

Syllabus area C2(d)

11.8 **C** C relates to just-in-time. It is not a drawback of EOQ.

Syllabus area C2(c)

11.9 **D** D relates to receivables, not payables.

Syllabus area C2(e)

11.10 **B** Inventory shortages are the most likely problem with a JIT inventory ordering system.

Syllabus area C2(c)

12 MCQ bank – Working capital finance

12.1	**A**	Receipts for March:	$
		50% March sales for cash (50% × $150,000)	75,000
		80% × February credit sales less 4% discount (50% × 80% × $501,500 × 96%)	192,576
		15% × January credit sales (50% × 15% × $300,100)	22,508
			290,084

Syllabus area C2(b)

12.2 C The Baumol model applies here. This is effectively economic order quantity applied to cash draw-downs as follows:

$$\sqrt{\frac{2 \times \cos t \text{ of ordering} \times \text{annual cash required}}{\text{Net interest of holding \$1 for 1 year}}}$$

$$= \sqrt{\frac{2 \times 200 \times \$10m}{0.06}}$$

= $258,199 = $258,000 to the nearest $'000

Syllabus area C2(f)

12.3 D Miller Orr defines the difference between the upper limit and lower limit as the 'spread'.

TB Co's spread is $10m – $1m = $9m.

Miller Orr also defines the return point as the lower limit plus a third of the spread. In this case:

1 + [(1/3) × 9] = $4m

When the upper limit is reached, sufficient securities are purchased to reduce the cash balance back to the return point. In this case $10m – $4m = $6m. Therefore statement 1 is correct.

When the lower limit is reached, sufficient securities are sold to increase the cash balance back up to the return point. In this case $4m – $1 = $3m. Therefore statement 2 is correct.

The spread is calculated as:

$$3\left[\frac{\frac{3}{4} \times \text{transaction} \cos t \times \text{variance of cash flows}}{\text{int erest rate}}\right]^{\frac{1}{3}}$$

An increase in variance will therefore increase the spread. Therefore statement 3 is correct.

Syllabus area C2(f)

12.4 A Aggressive working capital finance means using more short-term finance (and less long-term). Short-term finance is cheaper but it is risky – it may not be renewed when required and finance rates may change when they are renewed. C describes a conservative financing policy. D is describing a more aggressive working capital investment policy (not finance).

Syllabus area C3(b)

12.5 A Rate risk refers to the fact that when short-term finance is renewed, the rates may vary when compared to the previous rate. This risk is less with long-term finance as it is renewed less frequently.

Renewal risk refers to the fact that finance providers may not renew the source of finance when it matures. This risk will be more acute with short-term finance as it needs renewing more often.

Short-term finance tends to be more flexible than long-term finance (eg overdraft, or supplier credit) so C and D are incorrect. Maturity mismatch is not a risk specifically related to short-term finance so D is incorrect.

Syllabus area C3(b)

13 JIT

(a) **Improvement in first year profit before tax attributable to the JIT agreement**

		$'000	$'000
Equipment: interest cost	13% × $0.5m		(65.00)
depreciation cost	$0.5m/5		(100.00)
Main customer:			
Original value of annual sales	20% × $20m	4,000.00	
Increased value of annual sales	1.05 × $4m	4,200.00	
Increase in sales			200.00
Original receivables	90/365 × $4m	986.30	
Revised receivables	60/365 × $4.2m	690.41	
Reduction in receivables		295.89	
Annual interest saving from			
reduction in receivables	13% × 295.89		38.47
Penalty payment for default	10% × $4.2m	420	
Expected value of penalty	5% × $420,000		(21.00)
Net benefit to year 1 profits			52.47

The **JIT arrangement** appears to be worthwhile in profit terms.

Other considerations

However, the expected value figure conceals the risk of adverse results if the company fails to meet delivery guarantees: the 'worst case' scenario in one year is that a penalty of $420,000 is payable (more than 5% of operating profit). The directors should make sure that the company is insured against all the normal risks outside its direct control (eg fire, theft, flood) and also invest in a total quality programme to underpin the JIT arrangement by eliminating any defective output.

(b) **Other benefits from the JIT agreement**

Closer relationship between organisations

The just in time arrangement with its major customer will promote a closer relationship between the two organisations. This will lower PS's **medium term operating risk** and enable it to plan its own materials requirements, although in the short term the company must be prepared to be very flexible in its delivery procedures. It may also result in PS entering into JIT arrangements with its own suppliers. The strengthened link between the companies may result in further co-operation in other fields (eg design of new products).

Just in time and total quality

A **just in time arrangement** with a customer works best when the company uses a **total quality** approach to eliminate defective products from its output. The growing reputation for 'zero defectives' is an advantage of implementing the system effectively. This growing reputation will boost PS's sales and enable it to negotiate JIT arrangements with other customers.

14 EOQ

(a) The **Economic Order Quantity (EOQ)** can be found as follows.

$$EOQ = \sqrt{\frac{2 \times \text{demand (units)} \times \text{ordering cost}}{\text{holding cost}}}$$

Before reorganisation

Demand   =   40,000 units per annum

Ordering cost = $100 per order

Holding cost =   20% × $2.50

$$EOQ = \sqrt{\frac{2 \times 40,000 \times 100}{0.2 \times 2.50}}$$

$$EOQ = \sqrt{16,000,000} = 4,000 \text{ units}$$

After reorganisation

Demand   =   40,000 units per annum

Ordering cost = $25 per order

Holding cost =   20% × $2.50

$$EOQ = \sqrt{\frac{2 \times 40,000 \times 25}{0.2 \times 2.50}}$$

$$EOQ = \sqrt{4,000,000} = 2,000 \text{ units}$$

(b) Implementation of the new system will affect both the total ordering costs per annum and the inventory holding cost. **Under the existing system** these costs are as follows.

Ordering cost

	$
EOQ is 4,000 units; demand is 40,000 units.	
Number of orders per year is therefore 10.	
Cost per order is $100.	
Total ordering cost per annum ($100 × 10) =	1,000

Carrying cost

	$
EOQ is 4,000 units.	
Average inventory is therefore 2,000 units.	
Cost is 2,000 × $2.50 × 20% =	1,000
Total annual cost	2,000

Under the proposed system the costs would become as follows.

Ordering cost

	$
EOQ is 2,000 units; demand is 40,000 units.	
Number of orders per year is therefore 20. Cost per order is $25.	
Total ordering cost per annum ($25 × 20) =	500

Carrying cost

EOQ is 2,000 units. Average inventory is therefore 1,000 units.
Cost is 1,000 × $2.50 × 20%   500
Total annual cost   1,000

The **annual cost saving** is therefore $1,000 ($2,000 − $1,000). This will give rise to an **after tax cash flow** of $700 ($1,000 × (1 − 0.3)). The cash flows can now be **discounted** at the cost of finance of 12%. It is **assumed** that tax is payable in the year in which it arises, and that the reorganisation costs are fully tax allowable.

		$
Year 0	$4,000 × (1 − 0.3) × 1.000 =	(2,800.00)
Years 1-8	$700 × 4.968 =	3,477.60
NPV of reorganisation		677.60

15 Thorne Co

Text reference. Cash management is covered in Chapter 6.

Top tips. This question focuses on the need to understand cash management and the amount and timing of future cash flows. Make sure you mention the company Thorne Co in your answers.

Easy marks. There are lots of opportunities for gaining at least a couple of marks in each of the parts.

Marking scheme

			Marks
(a)	Discussion of factors		5
(b)	Discussion of advantages and disadvantages		5
(c)	Discussion of Baumol model	2-3	
	Discussion of applicability in this case	2-3	
			5
			15

(a)   **Factors to consider when investing any cash surplus**

The cash budget for Thorne Co shows an increase in sales over the period, which suggests higher sales as the spring approaches. However, the payment of tax in April meant that a trend of increasing net cash flows was temporarily reversed.

Thorne needs to consider the following when investing any surpluses:

(i)   Short-term investments with no capital risk as these may be called upon at any time. Short-term investments include bank deposit accounts, certificates of deposit, term bills and gilts, which are short-dated.

In choosing between these, Thorne Co will consider the **size of the surplus**, the **length of time** it is available, the **yield offered** and the **risk** associated with each instrument.

(ii)   On an annual basis, look at any surpluses and invest these in longer-term higher yield assets. The company will most probably call on these at some stage to fund expansion but needs to pick the investments carefully.

The investment of cash balances is part of the treasury function of a company. It is unlikely that Thorne Co is of a size to sustain a full time treasury activity but nonetheless there is a definite benefit in closely managing any surpluses.

(b)	**Advantages and disadvantages of using overdraft finance to fund cash shortages**

Thorne Co has budgeted deficits in two of the months in the forecast. These are short term in nature so it is unlikely that a long-term loan will be required to fund these.

Typically, temporary deficits are funded by an **overdraft** granted by the company's bank where interest is charged on the overdrawn amount at a rate over base.

Advantages of overdraft finance include its flexibility and that interest is only due on the actual overdrawn amount. The rate of interest is flexible as it is variable and linked to a base rate and so can go down as well as up.

Disadvantages of overdraft finance include the risk of an interest rate increase as the rate is not fixed. Also, the overdraft is repayable on demand. Banks usually ask for some collateral when lending such as a fixed or floating charge on the company's assets.

(c)	**The Baumol model and cash management**

A number of different cash management models indicate the **optimum amount of cash** that a company should hold. One such model is based on the idea that deciding on optimum cash balances is like deciding on optimum inventory levels, and suggests the optimum amount to be transferred regularly from investments to current account.

We can distinguish two types of cost which are involved in obtaining cash:

(i)	The **fixed cost** represented, for example, by the issue cost of equity finance or the cost of negotiating an overdraft

(ii)	The **variable cost** (opportunity cost) of keeping the money in the form of cash

The Baumol approach has the following drawbacks for companies such as Thorne Co.

(i)	In reality, it is unlikely to be **possible** to **predict amounts required** over future periods with much certainty.

(ii)	No **buffer inventory** of cash is allowed for. There may be costs associated with running out of cash.

(iii)	There may be other **normal costs** of holding cash, which increase with the average amount held.

(iv)	It assumes **constant transaction costs** and **interest rates**.

16 Anjo Co

Text reference. Working capital management is covered in Chapters 4, 5 and 6.

Top tips. In parts (a) and (b) you were asked for calculations based on formulae you should have learnt. As a starting point for answering these types of questions write out the formula first and then slot in the numbers.

Note that there are two separate elements to part (b).

Easy marks. Part (a) and (b) were both very straightforward calculations followed by brief discussion parts. Note that there were as many marks for the discussion elements as the calculation.

Marking scheme

			Marks
(a)	Ratio calculations	3	
	Comment	3	
			6
(b)	Calculation of cash operating cycle	2	
	Significance of cash operating cycle	2	
			4
			10

(a) **Inventory days**

$$\text{Inventory Days} = \frac{\text{Inventory level at year end}}{\text{Cost of sales}} \times 365$$

20X6: (3,000/9,300) × 365 = 118 days

20X5: (1,300/6,600) × 365 = 72 days

Sector average: 90 days

Receivable days

$$\text{Receivable Days} = \frac{\text{Receivables at year end}}{\text{Revenue}} \times 365$$

20X6: (3,800/15,600) × 365 = 89 days

20X5: (1,850/11,100) × 365 = 61 days

Sector average: 60 days

Payable days

$$\text{Payable Days} = \frac{\text{Trade payables at year end}}{\text{Cost of sales}} \times 365$$

20X6: (2,870/9,300 × 0.95) × 365 = 119 days

20X5: (1,600/6,600 × 0.95) × 365 = 93 days

Sector average: 80 days

Commentary

In each case, the ratio in 20X6 is **higher** than the ratio in 20X5, indicating that deterioration has occurred in the management of inventory, receivables and payables in 20X6.

Inventory days have increased by 46 days or 64%, moving from below the sector average to 28 days – one month – more than it. Given the rapid increase in revenue (40%) in 20X6, Anjo Co may be expecting a continuing increase in the future and may have built up inventories in preparation for this, ie inventory levels reflect future sales rather than past sales. Accounting statements from several previous years and sales forecasts for the next period would help to clarify this point.

Receivable days have increased by 28 days or 46% in 20X6 and are now 29 days above the sector average. It is possible that more generous credit terms have been offered in order to stimulate sales. The increased revenue does not appear to be due to offering lower prices, since both gross profit margin (40%) and net profit margin (34%) are unchanged.

Payable days. In 20X5, only management of payables was a cause for concern, with Anjo Co taking 13 more days on average to settle liabilities with trade payables than the sector. This has increased to 39 days more than the sector in 20X6. This could lead to difficulties between the company and its suppliers if it is exceeding the credit periods they have specified.

Anjo Co has no long-term debt and the statement of financial position indicates an **increased reliance** on short-term finance, since cash has reduced by $780,000 or 87% and the overdraft has increased by $850,000 to $1 million. Perhaps the company should investigate whether it is **undercapitalised** (overtrading). It is unusual for a company of this size to have no long-term debt.

(b) Cash operating cycle = Inventory days + Receivable days – Payable days

Cash operating cycle (20X5) = 72 + 61 – 93 = 40 days

Cash operating cycle (20X6) = 118 + 89 – 119 = 88 days

Significance

The cash operating cycle or working capital cycle gives the average time it takes for the company to receive payment from receivables after it has paid its trade payables. This represents the period of time for which receivables require financing. The cash operating cycle of Anjo Co has lengthened by 48 days in 20X6 compared with 20X5. This represents an increase in working capital requirement of approximately $15,600,000 × 48/365 = $2.05 million.

17 Joan Co

Marking scheme

			Marks
(a)	New level of receivables	1	
	Finance saving	1	
	Administration cost savings	1	
	Interest on advance from factor	2	
	Factor annual fee	1	
	Net benefit of factor's offer	1	
	Conclusion and discussion	1	8
(b)	Working capital and business solvency	3-4	
	Factors influencing optimum cash level	4-5	
		Maximum	7
			15

(a)

	$000
Current receivables	3,800
Receivables under factor = 3,800 × 0.7	2,660
Reduction in receivables	1,140

	$000
Finance cost saving = 1,140 × 0.08	91.2
Administration cost saving = 1,000 × 0.02	20.0
Interest on advance = 2,660 × 0.8 × 0.01	(21.3)
Factor's annual fee = 15,600 × 0.005	(78.0)
Net benefit of accepting factor's offer	11.9

Although the terms of the factor's offer are financially acceptable, suggesting a net financial benefit of $11,900, this benefit is small compared with annual turnover of $15.6 million. Other benefits, such as the application of the factor's expertise to the receivable management of Joan Co, might also be influential in the decision on whether to accept the offer.

(b) The objectives of working capital management are **liquidity** and **profitability**, but there is a tension between these two objectives. Liquid funds, for example cash, earn no return and so will not increase profitability. Near-liquid funds, with short investment periods, earn a lower return than funds invested for a long period. Profitability is therefore decreased to the extent that liquid funds are needed.

The main reason that companies fail, though, is because they **run out of cash** and so good cash management is an essential part of good working capital management. Business solvency cannot be maintained if working capital management in the form of cash management is of a poor standard.

In order to **balance** the twin objectives of liquidity and profitability in terms of cash management, a company needs to decide on the **optimum** amount of cash to hold at any given time. There are several factors that can aid in determining the optimum cash balance:

First, it is important to note that cash management is a forward-looking activity, in that the optimum cash balance must reflect the expected need for cash in the next budget period, for example in the next month. The cash budget will indicate expected cash receipts over the next period, expected payments that need to be made, and any shortfall that is expected to arise due to the difference between receipts and payments. This is the **transactions need** for cash, since it is based on the amount of cash needed to meet future business transactions.

However, there may be a degree of **uncertainty** as to the timing of expected receipts. Receivables, for example, may not all pay on time and some may take extended credit, whether authorised or not. In order to guard against a possible shortfall of cash to meet future transactions, companies may keep a **'buffer inventory'** of cash by holding a cash reserve greater than called for by the transactions demand. This is the **precautionary demand** for cash and the optimum cash balance will reflect management's assessment of this demand.

Beyond this, a company may decide to hold additional cash in order to take advantage of any business opportunities that may arise, for example the possibility of taking over a rival company that has fallen on hard times. This is the **speculative demand** for cash and it may contribute to the optimum cash level for a given company, depending on that company's strategic plan.

18 Special Gift Suppliers

Text references. Working capital management is covered in Chapters 4, 5 and 6.

Top tips. This question offers good opportunities to score marks although you must make sure you spend sufficient time discussing permanent working capital. It is easy to spend too long on discussion of credit status. Credit control's role covers monitoring as well as initial granting of credit, and possibly a factor might be able to manage receivables more efficiently as well as providing finance.

Examiner's comment. Answers were generally good, particularly on credit control. Discussion of the permanent elements of working capital tended to be more variable.

To: Financial Controller, Special Gift Department

From: Adviser

Subject: Working capital

Date: 27 September 20X2

This report covers a number of aspects of managing working capital.

(a)   **Functioning of a credit control department**

The credit control department should be involved with customers at all stages of the credit control cycle.

(1)   When customers **first request credit**, the credit control department should **obtain references** and **credit ratings, analyse their accounts** and obtain other information such as **press comment** as appropriate. Staff may also **visit the customer**. A **credit limit** should be recommended based on the information obtained; initially the limit should be **low**, and only raised over time if the **customer's payment record** is good.

(2)   When the customer makes an order, the credit control department should check whether the **new order** will cause the customer to **exceed** their limits.

(3)   Staff should also review regularly the appropriateness of credit limits, and check the aged receivable listing to see if debts are overdue and report problems to designated senior managers.

(4)   The credit control department will be responsible for issuing documentation such as monthly statements and demands for payment. Staff should maintain contacts with other departments, trying

to ensure that orders are not accepted from customers who are in difficulties. The department will pursue slow payers, ultimately employing debt collectors and initiating legal action.

(5)   The department's procedures should be set out in a credit control manual.

(b)   **Benefits of factoring**

(1)   The business can **pay** its **suppliers promptly**, and so be able to take advantage of any early payment discounts that are available.

(2)   **Optimum inventory levels** can be **maintained**, because the business will have enough cash to pay for the inventories it needs.

(3)   **Growth** can be **financed** through **sales** rather than by injecting fresh external capital.

(4)   The business gets **finance linked** to its **volume of sales**. In contrast, overdraft limits tend to be determined by historical balance sheets.

(5)   The **managers** of the business **do not** have to **spend** their **time** on the problems of **slow paying receivables**.

(6)   The business does **not incur** the **costs** of **running** its own **sales ledger department**, and can use the **expertise** of receivable management that the factor has.

(7)   Because they are managing a number of sales ledgers, factors can **manage receivables more efficiently** than individual businesses through economies of scale.

(c)   **Financing of working capital**

Types of current assets

(i)   The **permanent current assets** businesses hold will include a minimum level of receivables owing money, and minimum balances of inventory and cash held for safety reasons. These minimum levels represent permanent working capital.

(ii)   **Fluctuating current assets** are assets held over and above the minimum amounts.

Aggressive management

If working capital is managed **aggressively**, all **fluctuating assets** plus a **certain proportion of permanent current assets** will be **financed by short-term capital** such as **bank overdrafts** and **trade payables**. Aggressive management will mean that there is an **increased risk** of **cash flow** and **liquidity problems**. Businesses may also suffer **higher interest costs** on short-term sources of finance.

Use of long-term capital

If short-term methods cannot be used, **long-term funding** such as **long-term loans** or **share capital** not tied up in funding non-current assets will be used to support **working capital**. This will mean that working capital is managed **conservatively**, with **all non-current assets** and **permanent current assets**, as well as part of **fluctuating current assets**, being **financed by long-term capital**. When fluctuating current assets are low, there will be surplus cash which the company will be able to invest in marketable securities.

19 Ulnad Co

Text references. Working capital management is covered in Chapters 4, 5 and 6.

Top tips. In part (a), think logically about the change in costs as a result of the credit policy and set out your workings clearly. In part (b) don't forget to explain your findings as well as do the calculation.

Easy marks. There are 4 easy marks available in part (b) for simply using the Miller-Orr formulae given to you in the exam.

		Marks
(a)	Increase in financing cost	1
	Incremental costs	1
	Cost of discount	1
	Contribution from increased sales	1
	Conclusion	1
		5
(b)	Calculation of spread	1
	Calculation of upper limit	1
	Calculation of return point	1
	Explanation of findings	2
		5
		10

(a) **Evaluation of change in credit policy**

Current average collections period = 30 + 10 = 40 days

Current accounts receivable = $6m × 40/365 = $657,534

Average collection period under new policy = (30% × 15 days) + (70% × 60 days) = 46.5 days

New level of credit sales = $6m × 1.05 = $6.3m

Accounts receivable after policy change = $6.3m × 46.5/365 = $802,603

Increase in financing cost = $(802,603 − 657,534) × 7% = $10,155

	$
Increase in financing cost	10,155
Incremental costs ($6.3m × 0.5%)	31,500
Cost of discount (30% × $6.3m × 1.5%)	28,350
Increase in costs	70,005
Contribution from increased sales ($6m × 5% × 60%)	180,000
Net benefit of policy change	109,995

The proposed policy will therefore increase the profitability of Ulnad Co.

(b) **Determination of spread**

Daily interest rate = 5.11/365 = 0.014% per day

Variance of cash flows = 1,000 × 1,000 = $1,000,000 per day

Transaction cost = $18 per transaction

Spread = 3 × ((0.75 × transaction cost × variance)/interest rate)$^{1/3}$

= 3 × ((0.75 × 18 × 1,000,000)/0.00014)1/3 = 3 × 4,585.7 = $13,757

Lower limit = $7,500

Upper limit = $(7,500 + 13,757) = $21,257

Return point = 7,500 + (13,757/3) = $12,086

Relevance of the values

The Miller-Orr model takes account of **uncertainty** in relation to cash flows. The cash balance of Renpec Co is allowed to vary between the lower and upper **limits** calculated by the model.

If the cash balance reaches an **upper limit** the firm **buys sufficient securities** to return the cash balance to a normal level (called the 'return point'). When the cash balance reaches a lower limit, the firm sells securities to bring the balance back to the return point.

The Miller-Orr model therefore helps Renpec Co to decrease the risk of running out of cash, while avoiding the loss of profit caused by having unnecessarily high cash balances.

20 Danul Co

Text references. Working capital management is covered in Chapters 4, 5 and 6.

Top tips. Both parts require full explanations so don't just simply write a list of points.

Easy marks. If you have learnt the subject matter the question should be straightforward.

Marking scheme

			Marks
(a)	Policy formulation	1-2	
	Credit analysis	1-2	
	Credit control	1-2	
	Collection of amounts due	1-2	
Maximum			5
(b)	Analysis of assets	1-2	
	Short-term and long-term debt	1-3	
	Discussion of policies	1-3	
	Other factors	1-2	
Maximum			5
			10

(a) **Key areas of accounts receivable management**

There are four key areas of accounts receivable management.

(i) **Formulation of policy**

A **framework** needs to be established within which the management of accounts receivable in an organisation takes place. Elements of the framework to be considered include establishing the **terms of trade** such as the period of credit offered and **early settlement discounts.** The organisation must also consider whether to **charge interest** on overdue accounts. Laid-down procedures will be needed for granting credit to new customers and determining what to do when accounts become overdue.

(ii) **Assessment of creditworthiness**

Information relating to a new customer needs to be analysed. The information may come from bank references, trade references or credit reference agency reports.

The greater the amount of credit being granted and the possibility of repeat business, the more credit analysis is needed.

(iii) **Credit control**

Accounts receivable' payment records must be **monitored** continually. This depends on successful sales ledger administration.

Credit monitoring can be simplified by a system of **in-house credit ratings**. For example, a company could have five credit-risk categories for its customers. These credit categories or ratings could be used to decide either individual credit limits for customers within that category or the frequency of the credit review.

A **customer's payment record** and the **accounts receivable aged analysis** should be examined regularly, as a matter of course. Breaches of the credit limit, or attempted breaches of it, should be brought immediately to the attention of the credit controller.

(iv) **Collection of amounts due**

A company needs to have in place agreed procedures for dealing with overdue accounts. Examples include instituting reminders or final demands, chasing payment by telephone or making a personal approach. If this does not work, the company could refuse to grant any more credit to the customer, hire a specialist debt collecting agency or, as a last resort, take legal action.

The overall **debt collection policy** of the firm should be such that the administrative costs and other costs incurred in debt collection do not exceed the benefits from incurring those costs.

(b) **Formulating a working capital funding policy**

In order to understand working capital financing decisions, assets can be divided into three different types.

Non-current (fixed) assets are long-term assets from which an organisation expects to derive benefit over a number of periods. For example, buildings or machinery.

Permanent current assets are the amount required to meet long-term minimum needs and sustain normal trading activity. For example, inventory and the average level of accounts receivable.

Fluctuating current assets are the current assets which vary according to normal business activity. For example due to seasonal variations.

Fluctuating current assets together with **permanent** current assets form part of the working capital of the business, which may be financed by either long-term funding (including equity capital) or by current liabilities (short-term funding).

Short-term sources of funding are usually **cheaper** and **more flexible** than long-term ones. However short-term sources are **riskier** for the borrower as interest rates are more volatile in the short term and they may not be renewed.

The matching principle suggests that long-term finance should be used for long-term assets. A **balance** between risk and return might be best achieved by a **moderate approach** to working capital funding. This is a policy of **maturity matching** in which long-term funds finance permanent assets while short-term funds finance non-permanent assets. This means that the maturity of the funds **matches** the maturity of the assets.

A **conservative approach** to financing working capital involves all non-current assets and permanent current assets, as well as part of the fluctuating current assets, being financed by long-term funding. This is less risky and less profitable than a matching policy. At times when fluctuating current assets are low, there will be **surplus cash** which the company will be able to invest in marketable securities.

Finally, an organisation may adopt an **aggressive approach** to financing working capital. Not only are fluctuating current assets all financed out of short-term sources, but so are some of the permanent current assets. This policy represents an **increased risk** of liquidity and cash flow problems, although potential returns will be increased if short-term financing can be obtained more cheaply than long-term finance.

Other factors that influence a working capital funding policy include **previous management attitudes to risk**; this will determine whether there is a preference for a conservative, aggressive or moderate approach. Secondly, **previous funding decisions** will determine the current position being considered in policy formulation. Finally, the **size of the organisation** will influence its ability to access different sources of finance. For example, a small company may have to adopt an aggressive working capital funding policy because it cannot raise additional long-term finance.

21 PKA Co

Marking scheme

			Marks
(a)	Profitability and liquidity	1	
	Discussion of conflict between objectives	2	
			3
(b)	Cost of cutting ordering policy	3	
	Cost of EOQ–based ordering policy	3	
	Saving by using EOQ model	1	
			7
			10

(a) **Objectives of working capital management**

The two main objectives of working capital management are to ensure it has **sufficient liquid resources** to continue in business and to **increase its profitability**.

Every business needs adequate **liquid resources** to maintain day-to-day cash flow. It needs enough to pay wages, salaries and accounts payable if it is to keep its workforce and ensure its supplies.

Maintaining adequate working capital is not just important in the short term. Adequate liquidity is needed to ensure the **survival** of the business in the long term. Even a profitable company may fail without adequate cash flow to meet its liabilities.

On the other hand, an excessively conservative approach to working capital management resulting in high levels of cash holdings will **harm profits** because the opportunity to make a return on the assets tied up as cash will have been missed.

These two objectives will often **conflict** as liquid assets give the lowest returns.

(b) **Cost of current ordering policy**

Minimum inventory level = re-order level – (average usage × average lead time)

Average usage per week = 625,000 units/50 weeks = 12,500 units

Average lead time = 2 weeks

Re-order level = 35,000 units

Minimum inventory level = 35,000 – (12,500 × 2) = 10,000 units

Average inventory = Minimum level + $\dfrac{\text{reorder quantity}}{2}$

$\qquad$ = 10,000 + (100,000/2)

$\qquad$ = 60,000 units

Annual holding cost = 60,000 × €0.50 = €30,000

Annual ordering cost = €250 × (625,000/100,000) = €1,563

Annual total cost = 30,000 + 1,563 = **€31,563**

Economic order quantity

EOQ = $\sqrt{\dfrac{2C_0D}{C_h}}$ = $\sqrt{\dfrac{2 \times 250 \times 625,000}{0.5}}$ = 25,000 units.

Number of orders per year = 625,000/25,000 = 25

Annual ordering cost = €250 × 25 = €6,250

Annual holding cost = (10,000 + (25,000/2)) × €0.50 = €11,250

Annual total cost = 11,250 + 6,250 = **€17,500**

Saving as a result of using the economic order quantity model = 31,563 − 17,500 = **€14,063** per year

22 HGR Co

Text reference. Working capital financing and cash flow forecasting are covered in Chapter 6 and receivables management in Chapter 5.

Top tips. This question demonstrates the importance of being able to forecast cash flow and financial position. This is a time pressured question that will need to be carefully planned to obtain the maximum marks. Part (a) should be a straightforward discussion, provided you answer the specific requirement. Part (b) has some tricky parts in calculating the effect of the finance director's proposals. If you get stuck, make an assumption and move on.

Easy marks. The easiest marks are probably for the discussion parts, provided you have sufficient knowledge of this area of the syllabus.

Examiner's comments. In part (a) some candidates ignored the word 'financing' and discussed working capital strategy in general. Better answers recognised the aggressive financing strategy and discussed how current assets could be divided into fluctuating and permanent current assets, linking this via the matching principle to the use of short-term and long-term finance.

Many candidates had great difficulty in part (b). Common errors included failing to recognise that the opening balance was the overdraft, calculating annual rather than monthly interest and including cash flows other than those given in the question. The general standard of answers showed that many candidates need further preparation in the important area of cash flow preparation.

			Marks
(a)	Analysis of current assets		
	Short-term and long-term finance	1-2	
	Matching principle	2-3	
	Financing approach used by company	1-2	
		1-2	
		Maximum	5
(b)	Bank balance if no action is taken	2	
	Bank balance if action is taken	5	
	Working capital management implications	1-2	
	Advice on course of action	1-2	
		Maximum	10
			15

(a) Working capital financing strategy of HGR Co

Working capital can be financed using **short-term** finance or **long-term** finance or a mixture of the two.

Short-term finance

An **overdraft** is an example of short-term finance. It is **flexible** as it is used as and when it is needed and **variable interest** is charged. It is however **risky** as it can be withdrawn at any time by the bank and the **interest rate** charged may be **higher** than a short-term loan. In general, the **term structure** of interest rates suggests that short-term debt finance has a **lower cost** than long-term debt finance.

HGR Co has an overdraft facility of $4 million and at the current date is using nearly all of this facility. 83% (14,000,000/16,935,000 × 100) of current assets are financed from short-term sources in the form of the overdraft and trade payables.

Long-term finance

The **matching principle** suggests that long-term finance should be used for long-term investments. In terms of working capital finance, this means that long-term finance should be matched with **permanent current assets** and **non-current assets**.

Permanent current assets are the amount required to meet long-term minimum needs and sustain normal trading activity. For example, inventory and the average level of accounts receivable. As a business grows, the level of permanent current assets will grow.

17% (2,935,000/16,935,000 × 100) of HGR's current assets are financed from equity finance and traded bonds, which are long-term sources of finance.

HGR Co's policy

HGR Co's working capital financing policy is **aggressive** as it mostly consists of short-term finance. This policy represents an **increased risk** of liquidity and cash flow problems, although potential returns will be increased if short-term financing can be obtained more cheaply than long-term finance.

(b) Bank balance in three months' time if no action is taken

Month	1	2	3
	$000	$000	$000
Receipts	4,220	4,350	3,808
Payments	(3,950)	(4,100)	(3,750)
Interest on bonds		(200)	
Overdraft interest (W3)	(19)	(18)	(18)
Capital investment			(2,000)
Net cash flow	251	32	(1,960)
Opening balance	(3,800)	(3,549)	(3,517)
Closing balance	(3,549)	(3,517)	(5,477)

Bank balance in three months' time if the finance director's proposals are implemented

Month	1	2	3
	$000	$000	$000
Receipts	4,220	4,350	3,808
Payments	(3,950)	(4,100)	(3,750)
Interest on bonds		(200)	
Overdraft interest (W3)	(19)	(15)	(13)
Capital investment			(2,000)
Accounts receivable (W1)	270	270	270
Inventory (W2)	204	204	204
Net cash flow	725	509	(1,481)
Opening balance	(3,800)	(3,075)	(2,566)
Closing balance	(3,075)	(2,566)	(4,047)

Workings

(1) Reduction in accounts receivable days

Current accounts receivable days = (8,775/49,275) × 365 = 65 days

Reduction in days over 6 months = 65 − 53 = 12 days

Monthly reduction = 12/6 = 2 days

Each receivables day is equivalent to 8,775,000/65 = $135,000

Monthly reduction in accounts receivable = 2 × 135,000 = $270,000

(2) Reduction in inventory days

Current inventory days = (8,160/37,250) × 365 = 80 days

Each inventory day is equivalent to 8,160,000/80 = $102,000

Monthly reduction in inventory = 102,000 × 2 = $204,000

(3) Overdraft interest

Monthly overdraft interest rate $= \sqrt[12]{1.0617} - 1$

$= 1.005 - 1$

$= 0.005$ or 0.5%

If no action is taken:

Period 1 interest = 3,800,000 × 0.5% = $19,000

Period 2 interest = 3,549,000 × 0.5% = $17,745

Period 3 interest = 3,517,000 × 0.5% = $17,585

If action is taken:

Period 1 interest = 3,800,000 × 0.5% = $19,000

Period 2 interest = 3,075,000 × 0.5% = $15,375

Period 3 interest = 2,566,000 × 0.5% = $12,830

Comment

The cash flow forecast shows that, if no action is taken, HGR Co will **exceed its overdraft limit** of $4 million by $1.48 million in three months' time.

If the finance director's suggestions for action are taken, the bank balance will **improve** but the overdraft limit will still be exceeded by $47,000.

Following this 3 month period, the bank balance will continue to improve by $270,000 per month due to the **reduction in accounts receivable**. Further information would be needed on other future cash flows to forecast whether the overdraft would then return to under the limit.

The main reason why there is a cash shortfall is the **capital expenditure** of $2 million. This is a **long-term** investment that should be financed using long-term sources of finance, such as equity or bonds. If this were to happen, the overdraft balance would be $3.48 million at the end of three months if no action was taken, and $2.05 million if the finance director's suggestions were implemented.

HGR Co could raise finance through **long-term debt** using the $48,965,000 of non-current assets as security. The six-monthly interest payment of $200,000 suggests that HGR Co is not highly geared so there is room for more long-term debt finance.

Recommendation

HGR Co should implement the finance director's suggestion for working capital management and use long-term debt to finance the capital expenditure.

23 RGH Co

Text reference. Working capital financing and cash flow forecasting are covered in Chapter 6 and receivables management in Chapter 5.

Top tips. This question should be a straightforward discussion, provided you answer the specific requirement.

Easy marks. This was fairly straightforward provided you have sufficient knowledge of this area of the syllabus.

Examiner's comments. Some answers were one-sided concentrating on exchange rate risk rather than on credit risk.

Risks arising from granting credit to foreign customers

Foreign debts raise the following special problems. When goods are sold abroad, the customer might ask for credit. Exports take time to arrange, and there might be complex paperwork. Transporting the goods can be slow, if they are sent by sea. These **delays in foreign trade** mean that exporters often build up **large investments** in inventories and accounts receivable. These working capital investments have to be financed somehow.

The **risk of bad debts** can be greater with foreign trade than with domestic trade. If a foreign customer refuses to pay a debt, the exporter must pursue the debt in the debtor's own country, where procedures will be subject to the laws of that country.

How risks can be managed and reduced

A company can reduce its investment in foreign accounts receivable by insisting on **earlier payment** for goods. Another approach is for an exporter to arrange for a **bank to give cash for a foreign debt**, sooner than the exporter would receive payment in the normal course of events. There are several ways in which this might be done.

Where the exporter asks his bank to handle the collection of payment (of a bill of exchange or a cheque) on his behalf, the bank may be prepared to make an **advance** to the exporter against the collection. The amount of the advance might be 80% to 90% of the value of the collection.

Negotiation of bills or cheques is similar to an advance against collection, but would be used where the bill or cheque is payable outside the exporter's country (for example in the foreign buyer's country).

Discounting bills of exchange is where a bank buys the bill before it is due and credits the value of the bill after a discount charge to the company's account.

Export factoring could be considered where the exporter pays for the specialist expertise of the factor in order to reduce bad debts and the amount of investment in foreign accounts receivable.

Documentary credits provide a method of payment in international trade, which gives the exporter a secure risk-free method of obtaining payment. The buyer (a foreign buyer, or a UK importer) and the seller (a UK exporter or a foreign supplier) first of all agree a contract for the sale of the goods, which provides for payment through a documentary credit. The buyer then requests a bank in his country to issue a letter of credit in favour of the exporter. The issuing bank, by issuing its letter of credit, guarantees payment to the beneficiary.

Countertrade is a means of financing trade in which goods are exchanged for other goods.

Export credit insurance is insurance against the risk of non-payment by foreign customers for export debts. If a credit customer defaults on payment, the task of pursuing the case through the courts will be lengthy, and it might be a long time before payment is eventually obtained.

Premiums for export credit insurance are however very high and the benefits are sometimes not fully appreciated.

24 APX Co

Text references. Forecasting and working capital financing are covered in Chapters 4, 5 and 6.

Top tips. This question covers the key skills of forecasting financial statements as well as using and interpreting provided financial information.

Part (a) may throw you as it requires a forecast statement and statement of profit and loss. However, the format is provided in the question and the workings require logical manipulation of the accounting ratios provided. Fill in as many figures as you can and you will gain a mark for each correct calculation.

Easy marks. This question may look daunting initially but there are plenty of easy marks available if you tackle it logically and move on quickly if you get stuck.

Examiner's comments. For part (a) many answers were of a very good standard and gained full marks. Some candidates ignored the forecast financial ratios and applied the expected turnover growth rate to cost of sales and other expenses. Other candidates showed a lack of knowledge of the structure of the statement of profit or loss by calculating the tax liability before subtracting the interest payments.

Part (b) asked for an analysis and discussion of the working capital financing policy of the company in the question. Many students were not aware of the conservative, aggressive and matching approaches to working capital financing policy, and so were ill-prepared for this question.

Marking scheme

			Marks
(a)	Gross profit	1	
	Net profit	1	
	Profit before tax	1	
	Retained profit	1	
	Inventory	1	
	Trade receivables	1	
	Trade payables	1	
	Reserves	1	
	Overdraft	1	
	Layout and format	1	
		Maximum	9
(b)	Working capital financing policies	2-3	
	Financial analysis	1-2	
	Working capital financing policy of company	2-3	
		Maximum	6
			10

(a) (i) **Forecast statement of profit or loss**

		$m
Turnover (16.00m × 1.084)		17.344
Cost of sales (17.344m – 5.203m)		12.141
Gross profit (17.344m × 30%)		5.203
Other expenses (5.203m – 3.469m)		1.734
Net profit (17.344m x 20%)		3.469
Interest (10m x 0.08) + 0.140m		0.940
Profit before tax		2.529
Tax (2.529m × 0·3)		0.759
Profit after tax		1.770
Dividends (1.770m × 50%)		0.885
Retained profit		0.885

(ii) **Forecast statement of financial position**

	$m	$m
Non-current assets		22.00
Current assets		
Inventory (12.141m × (110/365))	3.66	
Trade receivables (17.344m × (65/365))	3.09	
		6.75
Total assets		28.75
Equity finance		
Ordinary shares	5.00	
Reserves (7.5m + 0.885m)	8.39	
		13.39
Long-term bank loan		10.00
		23.39
Current liabilities		
Trade payables(12.141m × (75/365))	2.49	
Overdraft (28.75m – 23.39m – 2.49 balancing figure)	2.87	
		5.36
Total liabilities		28.75

(b) **Working capital financing policy**

Working capital financing policies can be described as **conservative, moderate** or **aggressive**, depending on the extent to which fluctuating current assets and permanent current assets are financed by short-term sources of finance.

Permanent current assets are the amount required to meet long-term minimum needs and sustain normal trading activity, for example inventory and the average level of accounts receivable.

Fluctuating current assets are the current assets which vary according to normal business activity, for example due to seasonal variations.

A **conservative** working capital financing policy uses **long-term funds** to finance non-current assets and permanent current assets, as well as a proportion of fluctuating current assets.

An **aggressive** working capital financing policy uses **short-term funds** to finance fluctuating current assets and a proportion of permanent current assets as well. This is riskier but potentially more profitable.

A **balance** between risk and return might be best achieved by a **moderate** policy, which uses long-term funds to finance long-term assets (non-current assets and permanent current assets) and short-term funds to finance short-term assets (fluctuating current assets).

The **current** statement of financial position shows that APX Co uses **trade payables** and an **overdraft** as sources of **short-term** finance. 89% (100 x 4.1/4.6) of current assets are financed from short-term sources and only 11% are financed from long-term sources. This appears to be a **very aggressive** working capital financing policy which carries significant risk. For example, if the bank called in the overdraft, APX Co might have to resort to more expensive short-term financing.

The **forecast** statement of financial position shows a **reduced** reliance on short-term finance. 79% (100 × 5.36/6.75) of current assets are now financed from short-term sources and 21% are financed from long-term sources. This reduces the risk of the working financing capital policy.

Further moves away from an aggressive policy would be hampered by a lack of ability to pay interest on more long-term debt. The forecast **interest coverage ratio** is only 3.7 times (3.469/0.94). Alternatively, APX Co could consider an **increase in equity funding** to decrease reliance on short-term finance.

25 ZSE Co

Text references. Joint probability is covered in Chapter 10 and working capital objectives are covered in Chapter 4.

Top tips. If the joint probability calculation looks daunting, then it may be better to attempt part (b), which is unrelated to the calculations, before returning to part (a). Also don't forget to discuss the results from part (a), where a discussion of issues with the use of expected values will gain marks.

To tackle part (a) the two periods should be looked at separately with all of the possible outcomes from the first period being included as opening balances for period two. As a check that the calculations have been done correctly the sum of the joint probabilities should be 1.

Easy marks. The discussions on profitability vs liquidity in part (b) are straightforward.

Examiner's comments. In part (a) many candidates were unable to calculate these probabilities because they did not appreciate the importance of the joint probabilities used in a probability table.

Candidates were then asked to discuss whether the expected value analysis could assist the company to manage its cash flows. Many candidates tended to discuss ways in which the company could manage cash flows in general, even in some cases discussing cash management models, rather than discussing the usefulness of an expected value analysis. Better answers discussed the benefits and limitations of the analysis that had been undertaken.

Marking scheme

			Marks
(a)	Expected value of period 1 closing balance	2	
	Expected value of period 2 closing balance	3	
	Probability of negative cash balance	1	
	Probability of exceeding overdraft limit	2	
	Discussion of expected value analysis	2	
			10
(b)	Relevant discussion		5
			15

(a) (i)

Opening balance $'000	Period 1 cash flow $'000	Closing balance for period 1 $'000	Probability	Expected value $'000
(500)	8,000	7,500	0.1	750
(500)	4,000	3,500	0.6	2,100
(500)	(2,000)	(2,500)	0.3	(750)
				2,100

The expected value of the cash balance at the end of period 1 is $2,100,000.

(ii)

Period 1 closing balance $'000	Probability	Period 2 cash flow $'000	Probability	Period 2 closing balance $'000	Joint probability	Expected value $'000
(a)	(b)	(c)	(d)	(a) + (c)	(b) × (d)	
7,500	0.1	7,000	0.3	14,500	0.03	435
7,500	0.1	3,000	0.5	10,500	0.05	525
7,500	0.1	(9,000)	0.2	(1,500)	0.02	(30)
3,500	0.6	7,000	0.3	10,500	0.18	1,890
3,500	0.6	3,000	0.5	6,500	0.30	1,950
3,500	0.6	(9,000)	0.2	(5,500)	0.12	(660)
(2,500)	0.3	7,000	0.3	4,500	0.09	405
(2,500)	0.3	3,000	0.5	500	0.15	75
(2,500)	0.3	(9,000)	0.2	(11,500)	0.06	(690)
						3,900

The expected value of the cash balance at the end of period 2 is $3,900,000.

(iii) There is a 0.20 (0.02 + 0.12 + 0.06) or 20% chance of a negative cash balance at the end of period 2. (These are the joint probabilities of the negative period two closing balances.)

(iv) There is a 0.18 (0.12 + 0.06) or 18% chance that the overdraft limit will be exceeded at the end of period 2. (These are the joint probabilities of the period two closing balances in excess of the overdraft limit of $2million.)

Discussion

Expected values do not work well for one-off activities as they are based on averages. As such the expected value may not be a possible outcome. For example in period one the expected value of $2.1million is not a possible outcome and nor is the period two expected balance of $3.9million. Expected values work best for repeat decisions as they give the average outcome from an activity repeated many times.

ZSE is at risk of exceeding its overdraft limit in both periods. There is a 30% chance of this in period 1 and an 18% chance in period 2. However, extra financing of $500,000 will only be needed to guard against this in period 1, but $9.5million may be required in period 2.

Extending the overdraft facility may be appropriate for period 1, but not for period 2.

The model is useful in highlighting the risk faced by ZSE, but assigning probabilities is subjective, even when external experts are used. Whether these probabilities represent realistic outcomes is questionable.

(b) The two main objectives of working capital management are profitability and liquidity. These are said to be twin objectives because they conflict with each other.

A business will need to have a level of liquidity that is sufficient to maintain day-to-day cash flow. Wages, salaries and expenses will have to be paid for the business to continue operations.

Although this liquidity level is needed to ensure day-to-day expenses can be met, adequate liquidity is also required to ensure the survival of the business in the long term. A profitable company can still fail if it is unable to generate cash to meet its liabilities.

However, a conservative approach will result in high levels of liquid assets such as cash. High levels of liquid assets will reduce profitability as they have the lowest returns.

In conclusion, liquidity will be more important when short-term finance is difficult to obtain and profitability is more important when there are high levels of liquid assets. However, neither objective should be ignored in any situation.

26 WQZ Co

Marking scheme

			Marks
(a)	Reduction in trade receivables	2	
	Financing cost saving	1	
	Cost of early settlement discount	1	
	Comment on net benefit	2	
	Maximum early settlement discount	1	
			7
(b)	Relevant discussion		8
			15

(a) **Change of receivables policy**

Receivables payment period is currently $(18/87.6) \times 365 = 75$ days

Under the new policy only 25% will pay in 30 days, so the revised payment period would be

$(0.25 \times 30) + (0.75 \times 60) = 52.5$ days

Current trade receivables = $18m

Revised level using the revised payment period = $87.6 \times (52.5/365) = \$12.6m$

Reduction in receivables = $18 - 12.6 = \$5.4m$

Short-term finance cost is 5.5%

Finance cost savings = $5.4m \times 0.055 = \$297,000$

Administration savings = $753,000

Total savings = $297,000 + 753,000 = \$1,050,000$

Cost of the discount = credit sales $\times$ % customers taking discount $\times$ discount %

Cost of the discount = $87.6m \times 0.25 \times 0.01 = \$219,000$

Benefit of the discount = $1,050,000 - 219,000 = \$831,000$

The proposed change in receivables management should be accepted, although this does depend on the forecast cost savings being achieved.

Maximum discount

25% of the customers will take the discount. Therefore the total sales value affected by the discount will be 25% of $87.6milion, which is $21.9million

The maximum discount will be where the costs equal the benefits of $1,050,000. This would occur at

$1.05/21.9 = 0.048 = 4.8\%$

(b)   The policy on the management of trade receivables will depend on a number of factors.

The level of trade receivables

If there is a substantial amount of capital tied up in trade receivables, then the policy may be aimed at reducing the level of investment by not granting credit as freely as before or shortening the credit terms.

The cost of trade credit

Where the cost of trade credit (including opportunity costs) is high, a company will want to reduce the level of investment in trade receivables.

Competitor trade terms

Unless a company can differentiate itself from its competitors, it will need to, at least, match the credit terms offered by its competitors to avoid a loss of customers.

Liquidity needs

Where a company needs to improve its liquidity they may want to reduce credit terms or consider debt factoring or invoice discounting.

Risk appetite

A company may be prepared to risk higher levels of bad debts by offering credit terms that are relatively relaxed as this will increase sales volume.

Expertise in credit management

If a company lacks expertise in credit management, particularly in monitoring level of receivables then the may choose to factor their debts.

27 Bold Co

Text references. The cash operating cycle is covered in Chapter 4.

Top tips. For part (a) the requirement leads you to what should be included in your answer, make sure that you have covered these areas.

Easy marks. Part (b) provides easy marks for straightforward calculation of the cash operating cycle.

Marking scheme

			Marks
(a)	Explanation of cash operating cycle	1-2	
	Cash operating cycle and working capital policy	2-3	
	Cash operating cycle and business operation	2-3	
	Other relevant discussion	1-2	
		Maximum	6
(b)	Inventory days	1	
	Receivables days	1	
	Payables days	1	
	Cash operating cycle	1	
			4
			10

(a)   The cash operating cycle is the period of time which elapses between the point at which cash begins to be expended on the production of a product and the collection of cash from a customer. The cash operating cycle in a manufacturing business equals the average time that raw materials remain in inventory less the average period of credit taken from suppliers plus the average time taken to produce the goods plus average the time taken by customers to pay for the goods.

There is a relationship between the cash operating cycle and the level of investment in working capital. If the turnover periods for inventories and accounts receivable lengthen, or the payment period to accounts payable shortens, then the operating cycle will lengthen and the investment in working capital will increase. The length of the cash operating cycle depends on the working capital policy which will determine the level of investment in working capital and also of the nature of the business operations.

Working capital policy

The level of investment in working capital depends on the company's working capital policy. Two companies with similar business operations may have significantly different levels of investment depending on whether they adopt a conservative or an aggressive approach. An aggressive policy involves having lower levels of inventory and trade receivables and will therefore mean there is a shorter cash operating cycle. A conservative policy involves having higher levels of inventory and trade receivables and will give rise to a longer cash operating cycle. The longer cash operating cycle will mean profitability is less than under the aggressive approach, but it reduces risk such of the risk of a stock-out.

Nature of business operations

Business operations will have a significant effect on the cash operating cycle. A business supplying services may have very low levels of inventory whereas a manufacturer may have very high levels of inventory. A retailer who operates mainly using cash sales will have a significantly lower level of trade receivables than a company who conducts most of its sales by offering credit terms.

(b)   Inventory days = 4,500 / 16,400 × 365 = 100 days

Trade receivables days = 3,500 / 21,300 × 365 = 60 days

Trade payables days = 4,500 / 16,400 × 365 = 67 days

Cash operating cycle = 100 + 60 − 67 = 93 days

28 Wobnig Co

Text references. The signs of overtrading are covered in Chapter 4. The Miller-Orr model is covered in Chapter 5.

Top tips. In part (a), concentrate on what the question asks for – you will not gain any marks by discussing how Wobnig can improve its working capital position! Start by listing the typical signs of overtrading, before calculating the ratios to support each point.

Easy marks. Easy marks are available in part (b), for calculating the upper limit and return point using the Miller-Orr model.

Examiner's comments. Most answers to part (a) gained good marks. Answers that did not focus on the question asked, which was whether or not the company was overtrading, lost marks as a result.

In part (b), few answers went on to discuss or explain the objective of keeping the cash balance between the two limits, ie the importance of the return point.

Marks

(a) Rapid increase in revenue   1-2
Increase in trade receivables days   1-2
Decrease in profitability   1-2
Rapid increase in current assets   1-2
Increased dependence on short-term finance   2-3
Decrease in liquidity   2-3
Conclusion as regards overtrading   1
          Maximum   __12__

(b) Calculation of upper limit   0.5
Calculation of return point   0.5
Explanation of use in managing cash balances   __2__

          __3__
          __15__

(a) Signs of overtrading:

Rapid increase in sales revenue: Wobnig's sales revenue has increased by 40% from $10,375k in 20X0 to $14,525k in 20X1. This rapid growth in revenue is not supported by a similar increase in long-term financing, which has only increased by 4.7% ($16,268k in 20X1 compared to $15,541k in 20X0).

Rapid increase in current assets: Wobnig's current assets have also nearly doubled, increasing from $2,826k in 20X0 to $5,349k in 20X1 (89%). This is striking, given that long-term financing has only increased by 4.7%. Trade receivables have increased by 85% ($1,734k in 20X0 and $3,200k in 20X1), and inventory levels have increased by 97% ($2,149k from $1,092k in 20X0).

Increase in inventory days: Linked to the above, Inventory turnover has slowed noticeably, from 60 days in 20X0 to 75 days in 20X1, well above the industry average of 55 days. This may indicate that Wobnig is expecting further increases in sales volumes in the future.

Increase in receivable days: Perhaps a matter of greater concern is the fact that trade receivables are being paid much more slowly. Receivable days have increased from 61 days in 20X0 to 80 days in 20X1, again significantly above the industry average. It could be that in order to encourage sales, Wobnig has offered more favourable credit terms to its customers. However, the increase in receivable days may also indicate that Wobnig is lacking sufficient resources to effectively manage its receivables, and/ or that its customers may be unable to settle their debts on time, as they are struggling financially.

Reduction in profitability: Although Wobnig's sales revenue has increased by 40% over the past year, its PBIT has only increased by 8.8%. The net profit margin has actually decreased, from 36% in 20X0 to 28% in 20X1. This may be due partly to the company selling at lower margins to increase sales volumes, but most likely points to increased costs of sales and operating costs.

With the additional costs associated with holding larger inventories, and increasing financing costs from overdrafts (see below), the company's profitability is likely to suffer even more going forward.

Increase in current liabilities: Wobnig is increasingly financed through current liabilities, which has increased by 131% (from $1,887k in 20X0 to $4,365k in 20X1) while long-term financing has increased only marginally by 4.7%. The sales revenue/ net working capital ratio has increased from 11 times to 15 times in 20X1. In particular, overdraft has increased five-fold from 20X0 to 20X1. Payables days have lengthened from 90 days to 100 days, indicating that Wobnig is finding it more difficult to settle trade debts.

All of this will put further strain on financing costs, eroding the distributable profits. The company's interest expense has increased from $292k to $355k.

Reduced liquidity: The cause of Wobnig's increasing dependence on overdrafts and lengthening payables days lies in its reduced liquidity. Wobnig's current ratio has reduced from 1.5 times to 1.2 times, compared to the industry average of 1.7 times. The more sensitive quick ratio has reduced from 0.9 times to 0.7 times, against the average of 1.1 times. Wobnig does not yet have a liquid deficit though, as its current assets still exceed its current liabilities.

Conclusion

From the trends discussed above, we can conclude that Wobnig is overtrading.

Workings

Ratio	Formula	20X1	20X0
Net profit margin	PBIT/Revenue × 100%	28%	36%
Current ratio	Current assets/current liabilities	1.2 times	1.5 times
Quick ratio	(Current assets – inventory)/current liabilities	0.7 times	0.9 times
Inventory days	Inventory/cost of sales x 365	75 days	60 days
Receivables days	Trade receivables/revenue × 365	80 days	61 days
Payables days	Trade payables/cost of sales × 365	100 days	90 days
Net working capital	Current assets – current liabilities	$984,000	$949,000
Revenue/net working capital	Revenue/net working capital	15 times	11 times

(b)   Upper limit = lower limit + spread = $200,000 + $75,000 = $275,000

Return point = Lower limit + (spread/3) = $200,000 + $75,000/3 = $225,000

The Miller-Orr model would help to indicate when Wobnig should invest surplus cash, and when it should sell securities to bring more cash back into the business. Based on the calculations above, the directors at Wobnig would invest $50,000 of cash when the cash balance in the company reaches $275,000, to bring the cash balance to the return point. They would look to sell $25,000 of securities for cash when the cash balance reduces to $200,000.

29 ZPS Co

Text references. The working capital policy factors and bulk purchase discounts are covered in Chapter 6 and early settlement discounts are covered in Chapter 5.

Top tips. This question looks at working capital management. Part (a) requires candidates to identify factors that will affect working capital **policy**, not a discussion of working capital financing or working capital investment. Part (b) involves some logical calculations, but don't try to use the EOQ formula for the bulk purchase discount part.

Easy marks. The discussion in part (a) should award marks quickly provided you've done your homework.

Examiner's comments. A number of students lost valuable time in part (b) with economic order quantity calculations, which were not required by the question and which were completely unnecessary. The two offered discounts needed to be compared with the current costs of the company.

Marking scheme

			Marks
(a)	Nature of the business	1-2	
	Operating cycle	1-2	
	Terms of trade	1-2	
	Risk appetite	1-2	
	Other relevant factors	1-2	
		Maximum	8

		Marks
(b)	Value of early settlement discount offered	1
	Increase in financing cost	1
	Loss if early settlement discount taken	1
	Inventory cost under current ordering policy	1
	Revised holding and ordering costs	1
	Inventory cost if discount is taken	1
	Benefit if bulk purchase discount taken	1
		7
		15

(a) Working capital policies cover a number of areas: the level of investment in current assets, the financing of current assets and the procedures for day-to-day management of working capital components (trade payables, trade receivables, inventory and cash). There are two objectives of working capital management, namely profitability and liquidity. Working capital policies help achieve these objectives. A number of factors influence working capital policies.

Nature of the business

The type of business will have an effect on the working capital policy as this can influence the components of working capital. Manufacturing companies are likely to have high levels of inventory and trade receivables whereas service companies will have low levels of inventory. High street retail companies are likely to have low levels of trade receivables.

Operating cycle

The length of the operating cycle combined with the desired investment in current assets determines the amount of working capital finance required. Working capital policies should be designed to optimise the length of the components of the operating cycle which are the inventory turnover days, the trade receivables days and the trade payables days.

Terms of trade

It will be difficult to offer a much shorter payment period than competitors as this is likely to lead to a loss of customers. The level of receivables is determined by the credit level offered and the average credit period taken by customers.

Risk appetite

Risk-averse companies will usually operate with higher levels of inventory and receivables than companies that are more prepared to take risks. A risk-averse company will also employ a conservative policy and use long-term finance for its permanent current assets and some fluctuating current assets, but a company more prepared to take risks will employ an aggressive policy and use short-term finance for fluctuating current assets as well as some permanent current assets.

(b) **Early settlement**

Annual cost of components = 120,000 × 7.50 = $900,000 per year

Value of discount offered = 900,000 × 0.005 = $4,500

Current level of payables = 900,000 × 90 / 365 = $221,918

Revised level of payables = 900,000 × 30 / 365 = $73,973

(Alternatively $221,918 × ⅓ = $73,973)

Reduction in payables = 221,918 – 73,973 = $147,945

(Alternatively 221,918 × ⅔ = $147,945, or 900,000 × 60 / 365 = $147,945)

Annual borrowing cost 4.5%

Increase in financing costs by taking discount = 147,945 × 0.045 = $6,657

The cost of the discount is greater than the discount offered by $6,657 – $4,500 = $2,157, therefore ZPS will not benefit financially from taking the discount.

Bulk purchase discount

Current number of orders = 120,000/10,000 = 12 orders

Current ordering cost = 12 × $200 = $2,400 per year

Current holding cost = (10,000/2) × $1 = $5,000 per year

Annual cost of components = 120,000 × $7.50 = $900,000 per year

Inventory cost of current policy = 900,000 + 2,400 + 5,000 = $907,400 per year

To obtain the bulk purchase discount orders must be 30,000 components

The number of orders will be 120,000/30,000 = 4 orders per year

The new ordering cost will be 4 × 200 = $800 per year

The revised holding cost will be (30,000/2) × 2.2 = $33,000 per year

The annual cost of the components will be 120,000 × 7.50 × 0.964 = $867,600 per year

Inventory cost using discount = 867,00 + 800 + 33,000 = $901,400 per year

The bulk discount saves $907,400 – $901,400 = $6,000 per year in inventory costs

30 KXP Co

Text references. Early settlement discounts, the effect of a change in credit policy, bulk discounts and the factors to be considered in managing trade receivables are all covered in Chapter 5.

Top tips. The calculations in parts (a) and (b) should pose no problems if you work through them logically.

Easy marks. Parts (a) and (b) contain straightforward calculations.

Examiner's comments. In part (a), weaker answers showed a lack of understanding of how the receivables days' ratio links credit sales for a period with the trade receivables balance at the end of the period. Some answers, for example, tried to calculate the revised trade receivables balance by applying changed receivables days ratios to current receivables, instead of applying them to credit sales. In part (b), perhaps because information on holding cost and order cost was provided in the question, many candidates calculated the economic order quantity (EOQ). The question made no reference to the EOQ and an EOQ calculation was not necessary.

Marking scheme

		Marks	
(a)	Revised trade receivables	0.5	
	Reduction in trade receivables	0.5	
	Reduction in financing cost	1	
	Cost of early settlement discount	1	
	Net cost of change in receivables policy	1	
	Comment on findings	1	
			5
(b)	Current annual ordering cost	0.5	
	Current holding cost	0.5	
	Total cost of current inventory policy	0.5	
	Revised cost of materials	0.5	
	Revised number of orders	0.5	
	Revised ordering cost	0.5	
	Revised holding cost	0.5	
	Net benefit of bulk purchase discount	0.5	
	Comment on assumptions	1	
			5
			10

(a) **Cost/benefit of changing trade receivables policy**

Receivables paying within 30 days = 50% × $15m × 30/365 = $616,438

Receivables paying after 45 days = 30% × $15m × 45/365 = $554,795

Total receivables changing their payment patterns = $616,438 + $554,795 = $1,171,233

Original value of these receivables = 80% × $2,466k = $1,972,800

Reduction in receivables = **$801,567**

Cost of early payment discount = 50% × $15m × 1% = $75,000

Reduction in financing cost = $801,567 × 6% = $48,094

Net cost of changing trade receivables policy = $75,000 – $48,094 = **$26,906**

Alternative calculation for the reduction in receivables

Current receivable days = $2,466k/ $15,000k × 365 = 60 days

Receivable days under new trade receivables policy = 50% × 30 + 30% × 45 + 20% × 60 = 40.5 days

Decrease in receivable days = 60 – 40.5 = 19.5 days

Reduction in receivables = $15m × 19.5/365 = **$801,370** (difference due to rounding)

Conclusion

The benefit of the new trade receivables policy is outweighed by the associated costs. KXP Co should not adopt the proposed policy. However, the analysis currently excludes bad debts and assumes constant sales throughout the year – the company may need to take these into account. Given that receivables on average are failing to meet the credit period, KXP Co may still want to consider how the trade receivables policy may be changed in order to encourage earlier payment.

(b) Total annual cost of inventory policy = cost of materials + ordering cost + holding cost

Current policy

Annual ordering cost = 12 × $150 = $1,800

Annual holding cost = $0.24 × (15,000/2) = $1,800

Total annual cost = $540,000 + $1,800 + $1,800 = $543,600

Proposed policy

Annual cost of materials = $540,000 × (1 – 2%) = $529,200

KXP Co currently requires 180,000 units of Product Z per year (12 × 15,000).

To benefit from the bulk discount, KXP Co needs to order 30,000 units each time. This means KXP Co will make 6 orders per year (180,000 / 30,000).

Revised annual ordering cost = 6 × $150 = $900

Revised annual holding cost = $0.24 × (30,000/2) = $3,600

Total annual cost = $529,200 + $900 + $3,600 = $533,700

Net benefit

Net benefit of taking bulk purchase discount = $543,600 – $533,700 = $9,900

Conclusion

The analysis shows that the bulk discount should be accepted. However, KXP Co may wish to evaluate the appropriateness of a number of key assumptions first:

- Demand for Product Z is constant throughout the year, and does not change from year to year
- Ordering costs and holding costs are both constant throughout the year

31 PXK Co

Marking scheme

			Marks
(a)	Transactions need for cash	1-2	
	Precautionary need for cash	1-2	
	Speculative need for cash	1-2	
	Other relevant discussion	1-2	
			5
(b)	Credit analysis	1-2	
	Credit control	1-2	
	Receivables collection	1-2	
	Cost and benefits of trade receivables policy	1-2	
		Maximum	5
			10

(a)   The optimum level of cash to be held by a company depends on the following factors:

The level of cash required for the company's operations

This includes holding enough cash to:

- Pay for the transactions expected to occur during the period (including the payment of suppliers, finance costs, etc). This can be achieved by drawing up a cash budget.

- Cover unexpected expenditure and account for uncertainty in the cash budget. In addition to the cash needs forecasted in the cash budget, the company needs to have a precautionary 'buffer' for unexpected events. This can be estimated based on previous experience.

The availability of finance

Not all sources of finance may be available to a company. A small and medium company, for example, may not be able to obtain or extend bank loans as easily. An unlisted company will find it very difficult, and expensive, to raise funds through issuing securities. Where it is difficult and/ or expensive to raise new finance, a company will need to hold more cash.

The availability and attractiveness of other uses for the cash

The amount of cash that a company holds will also depend on whether there are other, more attractive, ways to use the cash. Instead of holding cash for no return, a company usually has the option of putting the cash in a deposit account with a bank, investing it in short or long term debt instruments, or investing in equity shares of listed companies. The extent to which the company will consider these alternative uses depends on the amount of investment required, the expected level of return (interest, dividends or capital growth), the term to maturity, the ease of realising the investment.

A company may also wish to hold cash in order to be able take advantage of an unexpected speculative opportunity when it arises.

(b) Factors to consider in formulating a trade receivables management policy

The total credit

Each company must determine the level of total credit it is willing to offer. This involves finding a balance between maximising revenue from customers, and minimising the finance costs associated with funding the period of credit and also minimising bad debts.

Allowing a long period of credit may attract more sales, but the company may suffer from high finance costs. A short period of credit will reduce the need for additional finance, but the company may lose out on sales opportunities.

The cost of the additional finance – be it bank overdraft interest, loans or equity – must be considered.

Credit control

Companies need to have a policy in place for assessing the creditworthiness of customers. Verifying that new customers are creditworthy before concluding the sale reduces the risk of customer default.

This may involve requiring references for new customers, checking credit ratings through a credit rating agency, and offering a lower level of credit for new customers. A credit-rating system may be devised to determine the appropriate level of credit to offer to new customers based on their characteristics (age, occupation, etc).

Collection

A credit policy can only be maintained if it is policed effectively and the amounts owing collected. The company will need to monitor customers' payment records to ensure that the credit limits are maintained. An aged receivables analysis should be performed on a regular basis. Any breaches of credit limits should be brought to the attention of the credit controller.

Factors which would influence how tightly a company polices its credit policy includes on the number of customers requiring more credit, and the extent to which the company is exposed to accounts receivable.

The associated costs of collection – either internal or external – also needs to be considered. The costs of collection should not be greater than the amount collected.

Changes to the credit policy

The credit policy needs to be reviewed regularly and revised, as economic conditions and customer payment patterns change. The company may assess whether it is beneficial to offer an early payment discount to encourage customers to pay earlier, or extend the credit period to encourage custom.
The associated costs and impact on the company's working capital must be considered. Only when the financial benefit of the change in policy outweighs the additional costs should the change go ahead.

32 Gorwa (2) Co

Text references. Overtrading in Chapter 4.

Top tips. This question is a time pressured question and you will need to do the necessary calculations as quickly as possible, making sure you allow sufficient time to write enough explanations and discussion.

Easy marks. There are plenty of easy marks available for some straightforward ratio analysis and the calculation.

Examiner's comments. Better answers calculated a series of accounting ratios, perhaps adding some growth rates and changes in financial statement entries, and used this analysis to look at the increasing dependence of the company on short-term sources of finance while sales were expanding at a high rate. Weaker answers often did not explain how or why the identified changes supported the idea that the company was overtrading.

	Marks
Financial analysis	5-6
Discussion of overtrading	4-5
Conclusion as to overtrading	1
Maximum	10

Overtrading

Overtrading happens when a business tries to **do too much too quickly** with **too little long-term capital**, so that it is trying to support too large a volume of trade with the capital resources at its disposal.

Even if an overtrading business operates at a profit, it could easily run into serious trouble because it is **short of money**. Such liquidity troubles stem from the fact that it does not have enough capital to provide the cash to pay its debts as they fall due.

	20X7	*20X6*
Inventory days	4,600/34,408 × 365 = 49 days	2,400/23,781 × 365 = 37 days
Receivables days	4,600/37,400 × 365 = 45 days	2,200/26,720 × 365 = 30 days
Payables days	4,750/34,408 × 365 = 50 days	2,000/23,781 × 365 = 31 days
Current ratio	9,200/7,975 = 1.15 times	4,600/3,600 = 1.28 times
Quick ratio	4,600/7,975 = 0.58 times	2,200/3,600 = 0.61 times
Sales/net working capital	37,400/(9,200 – 7,975) = 30.53 times	26,720/(4,600 – 3,600) = 26.72 times

Increase in sales	(37,400 – 26,720)/ 26,720 × 100% = 40%
Increase in non-current assets	(13,632 – 12,750)/12,750 × 100% = 7%
Increase in inventory	(4,600 – 2,400)/2,400 × 100% = 92%
Increase in receivables	(4,600 – 2,200)/2,200 × 100% = 109%
Increase in payables	(4,750 – 2,000)/2,000 × 100% = 138%
Increase in overdraft	(3,225 – 1,600)/1,600 × 100% = 102%

Symptoms of overtrading are as follows.

A rapid increase in turnover

Gorwa Co has experienced a 40% increase in turnover from 20X6 to 20X7 and working capital has not increased in line. The sales/net working capital ratio has increased from 26.72 times to 30.53 times.

A rapid increase in the volume of current assets

Inventories have increased by 92% and receivables by 109%. **Inventory turnover** and **accounts receivable turnover** have slowed down so the rate of increase in inventories and accounts receivable has been even greater than the rate of increase in sales. Inventory may have been stockpiled in anticipation of a further increase in turnover. The increase in sales could have partly arisen due to a relaxation of credit terms for receivables.

Most of the increase in assets is financed by credit

The payment period for **accounts payable** has lengthened from 31 days to 50 and there has been an overall increase of 138% in payables. The **bank overdraft** has also increased by 102%.

Falling liquidity ratios

Both the **current ratio** and the **quick ratio** have deteriorated.

Conclusion

There is clear evidence that Gorwa Co is overtrading. It would be helpful to have **benchmark information** such as key ratios from similar companies and more information from **prior years** to see if there is definitely a trend.

33 MCQ bank – Investment decisions

33.1 C   Return on capital employed = Average annual accounting profits / Average investment

Average annual accounting profits = (16,500 + 23,500 + 13,500 – 1,500)/4 = $13,000 pa.

Note accounting profits are *after* depreciation so no adjustment is required.

Average investment = (initial + scrap)/2 = ($46,000 + $7,000)/ 2 = $26,500

ROCE = 13,000/26,500 = 49%

Syllabus area D1(d)

33.2 A   Payback period is the amount of time taken to repay initial investment:

Time		Profit	Depreciation*	Cash flow	Cumulative cash flow
0	Investment			(46,000)	(46,000)
1	Cash inflow	16,500	9,750	26,250	(19,750)
2	Cash inflow	23,500	9,750	33,250	13,500

* Depreciation = (46,000 – 7000) / 4

Payback period = 1 + (19,750/33,250) = 1.59 years or 1 year 7 months to the nearest month.

Syllabus area D1(b)

33.3 B   1 is correct as a 'cut off' point is not reached unlike payback period.

2 is incorrect. ROCE is profit based.

3 is correct, and may well help explain ROCE's use in the real world.

Syllabus area D1(d)

33.4 B   The $1,000 is sunk. If the chemical is used in a new project it would save SW Co $400 that it would otherwise have to spend to dispose of the chemicals. This equates to an effective net cash inflow (or, more precisely, the avoidance of an outflow) of $400. Thus the project appraisal should show an inflow of $400 in relation to using this chemical.

Syllabus area D1(a)

33.5 C   We assume BLW would choose the cheapest source of labour.

Cost to buy in = $20 × 1,000 hours = $20,000

Cost to divert existing labour = lost contribution + labour cost ie ($10 + $15) × 1,000 hours = $25,000

The cheapest alternative is therefore to buy in at a cost of $20,000.

The labour cost is added back to the lost contribution as it would be paid anyway, hence to calculate how the existing BLW project suffers as a result of diverting labour, it is added back to the lost contribution to give the full impact of diverting labour away from its current role.

Syllabus area D1(a)

33.6 A   The current rental cost is $5,000. The net new rental cost should the project proceed would be ($17,000 + $5,000 – $3,000) = $19,000, so an increment of $19,000 – $5,000 = $14,000.

Syllabus area D1(a)

33.7 C   Option A is a benefit not a drawback. Option B is incorrect. Payback period does not take account of the time value of money. D is incorrect. The calculation is not based on profit. On the assumption that the basic reason for approving a project is that it will increase shareholder wealth, a major drawback of payback period is that it does not attempt to measure the impact on shareholder wealth should the project go ahead.

Syllabus area D1(b)

33.8   **A**   Project screening should be undertaken before stage 2 to sift out unsuitable ideas before further time and money is spent investigating further. Raising finance is impractical before knowing what the funding requirement is. Implementation can only occur once a suitable project has been selected.

Syllabus area D1(a)

33.9   **D**   A payback of 20 years suggests net annual inflow of 50,000/20 = $2,500 per annum.

Return on capital employed (ROCE) = Average annual accounting profit / Average investment.

Average annual accounting profit = $2,500 cash inflows less depreciation.

Depreciation = 50,000/40 = $1,250 p.a.

So average annual accounting profit = $2,500 – $1,250 = $1,250.

Average investment = (50,000 + 0)/2 = $25,000

Therefore ROCE = $1,250/$25,000 = 0.05 or 5% per annum

Syllabus area D1(d)

33.10 **B**   Even if the accountant's salary was not sunk (eg if they were PLANNING to work on the project next month) the cost should still not feature in the project appraisal as the accountant is paid anyway ie his salary is not incremental.

Syllabus area D1(a)

34 MCQ bank – Investment appraisal using DCF

34.1   **D**   The present value of the annuity = $7,000 \times AF_{3\text{-}7}$

where $AF_{3\text{-}7}$ is the 10% Annuity factor from years 3-7 inclusive.

$AF_{3\text{-}7}$ = $AF_{1\text{-}7}$ - $AF_{1\text{-}2}$

            = 4.868 – 1.736 (from tables)

            = 3.132

Therefore the present value = $7,000 \times 3.132 = $21,924

Syllabus area D1(e)

34.2   **C**   The present value of the perpetuity = $90,000 \times AF_{3\text{-}\infty}$

Where $AF_{3\text{-}\infty}$ = the perpetuity factor from year 3 onwards.

$AF_{3\text{-}\infty}$ = $AF_{1\text{-}\infty}$ - $AF_{1\text{-}2}$ = (1/0.1) – 1.736   (from tables)

          = 8.264

So the present value of the perpetuity = $90,000 \times 8.264 = $743,760

The present value of the lump sum = $910,000 \times DF_1$

Where DF_1 is the 1 year 10% discount factor from tables = 0.909

So present value of lump sum = $910,000 \times 0.909 = $827,180

The lump sum should be chosen because it has a higher net present value.

Syllabus area D1(e)

34.3 C   Remember that a cash outlay or receipt which occurs at the beginning of a time period is taken to occur at the end of the previous year. Therefore an inflow of $12,000 in advance for 5 years (ie starting now) is taken to occur in years 0, 1, 2, 3 and 4.

NPV at 10%:

Time		$	DF 10%	PV $
0	Investment	(40,000)	1	(40,000)
0-4	Net cash inflows	12,000	1+3.17 = 4.17	50,040
5	Decommissioning	(15,000)	0.621	(9,315)
	Net present value			725

= $700 to the nearest $100

Syllabus area D1(e)

34.4 A

$$IRR = a + \left[\frac{NPV_a}{NPV_a - NPV_b} \times (b-a) \right]\%$$

where   a = lower % discount rate

b = higher % discount rate

NPV_A = NPV at a%

NPV_B = NPV at b%

NPV at 10% = $725 (see question above)

NPV at 15%:

Time		$	DF 15%	PV $
0	Investment	(40,000)	1	(40,000)
0-4	Net cash inflows	12,000	1+2.855 =3.855	46,260
5	Decommissioning	(15,000)	0.497	(7,455)
	Net present value			(1,195)

Therefore IRR = 10%+ [(725/(725+1195)) × (15% – 10%)] = 11.9% (12% to the nearest whole %)

Syllabus area D1(f)

34.5 D   The project with the highest NPV will maximise shareholder wealth as NPV directly measures the impact on shareholder wealth.

Syllabus area D1(g)

34.6 C   Statement 1 is not an advantage. The decision rule depends on the shape of the IRR curve. There could be several IRRs and whether the IRR needs to be higher or lower than the cost of capital depends on the project cash flows.

Statement 2 is an advantage. IRR is a discounting technique hence takes into account the time value of money.

Statement 3 is a disadvantage. The 'reinvestment assumption' is a flaw in IRR. There is no reason to suppose that funds generated early on in a project will be reinvested at the IRR after that point. The funds may well be distributed elsewhere.

Statement 4 is an advantage: unlike payback period, the IRR considers *all* of the future incremental cash flows associated with a decision in its calculation.

Syllabus area D1(g)

34.7 C   A higher cost of capital will discount future inflows more heavily, reducing the NPV of the project. The cost of capital does not feature in the calculation of the IRR, only in the decision rule that follows the calculation.

Syllabus area D1(e)(f)

34.8 B The net present value of the annuity is 26,496, hence:

26,496	$= (\$a \times AF_{1\text{-}4}) + 10,000$	Where $AF_{1\text{-}4}$ is the 4 year 8% annuity factor
16,496	$= \$a \times 3.312$	(from tables)
$a	$= 16,496/3.312$	
	$= \$4,981$	

Syllabus area D1(e)

34.9 A The IRR formula requires two NPV calculations at different rates to estimate the IRR.

B is inaccurate. Linear interpolation is still an estimate. It is not 100% precise.

C is inaccurate. There may be more than one IRR. It depends on whether the cash flows are conventional or not.

D is not necessarily true. For example, an unusual project with an initial large inflow followed by years of outflows will have a positive slope.

Syllabus area D1(h)

34.10 A The present value of the holiday home = $1.5m × (DF_5 10\%)$ = $1.5m × 0.621 = $931,500

Therefore the present value of the annuity = $931,500.

$931,500 = \$a \times AF_{0\text{-}4}$

Where $AF_{0\text{-}4}$ is the annuity factor from time 0 to time 4

$AF_{0\text{-}4} = 1 + AF_{1\text{-}4}$	$= 1 + 3.170 = 4.170$	
So 931,500	$= \$a \times 4.170$	
$a	$= 931,500/4.170$	
	$= 223,381$ or $223,400 to the nearest $100	

Syllabus area D1(e)

35 MCQ bank – Allowing for tax and inflation

35.1 C The asset is purchased on 31 December 20X4 (T0) so the first portion of tax allowable depreciation is accounted for on that date (as this is the end of the year). The amount of the depreciation would be $1m × 25\% = $250,000.

Claiming this allowance will save ($250,000 × 30\%=) $75,000 tax when it is paid at T_1 (one year delay) hence the present value = $75,000 × DF_1$ = $75,000 × 0.909 = $68,175

Syllabus area D2(b)

35.2 B As tax is paid one year in arrears, the $20,000 and associated tax are treated separately:

PV of perpetuity: $20,000 × 1/0.1	$=$	$200,000
Less PV of tax: ($20,000 × 30\%) × (AF_{2\text{-}\infty})$		
$AF_{2\text{-}\infty} = (1/0.1) - DF_1 = 10 - 0.909 = 9.091$		
PV of tax = $20,000 × 30\% × 9.091	$=$	$(54,546)
After tax	$=$	$145,454

Syllabus area D2(b)

35.3 C

$	Working capital required (10% × sales)	Increments = cash flow	Discount factor 10%	Present value
T0	10,000	(10,000)	1	(10,000.00)
T1	12,500	(2,500)	0.909	(2,272.50)
T2	10,500	2,000	0.826	1,652.00
T3	0	10,500	0.751	7,885.50
				(2,735.00)

Syllabus area D1(e)

35.4 A The working capital required will inflate year on year, then the inflated amount will be 'returned' at the end of the project:

$	Working capital required (with 10% inflation)	Increments = cash flow	Discount factor 12%	Present value
T0	100,000	(100,000)	1	(100,000)
T1	110,000	(10,000)	0.873	(8,730)
T2	0	110000	0.797	87,670
				(21,060)

Syllabus area D2(a)

35.5 C As not all cash flows will inflate at the same rate, cash flows will be inflated where necessary and discounted using the money rate.

(1 + money rate) = (1.08) × (1.02) = 1.1016 so m = 10% to the nearest whole %

Nominal income = $100,000 × (1 + income inflation) = $100,000 × 1.1 = $110,000

Nominal expenses = $35,000 (zero inflation)

Therefore NPV = [(110,000 − 35,000) × DF_1] − 10,000   where DF_1 = the 1 year 10% discount factor (tables)

= (75,000 × 0.909) − 10,000 = $58,175

Syllabus area D2(a)

35.6 C In order to use the perpetuity factor (1/r) the annual amount must be constant, so the calculation needs to be done in real terms.

The money cost of capital is given in the question, so the real rate needs to be calculated using:

(1 + r) × (1 + h) = (1 + i)   where r=real rate, h = inflation, i = money rate, so

(1 + r) × (1.02) = (1.102)

(1 + r) = 1.102 / 1.02 = 1.08 or 8%.

The perpetuity factor from $T_{2-\infty}$ = (1/r) − DF_1 = (1/0.08) − 0.926 = 11.574

Therefore the present value = 10,000 × 11.574 = $115,740

Syllabus area D2(a)

35.7 A Increased expectation of inflation will have two effects.

1   Higher expected nominal cash flow
2   Higher nominal discount rate

These will cancel each other out exactly.

Syllabus area D2(a)

35.8 B $(1 + r) \times (1 + h) = (1 + i)$ where r=real rate, h=inflation, i=money rate, so

$(1 + r) \times (1.04) = (1.10)$

$(1 + r) = 1.10/1.04 = 1.058$ or 5.8%.

Syllabus area D2(a)

35.9 D   The value of the tax allowable depreciation is $150,000 \times 100\% \times 30\% = \$45,000$ receivable immediately so the net initial outlay = $150,000 - 45,000 = \$105,000$

The future value of 105,000 in 2 years time (note....'receivable in 2 years....')

$= 105,000 \times 1.1^2 = \$127,050$.

The revenue is taxable, so the pre tax contract revenue needs to be $127,050/(1 - 0.3) = \$181,500$

Syllabus area D2(b)

35.10 D   The inflation included in the money cost of capital is required by the investors to compensate them for the loss of general purchasing power their money will suffer in the future as a result of investing in the business.

Syllabus area D2(a)

36 MCQ bank – Project appraisal and risk

36.1 C   Statement 1 is false. As an average the expected value probably won't actually occur in any single event so it does not represent a probable outcome. It is more appropriate for repeated events (for example expected sales each year for many years). By the same logic statement 3 is true.

Statement 2 is true. Expected values fail to show the spread of possible values, therefore hiding the best/worst outcomes from the decision making process.

Statement 4 is false. Risk is calculable (known or estimated probabilities and/or outcomes), uncertainty is not (either probabilities or some outcomes are unknown).

Syllabus area D3(c)

36.2 B   Expected sales = $(20,000 \times 0.6) + (25,000 \times 0.4) = 22,000$ units

Expected sales price = $(\$10 \times 0.3) + (\$15 \times 0.7) = \$13.50$

So expected revenue = 22,000 units $\times \$13.50 = \$297,000$

Expected margin = $(30\% \times 0.5) + (40\% \times 0.5) = 35\%$ therefore costs will be $1 - 35\% = 65\%$

So expected cost = $65\% \times \$297,000 = \$193,050$

Syllabus area D3(c)

36.3 B   Adjusted payback period is payback period based on discounted cash flows:

Time	Cash flow ($)	DF 8%	Discounted cash flow ($)	Cumulative discounted cash flow
0	(100,000)		(100,000)	(100,000)
1	40,000	0.926	37,040	(62,960)
2	40,000	0.857	34,280	(28,680)
3	40,000	0.794	31,760	3,080

Syllabus area D3(d)

36.4 **A**   To force an NPV = 0, the 4 year annuity factor, AF_{1-4} = 110,000/40,000 = 2.75

Proof: the NPV calculation would be (2.75 × 40,000) – 110,000 = 0

From tables, the 4-year annuity factor closest to 2.75 is 17%.

In terms of sensitivity: (17 – 10)/10 = 70% sensitivity

Note: alternatively IRR could be estimated to find the 17% instead of tables.

NPV when cost of capital is 18% = -110,000 + (40,000 × 2.69) = (2,400)

$$IRR = 0.1 + \frac{16,800}{16,800 + 2,400} \times (0.18 - 0.1) = 17\%$$

The cost of capital can therefore increase by $\frac{17-10}{10}$ = 70% before the NPV becomes negative.

Syllabus area D3(b)

36.5 **B**   A is incorrect. There is no decision rule with simulations – it is not an 'optimising' technique

B is a clear advantage that simulations have over sensitivity analysis

C is incorrect. The input variables and distributions are estimates

D has some validity potentially, but is not necessarily the case.

Syllabus area D3(d)

37 MCQ bank – Specific investment decisions

37.1 **C**   Net present cost of 1 year cycle = 20,000 – (10,000 × 0.909) = $10,910 cost

Net present cost of 2 year cycle = 20,000 – [(8,000 – 5,000) × 0.826] = $17,522 cost

EAC 1 year cycle = $10,910 / 0.909 = 12,002

EAC 2 year cycle = $17,522 / 1.736 = 10,093

The 2-year cycle should be chosen with an equivalent annual cost of $10,093

Syllabus area D4(b)

37.2 **A**   Statement 1 is incorrect: Lessee's acquire the risk and responsibility of ownership with finance leases.

Statement 2 is correct: Finance leases are accounted for as an asset and a payable – on the statement of financial position.

Statement 3 is incorrect: Finance leases have a primary period covering all or most of the useful economic life of the asset.

Syllabus area D4(a)

37.3 **C**   Interest should not be included as a cash flow as it is part of the discount rate.

As a financing decision the alternatives should be assessed at the after tax cost of borrowing – the risk associated with each is the risk of borrowing (or not), and not related to what is done with the asset.

Syllabus area D4(a)

37.4 **D**   A constraint being termed 'soft' means it is internally imposed. It may or may not be flexible so is not always true.

Whether a project may be considered divisible or not depends on the project – for example investing in a machine is unlikely to be divisible (half a machine will not generate half the return), however buying a chain of shops could be divisible; it might be possible to buy half the chain for half the cost and expect half the net present value.

Syllabus area D4(c)

37.5 B

Project	Initial cost ($m)	NPV ($m)	Profitability index*	Ranking
1	40	4	1.10	3
2	30	5	1.167	1
3	50	6	1.12	2
4	60	5	1.08	4

*(npv + initial cost) / initial cost

Investment plan:

Project	Investment ($m)	NPV ($m)
100% of project 2	30	5
100% of project 3	50	6
50% of project 1	20	2
	100	13

Syllabus area D4c

37.6 A Projects 2 and 3 give the highest NPV without breaking the $100 million constraint.

Syllabus area D4c

37.7 A 'A' is potentially a benefit. Tax exhaustion is when a business has negative taxable income so it cannot benefit from tax relief such as capital allowances. In this case, it may be beneficial to lease the asset from a business than *can* benefit from the tax allowable depreciation and share in that benefit via lower lease payments.

B is a potential benefit to a lessor, not a lessee.

C is a potential benefit for the purchaser, not the lessee.

D is a potential benefit for the purchaser, not the lessee as the lessee is not entitled to scrap proceeds.

Syllabus area D4a

37.8 C The NPVs cannot be directly compared as they relate to different time periods. Equivalent annual benefits (EAB) should be compared. This is similar in principle to equivalent annual cost.

EAB Gas = $50,000 / AF_{1-5} = 50,000 / 3.993 = $12,522 pa

EAB Electric = $68,000 / AF_{1-7} = 68,000 / 5.206 = $13,062 pa

Therefore electric should be chosen as its equivalent annual benefit is higher.

Syllabus area D4b

37.9 A Statement 1 is a benefit. Scrapped assets will be newer hence worth more.

Statement 2 is a benefit. Newer assets look better, motivate employees and are more efficient.

Statement 3 is not true hence not a benefit. Typically depreciation is higher in earlier years, meaning annual depreciation charges will be higher with a shorter replacement cycle.

Statement 4 is inaccurate hence not a benefit. Although owned for a shorter period, the asset will be replaced so ownership of that type of asset will be indefinite.

Syllabus area D4b

37.10 D Leasing may be possible. A joint venture partner may provide additional funding. Although delaying projects will probably reduce their NPV (time value of money, and competitor response), this may be better than not investing at all.

Syllabus area D4a

38 Calvic Co

Marking scheme

		Marks
(a)	Servicing costs	1
	Cleaning costs	1
	Present values of total costs	1
	Present values of trade-in values	1
	Net present values of costs of each cycle	3
	Annuity factors	1
	Equivalent annual costs	1
	Recommendation	1
		10
(b)	Causes of capital rationing	5
		15

(a)

Replace every year

Year	0	1
Initial cost	(15,000)	
Trade-in value		11,250
Service cost		(1,000)
Cleaning cost		(500)
Net cost	(15,000)	9,750
Discount factor @ 10%	1	0.909
Present value	(15,000)	8,863
NPV	(6,137)	
Annuity factor	0.909	
Equivalent annual cost	**(6,751) pa**	

Replace every 2 years

Year	0	1	2
Initial cost	(15,000)		
Trade-in value			9,000
Service cost		(1,000)	(1,400)
Cleaning		(500)	(625)
Net cost	(15,000)	(1,500)	6,975
Discount factor 10%	1	0.909	0.826
Present value	(15,000)	(1,364)	5,761
NPV	(10,603)		
Annuity factor	1.735 for 2 years		
Equivalent annual cost	**(6,111) pa**		

Replace every 3 years

Year	0	1	2	3
Initial cost	(15,000)			
Trade-in value				6,200
Service cost		(1,000)	(1,400)	(1,960)
Cleaning cost		(500)	(625)	(781)
Net cost	(15,000)	(1,500)	(2,025)	3,459
Discount factor @ 10%	1	0.909	0.826	0.751
Present value	(15,000)	(1,364)	(1,673)	2,598
NPV	(15,439)			
Annuity factor	2.487 for 3 years			
Equivalent annual cost	**(6,208) pa**			

As the lowest cost option, the decision should be made to replace every two years.

(b) In order to invest in all projects with a positive net present value a company must be able to raise funds as and when it needs them: this is only possible in a **perfect capital market**. In practice capital markets are not perfect and the capital available for investment is likely to be **limited** or **rationed**. The causes of capital rationing may be external (hard capital rationing) or internal (soft capital rationing).

Soft capital rationing is more common than hard capital rationing. When a company cannot raise external finance even though it wishes to do so, this may be because providers of debt finance see the company as being **too risky**. In terms of **financial risk**, the company's gearing may be seen as too high, or its interest cover may be seen as too low. From a **business risk** point of view, lenders may be uncertain whether a company's future profits will be sufficient to meet increased future interest payments because its trading prospects are poor, or because they are seen as too variable.

When managers **impose restrictions** on the funds they are prepared to make available for capital investment, soft capital rationing is said to occur. One reason for soft capital rationing is that managers may not want to raise new external finance.

For example, they may not wish to raise new debt finance because they believe it would be unwise to commit the company to meeting future interest payments given the current economic outlook. They may not wish to issue new equity because the finance needed is insufficient to justify the **transaction costs** of a new issue, or because they wish to avoid **dilution of control**.

Another reason for soft capital rationing is that managers may prefer **slower organic growth**, where they can remain in control of the growth process, to the sudden growth arising from taking on one or more large investment projects.

A key reason for soft capital rationing is the desire by managers to make capital investments **compete** for funds, ie to create an internal market for investment funds. This competition for funds is likely to weed out weaker or marginal projects, thereby channelling funds to more robust investment projects with better chances of success and larger margins of safety, and reducing the risk and uncertainty associated with capital investment.

39 Trecor Co

Text references. Investment appraisal is covered in Chapters 7, 8 and 9.

Top tips. Set out your workings clearly to gain the maximum number of marks for your workings. Do as much of the NPV calculation as you possibly can, as marks are awarded for each stage. Make an assumption and carry on if you get stuck on any part. Nominal cash flows are used so the nominal discount rate must be calculated and used.

Easy marks. The easy marks include the inflation of the sales revenue, variable costs and fixed production overheads.

	Marks
Discount rate	1
Inflated sales revenue	2
Inflated variable cost	2
Inflated fixed production overheads	2
Taxation	2
Tax allowable depreciation tax benefits	3
Discount factors	1
Net present value	1
Comment	1
	15

Calculation of NPV

Nominal discount rate:

$(1 + i) = (1 + r)(1 + h) = 1.057 \times 1.05 = 1.10985$

i = 11%

	1	*2*	*3*	*4*	*5*
	$'000	$'000	$'000	$'000	$'000
Sales (W1)	433	509	656	338	
Variable cost (W2)	284	338	439	228	
Contribution	149	171	217	110	
Fixed production overheads	27	28	30	32	
Net cash flow	122	143	187	78	
Tax		(37)	(43)	(56)	(23)
TAD tax benefits (W3)		19	14	11	30
After-tax cash flow	122	125	158	33	7
Disposal				5	
After-tax cash flow	122	125	158	38	7
Discount factors (11%)	0.901	0.812	0.731	0.659	0.593
Present values	110	102	115	25	4

	$
PV of benefits	356,000
Investment	250,000
NPV	106,000

The NPV is positive and so the purchase is worthwhile.

Workings

(1)

Year	*1*	*2*	*3*	*4*
Demand (units)	35,000	40,000	50,000	25,000
Selling price ($/unit)	12.36	12.73	13.11	13.51
Sales ($/year)	432,600	509,200	655,500	337,750

(2)

Year	*1*	*2*	*3*	*4*
Demand (units)	35,000	40,000	50,000	25,000
Variable cost ($/unit)	8.11	8.44	8.77	9.12
Sales ($/year)	283,850	337,600	438,500	228,000

(3)

	Tax allowable depreciation		Tax benefits	
		$		$
1	250,000 × 0.25 =	62,500	62,500 × 0.3 =	18,750
2	62,500 × 0.75 =	46,875	46,875 × 0.3 =	14,063
3	46,875 × 0.75 =	35,156	25,156 × 0.3 =	10,547
4	By difference	100,469	100,469 × 0.3 =	30,141
	250,000 − 5,000 =	245,000		73,501

40 Corter Co

Marking scheme

			Marks
(a)	Calculation of average annual accounting profit	2	
	Calculation of average investment	2	
	Calculation of return on capital employed	1	
			5
(b)	Strengths of IRR	2-3	
	Weaknesses of IRR	2-3	
	Maximum		5
			10

(a) **Calculation of before-tax return on capital employed (ROCE)**

Cash flow before tax = 122 + 143 + 187 + 78 = $530,000

Total depreciation = (250,000 − 5,000) = $245,000

Average annual accounting profit = (530 − 245)/4 = $71,250

Average investment = (250,000 + 5,000)/2 = $127,500

ROCE = 71,250/127,500 × 100 = 56%

The target ROCE is 20% and the expected ROCE is significantly higher than this so the purchase of the machine can be recommended.

(b) **Strengths of IRR**

The main advantage of the IRR method is that the information it provides is **more easily understood** by managers than NPV, especially non-financial managers. It gives a **relative measure** of the value of a proposed investment in the form of a percentage which can be compared with the company's cost of capital or the rates of interest and inflation.

IRR is a **discounted cash flow method** and so takes account of the **time value** of money: the concept that $1 received today is not equal to $1 received in the future.

IRR considers cash flows over the **whole** of the project life and is sensitive to both the amount and the **timing** of cash flows.

Weaknesses of IRR

IRR ignores the **relative sizes** of investments. It therefore does not measure the absolute increase in company value, and therefore shareholder wealth, which will be created by an investment.

Where cash flow patterns are **non-conventional**, for example cash flows change from positive to negative during the life of the project, there may be **several IRRs** which decision makers must be aware of to avoid making the wrong decision. When **discount rates** are **expected to differ** over the life of the project, such **variations** can be incorporated easily into **NPV** calculations, but not into IRR calculations.

Mutually exclusive projects are two or more projects from which only one can be chosen. Examples include the choice of a factory location or the choice of just one of a number of machines. The IRR and NPV methods can, however, give **conflicting rankings** as to which project should be given priority. Where there is a conflict, NPV always offers the **technically correct investment advice.**

Despite the advantages of the NPV method over the IRR method, the **IRR method** is **widely used** in practice.

41 OKM Co

Text references. Net present value is covered in Chapters 8 and 9, investment appraisal issues are covered in Chapters 8 and 10.

Top tips. Part (a) is a different approach to NPV. One way to approach this question is to perform part (b) first and then check the differences between the calculations

Part (b) is a fairly straightforward NPV calculation. Do not be put off by the large positive value calculated.

Easy marks. Part (b) is fairly straightforward.

Examiner's comments. For part (a) candidates who did not gain full marks failed to identify clearly the errors they had identified, or did not comment on these errors, or identified errors that did not exist.

For part (b) candidates who did not amend the contribution figures provided were not aware that inflation must be applied every year and not just in the first year. The development costs had to be excluded from the fixed costs in the investment appraisal because they had already been incurred, i.e. they were not relevant costs. Depreciation had to be stripped out because it is not a cash flow, and NPV is an investment appraisal method that uses cash flows. Interest payments had to be excluded because they would be taken account of by the discount rate.

Marking scheme

			Marks
(a)	Identification of errors in the evaluation		5
(b)	Nominal weighted average cost of capital	1	
	Inflated selling prices	1	
	Inflated variable costs	1	
	Inflated contribution	1	
	Inflated fixed costs	1	
	Tax allowable depn and/or related tax benefits	1	
	Scrap value	1	
	Discount factors	1	
	Net present value	1	
	Comment	1-2	
	Maximum		10
			15

(a) The depreciation charge used is straight line depreciation, but this is not a relevant cost to the project and should be excluded, tax allowable depreciation tax benefits using the 25% reducing balance method should be included.

Inflation has not been applied correctly to either selling price or variable costs as only one year of inflation has been included in each year eg in year 2

$(12 \times 1.05) - (7 \times 1.04) \times 400,000 = \$2,128,000$ is what has been done

But there should be two years of inflation

$(12 \times 1.05^2) - (7 \times 1.04^2) \times 400,000 = \$2,263,520$

The \$200,000 fixed cost development charge is not a relevant cost for the project and should be excluded. Fixed costs have been inflated at 6% per annum including this charge.

Interest payments are already taken into account by the discount rate and so do not need to be included.

The discount rate used is the interest rate on the \$2million loan, but the nominal weighted average cost of capital should be used. The nominal rate should be used as inflation has been factored into the cash flows.

(b) The nominal weighted average cost of capital is the real WACC multiplied by the inflation rate

$1.07 \times 1.047 = 1.120$ Therefore use 12%

	Year 0 $'000	Year 1 $'000	Year 2 $'000	Year 3 $'000	Year 4 $'000	Year 5 $'000
Contribution (W1)		1,330	2,264	3,010	1,600	
Fixed costs (W3)		(318)	(337)	(357)	(379)	
Taxable cash flow		1,012	1,927	2,653	1,221	
Taxation			(304)	(578)	(796)	(366)
Capital expenditure	(2,000)					
Scrap value					250	
Tax benefit of tax depn (W2)			150	112	84	178
	(2,000)	1,012	1,773	2,187	759	(188)
Discount factors @ 12%	1	0.893	0.797	0.712	0.635	0.567
Present value	(2,000)	904	1,413	1,557	482	(107)

Net present value = (2,000) + 904 + 1,413 +1,557 + 482 – 107 = 2,249

The net present value is positive and the investment should be accepted.

Workings

(1) *Contribution*

	Year 1	Year 2	Year 3	Year 4
Selling price ($12 × 1.05^t)	12.60	13.23	13.89	14.59
Variable cost ($7 × 1.04^t)	(7.28)	(7.57)	(7.87)	(8.19)
Contribution per unit	5.32	5.66	6.02	6.40
Sales volume	250,000	400,000	500,000	250,000
Total contribution	1,330,000	2,264,000	3,010,000	1,600,000

(2) *Tax allowable depreciation tax benefits*

Year		Tax allowable depn ($)	Tax benefit ($)
1	2,000,000 × 25%	500,000	150,000
2	500,000 × 75%	375,000	112,500
3	375,000 × 75%	281,250	84,375
4	Balancing charge	593,750	178,125
Scrap value		250,000	
		2,000,000	

Tax benefits like tax charge affects following period due to timings.

(3)   *Fixed costs*

Fixed costs $300,000 per year inflating at 6%

Year		Fixed costs ($'000)
1	300×1.06	318
2	300×1.06^2	337
3	300×1.06^3	357
4	300×1.06^4	379

42 CJ Co

Text references. Investment appraisal is covered in Chapters 7, 8 and 9.

Top tips. This is a good example of an investment appraisal question which also includes the concept of project-specific cost of capital. You need to be very careful with the inflating of the cash flows. Ensure that the right inflation rate is used with the appropriate price or cost. Remember that the current price levels will need to be inflated for the first year cash flows. Do not use the Fisher equation to calculate a discount rate as you are already given the nominal discount rate.

Easy marks. There are easy marks available in the calculations.

Examiner's comments. Most candidates gained good marks.

The treatment of working capital was a problem for some candidates. Working capital recovery was excluded by the directors' views on investment appraisal. Even though working capital investment was specified in the question as an initial investment, some candidates inflated the initial investment and placed it at the end of year one.

Marking scheme

		Marks
Sales revenue	1	
Selling costs	1	
Variable costs	1	
Tax allowable depreciation, years 1 to 3	1	
Tax allowable depreciation/balancing allowance, year 4	1	
Tax liabilities and timing of tax	1	
Incremental working capital	1	
Discount factors	1	
NPV calculation	1	
Decision as to financial acceptability	1	
		10

Calculation of NPV

Year	0	1	2	3	4	5
	$'000	$'000	$'000	$'000	$'000	$'000
Investment	(3,500)					
Sales revenue (W1)		1,575	1,654	1,736	1,823	
Selling costs (W2)		(32)	(33)	(35)	(37)	
Variable costs (W3)		(624)	(649)	(675)	(702)	
Before-tax cash flows		919	972	1,026	1,084	
Taxation at 30%			(276)	(292)	(308)	(325)
Tax benefits (W4)			263	197	148	443
Working capital (W5)	(250)	(11)	(12)	(12)	(13)	
Project cash flows	(3,750)	908	947	919	911	118
Discount factor 10%	1.000	0.909	0.826	0.751	0.683	0.621
Present value	(3,750)	825	782	690	622	73
NPV	**(758)**					

The net present value is negative and therefore Project A is not financially acceptable.

Workings

(1)   Calculation of sales revenue (inflates at 5% per year from $2.00)

Year	1	2	3	4
Inflated selling price ($/unit)	2.100	2.205	2.315	2.431
Demand (units/year)	750,000	750,000	750,000	750,000
Income ($/year)	1,575,000	1,653,750	1,736,250	1,823,250

(2)   Calculation of selling costs (inflates at 5% per year from $0.04)

Year	1	2	3	4
Inflated selling cost ($/unit)	0.042	0.044	0.046	0.049
Demand (units/year)	750,000	750,000	750,000	750,000
Selling costs ($/year)	31,500	33,000	34,500	36,750

(3)   Calculation of operating costs (inflates at 4% per year from $0.80)

Year	1	2	3	4
Inflated variable cost ($/unit)	0.832	0.865	0.900	0.936
Demand (units/year)	750,000	750,000	750,000	750,000
Variable costs ($/year)	624,000	648,750	675,000	702,000

(4)   Calculation of tax benefits

Year	Tax allowable depn $		30% Tax benefit $	Year taken
1	875,000	(3.5m × 0.25)	262,500	2
2	656,250	(875,000 × 0.75)	196,875	3
3	492,188	(656,250 × 0.75)	147,656	4
4	*1,476,562	(3.5m – 875,000 – 656,250 – 492,188)	442,969	5

* This includes the year 4 balancing allowance

(5)   Calculation of working capital requirements (Increases at 4.5% per year)

Year	Working capital $	Incremental investment $
0	250,000	
1	261,250	11,250
2	273,006	11,756
3	285,292	12,286
4	298,130	12,838

43 BRT Co

Text references. Net present value is covered in Chapters 8 and 9.

Top tips. It is a fairly straightforward NPV calculation, although with an artificial cut-off point.

Easy marks. You can pick up easy marks by correctly inflating the selling price and variable costs and calculating the tax.

Examiner's comments. Some candidates said that, because the same rate of inflation was applied to selling price, variable cost and fixed cost, inflation could be ignored and their answers used a real terms approach. This ignores the stated requirement to use a nominal terms approach and is also not correct in this case. Although the question required that the candidate advise on the financial acceptability of the proposed investment, some answers did not do this, or made a casual comment that did not gain full marks.

	Marks
Inflated selling price per box	1
Sales	1
Inflated variable cost per box	1
Variable cost	1
Inflated fixed costs	1
Tax payable	1
Tax allowable depreciation tax benefits	1
Balancing allowance	1
Timing of tax payments or benefits	1
Initial working capital investment	1
Incremental working capital investment	1
Working capital recovery	1
Discount factors	1
Net present value	1
Comment on acceptability	1
	15

	0	1	2	3	4	5
	$'000	$'000	$'000	$'000	$'000	$'000
Sales (W1)		3,605	8,488	11,474	16,884	
Variable cost (W2)		(2,019)	(5,093)	(6,884)	(10,299)	
Fixed costs (W3)		(1,030)	(1,910)	(3,060)	(4,277)	
Net cash flow		556	1,485	1,530	2,308	
Tax @ 30%			(167)	(446)	(459)	(692)
TAD tax benefits (W4)			150	113	84	253
Investment	(2,000)					
Working capital (W5)	(750)	(23)	(23)	(24)	820	
After-tax cash flow	(2,750)	533	1,445	1,173	2,753	(439)
Discount factors	1.000	0.893	0.797	0.712	0.636	0.567
Present values	(2,750)	476	1,152	835	1,751	(249)

Net present value = $1,215,000

Since the NPV is positive the proposed investment is financially acceptable.

Workings

(1)

Year	1	2	3	4
Demand (units)	700,000	1,600,000	2,100,000	3,000,000
Selling price ($/unit)				
(Inflated from $5 at 3% pa)	5.15	5.305	5.464	5.628
Sales ($000/year)	3,605	8,488	11,474	16,884

(2)

Year	1	2	3	4
Demand (units)	700,000	1,600,000	2,100,000	3,000,000
Variable cost ($/unit)	2.800	3.000	3.000	3.050
Inflated variable cost ($/unit)				
(Inflated at 3% pa)	2.884	3.183	3.278	3.433
Variable cost ($000/year)	2,019	5,093	6,884	10,299

(3)

Year	1	2	3	4
Fixed cost ($000)	1,000	1,800	2,800	3,800
Inflated fixed cost ($000)	1,030	1,910	3,060	4,277
(Inflated at 3% pa)				

(4)

	Tax allowable depreciation	$	Tax benefits	$
1	2,000,000 × 0.25 =	500,000	500,000 × 0.3 =	150,000
2	500,000 × 0.75 =	375,000	375,000 × 0.3 =	112,500
3	375,000 × 0.75 =	281,250	281,250 × 0.3 =	84,375
4	By difference	843,750	843,750 × 0.3 =	253,125
		2,000,000		600,000

(5)

Year	0	1	2	3	4
Working capital $	750,000	772,500	795,675	819,545	0
(Inflated at 3% pa)					
Increment $	750,000	22,500	23,175	23,870	(819,545)

44 Umunat Co

Marking scheme

			Marks
(a)	Discussion of risk	2	
	Discussion of uncertainty	1	
	Value of considering risk and uncertainty	2	
			5
(b)	Calculation of payback period	2	
	Discussion of payback period	3	
			5
			10

(a) The terms **risk** and **uncertainty** are often used interchangeably but a distinction should be made between them. With risk, there are **several possible outcomes**, which upon the basis of past relevant experience, can be **quantified**. In areas of uncertainty, again there are several possible outcomes, but with little past experience, it will be **difficult to quantify** its likely effects.

A risky situation is one where we can say that there is a 70% probability that returns from a project will be in excess of $100,000 but a 30% probability that returns will be less than $100,000. If, however, no information can be provided on the returns from the project, we are faced with an uncertain situation. Managers need to exercise caution when assessing future cash flows to ensure that they make appropriate decisions. If a project is too risky, it might need to be rejected, depending upon the prevailing **attitude to risk**.

In general, risky projects are those whose future cash flows, and hence the project returns, are likely to be **variable**. The greater the variability is, the greater the risk. The problem of risk is more acute with capital investment decisions than other decisions because estimates of cash flows might be for several years ahead, such as for major construction projects. Actual costs and revenues may vary well above or below budget as the work progresses.

(b) Assuming that cash flows occur evenly throughout the year:

Contribution per unit = $3.00 − $1.65 = $1.35

Total contribution = 20,000 units × $1.35 = $27,000 per year

Annual cash flow = $27,000 − $10,000 = $17,000

Payback = $50,000/$17,000 = 2.9 years

This **exceeds** the company's **hurdle payback period** of two years. Payback is often used as a first screening method. By this, we mean that the first question to ask is: 'How long will it take to pay back its cost?' Umunat has a **target payback**, and so it might be tempted to reject this project. However, a project should not be evaluated on the basis of payback alone. If a project gets through the payback test, it ought then to be evaluated with a more sophisticated investment appraisal technique, such as NPV. Payback ignores the **timing of cash flows** within the payback period, the cash flows **after the end** of payback period and therefore the total project return. It also ignores the **time value of money** (a concept incorporated into more sophisticated appraisal methods).

45 Tanumu Co

Text references. Dealing with risk is covered in Chapter 10.

Top tips. Make sure that you use an annuity factor in part (b) to save time.

Easy marks. There are easy marks for the calculation of the NPV in part (a).

Examiner's comments. The answers offered for part (a) were of variable quality, with only a small number of answers correctly evaluating the sensitivity of the project's NPV to changes in the specified variables. In part (b), the majority of candidates calculated the expected sales volume but did not comment on the ENPV. Few noted that the NPV of the worst case was negative, and that there was a 30% chance of this occurring. Some managers might regard a 30% chance of negative returns as an unacceptable risk. As in part (b), many candidates calculated and discounted itemised annual cash flows for each year of the project life, when an annuity factor approach would have saved a considerable amount of time.

Marking scheme

			Marks
(a)	Calculation of net present value	2	
	Sensitivity of NPV to sales volume	2	
	Sensitivity of NPV to sales price	2	
	Sensitivity of NPV to variable cost	1	
	Discussion of sensitivity analysis	3	
			10
(b)	Calculation of expected value of sales	1	
	Calculation of expected net present value	1	
	Discussion of expected net present value	3	
			5
			15

(a)

Year	Investment $	Contribution $	Fixed costs $	Net $	Discount factor 12%	Total $
0	(50,000)			(50,000)	1.000	(50,000)
1-5		27,000	(10,000)	17,000	3.605	61,285
						11,285

NPV of sales revenue = 20,000 × $3.00 × 3.605 = $216,300
NPV of variable costs = 20,000 × $1.65 × 3.605 = $118,965
NPV of contribution = $97,335.

(i) **Sensitivity to sales volume**

For an NPV of zero, contribution has to decrease by $11,285. This represents a reduction in sales of 11,285/97,335 = 11.6%

(ii) **Sensitivity to sales price**

As before, for an NPV of zero, contribution has to decrease by $11,285. This represents a reduction in selling price of 11,285/216,300 = 5.2%

(iii) **Sensitivity to variable cost**

As before, for an NPV of zero, contribution has to decrease by $11,285. This represents an increase in variable costs of 11,285/118,965 = 9.5%

The basic approach of sensitivity analysis is to calculate the project's NPV under alternative assumptions to determine how sensitive it is to changing conditions. An indication is thus provided of those variables to which the NPV is most sensitive (critical variables) and the extent to which those variables may change before the investment results in a negative NPV.

Sensitivity analysis therefore provides an indication of why a project might fail. Management should review critical variables to assess whether or not there is a strong possibility of events occurring which will lead to a negative NPV. Management should also pay particular attention to controlling those variables to which the NPV is particularly sensitive, once the decision has been taken to accept the investment.

(b) Expected sales = (17,500 × 0.3) + (20,000 × 0.6) + (22,500 × 0.1) = 19,500 units

Expected contribution = 19,500 units × $1.35 = $26,325

Year	Investment $	Contribution $	Fixed costs $	Net $	Discount factor 12%	Total $
0	(50,000)			(50,000)	1.000	(50,000)
1-5		26,325	(10,000)	16,325	3.605	58,852
						8,852

The expected net present value is positive, but it represents a value that would never actually be achieved, as it is an amalgamation of various probabilities. Examining each possibility:

Worst case (sales of 17,500 units, 30% probability):

Year	Investment $	Contribution $	Fixed costs $	Net $	Discount factor 12%	Total $
0	(50,000)			(50,000)	1.000	(50,000)
1-5		23,625	(10,000)	13,625	3.605	49,118
						(882)

We already know the NPV of sales of 20,000 units to be $11,285
Best case (sales of 22,500, 10% probability):

Year	Investment $	Contribution $	Fixed costs $	Net $	Discount factor 12%	Total $
0	(50,000)			(50,000)	1.000	(50,000)
1-5		30,375	(10,000)	20,375	3.605	73,452
						23,452

The managers of Tamumu will need to satisfy themselves as to the accuracy of this latest information, but the fact that there is a 30% chance that the project will produce a negative NPV could be considered too high a risk.

It can be argued that assigning probabilities to expected economic states or sales volumes gives the managers information to make better investment decisions. The difficulty with this approach is that probability estimates of project variables can carry a high degree of uncertainty and subjectivity.

46 Duo Co

Text references. Investment appraisal is covered in Chapters 8 and 9.

Top tips. In part (a), set out your workings clearly to gain the maximum number of marks for your workings. Do as much of the NPV calculation as you possibly can, as marks are awarded for each stage. Make an assumption and carry on if you get stuck on any part. Don't forget to comment on the acceptability of the proposed purchase in both parts (a) and (b).

Easy marks. There are plenty of easy marks available throughout this question provided you have done your revision thoroughly.

Examiner's comments. Many candidates gained very high marks in part (a).

A number of candidates lost straightforward marks by failing to comment on the calculated NPV, or by simply saying 'accept' without referring to the NPV decision rule. The reason for accepting an investment project must be clearly explained.

Many candidates gained full marks in part (b). Some candidates lost marks through the incorrect application of linear interpolation in calculating IRR. A number of candidates lost a straightforward mark by not commenting on their calculated IRR.

Marking scheme

		Marks	
(a)	After-tax weighted average cost of capital	2	
	Annual contribution	2	
	Fixed costs	1	
	Taxation	1	
	Tax allowable depreciation tax benefits	2	
	Scrap value	1	
	Discount factors	1	
	Net present value	1	
	Comment	1	
			12
(b)	Internal rate of return calculation	2	
	Comment	1–2	
		Maximum	3
			10

(a) **Weighted average cost of capital**

$$\text{WACC} = \left[\frac{V_e}{V_e + V_d}\right] k_e + \left[\frac{V_d}{V_e + V_d}\right] k_d (1 - T)$$

$$= (0.8 \times 11\%) + (0.2 \times 8.6\%(1 - 30\%))$$

$$= 8.8\% + 1.2\%$$

$$= 10\%$$

Calculation of NPV

	1	2	3	4	5
	$'000	$'000	$'000	$'000	$'000
Contribution (W1)	440	550	660	660	
Fixed costs	(240)	(260)	(280)	(300)	
Net cash flow	200	290	380	360	
Taxation		(60)	(87)	(114)	(108)
TAD tax benefits (W2)		60	45	34	92
Scrap value				30	
After-tax cash flow	200	290	338	310	(16)
Discount factor @10%	0.909	0.826	0.751	0.683	0.621
Present values	182	240	254	212	(10)

	$'000
PV of benefits	878
Investment	800
NPV	**78**

Workings

(1)

Year	1	2	3	4
Additional demand (kg)	400,000	500,000	600,000	700,000
Output of new machine	400,000	500,000	600,000	600,000
Contribution per kg (8 – 5 – 1.9)	1.10	1.10	1.10	1.10
Contribution per year	440,000	550,000	660,000	660,000

(2)

	Tax allowable depn			**Tax benefits**	
Year		$	Year		$
1	$800,000 \times 0.25 =$	200,000	2	$200,000 \times 0.3 =$	60,000
2	$200,000 \times 0.75 =$	150,000	3	$150,000 \times 0.3 =$	45,000
3	$150,000 \times 0.75 =$	112,500	4	$112,500 \times 0.3 =$	33,750
		462,500			
	Scrap value	30,000			
		492,500			
4	By difference	307,500	5	$307,500 \times 0.3 =$	92,250
		800,000			

The acceptability of the proposed purchase

The net present value is **positive** so the proposed purchase is **financially acceptable**. However the machine has a maximum output of only 600,000 kg and additional demand **exceeds this** in the fourth year. The machine is also only viable for four years so more investment will be needed in the relatively short term. It would therefore be advisable to include these additional investment requirements in a **more detailed and longer reaching appraisal**.

It would also be advisable to look in more detail at **other issues** raised by this analysis. For example **constant selling prices and variable costs** have been assumed but it might be more realistic to build in an element of **inflation. Fixed costs** and demand may also increase in a **less linear**, controlled manner.

It is important to bring these issues into this project appraisal so that an informed decision can be made and uncertainties dealt with.

(b) **Internal rate of return**

$$IRR \approx a + \left[\left(\frac{NPV_a}{NPV_a - NPV_b} \right)(b-a) \right]\%$$

where a	=	10%
b	=	15%
NPV_a	=	78
NPV_b	=	(16)

$$IRR \approx 10 + \left[\left(\frac{78}{78 + 16} \right) \times (15 - 10) \right]$$

$$\approx 10 + 4.15$$
$$\approx 14.2\%$$

The acceptability of the proposed purchase

The internal rate of return is approximately 14% which is greater than the 10% weighted average cost of capital used for investment appraisal by Duo Co. This means that the project is financially acceptable using the IRR criteria but the limitations of the NPV method discussed above also apply to IRR.

47 SC Co

Text references. Investment appraisal is covered in Chapters 8 and 9.

Top tips. Read the detail in the question carefully so that you deal with part (a) correctly. For example, the question specifies straight-line tax allowable depreciation, not reducing balance. Working capital is recovered in the last two years of the investment. Make an assumption and carry on if you get stuck on any part.

Easy marks. Using the standard proforma for the calculations in part (a) will help you to gain easy marks even if you get stuck on the harder aspects. Part (b) should provide an easy three marks if you are sufficiently familiar with this technique.

Examiner's comments. Many answers to part (a) gained high marks and dealt correctly with most of the issues involved with the calculation. The treatment of working capital investment was a source of regular errors, however. Many answers put the investment in working capital at the end, rather than at the start, of each year, and included total investment rather than incremental investment. Another common error was to treat investment in working capital as tax-allowable (and even to call it a fixed cost), when in fact it has no tax effect at all.

Many answers gained high marks in part (b) and produced a result consistent with findings in part (a). Markers noted that some candidates made illogical choices of discount rates in their calculations, choosing to work for example with two negative NPV values, rather with one positive and one negative NPV value. While linear interpolation and linear extrapolation use the same mathematical approach, candidates should note that interpolation is more likely to be accurate than extrapolation in calculating IRR.

It was pleasing to note that very few candidates confused IRR with accounting rate of return (return on capital employed).

Marking scheme

			Marks
(a)	Inflated sales revenue	2	
	Inflated variable costs	2	
	Tax allowable depreciation	2	
	Taxation	1	
	Working capital	3	
	Discount factors	1	
	Net present value calculation	1	
			12
(b)	Net present value calculation	1	
	Internal rate of return calculation	2	
			3
			15

(a) **Calculation of NPV**

Year	0	1	2	3	4
	$	$	$	$	$
Sales revenue (W1)		728,000	1,146,390	1,687,500	842,400
Variable costs (W2)		441,000	701,190	1,041,750	524,880
Contribution		287,000	445,200	645,750	317,520
Taxation @ 30%		(86,100)	(133,560)	(193,725)	(95,256)
Capital expenditure	(1,000,000)				
Working capital (W3)	(50,960)	(29,287)	(37,878)	59,157	58,968
Tax benefit of tax depreciation (W4)		75,000	75,000	75,000	75,000
Net cash flow	(1,050,960)	246,613	348,762	586,182	356,232
Discount factor @ 12%	1.000	0.893	0.797	0.712	0.636
Present value	(1,050,960)	220,225	277,963	417,362	226,564
NPV	**$91,154**				

Workings

(1) Sales revenue

Year	1	2	3	4
Selling price ($\times$ 1.04)	$20.80	$21.63	$22.50	$23.40
Sales volume in units	35,000	53,000	75,000	36,000
Sales revenue	$728,000	$1,146,390	$1,687,500	$842,400

(2) Variable costs

Year	1	2	3	4
Variable cost ($\times$ 1.05)	$12.60	$13,23	$13.89	$14.58
Sales volume in units	35,000	53,000	75,000	36,000
Variable cost	$441,000	$701,190	$1,041,75	$524,880

(3) Working capital

Year	0	1	2	3	4
	$	$	$	$	$
Sales revenue		728,000	1,146,390	1,687,500	842,400
Working capital requirement @ 7%		50,960	80,247	118,125	58,968
Incremental working capital cash flow	(50,960)	(29,287)	(37,878)	59,157	58,968

(4) Tax benefit of tax depreciation

Depreciation = $1,000,000/4 = $250,000 per year

Tax benefit = 30% $\times$ $250,000 = $75,000

(b) **Calculation of internal rate of return**

Net cash flow	(1,050,960)	246,613	348,762	586,182	356,232
Discount factor @ 20%	1.000	0.833	0.694	0.579	0.482
Present value	(1,050,960)	205,429	242,041	339,399	171,704
NPV	**(92,387)**				

$$IRR \approx a + \left[\left(\frac{NPV_a}{NPV_a - NPV_b} \right)(b-a) \right]\%$$

$$IRR \approx 12 + \left[\frac{91,154}{91,154 + 92,387} \times (20-12) \right]\% = 16\%$$

BPP
LEARNING MEDIA

48 PV Co

Marking scheme

		Marks
(a)	Inflated income	1
	Inflated operating costs	1
	Discount factors	1
	Net present value	1
	Internal rate of return	3
	Return on capital employed	2
	Discounted payback	1
		10
(b)	Discussion of investment appraisal findings	4
	Advice on acceptability of project	1
		5
		15

(a) (i) **Calculation of NPV**

Year	0	1	2	3	4
	$	$	$	$	$
Investment	(2,000,000)				
Income (W1)		1,236,000	1,485,400	2,622,000	1,012,950
Operating costs (W2)		(676,000)	(789,372)	(1,271,227)	(620,076)
Net cash flows	(2,000,000)	560,000	696,028	1,350,773	392,874
Discount factor 10%	1.000	0.909	0.826	0.751	0.683
Present value	(2,000,000)	509,040	574,919	1,014,430	268,333
NPV	**366,722**				

Workings

(1) Calculation of income

Year	1	2	3	4
Inflated selling price ($/unit)	20.60	21.22	21.85	22.51
Demand (units/year)	60,000	70,000	120,000	45,000
Income ($/year)	1,236,000	1,485,400	2,622,000	1,012,950

(2) Calculation of operating costs

Year	1	2	3	4
Inflated variable cost ($/unit)	8.32	8.65	9.00	9.36
Demand (units/year)	60,000	70,000	120,000	45,000
Variable costs ($/year)	499,200	605,500	1,080,000	421,200
Inflated fixed costs ($/year)	176,800	183,872	191,227	198,876
Operating costs ($/year)	676,000	789,372	1,271,227	620,076

(ii) **Calculation of IRR**

Year	0	1	2	3	4
	$	$	$	$	$
Net cash flow	(2,000,000)	560,000	696,028	1,350,773	392,874
Discount factor 20%	1.000	0.833	0.694	0.579	0.482
Present values	(2,000,000)	466,480	483,043	782,098	189,365
NPV	**(79,014)**				

$$IRR = a + \left[\left(\frac{NPV_a}{NPV_a - NPV_b} \right)(b-a) \right]\%$$

$$IRR = 10 + \left[\frac{366,722}{366,722 + 79,014} \times (20-10) \right]\% = \mathbf{18.2\%}$$

(iii) **Calculation of ROCE**

Total cash inflow = 560,000 + 696,028 + 1,350,773 + 392,874

$\qquad$ = $2,999,675

Total depreciation = initial investment as there is no scrap value

Total accounting profit $\qquad$ = 2,999,675 − 2,000,000

$\qquad$ = $999,675

Average annual accounting profit $\quad$ = 999,675/4

$\qquad$ = $249,919

Average investment = 2,000,000/2

$\qquad$ = $1,000,000

ROCE = 249,919/1,000,000 × 100

$\qquad$ = **25%**

(iv) **Calculation of discounted payback**

Year	0	1	2	3
	$	$	$	$
Present value of cash flows	(2,000,000)	509,040	574,919	1,014,430
Cumulative PV	(2,000,000)	(1,490,960)	(916,041)	98,389

Discounted payback period = 2 + (916,041/1,014,430)

$\qquad$ = **2.9 years**

(b) **NPV**

The investment proposal has a positive NPV of $366,722 and is therefore **financially acceptable**. The NPV decision rule will always give the **correct investment advice** on financial grounds.

IRR

The result of the IRR calculation also indicates that the investment proposal is acceptable as the calculated IRR of 18.2% is **higher** than the 10% **return required** by PV Co. If the IRR result had been less than 10%, the NPV result would still have been preferred.

ROCE

The calculated ROCE of 25% is **less** than the target return of 30% but this is not a reliable method compared to NPV. The hurdle rate appears to be too high and may be **out of date**.

Discounted payback

There is no target given for a payback period but payback is expected to be well into the lifecycle of the project. The project's lifecyle is quite **short** at 4 years and it would therefore be useful to conduct a **sensitivity analysis** of demand to ensure the risk is acceptable.

Conclusion

The NPV and IRR both indicate that the project is financially acceptable, and subject to further analysis of the risks of the project, it should go ahead.

49 AGD Co

Text references. Leasing is covered in Chapter 11.

Top tips. This question is in two parts covering leasing versus borrowing to buy, as well as calculating the equal payments on a bank loan.

Each part of the question could be answered separately.

Easy marks. The question is split into two smaller calculation elements in part (b) that will gain you easy marks if you know how to calculate APRs and repayments. Look at using pro forma workings for the investment appraisal in part (a).

Examiner's comments. While many candidates made errors in this popular question, answers were usually of a satisfactory overall standard. Common errors included timing the investment when borrowing to buy as occurring at the end of the first year, omitting the tax savings on the maintenance costs incurred by buying the asset, and omitting the tax savings on the lease rental payments.

Many candidates either did not answer part (b) or gave answers that were incorrect. The overall standard of answers was very poor.

Marking scheme

			Marks
(a)	Purchase price	1	
	Sale proceeds	1	
	Tax allowable depreciation and balancing allowance	1	
	Tax allowable depreciation tax benefits	1	
	Maintenance costs after tax	1	
	PV of borrowing to buy	1	
	Lease rentals	1	
	Lease rental tax benefits	1	
	PV of leasing	1	
	Selection of cheapest option	1	10

(b) Annual percentage rate   2
     Amount of equal instalments   3

5
15

(a) (i) **Present value of purchase costs**

	Year 0 $'000	Year 1 $'000	Year 2 $'000	Year 3 $'000	Year 4 $'000
Cash outflows					
Capital costs	(320)				
Annual maintenance costs		(25)	(25)	(25)	
	(320)	(25)	(25)	(25)	0
Cash inflows					
Disposal proceeds				50	
Taxation (at 30% in following year)			8	8	8
Tax allowable depn (W)			24	18	39
			32	76	47
Net cash flows	(320)	(25)	7	51	47
Discount at 7%	1.000	0.935	0.873	0.816	0.763
PV of cash flow	(320)	(23)	6	42	36
NPV of cash flow	**($259,000)**				

Working

Tax allowable depreciation

	$'000	Tax Allowable depn $'000	Tax benefit $'000	Year of cash flow
Initial investment	320			
Allowances at 25% pa on a reducing balance basis over 3 years				
Year 1	(80)	(80)	24	Y2
	240			
Year 2	(60)	(60)	18	Y3
	180			
Year 3				
Proceeds on sale	(50)			
Balancing allowance	130		39	Y4

(ii) **Present value of leasing costs**

	Year 0 $'000	Year 1 $'000	Year 2 $'000	Year 3 $'000	Year 4 $'000
Cash outflows					
Annual lease rentals	(120)	(120)	(120)		
	(120)	(120)	(120)		
Cash inflows					
Taxation (at 30% in following year) – tax deduction for lease rentals			36	36	36
Net cash flows	(120)	(120)	(84)	36	36
Discount at 7%	1.000	0.935	0.873	0.816	0.763
PV of cash flow	(120)	(112)	(73)	29	27
NPV of cash flow	**$249,000)**				

Therefore the machine should be **leased** rather than purchased.

(b)　(i)　**Annual percentage rate (APR)** on a 10% loan by the bank with two six-monthly interest payments.

As interest is due every six months, this is equivalent to 5% every six months.

As this would be compounded, therefore the APR would be (1.05 × 1.05 − 1) = 0.1025 or 10.25%

(ii)　The term of the loan is $320,000 at 10% pa over 5 years with six-monthly payments of interest.

In (i) above, we established that the rate was 5% every six months. There are 10 equal payments due. Treating this as an annuity at 5% over 10 periods gives a discount rate of 7.722.

Therefore dividing $320,000/7.722 gives **$41,440** as each equal payment due.

50 Leaminger Co

Text references. Leasing and capital rationing are covered in Chapter 11.

Top tips. Make sure you take into account all the detail given in the question; it's easy to miss or misinterpret the timing of flows or the maintenance costs. Note that annuity factors can be used to save time in (a) (ii) and (iii), whereas in (a) (i) a more complicated calculation is required. Most points in the NPV calculation were worth 1 mark, although 3 marks were available for the tax allowable depreciation.

The key point in (b) is that capital rationing affects the purchase and operating lease options, but does not affect the finance lease option since the first payments do not take place until capital rationing has ended.

Examiner's comment. There were a number of errors in (a) that many candidates made including: omitting maintenance costs and their tax benefits from the purchase and finance lease calculations; including the tax allowable depreciation rather than the tax benefit of the tax allowable depreciation in the purchase calculation; including the tax benefits of tax allowable depreciation in the lease calculations (they were only available on ownership); only considering one year of the operating lease.

In (b) few candidates recognised the opportunity cost element in the purchase and operating lease options. Candidates gained marks for using a profitability index approach.

(a)　(i)　**Present value of purchasing the machine**

	20X2 $	20X3 $	20X4 $	20X5 $	20X6 $	20X7 $
Purchase price	(360,000)					
Maintenance		(15,000)	(15,000)	(15,000)	(15,000)	
Tax on maintenance			4,500	4,500	4,500	4,500
Tax allowable depreciation (W)		27,000	20,250	15,188	11,391	28,172
Disposal proceeds					20,000	
Net cash flow	(360,000)	12,000	9,750	4,688	20,891	32,672
Discount factor	1.000	0.909	0.826	0.751	0.683	0.621
Present value	(360,000)	10,908	8,054	3,521	14,269	20,289

Present value = **$(302,959)**

Working

Tax allowable depreciation

Year of claim	Depreciation $	Tax saved $	Year of tax payment/saving
20X2	90,000	27,000	20X3
20X3	67,500	20,250	20X4
20X4	50,625	15,188	20X5
20X5	37,969	11,391	20X6
20X6	93,906	28,172	20X7

Depreciation

20X2	$360,000 \times 25\% = 90,000$
20X3-5	75% of previous year
20X6	Balancing allowance = Purchase price − Depreciation − Sale proceeds
	$= 360,000 - 90,000 - 67,500 - 50,625 - 37,969 - 20,000$
	$= 93,906$

(ii) **Present value of the finance lease**

Year		Cash flow $	Discount factor 10%	Present value $
20X3-6	Rental and maintenance			
	(135,000 + 15,000)	(150,000)	3.170	(475,500)
20X4-7	Tax on payments	45,000	2.882*	129,690
	Present value			(345,810)

20X4-7 factor	= Year 1-5 Factor − Year 1 Factor
	= 3.791 − 0.909
	= 2.882

(iii) **Present value of the operating lease**

Year		Cash flow $	Discount factor 10%	Present value $
20X2-5	Rental	(140,000)	3.487	(488,180)
20X3-6	Tax on rental	42,000	3.170	133,140
	Present value			(355,040)

Based on these calculations, **purchase** would appear to be the best option.

(b) Every $ of year 0 expenditure will involve a loss of profit of 100,000/500,000 = 20c

Purchase

	$
Present value	(302,959)
Profits foregone (360,000 × 0.20)	(72,000)
Revised present value	(374,959)

Finance lease

$345,810 as before.

Operating lease

	$
Present value	(355,040)
Profits foregone (140,000 × 0.20)	(28,000)
Revised present value	(383,040)

If capital rationing applies, the finance lease is the best option.

51 ASOP Co

Marking scheme

		Marks
(a)	Present value of lease rentals	2
	Present value of lease rental tax benefits	1
	Present value of cost of leasing	1
	Investment and scrap values	1
	Licence fee	1
	Tax allowable depreciation tax benefits	1
	Licence fee tax benefits	1
	Present value of cost of borrowing to buy	1
	Appropriate decision on leasing versus buying	1
		10
(b)	Inflated cost savings	1
	Tax liabilities	1
	Present values of net cash flows	1
	Net present value	1
	Advice on acceptability of investment	1
		5
		15

(a) **Present value of purchasing new technology**

Discount rate = 8.6% × (1 - 30%) = 6%

	Year 0 $'000	Year 1 $'000	Year 2 $'000	Year 3 $'000	Year 4 $'000	Year 5 $'000
Capital costs	(1,000)					
Licence fee		(104)	(108)	(112)	(116)	
Disposal proceeds					100	
Tax deduction @30% for licence payments			31	32	34	35
Tax allowable depn (W)			75	56	42	96
Net cash flows	(1,000)	(104)	(2)	(24)	60	131
Discount at 6%	1.000	0.943	0.890	0.840	0.792	0.747
	(1,000)	(98)	(2)	(20)	48	98
PV of cash flow	**$(974)**					

Working

Tax allowable depreciation

	$'000	Capital allowance $'000	Tax benefit $'000	Year of cash flow
Initial investment	1,000			
Allowances at 25% pa on a reducing balance basis over 4 years				
Year 1	(250)	(250)	75	Y2
	750			
Year 2	(188)	(188)	56	Y3
	562			
Year 3	(141)	(141)	42	Y4
	421			
Year 4				
Proceeds on sale	(100)			
Balancing allowance	321		96	Y5

Present value of leasing new technology

	Year 0 $'000	Year 1 $'000	Year 2 $'000	Year 3 $'000	Year 4 $'000	Year 5 $'000
Annual lease rentals	(380)	(380)	(380)	(380)		
Taxation deduction @ 30% for lease rentals			114	114	114	114
Net cash flows	(380)	(380)	(266)	(266)	114	114
Discount at 6%	1.000	0.943	0.890	0.840	0.792	0.747
	(380)	(358)	(237)	(223)	90	85
PV of cash flow	**$(1,023)**					

Therefore the new technology should be **purchased** rather than leased.

(b) **Present value of buying the new technology**

	Year 0 $'000	Year 1 $'000	Year 2 $'000	Year 3 $'000	Year 4 $'000	Year 5 $'000
Saving in operating costs (W)		365	480	638	564	
Licence fee		(104)	(108)	(112)	(116)	
Net additional cash flow		261	372	526	448	
Tax @ 30%			(78)	(112)	(158)	(134)
Capital costs	(1,000)					
Disposal proceeds					100	
Tax allowable depn			75	56	42	96
Net cash flows	(1,000)	261	369	470	432	(38)
Discount at 11%	1.000	0.901	0.812	0.731	0.659	0.593
	(1,000)	235	300	344	285	(23)
PV of cash flow	**$141**					

Working

Operating costs

	Year 1	Year 2	Year 3	Year 4
Production units	60	75	95	80
Cost saving @ $5.80	348	435	551	464
Inflation	× 1.05	× 1.05^2	× 1.05^3	× 1.05^4
Saving in operating costs cash flow	365	480	638	564

Advice on proposed investment

The present value of the investment proposal is **positive** and is $141,000. According to this criteria, ASOP Co should therefore undertake the proposed investment.

52 Capital rationing

Text references. Capital rationing is covered in Chapter 11.

Top tips. (a) is a good summary of why long-term profits don't always lead to positive cash flows. (b) demonstrates why capital rationing may be a matter of choice; certain sources of funds may not be felt desirable and projects have to be properly controlled.

(a) **Cash shortages**

A period of capital rationing is often associated with more general problems of cash shortage. Possible reasons for this include the following.

(i) The business has become **loss making** and is unable to cover the depreciation charge. Since one purpose of the depreciation charge is to allow for the cost of the assets used in the profit and loss account, the implication is that there will be insufficient cash with which to replace these assets when necessary.

(ii) High inflation may mean that even though the business is profitable in historical cost terms, it is still failing to **generate sufficient funds** to replace assets.

(iii) If the business is growing it may face a **shortage of working capital** with which to finance expansion, and this may result in a period of capital rationing.

(iv) If the business is **seasonal or cyclical** it may **face times of cash shortage** despite being fundamentally sound. In this situation, there may be a periodic need for capital rationing.

(v) A **large one-off item** of **expenditure** such as a property purchase may mean that the company faces a temporary shortage of cash for further investment.

Investment opportunities

A further reason for capital rationing arises in the situation where the company has **more investment opportunities** available than the **funds allocated** to the capital budget permit. This means that projects must be ranked for investment, taking into account both financial and strategic factors.

(b) **Hard capital rationing** describes the situation when a firm is prevented from undertaking attractive investments for reasons external to the firm.

Soft capital rationing describes the position when management places a limit on the amount of capital investment that may be undertaken: it is due to factors internal to the firm.

Reasons for the deliberate restriction of capital expenditure include the following.

(i) Management may decide to **limit the funds available** to those which can be generated from retained earnings, for the following reasons.

   (1) They **do not wish** to **issue further equity** to prevent outsiders from gaining control of the business.

   (2) They **do not wish** to **raise further equity** to avoid earnings dilution.

   (3) They **do not wish to commit the company** to meeting large fixed interest payments on additional debt capital.

(ii) A **capital budgeting procedure** may be used to ensure that only the best projects are undertaken.

(iii) The **number of projects** undertaken may be **restricted** in order to ensure that there are adequate management resources available for them to realise their full potential.

53 Filtrex Co

Text references. Capital rationing is covered in Chapter 11.

Top tips. (a)(i) of the question can be approached by means of the Profitability Index (PI); the optimal mix of project can then be found by trial and error. In addition you need to be clear about mutual exclusivity and indivisibility. Mutual exclusivity means that if you choose one project, you cannot choose other projects with which the chosen project is mutually exclusive. Indivisibility means that you cannot carry out part of a project; it is all or nothing.

In (b) it is helpful to consider the situation from the point of view of developing the projects themselves and in terms of alternative sources of funds.

(a) (i) **Profitability index**

When resources are limited, the aim must be to maximise the productivity of the scarce resource, in this case capital. It is therefore helpful to calculate the **Profitability Index (PI)** for each project to determine which delivers the most NPV per dollar of investment.

Project	Outlay	NPV	PI(NPV/Outlay)
	$	$	
A	150,000	65,000	0.43
B	120,000	50,000	0.42
C	200,000	80,000	0.40
D	80,000	30,000	0.38
E	400,000	120,000	0.30

On this basis, project A is the most attractive since it shows the highest PI, and project E is the least attractive. Since the projects are not divisible and projects A and C are mutually exclusive it is not possible simply to work down the rankings to determine the optimum combination. Instead this must be done algebraically or by trial and error. Various combinations of projects can be evaluated using the latter approach.

	Outlay	NPV
	$	$
A, B, D	350,000	145,000
B, C, D	400,000	160,000
E	400,000	120,000

It appears that the **optimum combination** of projects is B, C and D. As well as delivering the highest NPV it also has the **benefit that all the funds available** for investment are used and Filtrex does not face the choice between investments showing a poorer return or returning excess funds to its shareholders.

(ii) **Useful further information**

(1) The **possibility** of **raising additional finance** and at what cost.

(2) If **rationing** is to continue, then the **effect on the NPV** of **postponing projects becomes relevant**. If all the projects are equally postponable than Filtrex should select those which provide the fastest flow of funds in order to finance those which have been postponed as quickly as possible.

(3) It has been assumed that all the projects carry a **similar degree of risk**. If this is not the case then Filtrex should allow for this, for example by the use of sensitivity analysis in its evaluations.

(4) It may be that some of the projects carry a **greater strategic significance** than others. Information on this area should also be taken into account in the investment decision.

(b) **Further opportunity**

Filtrex might consider some of the **following options** as a means of exploiting more of these opportunities.

(i) **Sale of patent rights**

It could accept that it will be **unable to manage** all the **later stages** of development itself and could decide to sell some of the patent rights once they have been obtained.

(ii) **Joint ventures**

It could seek **joint venture partners** to share in the development.

(iii) **Licensing or franchising**

Some of the areas may be appropriate **for licensing or franchising** with a royalty being payable to Filtrex. This in turn could help to finance the development of those projects which are retained for in-house promotion.

(iv) **Additional finance**

It could seek additional finance in the following forms.

(1) **Further equity** by way of a rights issue or, by agreement with existing shareholders, via a public issue.

(2) **Debt finance secured** on the **assets**. This should be possible since the company is currently ungeared.

(3) **Debt finance secured** against the **working capital** ie factoring or invoice discounting.

(4) It may be possible to arrange a **sale and leaseback** of some of the company's property or equipment.

(5) Depending on its location and business there may be the possibility of applying for **grant aid**, for example from one of the EU regional development funds.

54 Warden Co

Marking scheme

			Marks
(a)	Sales revenue	0.5	
	Variable costs	0.5	
	Fixed costs	0.5	
	Tax liabilities	1	
	Working capital recovered	0.5	
	Scrap value	0.5	
	Initial working capital	0.5	
	Initial investment	0.5	
	Discount factors	0.5	
	NPV calculation	1	
	Decision as to financial acceptability	1	
			7
(b)	(i) Explanation of sensitivity analysis		2
	(ii) After-tax present value of sales revenue	2	
	Selling price sensitivity	2	
	Discount rate sensitivity	1	
	Comment on findings	1	
			6
			15

(a) **Calculation of NPV**

Year	0	1	2	3	4	5	6
	$'000	$'000	$'000	$'000	$'000	$'000	$'000
Sales revenue		1,600	1,600	1,600	1,600	1,600	
Variable costs		(1,100)	(1,100)	(1,100)	(1,100)	(1,100)	
Fixed costs		(160)	(160)	(160)	(160)	(160)	
Before-tax cash flows		340	340	340	340	340	
Taxation at 30%			(102)	(102)	(102)	(102)	(102)
Capital investment	(800)					40	
Working capital	(90)					90	
Project cash flows	(890)	340	238	238	238	368	(102)
Discount factor 11%	1.000	0.901	0.812	0.731	0.659	0.593	0.535
Present value	(890)	306	193	174	157	218	(55)
NPV	**103**						

The net present value is positive and therefore the project is financially acceptable.

(b)   (i)   The sensitivity of an investment project to a change in a variable can be calculated as the ratio of the NPV to the present value (PV) of the variable. This shows the relative change in the variable which will make the NPV of the project zero. Sensitivity analysis can be used to calculate the key variable for a project and show the area on which management should focus in order to make the project successful.

   (ii)   **Selling price sensitivity**

As sales revenue is a five-year annuity the present value can be calculated as follows

100,000 units × $16 × Five year annuity factor at 11%

100,000 × $16 × 3.696 = $5,913,600

The tax liability from this revenue also needs to be considered as the NPV includes the tax paid.

Tax liability (before taking account of paying in arrears) = $5,913,600 × 30% = $1,774,080

Discounting by one year to give PV of tax liability = $1,774,080 × 0.901 = $1,598,446

Total PV relating to sales revenue = $5,913,600 – $1,598,446 = $4,315,154

Sensitivity of project to sales revenue = (103,000 / 4,315,154) × 100% = 2.4%

Discount rate sensitivity

Change in discount rate required for NPV to be zero = 16 – 11 = 5%

Sensitivity of project to the discount rate = (5/11) × 100% = 45.5%

As can be seen from the analysis above the critical variable is the selling price as the investment is significantly more sensitive to changes in the sales price than the discount rate.

55 Ridag Co

Text references. NPV are covered in Chapter 8.

Top tips. This is a fairly straightforward NPV calculation. Remember that inflation has to be compounded from year to year. Since we have nominal after-tax cash flows, the nominal after-tax WACC should be used – 'discount like with like.'

Easy marks. Don't forget to conclude on whether the project is financially acceptable. There are marks available for doing so.

Examiner's comments. Some students encountered difficulty including inflation in their NPV calculation. Too often, answers applied one year's inflation to every year's figures.

Marking scheme

		Marks
Sales revenue	2	
Variable and fixed costs	1	
Tax liabilities	1	
Balancing allowance	1	
Tax allowable depreciation tax benefits	1	
Timing of taxation benefits and liabilities	1	
Initial investment and scrap value	0.5	
Using the correct discount rate	0.5	
NPV	1	
Decision as to financial acceptability	1	
		10

Year	0	1	2	3	4	5
	$'000	$'000	$'000	$'000	$'000	$'000
Capital cost	(1,500)					
Sales revenue		1,300	2,466	3,622	2,018	
Variable costs		(513)	(1,098)	(1,809)	(1,035)	
Fixed costs		(105)	(115)	(125)	(125)	
Taxable cash flow		682	1,253	1,688	858	
Tax liabilities			(205)	(376)	(506)	(258)
Tax allowable depn			113	84	63	160
After-tax cash flow		682	1,161	1,396	415	(98)
Scrap value					100	
Net cash flow	(1,500)	682	1,161	1,396	515	(98)
Discount at 7%	1	0.935	0.873	0.816	0.763	0.713
Present values	(1,500)	638	1,014	1,139	393	(70)
PV	**1,614**					

Project 1 has a positive NPV which indicates it should be undertaken.

However, this NPV has been calculated based on the company's current weighted average cost of capital. Since the investment involves a new product, it may be more appropriate to base the NPV calculation on a discount rate that is specific to this project, so that it takes the risks associated with the recently-developed product into account.

Workings

(1) Sales revenue

Year	1	2	3	4
Selling price ($/unit)	25.00	24.00	23.00	23.00
4% inflated selling price ($/unit)	26.00	25.96	25.87	26.91
Sales quantity	50,000	95,000	140,000	75,000
Total sales revenue (nearest $'000)	1,300	2,466	3,622	2,018

(2) Variable costs

Year	1	2	3	4
Variable cost ($/unit)	10.00	11.00	12.00	12.50
2.5% inflated cost ($/unit)	10.25	11.56	12.92	13.80
Sales quantity	50,000	95,000	140,000	75,000
Total variable cost (nearest $'000)	513	1,098	1,809	1,035

(3) Tax allowable depn

	TWDV b/fwd ($'000)	25% ($'000)	TWDV c/fwd ($'000)	Tax benefit × 30%	Year benefit is received
Year 1	1,500	375	1,125	113	2
Year 2	1,125	281	844	84	3
Year 3	844	211	633	63	4
Year 4	633	533*	-	160	5

*Balancing allowance: TWDV $633k – proceeds $100k = $533k.

56 Gadir Co

Marking scheme

			Marks
(a)	Equivalent annual cost of Machine 1	2	
	Equivalent annual cost of Machine 2	2	
	Discussion on which machine to purchase	3	
			7
(b)	Explanation of risk and uncertainty	1	
	Discussion of sensitivity analysis	2-3	
	Discussion of probability analysis	2-3	
	Other relevant discussion	1-2	
		Maximum	8
			15

(a) Since tax is to be ignored, the weighted average pre-tax cost of capital of 12% should be used.

Machine 1

Year	0	1	2	3	4
Cost/ scrap ($'000)	(200)				25
Maintenance cost ($'000)		(25)	(29)	(32)	(35)
Net cash flow ($'000)	(200)	(25)	(29)	(32)	(10)
DF 12%	1	0.893	0.797	0.712	0.636
PV	(200)	(22)	(23)	(23)	(6)

PV of cash flows = $274k

To calculate equivalent annual cost, divide PV of cash flows by the cumulative DF (3.037).

$274k/3.037 = $90k

Machine 2

Year	0	1	2	3
Cost/ scrap ($'000)	(225)			50
Maintenance cost ($'000)		(15)	(20)	(25)
Net cash flow ($'000)	(225)	(15)	(20)	25
DF 12%	1	0.893	0.797	0.712
PV	(225)	(13)	(16)	18

PV of cash flows = $236k

To calculate equivalent annual cost, divide PV of cash flows by the cumulative DF (2.402).

$236k/2.402 = $98k

The machine with the lowest equivalent annual cost should be purchased. This is Machine 1. Machine 2 would have been selected if the investment were evaluated on the present value of cash flows alone – but this would have ignored the different useful lives of the machines.

(b)   Sensitivity analysis is used to show how a change in each of the key variables impacts the NPV calculation. By identifying the variables to which the outcome of the investment is most sensitive, this method gives an idea of where the main risks of a project lie.

The disadvantage of sensitivity analysis is that it tests only one individual variable at a time. Therefore, it ignores the interrelationships that often exist between variables. It also does not help to explain the probability of a change in the variable.

Being restricted to testing one variable at a time also means that sensitivity analysis is of limited use to managers. Firstly, managers may be more interested in the effect of a combination of variables. Secondly, management may not have control over critical factors.

There is also no 'decision rule' in sensitivity analysis. Carrying out the analysis therefore does not tell managers directly whether or not to invest in a project. It is up to the managers themselves to determine in which circumstances a project should be accepted.

Probability analysis is a more effective method for considering risk in the investment appraisal process. This analysis assigns probabilities to expected cash flows in order to arrive at an expected net present value which takes into account the likelihood of different cash flows arising. It provides one expected net present value figure which can be easily evaluated and benchmarked.

One disadvantage of probability analysis, however, is the fact that it depends upon probabilities which are difficult to estimate and are ultimately subjective.

57 BQK Co

Text references. NPV is covered in Chapter 8.

Top tips. This is a fairly straightforward NPV calculation without many of the difficulties that can be present. Ensure that you inflate each item of cost and revenue at the correct rates and the tax on profits is paid one year in arrears.

Easy marks. There are plenty of easy marks for calculations in this question.

Examiner's comments. Many candidates gained high marks on this part of question. Some answers mistakenly used the real after-tax cost of capital of 9%, or tried to calculate another discount rate altogether using the Fisher equation, but all that was needed was to use the 12% rate provided. Some answers chose not to comment on the financial acceptability of the investment project and so lost a relatively straightforward mark.

	Marks
Sales income without inflation	2
Inflation of sales income	1
Variable costs without inflation	1
Inflation of variable costs	1
Inflated fixed costs	1
Calculation of tax allowable depreciation	2
Correct use of tax allowable depreciation	1
Calculation of tax liabilities	1
Correct timing of tax liabilities	1
Selection of correct discount rate	1
Selection of discount factors	1
Calculation of net present value	1
Comment on financial acceptability	1
	15

Present value of cash flows

Year	0	1	2	3	4	5
	$'000	$'000	$'000	$'000	$'000	$'000
Capital cost	(4,000)					
Sales revenue (W1)		5,614	7,214	9,015	7,034	
Variable costs (W2)		(3,031)	(3,931)	(5,135)	(4,174)	
Fixed costs*		(1,530)	(1,561)	(1,592)	(1,624)	
Taxable cash flow		1,053	1,722	2,288	1,236	
Tax liabilities			(316)	(517)	(686)	(371)
TAD tax benefits**			300	300	300	300
After-tax cash flow		1,053	1,706	2,071	850	(71)
Discount at 12%	1	0.893	0.797	0.712	0.636	0.567
Present values	(4,000)	940	1,360	1,475	541	(40)
NPV	**276**					

This project has a positive NPV which indicates it should be undertaken.

*Fixed costs are inflated by 2% year on year.

**TAD tax benefits = Purchase cost $4,000k / 4 years × 30%

Workings

1 *Sales revenue*

Year	1	2	3	4
Small houses selling price ($'000/house)	200	200	200	200
Small houses sales quantity	15	20	15	5
Large houses selling price ($'000/house)	350	350	350	350
Large houses sales quantity	7	8	15	15
Total sales revenue (nearest $'000)	5,450	6,800	8,250	6,250
Inflated sales revenue ($'000/year) – sales revenue × 1.03^n	5,614	7,214	9,015	7,034

2   *Variable costs*

Year	1	2	3	4
Small houses selling price ($'000/house)	100	100	100	100
Small houses sales quantity	15	20	15	5
Large houses selling price ($'000/house)	200	200	200	200
Large houses sales quantity	7	8	15	15
Total sales revenue (nearest $'000)	2,900	3,600	4,500	3,500
Inflated sales revenue ($'000/year) – sales revenue × 1.045^n	3,031	3,931	5,135	4,174

58 MCQ bank – Sources of finance

58.1 **D**   Short-term loans are subject to a loan agreement giving the bank security and a definite repayment schedule. This lowers the risk from their perspective, hence the interest rate charged is lower.

Syllabus area E1a

58.2 **A**   Ordinary shares are most risky from the debt holder's perspective – the company can decide whether and how much of a dividend to pay.

Preference shares are next most risky – dividends are only payable if profit is available to pay dividends from.

Trade payables are next because they have to be paid before shareholders but are typically unsecured.

Finally, banks with fixed and floating charges face least risk.

Syllabus area E1b

58.3 **D**

$2	×	4	=	$8.00
$1.60	×	1	=	$1.60
		5		$9.60

Theoretical ex rights price = $9.60 / 5 = $1.92

Syllabus area E1c

58.4 **D**   Zero coupon bonds are issued at a discount to their redemption value and do not pay any interest.

Syllabus area E1b

58.5 **A**   B is mudaraba. C is murabaha. D is ijara. A key principle is that charging interest, and making money from money lending alone is forbidden under Sharia'a law, so providers of finance are more directly involved with the risks and rewards of the businesses they finance.

Syllabus area E1d

59 MCQ bank – Dividend policy

59.1 **A**   Modigliani and Miller ('M&M') assume perfect capital markets so there is no information content in dividend policy. They assume no taxes or tax preferences so investors will be indifferent between income and capital gains. They also assume no transaction costs so investors can switch between income and capital gains costlessly – eg if a company withholds a dividend when the investor would prefer cash, the investor can sell some of their shares (known as 'manufacturing a dividend'). M&M's theory is not contingent upon the existence or otherwise of inflation.

Syllabus area E1e

59.2 **B**   The signalling effect alludes to the information content in the dividend announcement. In semi-strong form capital markets with imperfect information, investors will 'interpret' dividend announcements and by comparing them to expectations they will adjust their perceptions of past, current and future performance.

Syllabus area E1e

59.3 B   M&M stated that income preference is irrelevant in deciding dividend policy, because if you 'assume away' taxation and transaction costs, it is costless for investors to switch from capital gain to dividends by selling some shares.

Syllabus area E1e

59.4 C   To incentivise investors to choose the shares alternative for their dividend, companies can offer an 'enhanced scrip' ie offer more value in shares than the cash alternative.

Syllabus area E1e

59.5 A   Company A dividends are growing at 10% per annum even though earnings are not.

Company B is paying 50% of its earnings out as a dividend consistently.

Company C's dividends are not obviously connected with reported earnings, so their policy is either random or residual (ie only paying dividends once investment plans are budgeted for).

Syllabus area E1e

60 MCQ bank – Gearing and capital structure

60.1 C   Operational gearing = Contribution / Profit before interest and tax.

Contribution = Turnover − variable cost = $10,123 − (70\% \times 7,222) − (10\% \times 999) = 4,967.70$

Operational gearing = $4,967.70 / 1,902 = 2.61$

Syllabus area E3d

60.2 D   Market value of equity = $\$5.50 \times \$100m = \$550m$

Market value of long term debt = $\$500m \times (125/100) = \$625m$

Therefore financial gearing = $625 / (625 + 550) = 53\%$

Syllabus area E3d

60.3 D   Statement A is incorrect. This may be true but is not the definition of financial risk.

Statement B is incorrect. This may be true but is not the definition of financial risk.

Statement C is incorrect. Overall dividends may be lower as gearing increases compared to an equivalent ungeared firm, however there are less shareholders/shares in the geared equivalent, meaning dividend per share could be higher, lower or the same as the ungeared firm.

Statement D is correct. As interest payments do not vary with profits, interest is effectively a fixed cost to the business. High financial gearing means that a company is more vulnerable to poor trading conditions. For example, reductions in turnover result in relatively large reductions in profits and dividends as there are less variable costs to cushion the reduction in turnover. The opposite is the case with increases in turnover, thus shareholders in a geared firm face higher variability in their returns.

Syllabus area E3a

60.4 B   All else being equal less interest to pay will mean a higher interest cover.

(Interest cover = Profit Before Interest and Tax / Interest)

Reducing debt will reduce the gearing ratio.

Syllabus area E3d

60.5 B   In relation to expectations, results being better than expected would boost share price. This would increase the Price / Earnings ratio.

By the same logic, dividend yield would reduce. Dividend yield is calculated as Dividend / Share price hence a higher share price would reduce the ratio.

Syllabus area E3d

61 MCQ bank – The cost of capital

61.1 **D** 20X9 to 20Y3 covers 4 years of growth,

so the average annual growth rate = $\sqrt[4]{(423/220)} - 1 = 0.178 = 17.8\%$

$$K_e = \frac{d_0(1+g)}{P_0} + g$$

$$K_e - g = \frac{d_0(1+g)}{P_0}$$

$$P_0 = \frac{d_0(1+g)}{K_e - g}$$

= (423,000 × 1.178) / (0.25 – 0.178)   = $6,920,750 for 4 million shares = $1.73 per share

Syllabus area F2c

61.2 **A** g = retention rate × return on investment.

Retention rate = proportion of earnings retained = ($1.50- $0.5)/$1.50 = 66.7%

Return on new investment = EPS / net assets per share = $1.5 / $6 = 0.25 so 25%

g = 66.7% × 25% = 16.7%

$$K_e = \frac{d_0(1+g)}{P_0} + g$$

$$= \frac{(\$0.50 \times 1.167)}{(\$4.50 - \$0.50)} + 0.167$$ Note: Share price given is cum div

= 31%

Syllabus area E2a

61.3 **D** A is incorrect. Systematic risk refers to return volatility.

B is incorrect. This describes TOTAL risk, which has both systematic and unsystematic elements

C is incorrect. Systematic risk cannot be diversified away

D is correct. It is the risk generated by undiversifiable systemic economic risk factors.

Syllabus area E2a

61.4 **C** The equity beta relates to the cost of equity, hence gearing and the debt beta are not relevant.

$E(r_i) = R_f + \beta(E(R_m) - R_f) = 3\% + (1.3 \times 8\%) = 13.4\%$

Syllabus area E2a

61.5 **A** $K_d = I(1-t) / P_o$

The loan note pays interest of $100 nominal × 10% = 10%. Ex-interest market price is $95 – $10 = $85.

Before the tax cut $K_d = 10(1 – 0.3) / 85 = 8.2\%$

After the tax cut $K_d = 10(1 – 0.2) / 85 = 9.4\%$

Decreasing tax reduces tax saved therefore increases the cost of debt.

Syllabus area E2b

61.6 **C** Conversion value: Future share price = $2.50 × $(1.1)^5$ = $4.03;

so conversion value = 20 × $4.03 = $80.60. The cash alternative = 100 × 1.1 = $110 therefore investors would not convert and redemption value = $110.

Kd = IRR of the after tax cash flows as follows:

Time	$	DF 10%	Present value 10% ($)	DF 15%	Present value 15% ($)
0	(90)	1	(90)	1	(90)
1-5	10(1 − 0.3) = 7	3.791	26.54	3.352	23.46
5	110	0.621	68.31	0.497	54.67
			4.85		(11.87)

$$IRR = a + \frac{NPV_a}{NPV_a - NPV_b} (b - a)$$

$$= 10\% + \frac{4.85}{(4.85 + 11.87)} (15\% - 10\%)$$

$$= 11.5\%$$

Syllabus area E2b

61.7 **C** $K_d = I(1 - T) / P_0 = 13(1 - 0.3) / 90 = 10.11\%$

$V_d = \$7m \times (90/100) = \$6.3m$

$K_e = 12\%$ (given)

$V_e = \$3 \times 10m$ shares = \$30m   Note: reserves are included as part of share price

$V_e + V_d = \$6.3m + \$30m = \$36.3m$

$$WACC = \left[\frac{V_e}{V_e + V_d}\right] k_e + \left[\frac{V_d}{V_e + V_d}\right] k_d$$

$$= [30/36.3]12\% + (6.3/36.3)10.11\% = 11.7\%$$

Syllabus area E2c

61.8 **D** Changes in capital structure will affect the WACC so need to stay constant. The current WACC reflects a risk premium commensurate with current operations, hence the new project should be of a similar risk profile to current operations. The project should be small in size; large projects are both riskier (commanding a risk premium) and likely to affect the value of equity, in turn affecting the WACC.

Syllabus area E3e

61.9 **D** A is a necessary assumption. Share price can be used to accurately calculate beta factors.

B is a necessary assumption. Shareholders only require compensation for systematic risk ie that risk that cannot be diversified away.

C is a necessary assumption. Beta factors are estimated using historical data, but the cost equity is to be used to appraise a future project, hence we need to assume the historical beta will continue.

D is not a necessary assumption. So long as investors are well diversified, any individual company need not be. Investors are assumed to invest in a diversified portfolio of projects; it doesn't matter how few or how many reside in any one company.

Syllabus area E2a

61.10 **B** ex-div share price = \$0.30 − (8% × \$0.50) = \$0.26

$K_p = \$0.50 \times 8\% / \$0.26 = 15.4\%$

Note: dividends are not tax deductible hence no adjustment for corporation tax is required.

Syllabus area E2b

62 MCQ bank – Capital structure

62.1 **B** Statement A refers to Modigliani-Miller ('MM') with tax: raising debt finance will increase interest payments and hence save tax, adding to the total returns a business generates.

Statement B is correct: the traditional view implies that once gearing has gone beyond optimal the weighted average cost of capital ('WACC') will increase if more debt is taken on. As A Co is significantly more highly geared than the industry standard, it is probably reasonable to assume its gearing is beyond optimal.

Statement C refers to MM with no tax: paying interest or paying dividends does not affect the overall returns generated by a non-tax paying business.

Statement D is incorrect: see 'B' above.

Syllabus area E4a&b

62.2 **B** Statement A: Although true, higher gearing increases the cost of equity (financial risk) therefore this doesn't in itself explain a reducing WACC.

Statement B is correct: The only different between MM (no tax) and MM (with tax) is the tax deductibility of interest payments. MM demonstrated that when a business does not pay tax, returns are not affected by capital structure. However, as interest is tax deductible (and dividends are not) paying relatively more interest will reduce tax payable and increase total returns to investors.

Statement C is similar to Statement A.

Statement D refers to the traditional view. MM assume financial risk is consistently proportionate to gearing across all levels.

Syllabus area E4b

62.3 **C** Statement 1. MM (with tax) assumes increased gearing will always reduce the weighted average cost of capital ('WACC').

Statement 2: At low levels of gearing, the traditional view states financial risk is low, hence more inexpensive debt will reduce the WACC.

Statement 3 is not relevant: pecking order theory relates to a logical order for choosing finance based on convenience and issue cost.

Statement 4: MM (no tax) concludes that the gearing level will not affect the WACC.

Syllabus area E4a&b

62.4 **B** The traditional view has a 'u' shaped weighted average cost of capital ('WACC') curve hence there is an optimal point where WACC is minimised.

MM (with tax) assumes 100% gearing is optimal, so no balance with equity.

MM (no tax) assumes the WACC is unaffected by the level of gearing. It therefore follows as the WACC is the discount rate for the projects of the business that the value of the business is unaffected by the gearing decision.

Syllabus area E4a&b

62.5 **B** Pecking order theory suggests that as internal funds are free to raise and immediate they should be used first. After that, debt is relatively quick and inexpensive to raise, interest is tax deductible and the cost of debt is lower than the cost of equity. New equity is relatively expensive hence is considered last.

Syllabus area E4d

62.6 A B Co is being used as a proxy company and has a different level of gearing to TR Co

Ungear B Co's equity Beta:

$$ß_a = ß_e \times \frac{V_e}{\left(V_e + V_d(1-t)\right)}$$

$$= 1.05 \times \frac{4}{\left(4 + 1(1-0.3)\right)}$$

$$= 0.89$$

Syllabus area E3e

62.7 C Regear $ß_a$ using TR assumption of a gearing level of 1:3 debt:equity

$$ß_e = ß_a \times \frac{V_e + V_d(1-T)}{V_e}$$

$$ß_e = 0.89 \times \frac{3 + 1(1-0.3)}{3}$$

$$ß_e = 1.10$$

Put into CAPM:

Ke $= R_f + ß(E(r_m) - R_f)$ R_f:4%, $E(R_m) - R_f = 4\%$ (market premium)

Ke $= 4 + 1.10(4)$

$= $ **8.4%**

Syllabus area E3e

62.8 A An equity beta reflects both business risk and financial risk. An asset beta only reflects the former.

Syllabus area E3e

62.9 C A project-specific cost of capital is relevant to appraise a project with a different risk profile from current operations. In these circumstances the current weighted average cost of capital is not relevant – so proxy information is used to calculate a project specific cost of capital for that particular appraisal.

Syllabus area E3e

62.10 B Tax exhaustion typically refers to a situation where although interest payments are tax deductible, because tax expenses have already been eliminated completely, further interest payments cannot save any more tax, hence the cost of the additional debt is the gross cost (more expensive).

Syllabus area E3c

63 Tirwen Co

Text references. Sources of finance are covered in Chapter 12.

Top tips. This question looks at key areas of business finance and needs to be answered in sequence.

Easy marks. In part (a), the calculation of the theoretical ex-rights price per share. Make sure you are confident in calculating this.

In part (c) calculation of current EPS and earnings.

Examiner's comments. In part (a), almost all candidates calculated correctly the theoretical ex-rights price per share, but some calculated the value of rights per new share rather than per existing share. Some candidates disregarded the instruction to ignore issue costs. Answers to part (b) indicated that many candidates are unclear about the effect of a rights issue on shareholder wealth. Candidates could have calculated the current EPS in part (c) by dividing the share price by the PE ratio, but a significant number divided reserves by the number of shares.

			Marks
(a)	Theoretical ex rights price per share	2	
	Values of rights per existing share	1	
			3
(b)	Effect on wealth of exercising rights	2	
	Effect on wealth of sale of rights	2	
	Discussion of rights issues and shareholder wealth	2	
			6
(c)	Current earnings per share	1	
	Current earnings	1	
	Funds raised via rights issue	1	
	Interest saved by redeeming loan notes	1	
	Revised earnings	1	
	Revised earnings per share	1	
			6
			15

(a) (i) Issue price of new shares = 85% × $4.00 = $3.40. The theoretical ex-rights price = ((5 × $4.00) + $3.40)/6 = $3.90.

(ii) The value of rights per existing share = ($3.90 – $3.40)/5 = 10c

(b) Choices open to the investor are to either **refuse the offer**, **take up the offered rights** or **sell the rights** (or a combination).

If the investor does not subscribe to the offer, a loss of $100 will occur, being the difference between the value of 1,000 shares before the rights issue ($4,000) and the value of 1,000 shares after the rights issue ($3,900).

If the investor takes up the offered rights, he will purchase an additional 200 shares at $3.40 = $680. This will give the investor 1,200 shares at $3.90 each = $4,680. This is equal to the sum of the value of 1,000 shares before the rights issue ($4,000) plus the cash subscribed. As a result there is no overall change in wealth. Some cash has merely been transferred into shares.

If the rights are sold (1,000 rights at 10c each) then again there is no overall change in wealth. The $100 proceeds plus the value of the shares after the rights issue (1,000 shares at $3.90 each = $3,900) is the same as the value of the holding before the rights issue. Part of the wealth has been converted from shares into cash.

(c) Current EPS = share price QPE ratio = $4.00 Q15.24 = 26.25c

Number of shares = $2,000,000 Q50c = 4 million

Earnings = number of shares × EPS = 4m × 0.2625 = $1,050,000

Funds raised from rights issue = 4m Q5 = 800,000 × $3.40 = $2,720,000

Net of issue costs = $2,500,000.

If this is entirely used to redeem loan notes, this will save $2,500,000 @ 12% = $300,000

	$	
Earnings before tax	1,500,000	$1.05 m grossed up for 30% tax rate
Loan note interest	540,000	$4.5m @ 12%
Overdraft interest	87,500	$1.25m @ 7%
Current PBIT	2,127,500	
Revised interest cost	(327,500)	$540k + $87.5k – $300k
	1,800,000	
Tax at 30%	(540,000)	
Revised profit after tax	1,260,000	
Total new shares	4,800,000	
Revised EPS	26.25	

64 Food retailers 1

Text references. Sources of finance are covered in Chapter 12 and shareholder ratios in Chapter 1.

Top tips. In (a), as well as commenting on the P/E ratios given in the table, you could also calculate high and low P/E ratios for the year and use this information to illustrate the meaning of the ratio to investors.

In (b), it is possible to calculate the level of dividends using the share price information and the dividend yield, and then to calculate earnings using the share price information and the P/E ratio. These figures can then be used to calculate the dividend cover. However, it is quicker to take the inverse of the product of the two ratios, and this is the method illustrated in the suggested solution.

(a)   **Price-earnings ratio**

The **price earnings (P/E) ratio** is regarded by many as the most important yardstick for assessing the relative worth of a share. It is calculated as:

$$\frac{\text{Market price of share}}{\text{EPS}}$$

This can also be expressed as:

$$\frac{\text{Total market value of equity}}{\text{Total earnings}}$$

The P/E ratio is a measure of the **relationship** between the **market value** of a company's shares and the **earnings** from those shares. It is an important ratio because it relates **two key variables** for investors, the market price of a share and its earnings capacity.

Stock market appraisal

The value of the P/E ratio reflects the **market's appraisal** of the share's future prospects. In other words, if one company has a higher P/E ratio than another it is because investors either expect its earnings to increase faster than the other's, or they consider that it is a less risky company or in a more secure industry.

Influence of market efficiency

The level of the ratio will change directly in response to changes in the share price and may vary widely during the course of the year as **events alter investor perceptions**. The extent and timing of changes will depend on the **efficiency** of the market; the stronger the level of efficiency, the more the market will be able to anticipate events.

Comparisons

Earnings potential is strongly related to the sector in which the business operates, and therefore P/E **comparisons** are only valid in respect of **companies in the same market** sectors. They can be used in this case since all the companies are publicly quoted food retailers.

Price earnings ratios of companies being compared

Using the information given in the table, the P/E ratio for Axis is 13.0. This means that it would take thirteen years for the earnings from the share to equal the price paid for it. The ratio for Spin is 21.1, the higher ratio meaning that the time taken for the earnings to equal the price of the share is 21.1 years. The reason for the higher level is that investors expect earnings from Spin to rise at a faster rate than those from Axis. The P/E ratio gives no indication of itself as to *why* earnings are expected to increase at different rates, although possibilities include superior management quality or more aggressive investment plans.

Ply has a current share price of 63 cents and a P/E ratio of 14.2. Earnings for last year were therefore 4.437 cents per share (63/14.2). At its high point for the year when the share price was 112, the P/E ratio was 25.2, while at its low point, the P/E ratio was 12.2. The figures also demonstrate that Spin has the lowest level of volatility, Axis the highest. This appears to reinforce the point made above that investors are confident about Spin's prospects (hence the P/E ratio has not altered much over the year), but are rather less sure about Axis's future.

(b)   **Dividend cover**

The dividend cover is the number of times that the actual dividend could be paid out of current profits. It indicates the **proportion** of **distributable profits** for the year that is being **retained** by the company and the level of risk that the company will not be able to maintain the same dividend payments in future years, should earnings fall.

Calculation of dividend cover

In this case, the ratio must be approached by means of the dividend yield and the P/E ratio:

$$P/E = \frac{\text{Market share price}}{\text{Earnings}} \qquad \text{Div yield} = \frac{\text{Dividend paid}}{\text{Market share price}}$$

$$P/E \times \text{Div yield} = \frac{\text{Dividend paid}}{\text{Earnings}} \text{ (since the Market share price cancels out)}$$

This is the inverse of the dividend cover, and therefore:

Dividend cover = 1 ÷ (P/E × div yield)

	P/E	Div yield	P/E × div yield	Dividend cover
Spin	21.1	2.3%	0.4853	2.06 times
Axis	13.0	2.1%	0.2730	3.66 times

Comparisons

As with the P/E ratio, comparisons with other companies in the same sector are a lot more valuable than comparisons with companies in different sectors, as the 'typical rate' for different business sectors will vary widely.

Dividend covers of companies being compared

The lower level of dividend cover for Spin means that the company has paid out nearly **half** of its **earnings** in the form of dividends, while Axis has only paid out less than one third. This suggests that Axis has **retained a higher proportion of profits** for **reinvestment** within the business. If earnings are very volatile, the figures could suggest that Spin might have **problems** in continuing to **pay out dividends** at this level in the future. However as indicated above, the market appears confident about Spin's future, and rates Axis rather lower despite Axis retaining more funds for future expansion.

65 Food retailers 2

Text references. Sources of finance are covered in Chapter 12.

Top tips. Part (a) is a good illustration of the importance of being able to predict market sentiment, as there are various different standpoints the market could take.

(a) **Payment of dividends from reserves**

If a company pays dividends in excess of earnings, then this payment must be made out of **reserves**. The effect of this will be to **reduce the net asset value** of the business.

Reasons for payment from reserves

(i) The company believes that it must continue to pay a **high level of dividends** in order to **support the share price**. If profits for the year are too low to support the previous level of dividends, the directors may decide that it should make a payment out of reserves rather than reduce the level of dividends.

(ii) If a company has a **high level of reserves** for which it **cannot find** an attractive **investment opportunity**, it may decide that it is appropriate to repay part of those reserves to investors by means of a dividend payment.

Problems with payment from reserves

(i) The fall in the net asset value of the business may make it **more vulnerable** to a **takeover** bid.

(ii) The market may see the payment out of reserves as a **desperate measure** on the part of the directors, and this may trigger a **significant drop in the share price**.

(iii) Payment of dividends that are in excess of earnings could lead to a **shortage of cash** for the business.

(b) **Reasons for using bonds**

(i) **Bonds** are a **cheaper form of finance** than preference shares because loan note interest is tax deductible, unlike preference dividends.

(ii) **Bonds** are **more attractive** to **investors** because they are secured against the company's assets.

(iii) **Bond holders rank before preference shareholders** in the event of a liquidation.

(iv) **Issue costs** should be **lower for bonds** than for preference shares.

66 TFR Co

Text references. Gearing and capital structure are covered in Chapter 14.

Top tips. This question looks at the important area of assessing the financial implications of a financing decision. This is a time consuming question, which requires you to first produce forecast statements of profit or loss for four years. You will need to plan your answers carefully and really watch the time.

Easy marks. Part (b) should provide some easy marks and is an important topic to have learnt.

Marking scheme

			Marks
(a)	Forecast statements of profit or loss	2	
	Interest cover	2	
	Debt/equity ratio	2	
	Return on equity	2	
	Return on capital employed	2	
			10
(b)	Discussion of difficulties faced by small companies		5
			15

(a)   **Statements of profit or loss for TFR Co for the four-year period**

Year	Current	Year 1	Year 2	Year 3	Year 4
	$	$	$	$	$
Turnover	210,000	255,000	300,000	345,000	390,000
Expenses (80%)	168,000	204,000	240,000	276,000	312,000
Net profit (20%)	42,000	51,000	60,000	69,000	78,000
Interest (W)	2,000	11,000	8,750	6,500	4,250
Profit before tax	40,000	40,000	51,250	62,500	73,750
Tax (25%)	10,000	10,000	12,812	15,625	18,438
Profit after tax	30,000	30,000	38,438	46,875	55,313
Dividend (50%)	15,000	15,000	19,219	23,438	27,656
Retained profit	15,000	15,000	19,219	23,438	27,656
Equity finance	200,000	215,000	234,219	257,657	285,313
Debt finance	nil	75,000	50,000	25,000	nil
Interest cover (times)	21·0	4·6	6·9	10·6	18·4
Debt/equity (%)	nil	35	21	10	nil
Return on equity (%)	15	14	16	18	19
ROCE (%)	21	18	21	24	27
ROCE (%)*	19	16	20	23	26

*Including the existing and continuing overdraft in capital employed

Working

Annual interest (assuming the continuing overdraft is maintained at the current level)

Year 1 interest payment = 100,000 × 0·09 = 9,000 + 2,000 = $11,000

Year 2 interest payment = 75,000 × 0·09 = 6,750 + 2,000 = $8,750

Year 3 interest payment = 50,000 × 0·09 = 4,500 + 2,000 = $6,500

Year 4 interest payment = 25,000 × 0·09 = 2,250 + 2,000 = $4,250

(b)   **Difficulties faced by small firms when seeking finance**

Debt finance

The main handicap that small companies such as TFR Co face in accessing funds is the problem of **uncertainty.** A small company may not have the **business** history **nor larger track record** that larger organisations possess. Larger enterprises are subject by law to **more public scrutiny**; their accounts have to contain more detail and be audited, they receive more press coverage and so on. Because of the uncertainties involved, banks often use **credit scoring** systems to **control exposure.**

Because the information is not available in other ways, small companies will have to provide it when they seek finance. They will need to give a business plan, list of the firm's assets, details of the experience of directors and managers and show how they intend to provide security for sums advanced.

A common problem is often that the banks will be **unwilling** to increase loan funding without an increase in **security** given (which the owners may be unwilling or unable to give), or an increase in equity funding (which may be difficult to obtain).

A further problem is the **maturity gap**. It is particularly difficult for small companies to obtain medium term loans due to a mismatching of the maturity of assets and liabilities. Longer term loans are easier to obtain than medium term loans as longer loans can be secured with mortgages against property.

In general, banks tend to ask for **personal guarantees** from owners and will set interest rates at **higher levels** than those charged to larger companies. TFR Co has non-current assets which are much greater in terms of value than the amount of its overdraft and so the company may be able to offer these as security for a loan.

Equity finance

Small firms such as TFR often face an equity gap. There are unlikely to be any wealthy individuals willing to invest in this company because there are likely to be more attractive investments elsewhere. A major problem with obtaining equity finance can be the inability of the small firm to offer an easy exit route for any investors who wish to sell their stake.

Solutions

There are a range of solutions which have been created to help with these problems. A Business Angel network can bring potential investors and small companies together, with the added bonus that the Business Angel may have expertise and experience to offer that could be useful in a small company situation. The owner of TFR Co may wish to look into this possibility.

There may be other government initiatives designed to help small businesses which could also be investigated.

67 Echo Co

Text references. Dividend policy is covered in Chapter 13, gearing and capital structure in Chapter 14, and sources of finance in Chapter 12.

Top tips. This is a wide-ranging sources of finance question which really tests your knowledge of this area of the syllabus. It is important to address the requirements and it is also quite time pressured. Make sure you compare like with like when you compare the debt/equity ratio with the industry average.

Easy marks. You should be able to discuss dividends as a signal to investors and Modigliani and Miller fairly easily.

Examiner's comments. In part (a), many candidates calculated correctly the increased dividend per share and then offered very little by way of discussion in order to gain any further marks.

In part (b), the sector average debt/equity ratio (D/E) was provided, but many candidates chose to calculate capital gearing (D/(D + E)) in the mistaken belief that this was the debt to equity ratio. Comparison with the sector average gearing was therefore pointless, since the gearing ratios were on a different basis. Some candidates also calculated incorrectly the interest coverage, dividing interest into profit before tax or profit after tax, rather than into profit before interest and tax.

It was surprising to see many candidates attempting to calculate the cost of debt (internal rate of return) of the bond issue. The bonds were to be issued and redeemed at nominal value and so their cost of debt was the same as their interest rate, as these unnecessary calculations confirmed (where they were made correctly).

Marking scheme

			Marks
(a)	Discussion of proposal to increase dividend		5
(b)	Evaluation of debt finance proposal	2–3	
	Discussion of debt finance proposal	2–3	
		Maximum	5
			10

(a) **Proposal A – Increasing the dividend per share**

The dividend paid last year was $2m which equates to 20c per share (2/5 × 0.5). A 20% increase would result in a dividend payment of **24c**, a total dividend of $2.4m (2 × 1.2). This would **reduce dividend cover** from 3 times (6/2) to 2.5 times (6/2.4).

Dividends as a signal to investors

The ultimate objective in any financial management decisions is to **maximise shareholders' wealth**. This wealth is basically represented by the **current market value** of the company, which should largely be determined by the **cash flows arising from the investment decisions** taken by management

Shareholders will look at a number of factors when analysing investments and not just dividends. They will be particularly interested in the **business** and **financial risk** of the company and will not necessarily be impressed with a large increase in dividends.

The dividend declared can be interpreted as a **signal** from directors to shareholders about the strength of underlying project cash flows. Investors usually expect a **consistent dividend policy** from the company, with stable dividends each year or, even better, **steady dividend growth**.

Modigliani and Miller

Modigliani and Miller (MM) proposed that in a tax-free world, shareholders are indifferent between dividends and capital gains, and the value of a company is determined solely by the 'earning power' of its assets and investments.

MM argued that if a company with investment opportunities decides to pay a dividend, so that **retained earnings** are **insufficient** to finance all its investments, the shortfall in funds will be made up by **obtaining additional funds** from outside sources. If a company pursues a consistent dividend policy, 'each corporation would tend to attract to itself a clientele consisting of those preferring its particular payout ratio, but one clientele would be entirely as good as another in terms of the valuation it would imply for the firm'.

Conclusion

The proposal to increase the dividend should be rejected as it will not generate any additional funds for the company and shareholders will not necessarily be attracted by the increase.

(b) **Proposal B – Bond issue**

Gearing

Echo Co current debt/equity (book value basis) = 30/20 × 100% = 150%

After bond issue debt/equity = 45/20 × 100% = 225%

Average debt/equity = 80%

Echo Co is currently **very highly geared** with a debt to equity ratio based on book values of almost twice that of the average of similar companies. A bond issue would increase the gearing to even higher levels.

Interest coverage

Echo Co interest coverage ratio = 12/3 = 4 times

After bond issue interest coverage ratio = 12/(3 + 1.5) = 2.7 times

Average interest coverage ratio = 8 times

Echo Co currently has **half** the interest coverage of similar companies which indicates a much higher level of **financial risk.** The bond issue would further increase this risk and Echo could have difficulty making the interest payments.

The interest on the existing loan notes is $2.4m (8% × $30m) and the total interest charge in the income statement is $3m. This implies that Echo Co also has an **overdraft** which further increases the level of financial risk.

Lack of investment opportunities

There are currently no suitable investment opportunities available and the bond issue proceeds would be invested short-term. The return on short-term investments will be **lower** than the interest charged on the loan notes, so there will be an **opportunity cost** which will decrease shareholder wealth. There is a significant **risk** that a suitable investment opportunity requiring exactly $15m will not be found.

Loan redemption

The current loan notes are due to be redeemed in three years' time and this would be followed five years later by a repayment of the bond issue. This raises issues for the **financial planning** of the company which needs to consider how best to **refinance.**

Conclusion

The proposal to make a bond issue should be rejected as the level of financial risk is already too high.

68 Echo Beach Co

Marking scheme

			Marks
(a)	Theoretical ex rights price per share	1	
	Amount of finance raised	1	
	Evaluation of rights issue proposal	2–3	
	Discussion of rights issue proposal	3–4	
		Maximum	8
(b)	Discussion of attractions of leasing		7
			15

(a) **Proposal – Rights issue**

Rights issue price = $2.30 × 80% = $1.84

Theoretical ex-rights price

	$
4 shares @ $2.30	9.20
1 share @ $1.84	1.84
5	11.04

Theoretical ex-rights price (TERP) = 11.04/5 = $2.21

Number of new shares to be issued = (5/0.5)/4 = 2.5 million

Amount of finance that would be raised = $1.84 × 2.5m = $4.6 million

Gearing

Current debt/equity = 30/20 = 150%

After rights issue debt/equity = 30/24.6 = 122%

The rights issue would reduce the level of gearing to 122% but this is still higher than the average for similar companies.

Interest coverage

Current interest coverage ratio = 12/3 = 4 times

Current return on equity = 6/20 × 100 = 30%

Assuming the rate of return on the new equity will be the same:

After-tax return on the new funds = 4.6m × 30% = $1.38 million

Before-tax return on the new funds = 1.38m × (9/6) = $2.07 million

After rights issue interest coverage = (12 + 2.07)/3 = 4.7 times

The interest coverage ratio would improve after the rights issue but again, is still worse than the average for similar companies.

Purpose of the rights issue

The aim of the rights issue is to **reduce the level of gearing and the financial risk** of the company. To some extent, this would be achieved but, in order to make more of a significant impact, the level of debt would need to be reduced much further. The amount of refinancing required is much greater than $4.6m and there is no indication that a suitable investment has been identified.

Unless more information can be provided on how the rights issue proceeds could be effectively used, the rights issue proposal cannot be recommended.

Note: You could sensibly have assumed that the equity raised will be used to reduce debt – this will result in a different gearing calculation and interest coverage ratio

(b)   ### Operating leases

An operating lease is a lease where the lessor retains most of the risks and rewards of ownership. It is a rental agreement between a lessor and a lessee with the lessor **supplying** the equipment to the lessee. The lessor is **responsible** for **servicing and maintaining** the leased equipment

Protection against obsolescence

A key advantage of an operating lease for the lessee is that the equipment is leased for a **shorter period** than its expected useful life. In the case of high-technology equipment, if the equipment becomes out of date before the end of its expected life, the lessee does not have to keep on using it. The lessor will bear the risk of having to sell obsolete equipment secondhand.

Source of finance

As a source of finance, leasing is particularly attractive to small companies or those who find it **difficult to raise debt finance**. There is no commitment to interest payments, and no need to use existing assets for security. If the lessee gets into financial difficulties, the asset will simply be returned to the lessor who retains legal title.

Cost

The lessor may be able to obtain the asset at a **cheaper** price than the lessee. This can be due to bulk buying economies, lower finance costs and/or more effective use of tax benefits. The lower cost can then be passed on to the lessee in the form of lower lease payments.

Off-balance sheet financing

The leased equipment does not have to be shown in the **lessee's** published **statement of financial position**, and so the lessee's statement of financial position shows no increase in its gearing ratio.

69 Nugfer Co

Marking scheme

	Marks
Analysis of recent financial performance	1-3
Discussion of recent financial performance	1-3
Analysis of current financial position	1-3
Discussion of current financial position	1-2
Consideration of suitable sources of finance	4-6
Recommendation of suitable source of finance	1
Maximum	15

Nugfer Co wants to raise $200m of finance to fund the purchase of a competitor. In order to recommend a source of finance, the financial position of the company must be examined, looking at both past and expected future performance following the acquisition.

Recent financial performance

Looking at the financial information given, the following analysis can be made:

Year	20W7	20W8	20W9	20X0
	$m	$m	$m	$m
Revenue	122.6	127.3	156.6	189.3
Operating profit	41.7	43.3	50.1	56.7
Net profit margin	34%	34%	32%	30%
Revenue growth		3.8%	23.0%	20.9%
Operating profit growth		3.8%	15.7%	13.2%
Finance charges	6.0	6.2	12.5	18.8
Interest coverage ratio	7 times	7 times	4 times	3 times
Finance charge growth		3.3%	101.6%	50.4%
Profit after tax growth		4.0%	1.2%	0.8%

Geometric revenue growth

$$\sqrt[3]{\frac{189.3}{122.6}} - 1 = 0.156 = 15.6\%$$

Geometric operating profit growth

$$\sqrt[3]{\frac{56.7}{41.7}} - 1 = 0.108 = 10.8\%$$

The revenue growth of Nufger Co is encouraging, with significant growth of 23.0% and 20.9% in 20W9 and 20X0 respectively. However this has not been matched in operating profit growth which was only 15.7% in 20W9 and 13.2% in 20X0. With this, the operating profit margin has fallen from 34% to 30%. This suggests a lack of control of costs. With increased control over these costs, operating profit should increase which would make Nugfer Co more attractive to providers of finance.

A major area of concern in the increasing finance costs. Interest coverage has been falling year on year and a level of 3 times would be dangerous for most businesses. The overall increase in finance charges is over three times as a result of substantially increased borrowings. The reason for the increase is unknown, but Nugfer Co is showing signs of overtrading. The level of risk from the finance costs must be taken into account when selecting a source of finance for the acquisition.

Financial position

The current level of gearing will interest potential providers of finance. As Nugfer Co has a significant level of short-term borrowings, the gearing position should also be looked at including these borrowings as debt.

Long-term debt / Total equity = 100 / 221 = 0.45 = 45%

Long-term + short-term debt / Total equity = (100 + 160) / 221 = 1.18 = 118%

The mix of long-term debt and equity is not particularly high at 45%, although there is no comparison to the industry and the potential target has no debt at all. However the interest coverage suggests borrowings may be dangerously high, which is why short-term borrowings should also be considered. Short-term borrowings are greater than long-term borrowings and they constitute 62% of the total level of debt.

When including short-term borrowings, the gearing level increases to 118% which would concern many potential providers of finance. Short-term borrowings are also attracting a higher rate of interest at 8% than the long-term borrowings at 6%, meaning that the short-term borrowings account for the majority (68%) of the total finance charge.

Another factor to consider is that the long-term debt is due for repayment in 20X2, so Nugfer Co needs to plan for the redemption of the bond and any necessary refinancing of this debt when considering the source of the $200million.

Sources of finance

From the analysis above, Nugfer is unlikely to attract providers of debt finance due to high gearing and low interest cover. Debt finance does not appear to be a viable option.

If no further debt is raised, other sources of finance may be acceptable as interest coverage should improve after the acquisition, as the competitor has no debt. As a conservative estimate, assuming no operating profit growth for Nugfer, interest coverage will be

Projected interest coverage following acquisition = (56.7 + 28) / 18.8 = 4.5 times

Assuming that debt of $200million could be provided at 8%, the interest coverage would be

Debt funded acquisition interest coverage = (56.7 + 28) /(18.8 + 16) = 2.4 times

In addition the gearing (including short-term debt) would worsen to

(260 + 200) / 221 = 2.08 = 208%

This again highlights that debt finance would not be suitable. Convertible debt could be an option, but in the short-term the interest coverage would fall and gearing would be very high.. This would improve on conversion of the debt, but this would depend on the share price of Nugfer being high enough to make the conversion attractive. The uncertainty of this combined with the short-term increased risk makes convertible debt unsuitable.

Venture capital is unlikely as Nugfer is a listed company.

If equity finance was used, the interest coverage would improve to 4.5 times and the gearing level would become

260 / (221 + 200) = 0.62 = 62%

This level may be acceptable and could improve further if the short-term debt was paid off. As Nugfer currently has no cash assets this may be difficult to achieve. This also will not help to address the issue of redeeming the bonds in two years time.

As Nugfer has not paid any dividends in the last four years, current shareholders are unlikely to favour a rights issue, unless they were confident that the acquisition would generate cash flows that would enable future dividend payments.

New shareholders would also need to be convinced that the acquisition would provide cashflows to enable dividends if Nugfer wanted to undertake a new public issue or a placing of equity.

Nugfer has $300m of non-current assets, meaning that it may look at sale and leaseback to fund the acquisition. This would depend on the nature of the non-current assets, which is unknown. With high levels of existing debt, some of these assets may already be provided as security, meaning that the scope for raising finance by this method is limited.

It is possible that finance could be raised via a combination of the methods covered, but realistically the analysis shows that Nugfer is in a poor financial position and may not be able to raise the funds for the acquisition.

70 Nug Co

Text references. Sources of finance are covered in Chapter 12 and capital market efficiency in Chapter 18.

Top tips. For part (a) make sure that you discuss company specific factors and economic factors.

Easy marks. Part (b) provides easy marks for students with a knowledge of the efficient markets hypothesis.

Examiner's comments. For part (a) poorer answers did not show understanding of the relationship for a bond between market value, interest rate, period to redemption, redemption value and cost of debt.

Some answers to part (b) incorrectly stated that capital market efficiency was about the information available in the market, when in fact capital market efficiency is concerned with pricing efficiency, ie the nature of the information reflected in the market prices of traded securities.

Marking scheme

			Marks
(a)	Company-specific factors	2-3	
	Economic environment factors	2-3	
		Maximum	4
(b)	Weak form efficiency	2	
	Semi-strong form efficiency	2	
	Strong form efficiency	2	
			6
			10

(a) Interest rates on bonds will depend and economic environment factors and company specific factors.

Economic factors

The rate of interest will largely depend on the overall level of interest rates within an economy. This can be influenced by the economic cycle as interest rates generally fall in a period of recession and rise during times of economic growth. Monetary policy decisions made by central governments or central banks will also effect interest rates.

The duration of the bond will also have an affect. Short-term debt is usually cheaper than long-term debt, which is shown by the upward sloping yield curve. The upward sloping yield curve can be explained by liquidity preference theory, market segmentation theory and expectations theory and cannot be affected by a single company.

Company-specific factors

The interest rate will be influenced by the risks associated with the company and whether the bonds are secured or not.

Where bonds are not secured, investors are likely to demand a higher interest rate to compensate for the additional level of risk. A bond issue will normally be secured on specific non-current assets such as land and buildings.

Potential debtholders will assess the risk by looking at the ability of the company to meet its mandatory interest payments in the future which will involve assessing future profitability and cash flows. The ability to redeem the bonds upon maturity will also need to be considered.

(b)   There are three forms of capital market efficiency: weak form, semi-strong form and strong form.

Weak form efficiency

Weak form efficiency is about the information content of security prices and it is suggested that the share price reflects all relevant past information. Information about past prices is in the public domain and equally available to all players in the market, and thus if this form of the hypothesis is correct, no one player should be able to outperform the market consistently using past information.

Semi strong efficiency

The semi-strong form of the theory holds that in addition to responding to past information, the market also reflects all other knowledge that is publicly available and relevant to the share valuation. Once again, this form of the theory is based upon the assumption that all the knowledge upon which share price movements are based is in **the public domain** and **freely available**. Thus no single player or group of players should be able consistently to outperform the market using past and publicly available information.

Strong form efficiency

The strong form of the theory holds that the market price of securities reflects **all information** that is **available**. This includes knowledge of past performance and anticipated events as in the semi-strong form, and also **'insider' knowledge**. Thus no single player or group of players should be able consistently to outperform the market. This does not exist in the real world where individuals with 'insider' knowledge can outperform the market with their knowledge.

71 YNM Co

Text references. Financial position measures are covered in Chapter 1, sources of finance are covered in Chapter 12.

Top tips. You will need to work through the question methodically. The question requires the calculation of financial performance and financial position ratios and then a discussion of what these mean for YNM.

Marking scheme

	Marks
Financial performance – analysis and comment	2-3
Financial position – analysis and comment	2-3
Comment on shareholder value	2-3
Comment on dividend choices	2-3
Comment on proposal to raise new debt	2-3
Maximum	10

Year	20X6	20X7	20X8
Growth in PBIT		-9%	-5%
Finance charges growth		10%	4%
Profit for the period growth		-13%	-7%
Interest coverage ratio (times)	6.1	5.0	4.6
Payout ratio	55%	64%	
Earnings per share (cents)	90.5	78.4	73.1
Price/earnings ratio (times)	5.6	5.9	5.7
Dividend per share (cents)	50	50	
Dividend yield (on opening price)	8.4%	9.8%	
Share price growth	-14.1%	-10.0%	-9.2%
Total shareholder return	-5.7%	-0.2%	
Gearing (before debt issue) %			47%
Gearing (after debt issue) %			93%

Financial performance

The recent financial performance of YNM Co has been poor. Net operating profit and profit after tax have fallen each year, meanwhile finance charges have been increasing year on year. The share price has been falling each year too.

Despite this, YNM has still been making profits rather than losses even though profits have been declining. The rate of decrease for both profit before and after tax has been slowing each year, as an example profit before tax fell by 9% between 20X6 and 20X7 but fell by only 5% between 20X7 and 20X8. Profit for the period decreased by 13% in 20X7 but only fell by 7% in 20X8. The rate of growth in finance charges has similarly fallen from an increase of 10% in 20X7 to an increase of 4% in 20X8. YNM may have started to recover from its difficult position which could explain why it is seeking further funding to support its existing operations.

Financial position

Interest cover has fallen from 6.1 times to 4.6 times showing that financial risk has increased. This is increasingly further away from the industry average of 10 times. The current level of gearing is also higher than the industry average at 47% compared to 40%. This indicates that increasing the amount of debt for YNM may be dangerous.

Shareholder wealth

Indications are that shareholder wealth has been decreasing as shown by the fall in share price and the negative shareholder returns generated in 20X6 and 20X7. However it could be claimed that YNM is doing better than its competitors because it maintained the level of dividend in 20X6 and 20X7 even though this caused the payout ratio to increase from 55% to 64%.

The dividend choice

If the same dividend of $9.5million is made in 20X8 then the payout ratio would be 68% which is a small increase on 20X7. The dividend yield would be 11.0% (50/459) which is relatively high. The total shareholder return would be 1.7% ((50 + 417-459)/459) which would be the first positive figure for three years. However new debt investors may have issues with the company making a dividend payment when they are looking to raise additional debt finance.

If no dividend is paid in 20X8 then the shareholders will be disappointed. The current share price is $4.17 per share and given a cost of equity of 12% the market is expecting an unchanged dividend since $0.50/0.12 = $4.17. Therefore paying no dividend is likely to reduce the share price further and increase difficulty in obtaining additional finance. If YNM were to explain the reason behind paying no dividend in 20X8 then the fall may be reduced or even prevented.

New debt finance

Given YNM's current financial position and their level of financial risk shown by the low level of interest cover it is unlikely that they would be successful in issuing new debt. If $50million of debt was raised at the current interest rate (8%) then interest cover would fall to 2.7 times (25.3/(5.5+4)) and gearing would increase to 93% as calculated above. Given the high level of financial risk already present in YNM it is possible that a higher interest rate would be charged which would mean interest cover would fall even further.

A decision should also be made on whether the debt should be short, medium or long-term or even a mix of maturities. As the debt is to support ongoing operations a mix of short-term, such as overdraft finance, and long-term debt such as a term loan or bonds may be considered. As a result YNM would be exposed to short-term variable and long-term fixed interest rates. This may be useful in managing interest rate risk.

Given the current financial position of YNM it would be appropriate to consider other sources of finance.

Note: The above answer is more than a candidate would be expected to produce under exam conditions.

72 Bar Co

Text references. Rights issues are covered in Chapter 12.

Top tips. For part (b) it is necessary to both calculate and discuss the effect of using the issue proceeds to buy back debt. Ensure that you also address the unlikely assumption that the price/earnings ratio remains unchanged.

Easy marks. The calculation of the theoretical ex-rights price is straightforward.

Marking scheme

			Marks
(a)	Rights issue price	1	
	Theoretical ex-rights price	2	
			3
(b)	Nominal value of bonds redeemed	1	
	Interest saved on redeemed bonds	1	
	Earnings after redemption	1	
	Current price/earnings ratio	1	
	Revised share price	1	
	Comment on acceptability to shareholders	1-2	
	Comment on constant price/earnings ratio	1-2	
	Maximum		7
			10

(a) The rights issue price is at a 20% discount

$7.5 × 0.8 = $6 per share

Number of shares to be issued = $90m / $6 = 15 million shares

Current number of shares in issue = 60 million

Therefore the rights issue will be a 1 for 4 issue

Theoretical ex-rights price

	$
4 shares @ $7.50	30.00
1 share @ $6.00	6.00
	36.00

Theoretical ex-rights price (TERP) = 36/5 = $7.20

(b) The proposal to buy back the bonds will only be acceptable to shareholders if it increases shareholder wealth.

The bonds would be bought back at market price ($112.50), which is higher than the nominal value ($100). The nominal value of bonds that will be bought back is $90 million / $112.50 × $100 = $80 million.

Interest saved on these bonds = $80m × 0.08 = $6.4m per year

New annual interest charge = $10m – $6.4m = $3.6m

Revised profit before tax = $49m – $3.6m = $45.4m

Revised profit after tax (earnings) = $45.4m × 0.7 = $31.78m

Revised earnings per share = $31.78m/75m = 42.37 cents per share

Current earnings per share = $27m/60m = 45 cents per share

Current price/earnings ratio = 750/45 = 16.7 times

Assuming the price/earnings ratio remains constant, the revised share price will be

Share price = 16.7 × 42.37 = 708 cents or $7.08 per share.

This revised share price is less than the theoretical ex-rights price and therefore using the issue proceeds to buy back debt will not be acceptable to the shareholders as their wealth will have decreased.

This conclusion has been reached based on the assumption that the price/earnings ratio remains unchanged. However, the share price will be determined by the stock market and this will determine the price/earnings ratio, rather than the price/earnings ratio determining the share price. Buying back debt would decrease the financial risk of Bar Co and this could cause the cost of equity to fall since shareholders will be taking on less risk. This means the share price is likely to rise and therefore the price/earnings ratio will also increase. If the share price were to increase above the theoretical ex-rights price, which would mean the price/earnings ratio would be at least 17 times, the shareholders would find the debt buy back to be an acceptable use of funds as they would experience a capital gain.

73 IML Co

Text references. CAPM is covered in Chapter 15 and the efficient market hypothesis in Chapter 18.

Top tips. Discussion of the assumptions and limitations of CAPM carried most marks so don't overrun on time in parts (a) and (b). It may be worth writing down a few headings before you start your answer so that you don't forget to mention any of the main points.

(a)   The required rate of return on equity can be found using the capital asset pricing model:

$$E(r_i) = R_f + \beta_i (E(r_m) - R_f)$$

AZT Co

$E(r_i)$ = 5% + 0.7(15% − 5%)

= **12%**

BOR Co

$E(r_i)$ = 5% + 1.4(15% − 5%)

= **19%**

(b)   The equity beta for IML can be found using the same expression:

17% = 5% + β(15% − 5%) $E(r_i)$

$$\beta = \frac{(17\% - 5\%)}{(15\% - 5\%)}$$

The equity beta factor = 1.2

The equity **beta factor** is a measure of the volatility of the return on a share relative to the stock market. If for example a share price moved at three times the market rate, its equity beta factor would be 3.0. The beta factor indicates the level of **systematic risk**, the risk of making an investment that cannot be diversified away. It is used in the capital asset pricing model to determine the level of return required by investors; the higher the level of systematic risk, the higher the required level of return.

(c) **Assumptions and limitations of CAPM**

Diversification

Under the CAPM, the return required from a security is **related** to its **systematic risk** rather than its total risk. Only the risks that **cannot** be **eliminated** by diversification are **relevant.** The assumption is that investors will hold a **fully diversified portfolio** and therefore deal with the unsystematic risk themselves. However, in practice, markets are **not totally efficient** and investors do not all hold fully diversified portfolios. This means that total risk is relevant to investment decisions, and that therefore the relevance of the CAPM may be limited.

Excess return

In practice, it is difficult to determine the excess return $(R_m - R_f)$. **Expected rather than historical returns** should be used, although historical returns are used in practice.

Risk-free rate

It is similarly difficult to **determine the risk-free rate**. A risk-free investment might be a government security; however, interest rates vary with the term of the debt.

Risk aversion

Shareholders are risk averse, and therefore **demand higher returns** in compensation for increased levels of risk.

Beta factors

Beta factors based on historical data may be a **poor basis** for future **decision making**, since evidence suggests that beta values fluctuate over time.

Unusual circumstances

The CAPM is unable to forecast accurately returns for companies with low price/earnings ratios, and to take account of seasonal 'month-of-the-year' effects and 'day-of-the-week' effects that appear to influence returns on shares.

74 Li Co

Text references. Cost of capital in Chapters 15 and 16.

Top tips. Part (a) is another weighted average cost of capital calculation with the complications of preference shares and tax. Part (b) demonstrates why WACC should be used by companies for assessing investment. If you are unsure about this, think about the effect of the new funding and investments on the overall capital structure of the firm, and the implications of this for raising finance in the future.

(a) **Assumptions**

It is assumed that the **market prices** of the shares and loan notes are **quoted excluding dividend** and interest. Since the WACC is to be calculated based on market values, the cost of reserves can be ignored.

Cost of equity

The dividend valuation model taking into account growth will be used.

$$k_e = \frac{d_1}{p_2} + g$$

where:	k_e	=	cost of equity
	d_1	=	next year's dividends
	g	=	annual rate of growth in dividends
	p_0	=	market price of shares (ex div)
In this case:	k_e	=	4/80 + 0.12
		=	17.0%

Cost of preference shares

$$k_{pref} = d/p_0$$

where:
k_{pref}	=	cost of preference shares
d	=	preference dividend (9c)
p_0	=	market price of shares (72c)
k_{pref}	=	9/72
	=	12.5%

Cost of loan notes

It is assumed that the loan notes are irredeemable. The after tax cost to the company will be calculated.

$$k_d = \frac{i(1-T)}{p_0}$$

where:
k_d	=	cost of loan notes
i	=	annual interest payment (14c)
p_0	=	market price of loan notes (100c)
T	=	rate of tax (33%)
k_d	=	$\dfrac{14(1-0.33)}{100}$
	=	9.4%

Weighted average cost of capital (WACC)

	No in issue $	Market price $	Market value $
Equity	10,400,000	0.80	8,320,000
Preference shares	4,500,000	0.72	3,240,000
Loan notes	5,000,000	1.00	5,000,000
			16,560,000

$$\text{WACC} = 17.0 \left[\frac{8,320}{16,560}\right] + 12.5 \left[\frac{3,240}{16,560}\right] + 9.4 \left[\frac{5,000}{16,560}\right] = 13.8\%$$

(b) **Required rate of return**

It is not usually correct to regard the **required rate of return** for an individual project as the cost of the actual source of funds that will be used to finance it, even where the funds can be traced directly. Debt is cheaper than equity only because there is an **equity base** which takes the risk – if the equity funds were not there then the company could not borrow. Each year some profits should be retained to increase the equity base, thus allowing further borrowing to take place. The borrowing is not independent of equity funds, and thus it is appropriate to combine the two in arriving at the cost of capital to be used in project appraisal.

WACC

The WACC reflects the company's **long-term capital structure**, and therefore capital costs. The capital structure generally changes only very slowly over time, and therefore the marginal cost of new capital should be approximately equal to the WACC. The **WACC** is therefore a more appropriate yardstick for the evaluation of new projects.

75 FAQ

(a) **After-tax cost of debt**

Year		Cash flow $	Discount factor 10%	PV $	Discount factor 5%	PV $
0	Market value	(90)	1.000	(90.00)	1.000	(90.00)
1–10	Interest (net of tax)	7	6.145	43.02	7.722	54.05
10	Capital repayment	100	0.386	38.60	0.614	61.40
				(8.38)		25.45

The approximate cost of redeemable debt capital is, therefore:

$$5 + [\frac{25.45}{25.45 - 8.38} \times (10 - 5)] = 8.76\%$$

(b) **Project-specific beta**

$$\beta_a = \beta_e \frac{V_e}{V_e + V_d(1-T)}$$

where: β_a = asset beta

β_e = equity beta

V_e = proportion of equity in capital structure

V_d = proportion of debt in capital structure

T = tax rate

For the competitor company:

$$\beta_a = 1.4 \left(\frac{35}{35 + 65(1 - 0.30)} \right) = 0.609$$

Re-gearing:

$$\beta_e = \frac{\beta_a(V_e + V_d(1-T))}{V_e}$$

$$\beta_e = \frac{0.609(40 + 60(1 - 0.3))}{40} = 1.248$$

Cost of equity

$$E(r_i) = R_f + \beta(E(r_m) - R_f)$$

where: $E(r_i)$ = cost of equity

R_f = risk free rate of return

$E(r_m)$ = market rate of return

$E(r_i)$ = 6.75% + (12.5% − 6.75%) × 1.248 = 13.93%

WACC

$(13.93 \times 0.4) + (8.76 \times 0.6) = 10.83\%$

Note: This final step of calculating the WACC is shown for completeness and is unlikely to be tested in the exam.

(c)   **The capital asset pricing model**

The discount rate has been calculated using the **capital asset pricing model** (CAPM). The CAPM produces a required return based on the expected return of the market $E(r_m)$, the risk-free interest rate (R_f) and the variability of project returns relative to the market returns (β). Its main advantage when used for investment appraisal is that it produces a discount rate which is based on the **systematic** risk of the individual investment. Systematic risk is the market risk which cannot be diversified away. It can be used to **compare projects of all different risk classes** and is therefore superior to an NPV approach which uses only one discount rate for all projects, regardless of their risk.

Practical problems

Problems in estimating

It is **hard to estimate** returns on projects under different economic environments, market returns under different economic environments and the probabilities of the various environments.

Single period model

The CAPM is really just a **single period model**. Few investment projects last for one year only and to extend the use of the return estimated from the model to more than one time period would require both project performance relative to the market and the economic environment to be reasonably stable.

Complications over time

In theory, it should be possible to apply the CAPM for each time period, thus arriving at successive discount rates, one for each year of the project's life. In practice, this would exacerbate the estimation problems mentioned above and also make the discounting process much more cumbersome.

Risk-free rate

It may be **hard to determine the risk-free rate of return**. Government securities are usually taken to be risk-free, but the return on these securities varies according to their term to maturity.

Beta formula

There are also problems with using the **geared and ungeared beta formula** for calculating a firm's equity beta from data about other firms. It is difficult to identify other firms with **identical operating characteristics** and there may be **differences in beta values** between firms caused by different cost structures or size differences between firms.

76 Droxfol Co

Text references. Cost of capital is covered in Chapter 15.

Top tips. In part (a), you need to rearrange the formula given for the dividend growth model so that you can calculate the cost of equity. Remember to use market values in the formula for weighted average cost of capital.

The discussion in part (b) covers a very important and highly examinable area and you must be familiar with both the traditional view and that of Modigliani and Miller.

Easy marks. The cost of capital calculations are straightforward marks if you have practised.

		Marks
(a)	Calculation of market values	2
	Calculation of cost of equity	2
	Calculation of cost of preference shares	1
	Calculation of cost of debt	2
	Calculation of WACC	2
		9
(b)	Relative costs of equity and debt	1
	Discussion of theories of capital structure	3-6
	Conclusion	1
	Maximum	6
		15

(a) **Weighted average cost of capital**

Market values	$ million
Equity (5m × $4.50)	22.500
Preference shares (2.5m × $0.762)	1.905
10% loan notes (5m × (105/100))	5.250
	29.655

Cost of equity using dividend growth model $\quad = \quad \dfrac{D_0(1+g)}{P_0} + g$

$$= \quad \frac{35(1+0.04)}{450} + 0.04$$

$$= \quad 12.09\%$$

Cost of preference shares $= \dfrac{D}{P_0} = \dfrac{9}{76.2} = 11.81\%$

Cost of debt:

Year		Cash flow	Discount factor	PV	Discount factor	PV
		$	10%	$	5%	$
0	Market value	(105)	1.000	(105)	1.000	(105)
1 – 8	After tax interest	7	5.335	37.34	6.463	45.24
8	Redemption	100	0.467	46.70	0.677	67.70
				(20.96)		7.94

Using interpolation, cost of debt $\quad = a + \left(\dfrac{NPV_a}{NPV_a - NPV_b}\right)(b-a)\,\%$

$$= 5 + \left(\frac{7.94}{7.94 + 20.96} \times 5\right)$$

$$= 6.37\%$$

WACC = [(12.09% × 22.5) + (11.81% × 1.905) + (6.37% × 5.25)]/29.655 = 11.05%

(b) **Sources of finance**

The sources of long-term finance for Droxfol Co are ordinary shares, preference shares and loan notes and the rate of return expected by investors depends on the **relative risks** of each type of finance. Equity is the most risky and therefore has the highest cost of capital and the loan notes are the least risky with the lowest cost of capital.

Therefore, if we ignore taxation, the weighted average cost of capital would be expected to decrease if equity is replaced by debt.

Traditional view

In the **traditional view** of capital structure, ordinary shareholders are relatively **indifferent** to the addition of small amounts of debt so the WACC falls as a company gears up.

However, as equity is replaced by debt and gearing increases, **financial risk** will increase so the cost of equity will rise and this will offset the effect of cheaper debt.

The before-tax cost of debt will also increase at high levels of gearing due to the risk of bankruptcy and this **bankruptcy risk** will further increase the cost of equity.

A company can therefore gear up using debt and reduce its WACC to a **minimum**. When the WACC is minimised, the **market value** of the company, equal to the present value of its cash flows, will be maximised.

Beyond this minimum point, the WACC will increase due to the effect of increasing financial and bankruptcy risk.

Modigliani and Miller

In contrast to this traditional view, **Modigliani and Miller**, assuming a perfect market and ignoring tax, demonstrated that the WACC remained constant as a company increased its gearing. They argued that the increase in the cost of equity due to financial risk **exactly balanced** the decrease in WACC caused by the lower before-tax cost of debt.

In a perfect capital market, there is no bankruptcy risk so the WACC and therefore the market value of the company is constant at all gearing levels. The market value of a company depends on its **business risk** only. This means that Droxfol Co cannot reduce its WACC to a minimum.

However, corporate tax does exist and interest payments on debt reduce tax liability, so it could be argued that WACC falls as gearing increases and Droxfol Co could reduce its WACC to a minimum by taking on as much debt as possible.

The assumption of a perfect capital market is unrealistic and so bankruptcy risk and other costs of servicing debt will increase as gearing increases and this will offset the value of the tax shield.

Conclusion

In conclusion, Droxfol Co should be able to reduce its WACC by gearing up, but the minimum WACC achievable may be hard to determine.

77 Burse Co

Marking scheme

	Marks
Calculation of cost of equity	2
Calculation of cost of convertible debt	3
Calculation of cost of bank loan	1
Calculation of market values	2
Calculation of WACC	2
	10

Cost of equity

The required rate of return on equity can be found using the capital asset pricing model:

$E(r_i)$ = $R_f + \beta_i (E(r_m) - Rf)$

$E(ri)$ = 4.7% + (1.2 × 6.5%)

= **12.5%**

Cost of convertible debt

Conversion value = $P_0 (1 + g)^n R$

Where P_0 is the current share price

g is the expected annual growth of the share price

n is the number of years to conversion

R is the number of shares received on conversion

Conversion value = $5.50 × $(1 + 0.06)^6$ × 15

= $117.03 per bond

BPP
LEARNING MEDIA

We can therefore assume that **conversion will take place** as the conversion value is much greater than nominal value.

The **annual interest cost** net of tax will be $7\% \times (1 - 0.3) = \$4.90$ per bond

The cash flows will be as follows:

Year		Cash flow $m	10% discount factors	PV $m	5% discount factors	PV $m
0	Market value	(107.11)	1.000	(107.11)	1.000	(107.11)
1-6	Interest	4.90	4.355	21.34	5.076	24.87
6	Conversion value	117.03	0.564	66.00	0.746	87.30
				(19.77)		5.06

Calculate the cost of convertible debt using an IRR calculation.

$$IRR = a\% + \left[\frac{NPV_a}{NPV_a - NPV_b} \times (b - a) \right]\%$$

$$= 5\% + \frac{5.06\,(10\% - 5\%)}{5.06 + 19.77} = 6.02\%$$

The after tax cost of convertible debt is therefore 6.02%

Cost of bank loan

After-tax interest rate $= 8\% \times (1 - 0.3)$

$= 5.6\%$

Market values

Market value of equity $= 20m \times \$5.50 = \$110m$

Market value of convertible debt $= 29m \times 107.11/100 = \$31.06m$

Market value of bank loan $= \$2m$

Total market value $= \$(110.00 + 31.06 + 2)m = \$143.06m$

Weighted average cost of capital

$$WACC = \left(\frac{V_E}{V_E + V_D} \right) k_e + \left(\frac{V_D}{V_E + V_D} \right) k_d$$

In this case, we have two costs of debt so:

$$WACC = \left(\frac{110}{143.06} \right) \times 12.5\% + \left(\frac{31.06}{143.06} \right) \times 6.02\% + \left(\frac{2}{143.06} \right) \times 5.6\%$$

$= 9.61\% + 1.31\% + 0.08\%$

$= \mathbf{11\%}$

78 Purse Co

Marking scheme

			Marks
(a)	Discussion of business risk	2-3	
	Discussion of financial risk	2-3	
	Discussion of other relevant factors	1-2	
	Maximum	Maximum	7
(b)	Discussion of dividend growth model	2-4	
	Discussion of capital asset pricing model	2-4	
	Conclusion	1-2	
	Maximum	Maximum	8
			15

(a)   The weighted average cost of capital is the **average** cost of the company's finance and represents the average return required as compensation for the **risks** of the investment.

Business risk

The WACC can only be used if the **business risk** of the proposed investment is similar to the business risk of existing operations. This would involve the **expansion of existing business**. If the proposed investment is in a different type of business, a **project-specific cost of capital** should be used which reflects the changing risk. The technique to use involves changing the beta in the capital asset pricing model.

Financial risk

The WACC can only be used where the **existing capital structure** will be maintained. This means that the finance for the project will be raised in the **same proportions** as the existing finance.

The finance that is raised to fund a new investment might substantially change the capital structure and the perceived **financial risk** of investing in the company. If this is the case, again a project-specific cost of capital can be calculated which reflects the changing financial risk.

Size of the project

The WACC can only be used if the project being appraised is **small** relative to the company. If the project is large in scale, it is more likely to cause a change in risk and make the WACC inappropriate.

(b)   **Dividend growth model**

There are a number of problems with the dividend growth model. It uses a set figure for g which assumes that **dividends grow smoothly**. In reality, dividends change according to decisions made by managers who do not necessarily repeat historical trends. It is therefore very difficult to accurately predict the future dividend growth rate.

The other main problem is how to incorporate **risk**. The dividend growth model does not explicitly consider risk, particularly **business risk**. The company may change its area of business operations and the economic environment is notoriously uncertain. The **share price** will however fall as risk increases, leading to an increased cost of equity.

The model also ignores the effects of **taxation** and assumes there are **no issue costs** for new shares.

Capital asset pricing model

The main advantage that the CAPM has over the dividend valuation model is that it does **explicitly consider risk.** The CAPM is based on a comparison of the **systematic risk** of individual investments with the risks of all shares in the market. Systematic risk is risk that cannot be diversified away and an investor will require a **higher return** to compensate for higher risk. This higher return is the higher cost of equity that is calculated using the CAPM formula.

The formula does however require **estimates** to be made of **excess return**, the **risk-free rate** and **beta values**. All of these can be difficult to estimate, but are more reliable than the dividend growth rate used in the dividend valuation model.

Conclusion

The CAPM does explicitly consider risk and uses estimated values that are more reliable than those used in the dividend valuation model. It can therefore be said that CAPM offers the better estimate of the cost of equity of a company.

79 DD Co

Text references. Cost of debt and cost of capital are covered in Chapter 15 and dividend policy in Chapter 13.

Top tips. This question has a number of quite small parts and covers WACC calculation and dividend policy so plenty of straightforward marks are available, even if you get stuck on one part. Use your knowledge of interest rate theory in part (b), the question is asking why interest rates differ on the bonds.

Easy marks. The calculations are mostly straightforward and logical and should provide easy marks if you have practised these techniques.

Examiner's comments. In part (a) weaker answers treated the debt as irredeemable by dividing the annual interest by the market value of the bond. Some candidates calculated the after-tax cost of debt, even though the question said to ignore taxation and did not provide a tax rate. It is clearly essential to follow the instructions given in the question.

Part (b) asked students to discuss the reasons why different bonds of the same company might have different costs of debt. Many students failed to gain full marks here because they did not appear to understand the link between risk and return. Candidates who discussed reasons that related to the company, rather than to the bonds, failed to recognise that reasons had to relate specifically to differences between the bonds.

In part (c) a significant number of students showed that they had not studied well this part of the syllabus as they were simply stating that if the dividend went up, the share price went up, and vice versa. Answers that gained higher credit referred to a number of key issues in the debate on dividend relevance and dividend irrelevance, such as the clientele effect, the bird-in-the-hand theory, the signalling properties of dividends and the perfect capital market-based view of Miller and Modigliani.

Marking scheme

			Marks
(a)	Calculation of cost of debt of Bond A		3
(b)	Term structure of interest rates	1-2	
	Liquidity preference theory	1-2	
	Expectations theory	1-2	
	Market segmentation theory	1-2	
	Other relevant discussion	1-2	
		Maximum	6

(c)   Dividend irrelevance   3-4
       Dividend relevance   2-4
                                                             Maximum   6
                                                                                   ──
                                                                                   15

(a)   **Cost of debt of bond A**

The cash flows will be as follows:

Year		Cash flow $	10% discount factors	PV $	8% discount factors	PV $
0	Market value	(95.08)	1.000	(95.08)	1.000	(95.08)
1-10	Interest	9.00	6.145	55.31	6.710	60.39
10	Capital repayment	100.00	0.386	38.60	0.463	46.30
				(1.17)		11.61

Calculate the cost of debt using an IRR calculation.

$$IRR = a\% + \left[\frac{NPV_a}{NPV_a - NPV_b} \times (b-a) \right]\%$$

$$= 8\% + \frac{11.61}{11.61 + 1.17} \times (10-8) = 9.82\%$$

The **cost of debt** is therefore **9.82%**

(b)   **Different bonds and different costs of debt**

Risk

In general, the cost of a source of finance is related to its level of risk. The **higher** the risk, the **greater** the return expected by investors and therefore the higher the cost to the company. In this case, the bonds were issued at the same time by the company so business risk will not be a reason for the difference in cost of debt.

Security

Connected with the concept of risk and return is the amount of security offered. For example, a bond may be secured on a specific asset or group of assets. An unsecured bond will generally have a **higher** interest rate than a secured one. A lack of security therefore raises the cost of debt. There is no information to suggest a difference in security for Bond A and Bond B.

Time

The **yield curve** is normally upward sloping which means that long-term financial assets offer a higher yield than short-term assets. This is due to **liquidity preference** theory which states that investors prefer cash now to later and want **compensation** in the form of a **higher return** for being unable to use their cash now.

Longer dated bonds can therefore be expected to have a higher cost of debt than shorter dated bonds. Bond A has a greater time to maturity than Bond B so would therefore be expected to have a higher interest rate and cost of debt.

Size of debt

The amount of finance raised by Bond A is twice that of Bond B and that may have contributed to the higher cost of debt.

(c) Dividend policy and the share price

Dividends as a signal to investors

The ultimate objective in any financial management decisions is to **maximise shareholders' wealth**. If shareholder wealth is increased, it can be expected that the share price will rise. Shareholder wealth and therefore the share price should largely be determined by the **cash flows arising from the investment decisions** taken by management

Shareholders will look at a number of factors when analysing investments and not just dividends. They will be particularly interested in the **business** and **financial risk** of the company and will not necessarily be impressed with a large increase in dividends.

The dividend declared can be interpreted as a **signal** from directors to shareholders about the strength of underlying project cash flows. Investors usually expect a **consistent dividend policy** from the company, with stable dividends each year or, even better, **steady dividend growth**.

Modigliani and Miller

Modigliani and Miller (MM) proposed that in a tax-free world, shareholders are indifferent between dividends and capital gains, and the value of a company is determined solely by the 'earning power' of its assets and investments.

MM argued that if a company with investment opportunities decides to pay a dividend, so that **retained earnings** are **insufficient** to finance all its investments, the shortfall in funds will be made up by **obtaining additional funds** from outside sources. If a company pursues a consistent dividend policy, 'each corporation would tend to attract to itself a **clientele** consisting of those preferring its particular payout ratio, but one clientele would be entirely as good as another in terms of the valuation it would imply for the firm'.

Conclusion

Capital markets are only **semi-strong efficient**, not perfect, so the signalling power of a dividend and the existence of clienteles can be important. This implies that a change in dividend policy could affect DD Co's share price.

80 YGV Co

Text references. Cost of debt and weighted average cost of capital are covered in Chapter 15, sources of finance are explained in Chapter 12 and interest coverage and gearing in Chapter 14.

Top tips. In part (a) the choice of discount factors is not crucial and other rates could be used to get a slightly different cost of debt, and therefore, WACC.

Easy marks. The cost of debt calculation in part (a) is quite straightforward as are the interest coverage and gearing calculations in part (c).

Examiner's comments. In part (a) some candidates wrongly used the redemption value of $110 as the issue price, or wrongly used a redemption value of $100, when the question said that redemption was at a 10% premium to par.

For part (b) there were two possible answers about the effect of the bond issue on the WACC. If an answer assumed that the current overdraft was not included in the WACC calculation (even though the bond issue was replacing the overdraft), the bond issue caused a decrease in the WACC. However, if an answer assumed that the overdraft was included in the WACC calculation, the bond issue led to an increase in WACC, since the more expensive bond issue (after-tax cost of debt of 7.2%) was replacing a cheaper overdraft (after-tax cost of debt of 3.5%).

Many candidates did not state any of the assumptions underlying their calculations. The most obvious ones, perhaps, were the assumptions that the cost of equity was not affected by the bond issue, and that the share price was unchanged.

For part (c) although the question said 'calculate', many answers chose to discuss their findings, sometimes at length. This discussion was not asked for in this part of the question and students must learn to follow the question requirement.

(a) The after tax interest charge per bond is 9 × 0.7 = $6.30

Two discounts should be chosen, 6% and 8%

Year	0	1-10	10
	$	$	$
Cash flow	(100)	6.30	110
Discount factor @ 8%	1.000	6.710	0.463
Present value	(100.00)	42.27	50.93

Net present value = (6.80)

Year	0	1-10	10
	$	$	$
Cash flow	(100)	6.30	110
Discount factor @ 6%	1.000	7.360	0.558
Present value	(100.00)	(46.37)	61.38

Net present value = 7.75

Cost of debt = 6 + [(8 − 6) × 7.75 / (7.75 + 6.8)] = 6 + 1.1 = 7.1%

(b) Since YGV does not have any long-term debt the current weighted average cost of capital (12%) will be the current cost of equity.

The current market value of the equity is $4.10 × 10 million shares = $41 million.

Using the cost of debt calculated in part (a) the WACC after the bond issue will be

[(41m × 12%) + (4m × 7.1%)] / (41m + 4m) = 11.6%

Therefore the bond issue will reduce the WACC from 12% to 11.6%.

This calculation includes the assumption that the share price is unaffected by the issue of the bonds. This may not be the case in practice. This calculation has also excluded the overdraft, but given its size there is a case for including it as it may affect the return required by investors.

NOTE Calculations including the overdraft as debt were accepted

(c) (i) The current level of interest charge per year is $4.5m × 5% = $225,000

Current interest coverage ratio = PBIT/Interest

1m / 0.225m = 4.4 times

Interest on bonds after issue = $4m × 9% = $360,000

Interest on overdraft = $0.5m × 5% = $25,000

Total interest per year = $385,000

Interest coverage ratio with bond issue = 1m / 0.385m = 2.6 times

(ii) The current market capitalisation is $4.10 × 10 million shares = $41 million

Current gearing = zero (as no long-term debt)

Gearing following bond issue (debt/equity) = 4m / 41m = 9.8%

Alternatively if the overdraft is included in the calculations

Current gearing = 4.5m / 41m = 11.0%

Gearing following bond issue (debt/equity) = 4.5m / 41m = 11.0%

81 NN Co

Marking scheme

		Marks
Profitability	1-2	
Liquidity	1-2	
Legal and other restrictions	1-2	
The need for finance	1-2	
The level of financial risk	1-2	
The signalling effect of dividends	1-2	
	Maximum	10
		10

Dividend policy will depend on a number of factors

Profits and retained earnings

The company needs to remain profitable. Dividends are paid out of profits, and an unprofitable company cannot for ever go on paying dividends out of retained profits made in the past.

Law

Company legislation may make companies bound to pay dividends solely out of accumulated net realised profits, as in the UK.

Other restrictions

There may be other dividend restraints that might be imposed, such as covenants in loan agreements.

Liquidity

Since dividends are a cash payment, and a company must have enough cash to pay the dividends it declares without compromising its day-to-day operations.

If the company has to repay any debt in the near future, then this will also need to be considered.

Gearing

If gearing is high, then low dividend payments can help to keep retained earnings high which will then reduce the level of gearing as the level of reserves will be higher.

The signalling effect

Although the market would like to value shares on the basis of underlying cash flows on the company's projects, such information is not readily available to investors in a semi-strong form efficient market. But the directors do have this information so information asymmetry exists. The dividend declared can be interpreted as a signal from directors to shareholders about the strength of underlying project cash flows.

Investors usually expect a consistent dividend policy from the company, with stable dividends each year or, even better, steady dividend growth.

The need for finance

Another factor is the ease with which the company could raise extra finance from sources other than retained earnings. Small companies which find it hard to raise finance might have to rely more heavily on retained earnings than large companies.

Inflation

The effect of inflation means that there is a need to retain some additional profit within the business just to maintain its operating capability unchanged.

82 NNN Co

Text references. Business valuations are covered in Chapter 17, cost of capital in Chapter 15.

Top tips. For part (a) it is important to remember to use the after tax interest payment in the IRR style calculations. Although the discount rate used can vary it is sensible to start off with the cost of debt if the debt was irredeemable and add in the annualised capital profit made between now and redemption.

In part (b) don't get confused by the fact that there are three elements to the WACC.

Easy marks. The business valuation calculations are straightforward.

Examiner's comments. Answers that did not gain full marks to part (a) contained errors such as using the wrong tax rate (it was 25%), addition or multiplication errors, using the before-tax interest payment, or putting incorrect values to variables in the linear interpolation calculation.

Marking scheme

			Marks
(a)	Correct use of taxation	1	
	Calculation of after-tax cost of debt	3	
			4
(b)	Cost of preference shares	1	
	Market value of equity	1	
	Market value of preference shares	1	
	Market value of debt	1	
	Weighted average cost of capital	2	
			6
			10

(a)   The cost of redeemable debt is found by an IRR style calculation using linear interpolation.

The annual after tax interest payment is $7 \times (1 - 0.25) = \$5.25$

Year		Cash flow $	Discount factor 5%	PV $	Discount factor 4%	PV $
0	Market value	(103.50)	1.000	(103.50)	1.000	(103.50)
1–6	Interest	5.25	5.076	26.65	5.242	27.52
6	Capital repayment	100.00	0.746	74.46	0.790	79.90
				(2.25)		3.02

The approximate cost of redeemable debt capital is, therefore:

$(4 + \dfrac{3.02}{(3.02 - 2.25)} \times 1) = 4.6\%$

Note: The cost of debt will vary depending on the discounts rates used. Other values calculated for the cost of debt would also be acceptable.

(b)   Preference dividend = 8% × 50 cents = 4 c per share

Cost of preference shares

$$k_p = \frac{d}{P_0} = 4/67 = 0.06 = 6\%$$

Number of ordinary shares = 100m (from part (a))

Market value of equity V_e = 100m × 8.30 = $830m

Number of preference shares = 25/0.5 = 50m shares

Market value of preference shares V_p =50m × 0.67= $33.5m

Market value of long-term borrowings = V_d =20m × 103.50/100 = $20.7m

Market value of company = $V_e + V_d + V_p$ =830 + 33.5 + 20.7 = $884.2m

$$WACC = \left[\frac{V_e}{V_e + V_d + V_p}\right] k_e + \left[\frac{V_d}{V_e + V_d + V_p}\right] k_d (1 - T) + \left[\frac{V_p}{V_e + V_d + V_p}\right] k_p$$

WACC = (830/884.2) × 0.12 + (33.5/884.2) × 0.06 + (20.7/884.2) × 4.6 = 11.6%

83 AQR Co

Text references. Weighted average cost of capital is covered in Chapter 15 as well as the factors that influence the market value of bonds.

Top tips. For part (b) you need to identify that the formula for the market value of bonds contains the elements to be discussed.

Easy marks. Part (a) is a WACC calculation that candidates should be able to obtain good marks for.

Examiner's comments. Some answers treated existing bonds as irredeemable and used the after-tax cost of debt provided as a before-tax interest rate. This implies learning a WACC calculation method without understanding the underlying principles, leading to an attempt to make the information provided fit the calculation method learned. There were also a significant number of errors in calculating the cost of equity using the dividend growth model. Alarm bells should sound if the calculated cost of equity is less than the cost of debt, or if the calculated cost of equity is quite large. A glance through past examination papers will show that a realistic approach has been used, with the cost of equity lying between say 5% and 15%.

Marking scheme

		Marks	
(a)	Calculation of cost of equity using DGM inc calc dividend growth rate	2	
	Calculation of market weights	1	
	Calculation of pre-issue WACC	1	
	Correct use of tax as regards new debt	1	
	Setting up linear interpolation calculation	1	
	Calculating after-tax cost of debt of new debt	1	
	Calculation of post issue WACC	1	
	Comment	2	
			10
(b)	Amount of interest payments	1-2	
	Frequency of interest payments	1-2	
	Redemption value	1-2	
	Period to redemption	1-2	
	Cost of debt	1-2	
	Convertibility	1-2	
	Maximum		5
			15

(a)   **Cost of equity**

Geometric average growth rate = $\sqrt[4]{(21.8/19.38)} - 1 = 0.0298 = 2.98\%$ or 3%

Putting this into the dividend growth model gives $k_e = 0.03 + ((21.8 \times 1.03)/250)$

= 0.03 + 0.09 = 0.12 = 12%

Market values of equity and debt

Market value of equity = V_e = 100m × 2.50 = \$250 million

Market value of bonds = V_d = 60m × (104/100) = \$62.4 million

Total market value = \$250 million + \$62.4 million = \$312.4 million

WACC Calculation

The current after tax cost of debt is 7%

$$WACC = ((k_e \times V_e) + (k_d(1-T) \times V_d)/(V_e + V_d))$$

$$= ((12 \times 250m) + (7 \times 62.4m))/312.4m$$

$$= 11\%$$

Cost of debt

After-tax interest payment = 100 × 8% × (1 − 30%) = 5.6%

Year		Cash flow $	5% discount factors	PV $	6% discount factors	PV $
0	Market value	(100.00)	1.000	(100.00)	1.000	(100.00)
1-10	Interest	5.60	7.722	43.24	7.360	41.22
10	Capital repayment	105.00	0.614	64.47	0.558	58.59
				7.71		(0.19)

Calculate the cost of debt using an IRR calculation.

$$IRR = a\% + \left[\frac{NPV_a}{NPV_a - NPV_b} \times (b-a) \right]\%$$

$$= 5\% + \frac{7.71(6\% - 5\%)}{7.71 + 0.19}$$

$$= 5.98\% \text{ or } 6\%$$

Note: Other discount factors and therefore costs of debt are acceptable.

Revised WACC Calculation

Market value of the new issue of bonds is \$40 million

New total market value = \$312.4m + \$40 m = \$352.4m

Cost of debt of bonds is 6% (from above)

$$WACC = ((12 \times 250m) + (7 \times 62.4m) + (6 \times 40m))/352.4m$$

$$= 10.4\%$$

The debt issue has reduced the WACC. This is because of the additional of relatively cheap debt. Gearing up in this manner would usually be assumed to increase financial risk however – this hasn't been included in the above calculations.

(b)   The factors influencing the market value of bonds can be found in the bond valuation formula

$$P_0 = \frac{i}{(1+k_{d\,net})} + \frac{i}{(1+k_{d\,net})^2} + ... + \frac{i+p_n}{(1+k_{d\,net})^n}$$

Interest payment amount

As the amount of the interest payment increases, so will the market value of the bond as the reward for owning the bond is higher.

Interest payment frequency

If interest payments are paid at a greater frequency than annually then the present value of the interest payments will be higher and so will the market value.

Cost of debt

The cost of debt is the rate of return required by bond investors and is influenced by the perception of the company and its level of risk. This may be indicated by the company credit rating. As the cost of debt increases, the present value of the interest payments decrease as does the market value of the bond.

Redemption value

Market value will increase with a higher redemption value as the reward for owning the bond increases.

Period to redemption

The period to redemption can affect the market value in two ways: the value of the bond may be lower as the capital repayment is further in the future or it may be higher as there will be more interest payments offered.

84 Corhig Co

Text references. The price/earnings ratio method and the dividend valuation model are covered in Chapter 17. CAPM is discussed in Chapter 15.

Top tips. For part (a), you will need to select the future earnings value to use for the P/E valuation, and justify your choice. As a rule, future earnings are better than past earnings. The dividend valuation in part (b) is slightly tricky, because dividend growth becomes constant only after year 3 – the dividend growth model valuation therefore has to be discounted from year 3 back to year 0. Remember to comment on the two WACCs in part (c).

Easy marks. Part (c) is a WACC calculation that candidates should be able to obtain good marks for.

Examiner's comments. Many students struggled with part (a).

In part (b), most answers struggled to use the dividend valuation model to value the company. Most answers limited their valuation attempt to using the valuation growth model, ignoring the dividend expected in year 2. A useful point to remember with a question such as this, is that it is essential to pin down the amount and timing of future cash flows when calculating present values.

Marking scheme

		Marks	
(a)	Price/earnings value using year 1 earnings	1	
	Price/earnings value using average earnings	1	
	Discussion of variables	2	
			4
(b)	Calculation of current cost of equity using CAPM	1	
	PV of year 2 dividends	1	
	PV of year 3 dividends	1	
	Year 3 DGM value	2	
	Company value using dividend valuation model	1	
			6

(c) After-tax cost of debt   1
After-tax WACC   1
Revised cost of equity using CAPM   1
Revised after-tax WACC   1
Comment on change in WACC   1
                                          5
                                          ──
                                          15

(a) The value of the company can be calculated using the P/E ratio valuation as:

Expected future earnings x P/E ratio

Using the Corhig Co's forecast earnings for Year 1, and taking the average P/E ratio of similar listed companies, Corhig Co can be valued at $3m x 5 = $15m.

Future earnings

The valuation above does not take into consideration the fact that earnings are expected to rise by 43% over the next three years. Instead of using Year 1 earnings, we may wish to use average expected earnings over the next three years of $3.63m. This would give us a valuation of $18.15m.

Although the valuation above still ignores the forecast 3% pa rise in earnings after Year 3 (which some may argue is too uncertain), the value of $18.15m may be more appropriate.

P/E ratio

The P/E ratio of 5 is taken from the average of similar listed companies. However, P/E ratios vary from company to company depending on each company's business operations, capital structures, gearing, and markets. The ratio used here is therefore subject to a high degree of uncertainty. An inaccurate P/E ratio would call the valuation into question, as it is so crucial to the calculation.

Corhig Co is listed, so it would be much more appropriate to use the company's own current P/E ratio instead.

(b) The current cost of equity can be calculated using the Capital Asset Pricing Model ('CAPM'):

$E(rf) = Rf + Bi (E(Rm) - Rf)$

$E(rf) = 4 + 1.6 \times 5 = 12\%$

PV of Year 2 dividend = 500,000 × 0.797 = $398,500

PV of Year 3 dividend = 1,000,000 × 0.712 = $712,000

PV of dividends after Year 3

PV at Year 3 using the dividend growth model = (1,000,000 × 1.03)/0.12 – 0.03) = $11,444,444

PV of these dividends at Year 0 = 11,444,444 x 0.712 = 8,148,444

Total market value based on PV of future dividends = $399k + $712k + $8,148k = $9,259k or approximately $9,300k.

Alternative calculation:

Using Year 3 dividend as D1

PV of dividends from Year 3 onwards at Year 2 = $1,000k/ (0.12 – 0.03) = $11,111,111

PV of these dividends at Year 0 = 11,111,111 × 0.797 = $8,855,555

Adding the PV of the Year 2 dividend of $398,500, this gives a market value of $9,254k which approximates to $9,300k.

(c) **Current WACC**

Cost of equity = 12% (CAPM as calculated in part b above)

After-tax cost of debt = 5% (1 − 0.2) = 4%

Current after-tax WACC = 12 × 75% + 4 × 25% = 10%

WACC after new debt issue

Cost of equity = Rf + Bi (E(Rm) − Rf) = 4 +2 × 5 = 14%

After-tax cost of debt = 6 × (1 − 0.2) = 4.8%

Revised after-tax WACC = 14 ×60% + 4.8 × 40% = 10.32%

Comment

Corhig Co's WACC will increase slightly after the new debt issue, from 10% to 10.32%. Both the cost of equity and the cost of debt will rise after the debt issue. However, their overall impact on WACC is reduced because Corhig Co will be relying more on debt finance (from 25% of long-term capital employed to 40%), which is cheaper than equity.

85 BKB Co

Text references. WACC is covered in Chapter 15.

Top tips. If you know your formulas well, the calculations in part (a) should be straightforward. You should know that overdrafts should not be considered as part of the capital structure.

You will need to apply logic in answering part (b).

Easy marks. Marks are available for straightforward calculations in part (a).

Examiner's comments. Part (a) Few answers were able to calculate correctly the cost of the preference shares and some answers chose to use the dividend percentage relative to nominal as the cost of capital, or to assume a value for the cost of capital. Some answers mistakenly calculated the after-tax cost of the preference shares. As preference shares pay a dividend, which is a distribution of after-tax profit, they are not tax-efficient. A common error was to mix bond-related values (such as the $4.90 after-tax interest payment) with total debt-related values (such as the $21 million market value of the bond issue), producing some very high values in the linear interpolation calculation. Some candidates were unable to calculate the future share price as part of the conversion value calculation. Most candidates were able to calculate a WACC value, although some omitted the cost of preference shares from the calculation. **Part (b)** Many answers were not of a high standard and tried to make some general points about market efficiency or about the window-dressing of financial statements. The important point here is that the weightings used in the WACC calculation need to reflect the relative importance of the different sources of finance used by a company if the WACC is to be used in investment appraisal.

Marking scheme

		Marks
(a)	Calculation of cost of equity using CAPM	1
	Calculation of bond market price	0.5
	Calculation of current share price	0.5
	Calculation of future share price	1
	Calculation of conversion value	1
	After-tax interest payment	1
	Setting up interpolation calculation	1
	Calculation of after-tax cost of debt	1
	Calculation of cost of preference shares	1
	Calculation of after-tax WACC	2
	Explanation of any assumptions made	1
		11

(b) Market values reflect current market conditions   1-2

     Market values and optimal investment decisions   1-2

     Other relevant discussion or illustration   1-2

                                           Maximum $\frac{4}{15}$

(a) **Equity**

The MV of equity is given as $125m.

CAPM: $E(r_i) = R_f + \beta_i(E(r_m) - R_f)$

R_f = Risk-free rate = 4%

β_i = Equity beta = 1.2

$(E(r_m) - R_f)$ = Equity risk premium = 5%

Therefore the cost of equity = 4% + 1.2 × 5% = 10%

Convertible bonds

Assume that bondholders will convert if the MV of 19 shares in five years' time is greater than $100.

MV per bond = $100 × $21m/$20m = $105

MV per share today = $125m/25m = $5

MV per share in five years' time = $5 × 1.04^5 = $6.08 per share

Conversion value = $6.08 × 19 = $115.52

The after-tax cost of the convertible bonds can be calculated by linear interpolation, assuming the bondholders will convert.

Time	Cash flow $	Discount factor (7%)	Present value $	Discount factor (5%)	Present value $
0	(105)	1	(105)	1	(105)
1-5	4.9**	4.100	20.09	4.329	21.21
5	115.52	0.713	82.37	0.784	90.57
			(2.54)		6.78

** after-tax interest payment = 7 × (1 − 0.3) = $4.90 per bond

Cost of convertible bonds = 5 + [(7 − 5) × 6.78/6.78 + 2.54)] = 5 + 1.45 = 6.45%

Preference shares

After-tax cost of preference shares = 5% × $10m/$6.25m = 8%

WACC

Total value = $125m + $21m + $6.25m = $152.25m

After-tax WACC = [($125m ×10%) + ($21m × 6.45%) + ($6.25m × 8%) / $152.25m]

After-tax WACC = 9.4% per year

Note: As overdraft represents a short-term source of finance, it has been assumed not to form part of the company's capital and has therefore been excluded from the WACC calculation. The overdraft is large, however, and seems to represent a fairly constant amount. The company should evaluate whether it should be taken into account.

(b) Market values are preferable to book values when calculating WACC, because they reflect the current value of the company's capital.

If book values are used instead of market values, this will seriously understate the proportion that equity represents in the company's capital structure. This is because the market value of ordinary shares is usually significantly higher than its nominal book value.

Understating the impact of the cost of equity on the WACC will most likely cause the WACC to be understated, since, as we can see in the answer above, the cost of equity is greater than the cost of debt. Under-estimating the WACC will skew the company's investment appraisal process as a lower discount rate is used, and cause the company to sub-optimal investment decisions.

Using book values instead of market values will also change the value of debt in the company's capital structure. The impact of understating or overstating the value of debt would be less significant than is the case for equity, because debt instruments are often traded at close to their nominal value (par).

86 Zigto Co

Text references. Interest rate risk is covered in Chapter 20, overtrading in Chapter 4 and factoring in Chapter 5.

Top tips. This is a fairly easy question on which good marks should be available. Start by thinking about how the objectives of shareholders may differ from those of the directors (the agency problem) and then apply the ideas to SMEs.

Easy marks. Easy marks are available in knowledge-based questions such as this.

Examiner's comments. Many answers gained high marks. Where answers did not gain high marks, it was usually because they did not focus on 'the factors to be considered', but discussed instead different sources of finance.

Marking scheme

		Marks
Factors to consider when choosing source of debt	4-6	
Factors considered by providers of finance	4-6	
	Maximum	10

Factors Zigto Co should consider

Availability. The kinds of debt finance available to Zigto Co will be restricted by the size of its business. A medium-sized unlisted company such as Zigto Co may not have access to capital markets, so traded securities may not be an option. Bank loans are more likely to be Zigto Co's chosen source of debt finance.

Cost. The issue cost, rate of interest on the borrowing and repayment terms all need to be considered. Some bank loans require an annual capital repayment, and there may be early repayment penalties. The more Zigto Co can reduce the risks associated with the borrowing, for example by offering security or a guarantee from the directors, would reduce the cost of borrowing.

Maturity. The term of the debt should match the period over which finance is required. Zigto Co will also need to consider for how long it can commit itself to financial obligations, and when it will be able to make the capital repayment. Short-term finance is usually more flexible than long-term finance.

Financial risk. Debt will increase Zigto Co's gearing, and thus increase its financial risk. Zigto Co will need to consider how this change in gearing may impact on how the company is perceived by future investors.

Factors finance providers will consider

Ability to meet financial obligations. Finance providers will want to be sure that Zigto Co will be able meet its financial obligations. The amount and terms of the debt funding they are willing to provide will depend on the risks associated with the company. The finance provider will consider Zigto Co's previous financial record as well as the business plan for the expansion to evaluate the risks involved. The higher the perceived risks, the more expensive the debt finance will be.

Security/guarantees. Especially when lending to an SME, finance providers are likely to require assets as security and/or a guarantee from the directors. This reduces the risk of loss should the company default on its debt. If security is not available, the finance providers will demand a higher level of return (a higher rate of interest) to compensate for the greater risks they undertake.

Legal restrictions on borrowing. The finance providers will ascertain that there are no legal restrictions on the amount of debt Zigto Co is able to take on, either in the company's Memorandum of Association or in existing debt contracts. At the same time, finance providers may also wish to add legal restrictions in their debt contract, in the form of restrictive covenants. Zigto Co should be aware of such covenants, as they are likely to affect the company's investment and funding policies going forward.

87 MCQ bank – Business valuations

87.1 **C**   The replacement value of the business attempts to calculate the cost of setting up an equivalent venture. This is more than simply tangible assets, it includes intangibles such as brand value, customer and supply networks, and intellectual property. It is practically very difficult to calculate.

Syllabus area F2a

87.2 **C**   Statement of financial position value of equity = ordinary shares + reserves = (1 + 5=) $6 million.

Net book value of revalued assets = $10m × 3/10 = $3m.

Professional valuation of revalued assets = $1m; (3 – 1 =) $2m lower than net book value.

Number of shares = $1m / $1 per share = 1 million shares.

Realisable value per share = ($6m – $2m) / 1 million shares = $4 per share.

Syllabus area F2a

87.3 **A** $P_0 = \dfrac{D_0(1+g)}{(r_e - g)}$ Given on the formula sheet

Growth 'g' – Dividends grew from ($0.50-$0.10=) $0.40 to $0.50 in 3 years. This is an average annual growth rate of:

$0.40 (1+g)^3 = $0.50

$(1+g) = {}^3\sqrt{(0.5/0.4)}$

g = 0.077 = 7.7%

$P_0 = \dfrac{\$0.50(1+0.077)}{(0.10-0.077)} = \$23.41$

Syllabus area F2c

87.4 **A**   Statement 1 needs to be assumed: If D_0 is not typical, a better valuation would include the dividend that would have been paid if D_0 were in line with historical trends.

Statement 2 needs to be assumed: Only one rate for growth is included in the formula.

Statement 3 needs to be assumed: Only one cost of equity is included in the formula.

Statement 4 does not need to be assumed: Minority shareholders are entitled to dividends only, hence this valuation technique is in fact best suited to a minority shareholding.

Syllabus area F2c

87.5 B The maximum A Co should pay is the value that B Co would add to the group.

Value of A Co currently	= $4m × 21	= $84 million
Value of combined group	= $6.5m × 19	= $123.5 million
Difference – value added		= $39.5m

Syllabus area F2b

87.6 C For DD Co, P/E = 12, Earnings yield (=1/(P/E ratio) = 0.0833 = 8.3%.

For competitor, P/E (= 1/earnings yield) = 10, Earnings yield = 10%.

Syllabus area F2b

87.7 D Corporation tax is not relevant as investors pay market price and they receive the gross dividend.

Redemption value = ($100 × 1.15=) $115 cash or conversion value = $P_0(1+g)R$ = $(4 \times 1.1^3 \times 25=)$ $133.10 worth of shares.

Investors would opt to convert, hence the redemption value built into market price will be $133.10.

Time		$	Discount factor 10%	Present value $
1-3	Interest	9	2.487	22.383
3	Redemption	133.10	0.751	99.9581
				122.3411

So current market value = $122.34

Syllabus area F3a

87.8 D Market capitalisation refers to the total value of a company's share capital as valued by the capital markets / stock exchange.

Syllabus area F4b

87.9 C Options 1 and 3 do not consider intangible assets such as brand value, intellectual property and supply networks.

As the cost of setting up an equivalent venture is less than the net present value of the current business, the former is the maximum HAL Co should pay for SO Co.

Syllabus area F2a

87.10 A Should NCW Co purchase CEW Co it will acquire a cash flow of ($10 + 2 =) $12m per annum assuming it invests the $6m in new machinery. (Note: it should do this as its net present value = $2m/0.1 – $6m = $14m.)

Therefore the value would be: $12m/0.1 – $6m = $114 million. Note the $12m is a perpetuity.

Syllabus area F2c

88 MCQ bank – Market efficiency

88.1 B As share price reaction appears to have occurred before the information concerning the new project was made public, this suggests a strong-form efficient market (and, practically, quite possibly insider dealing) because in a strong form efficient market share price reflects even privately held information.

Syllabus area E4a

88.2 **D** A weak form efficient market will not react to new, publicly announced information hence a strategy based around using publicly available information could work.

In a semi strong form market, all publically available information is already assumed to be reflected in share price, hence reading the newspaper to help formulate a strategy is unlikely to work.

In a strong form efficient market, all publicly available information is already reflected in share price. Again, reading the newspaper is therefore unlikely to add any value to any investment strategy.

Syllabus area E4a

88.3 **A** In a weak form efficient market, all investors know previous share price movements, which will stop patterns consistently and predictably repeating. Sarah must therefore believe the markets are not even weak form efficient.

Syllabus area E4a

88.4 **C** Statement A supports the view that markets are completely inefficient.

Statement B supports the view that markets are weak form efficient.

Statement C supports the view that markets are semi-strong form efficient because in such a market share prices reflect publicly available information, but not privately held information. Share price will therefore not reflect information before it is announced.

Statement D supports the view that markets are strong form efficient: they reflect all available information including that which is privately held.

Syllabus area E4a

88.5 **A** Fundamental analysis values shares according to the future incremental cash flows associated with owning that share, discounted by the investor's required rate of return which reflects the perceived risk associated with that investment.

Technical analysis (or charting) attempts to predict share price movements by anticipating repeating patterns following detailed analysis of past share price movements.

Syllabus area E4a

89 Phobis Co

Text references. Market efficiency is covered in Chapter 18.

Top tips. Make sure that you use headings including one for the significance to a listed company. It is easy to get carried away with the first part of the question about efficiency and forget to answer the second part.

Easy marks. The discussion should be easy if you have learnt the material on the efficient market hypothesis.

Examiner's comments. A number of candidates did not understand and could not discuss market efficiency and very few correctly discussed the significance of semi-strong market efficiency to a company. Overall, many answers to this question were not of a pass standard.

Marking scheme

		Marks
Weak form efficiency	2-3	
Semi-strong form efficiency	2-3	
Strong form efficiency	2-3	
Significance of semi-strong form efficiency	2-3	
	Max	10

Stock market efficiency

If a stock market is efficient, share prices should vary in a **rational way** and will reflect the **amount of relevant information** that is available. The **efficient market hypothesis** identifies three forms of efficiency; weak, semi-strong and strong.

Weak form efficiency

Under the weak form hypothesis of market efficiency, share prices reflect all available information about **past** changes in the share price.

Since new information arrives unexpectedly, changes in share prices should occur in a **random fashion.** If it is correct, then using technical analysis to study past share price movements will not give anyone an advantage, because the information they use to predict share prices is already reflected in the share price.

Semi-strong form efficiency

If a stock market displays semi-strong efficiency, current share prices reflect both:

- **All relevant information** about **past price movements** and their implications, and
- All **knowledge** which is **available publicly**

This means that individuals cannot 'beat the market' by reading the newspapers or annual reports, since the information contained in these will be reflected in the share price.

Stock markets are usually presumed to be semi-strong efficient.

Strong form efficiency

If a stock market displays a strong form of efficiency, share prices reflect **all** information whether publicly available or not:

- From past price changes
- From public knowledge or anticipation
- From specialists' or experts' insider knowledge (eg investment managers)

Significance to a listed company of semi-strong efficiency

The main consequence for financial managers will be that they simply need to **concentrate** on **maximising the net present value** of the **company's investments** in order to maximise the wealth of shareholders. Managers need not worry, for example, about the effect on share prices of financial results in the published accounts because investors will make **allowances** for **low profits** or **dividends** in the current year if higher profits or dividends are expected in the future.

There is little point in financial managers attempting strategies that will attempt to mislead the markets. There is no point for example in trying to identify a correct date when **shares** should be **issued**, since share prices will always reflect the true worth of the company.

The market will identify any attempts to **window dress the accounts** and put an optimistic spin on the figures.

90 Close Co

Text references. Business valuation methods are covered in Chapter 17.

Top tips. For part (a) the calculations are relatively straightforward with all of the information required given in the question.

Part (b) is a standalone requirement that can be answered even if you have struggled with the preceding calculations.

Easy marks. The calculations in part (a) are relatively straightforward as is the discussion of the limitations of the dividend growth model in part (b).

		Marks
(a)	Net assets value	1
	Dividend growth model value	2
	Earnings yield method	2
		5
(b)	Dividend growth rate	2-3
	The cost of equity	1-2
	Zero dividends and other relevant discussion	1-2
	Maximum	5
		10

(a) (i) **Net assets**

As no additional information is available, this is based on book values.

Net assets = 720 – 70 – 160 = $490million

(ii) **Dividend growth model**

Dividends are expected to grow at 4% per year and the cost of equity is 10%.

$$P_0 = \frac{40 \times 1.04}{0.10 - 0.04}$$

$$= 41.6/0.06$$

$$= \$693 \text{ million}$$

(iii) **Earnings yield**

Earnings are the profit after tax figure of $66.6 million and the earnings yield that can be used for the valuation is 11%.

ie 66.6/0.11 = $605.5 million.

(b) The dividend growth model (DGM) is a widely used method for valuing ordinary shares and therefore also companies, however there are a number of weaknesses to the model.

The dividend growth rate

The DGM assumes that there is a constant growth in dividends in perpetuity. This is extremely unlikely in practice. If the growth rate is assumed to be an average growth rate though, this may be seen as less of a problem.

The future growth rate can only be an estimate and it is often based on historical data. The assumption that the past can be used to predict the future may not hold as it is future decisions that will determine the future results of a company. The DGM is also very sensitive to changes in the growth rate, a 1% change in the growth rate can give a significantly different valuation.

Cost of equity

The DGM assumes a constant cost of equity, but it represents the return required by shareholders which will change frequently depending on many different factors. The cost of equity can be calculated by the CAPM formula, but again this is often based on historical information.

Zero dividends

It is claimed that DGM cannot be used where dividends have not been paid. However this is not true if dividends are expected to be paid at some point in the future. In this case the DGM can be applied at that point to create a value for the shares which can then be discounted to give the current ex dividend share price. In a situation where dividends are not paid and are not expected to be paid the DGM has no use.

91 Boluje Co

Marking scheme

			Marks
(a)	Relevant discussion		6
(b)	Market value of each foreign bond	3	
	Total market value of foreign bonds	1	
			4
			10

(a) **Debt finance**

A company has a choice when deciding how to finance a new investment. **Pecking order theory** suggests that the company will first choose **retained earnings** if they are available rather than go to the trouble of obtaining external finance and have to live up to the demands of external finance providers.

The next choice in the pecking order is **debt finance** which will be preferred to equity finance. Perhaps the current shareholders will be unwilling to **contribute additional capital**; possibly the company does not wish to involve outside shareholders who will have more onerous requirements than current members.

Other reasons for choosing debt finance may include **lesser cost** and **easier availability**, particularly if the company has little or no existing debt finance. Debt finance provides **tax relief** on interest payments.

According to the traditional theory of capital structure, the weighted average cost of capital will fall initially as debt is introduced, as debt has a **lower cost** than equity. It will continue to fall until the **optimal capital structure** is achieved. The company can therefore **increase its market value** by increasing the level of debt finance up to this point.

The use of debt is a **signal of confidence in the company's cash flows** and the use of debt is a **discipline on management** as careful cash flow management is needed. A new, growing business will find it difficult to forecast cash flows with any certainty so high levels of gearing are unwise.

(b) Annual interest paid per foreign bond = $500 \times 6.1\% = 30.5$ pesos

Redemption value of each foreign bond = 500 pesos

Cost of debt of peso-denominated bonds = 7% per year

Market value of each foreign bond

Period		Cash flow Pesos	Discount factor 7%	Present value Pesos
1-5	Interest	30.5	4.100	125.05
5	Redemption	500	0.713	356.50
				481.55

Current total market value of foreign bonds = 16m × (481.55/500) = **15,409,600 pesos.**

92 MCQ bank – Foreign currency risk

92.1 D A is a financial reporting implication of retranslating foreign assets/liabilities and not immediately related to cash.

B is the impact on business value of long-term exchange rate trends.

D is correct: transaction risk refers to the fact that the spot rate may move between point of sale (denominated in foreign exchange) and when the customer pays, such that the net domestic receipt differs from expected.

Syllabus area G1a

92.2 A A strengthening Euro means Euros are getting more expensive: they will cost more dollars.

The exchange rate becomes €1 : $2.40   ($2 × 1.2)

The Euro receipt will be $1,000 / 2.4 = $416.67

Syllabus area G1a

92.3 B The spot rate for translating $ to € is 2.0000 + 0.003 = $2.003 / € – the worst rate for someone selling dollars. The dollar is at a premium so subtract the premium because the exchange rate is to the Euro so if the $ is strengthening then the Euro is weakening on the forward market'. : $2.003 / € – $0.002 = $2.001 / €

The Euro receipt will be $2,000 / 2.001 = €999.50.

Syllabus area G3a

92.4 C Statements 1 and 2 are true: As they are binding contracts, forward contracts fix the rate to that rate noted in the contract. By the same token therefore they are not flexible (statement 3 is false.) The contract contains named parties so the contracts cannot be sold on to someone else (statement 4 is false).

Syllabus area G3a

92.5 D The US company should borrow US$ immediately and send it to Europe. It should be left on deposit in € for 3 months then used to pay the supplier.

The amount to put on deposit today = €3.5m × 1/(1+ (0.01/4)) = €3,491,272.

This will cost €3,491,272 × $2 = $6,982,544 today (note $2 is the worst rate for buying €)

Assuming this to be borrowed in US$, the liability in 3 months will be:

$6,982,544 × [1+(0.08/4)] = $7,122,195.

Syllabus area G3a

92.6 B Statement 1: False: Futures contracts are subject to a brokerage fee only (for example there is no spread on the rate) so are relatively cheap.

Statement 2: True: It is not possible to purchase futures contracts from every currency to every other currency – there are only limited combinations available.

Statement 3: False. Futures contracts can be 'closed out' so if, for example, customers pay early or late, the timing of the futures hedge can accommodate this.

Statement 4: True. Futures contracts are for standardised amounts so may not match the size of the transaction being hedged precisely.

Syllabus area G3a

92.7　**A**　The Farland business will want to sell the US $ when they receive them which implies either a US$ put (sell) option purchased in Farland, or a Splot call (buy) option purchased in America. In this second alternative payment would be in US$, effectively giving up US$ in return for Splot.

Syllabus area G3c

92.8　**B**　Using Interest Rate Parity:

$$F_0 = S_0 \times \frac{(1+i_c)}{(1+i_b)}$$

The quarterly rates are: US: 8%/4 = 2%; Europe 4%/4 = 1%

Forward rate = 2 × 1.02/1.01 = $2.0198 : €1

Syllabus area G2b

92.9　**D**　Purchasing power parity means the cost of identical goods in different economies should be the same. If they aren't the same, businesses will buy from one location and sell to the other to make a profit, thus the interaction of supply ad demand will bring the prices back into line. Any differences in inflation between countries therefore creates supply and demand for currencies that evens out the price differences inflation causes.

Syllabus area G2b

92.10　**C**　If a currency strengthens it gets more expensive (eg If the Euro strengthens it may move from $1:€1 to $2:€1) meaning exporters will receive fewer € for their given $ sales, and importers will pay fewer € to satisfy their given $ debts with suppliers.

Syllabus area G1a

93　MCQ bank – Interest rate risk

93.1　**B**　'A' describes gap exposure. C and D is interest rate risk but not specifically basis risk.

Syllabus area G1b

93.2　**A**　Gap exposure occurs when interest rates on deposits and on loans move at different times. The fact that the company has benefitted in this instance means the rates have moved favourably.

Syllabus area G1b

93.3　**D**　Expectations theory: The shape of the curve reflects market expectations about future interest rate movements.

Liquidity preference theory explains why the curve is generally upward sloping – implying a higher periodic rate of return is required to compensate for money being tied up for longer with longer term debt.

Market segmentation theory explains why the curve may be kinked or even discontinuous as different investors (with different risk appetites) invest in different types of debt. For example, many banks will invest in short dated bonds, but pension funds are more likely to invest in long dated ones. The differences in the investor risk/return preferences are reflected through changes in the shape and steepness of the curve in places.

Syllabus area G2c

93.4　**B**　The FRA guarantees a net interest payment of 8%.

As the loan has been signed for 7%, ADB Co will need to pay the bank 1% × $4million × (6/12) = $20,000.

Syllabus area G4a

93.5 **D** Statement 1: Options don't have to be exercised so if an option would otherwise yield a loss, it can be abandoned.

Statement 2: As the question refers to exchange traded options this is true. Over-the-counter options however cannot be traded.

Statement 3: Sizeable premiums are payable for the ability to abandon options that aren't in the investor's favour.

Statement 4: Exchange traded options are standardised contracts so are for standard sized loans/deposits. They aren't tailored to an investor's particular amounts or dates. In comparison, over-the-counter options are tailored.

Syllabus area G4b

94 ZPS Co

Text references. Interest rate parity, purchasing power parity, forward rate agreements and money market hedges are covered in Chapter 19.

Top tips. This question looks at risk management. Keep your explanations brief in part (a) – the mark allocation doesn't justify a long essay!

Easy marks. Part (a) is a textbook explanation of interest rate parity and purchasing power parity and part (b) contains straightforward money market and forward rate agreement calculations.

Examiner's comments. If a candidate was not aware of interest rate parity (IRP) and purchasing power parity (PPP), the answer offered was often very general in nature, discussing exchange rates, interest rates and exchange rates from a macroeconomic perspective. Some answers lost valuable time by explaining what an exchange rate was, what an interest rate was and what an inflation rate was, but this was not required. Better answers showed familiarity with the IRP and PPP formulae in the formula sheet and discussed correctly how the forward rate could be in equilibrium with the spot rate (IRP), and how the expected future spot rate could be in equilibrium with the current spot rate (PPP).

Marking scheme

				Marks
(a)	(i)	Explanation of interest rate parity	2-3	
	(ii)	Explanation of purchasing power parity	2-3	
			Maximum	5
(b)		Dollar cost of forward market hedge	1	
		Calculation of six-month interest rates	1	
		Use of correct spot rate	1	
		Dollar cost of money market hedge	1	
		Comparison of cost of hedges	1	
				5
				10

(a) Exchange rate movements can be related to changes in interest rate or inflation rates. The relationship between interest rates and exchange rates is known as interest rate parity. The relationship between inflation rates and exchange rates is known as purchasing power parity.

Interest rate parity is a method of predicting foreign exchange rates based on the hypothesis that the difference between the interest rates in the two countries should offset the difference between the spot rates and the forward foreign exchange rates over the same period. The forward rate can be found by multiplying the spot rate by the ratio of the two interest rates. The country with the higher nominal interest rate is forecast to have its currency weaken against the currency of the country with the lower interest rate.

Purchasing power parity theory states that the exchange rate between two currencies is the same in equilibrium when the purchasing power of currency is the same in each country.

Purchasing power parity theory predicts that the exchange value of foreign currency depends on the relative purchasing power of each currency in its own country and that spot exchange rates will vary over time according to relative price changes. The country with the higher rate of inflation is forecast to have its currency weaken against the currency of the country with the lower rate of inflation.

Purchasing power parity holds in the longer term, not in the short term and therefore can be used to provide long-term forecasts of exchange rate movements.

(b)   The two hedges should be compared at the same point in time (in six months' time)

Forward market

Interest payment = 5,000,000 pesos

Six-month forward rate = 12.805 pesos per $

Dollar cost of peso interest = 5,000,000/12.805 = $390,472

Money market hedge

As ZPS has a liability of 5 million pesos in six months' time it needs to create a 5 million peso asset at the same point in time.

The six month deposit rate for pesos is 7.5% / 2 = 3.75%

The quantity of pesos to be deposited now = 5,000,000/1.0375 = 4,819,277 pesos

Dollars required to purchase pesos now = 4,819,277 / 12.500 = $385,542 which ZPS would borrow now

The six month dollar borrowing rate is 4.5% / 2 = 2.25% so the interest charge is $385,542 × 0.0225 = $8,675

The total dollar cost of the money market hedge is $394,217

The forward market hedge should be used as it is the cheaper hedging option by $394,217 - $390,472 = $3,745.

95 Gorwa Co

Text references. Interest rate risk is covered in Chapter 20.

Top tips. This question looks at risk management. Use a logical approach and show your workings clearly to gain as many marks as possible in the time available.

Easy marks. If you know about interest rate risk then you should find this question fairly straightforward.

Examiner's comments. Some candidates were not aware of the difference between interest rate and interest payment, and consequently discussed how the company's finance costs (interest payments) had increased from one year to the next. Analysis would have shown that the increase in the finance cost was due to the increase in the overdraft and that the interest rate applied to the overdraft was 5% in each year, ie the interest rate had not changed. The bonds were fixed-rate in nature, as they were given in the statement of financial position as 8% bonds. As the question asked about hedging interest rate risk, looking at the balance between fixed rate debt (bonds) and floating rate debt (overdraft) was also relevant here, as was a consideration of gearing and interest cover. The question was, in fact, very open in nature, and a discussion of the effects of an increase in interest rates could look at an increase in financial risk, a decrease in sales due to a fall in demand, an increase in operating costs and a cutting back of investment plans.

	Marks
Discussion of effects of interest rate increase	3-4
Relevant financial analysis	3-4
Interest rate hedging	2-3
	Maximum 10

	20X7	*20X6*
	$'000	$'000
8% bonds	2,425	2,425
Overdraft	3,225	1,600
Total debt	5,650	4,025
Proportion of debt that has variable interest		
(1,600/4,025 × 100%)	57%	40%
Overdraft interest payments @ 5%	161	80
Bond interest payments @ 8%	194	194
	355	274
Proportion of interest payments that are variable		
(80/274 × 100%)	45%	29%
Interest coverage ratio		
(2,939/274)	8.4 times	10.7 times
Long-term debt/equity ratio		
(2,425/11,325 × 100%)	20%	21%
Total debt/equity ratio		
(4,025/11,325 × 100%)	45%	36%

Fixed interest debt

The 8% bonds are redeemable in ten years' time and are therefore sufficiently **long-term** to protect Gorwa Co against an increase in interest rates. In 20X6, fixed interest debt constituted 60% of total debt but this fell to 43% in 20X7. The company has therefore become **more exposed** to interest rate fluctuations.

Financial risk

The **interest coverage ratio** has fallen from 10.7 times to 8.4 times and this will be a problem if this trend continues.

Gearing has increased from 36% to 45%, if we look at the debt/equity ratio including the overdraft. Gearing has fallen slightly if we ignore the overdraft, but it is sufficiently large to justify its inclusion in the calculation.

These two ratios indicate that **financial risk** has increased and an increase in interest rates will worsen the situation further. The proportion of interest arising from variable rate debt has already risen from 29% to 45% and an increase in interest rates would further reduce profit before taxation and therefore interest coverage.

Protection against interest rate risk

Interest rate risk relates to the sensitivity of profit and cash flows to changes in interest rates. Variable rate debt increases the **volatility of cash flows**; therefore a **switch into long-term fixed rate debt** would reduce this risk. However, long-term debt tends to be **more expensive** than short-term debt, assuming a normal yield curve. If interest rates fall sharply, Gorwa Co could suffer a loss of **competitive advantage** compared with companies using floating rate borrowing whose interest rates and cost of capital will fall.

Gorwa Co could consider the use of **interest rate derivatives** such as **options** and **futures** in the short-term to limit its exposure to adverse interest rate movements. A **forward rate agreement** could also be considered which would fix the interest rate on future borrowing.

96 Ziggazigto Co

Marking scheme

		Marks	
(a)	Calculated value of a forward exchange contract	1	
	Calculated value of a money market hedge	3	
	Comment on hedge to select	1	
			5
(b)	Calculation of one-year future spot rate	3	
	Link between future spot rate and forward rate	2	
			5
			10

(a)   **Forward exchange contract**

500,000/1.990 = $251,256

Using the six-month forward rate under the forward exchange contract, Ziggazigto Co will receive $251,256.

Money market hedge

Expected receipt after 6 months = Euro 500,000

Euro interest rate over six months = 5%/2 = 2.5%

Euros to borrow now in order to have Euro 500,000 liability after six months = Euro 500,000/ 1.025 = Euro 487,805

Spot rate for selling euros today = 2 euro/$

Dollar deposit from borrowed euros at spot rate = 487,805/2 = $243,903

Dollar deposit rate over six months = 4%/2 = 2%

Value of the dollar deposit in six months time = 243,903 × 1.02 = $248,781

In conclusion, the forward contract gives a higher value in dollars, so is financially preferable to the money market hedge.

(b)   **Expected future spot exchange rate**

Purchasing power parity theory states that the movement in the exchange rate between two currencies is linked to the relative inflation rates in the two countries. Inflation rates in purchasing power parity theory represent the relative purchasing power of its currency in its own country.

Using purchasing power parity:

$F_0 = S_0 \times (1+i_c)/(1+i_b)$

Where:

F_0 = expected spot rate

S_0 = current spot rate

i_c = expected inflation in country c

i_b = expected inflation in country b

$F_0 = 2.00 \times 1.03/1.045 = $ Euro 1.971/$

This can be compared to the current forward exchange rate of Euro1.981/ $.

Relationship between the expected future spot rate and the current forward exchange rate

The expected future spot rate is calculated based on the relative inflation rates between two countries. The current forward exchange rates are set based on the relative interest rates between them.

Expectations theory states that there is an equilibrium between relative inflation rates and relative interest rates, so the expected spot rate and the current forward rate would be the same. Realistically, purchasing power parity tends to hold true in the longer term, so is used to forecast exchange rates a number of years into the future. Short-term differences are not unusual.

Mock Exams

ACCA

Paper F9

Financial Management

Mock Examination 1

Question Paper	
Time allowed	
Reading and Planning Writing	**15 minutes** **3 hours**
ALL questions are compulsory and MUST be attempted	
During reading and planning time only the question paper may be annotated	

DO NOT OPEN THIS PAPER UNTIL YOU ARE READY TO START UNDER EXAMINATION CONDITIONS

Section A

1   During the year AB Co paid a dividend of 15c per share. At the year-end share price was $3.15. Share price was $2.50 at the start of the year.

What is the total shareholder return over the period?

A   32%
B   25.4%
C   28.3%
D   30.8%   (2 marks)

2   J Co is considering investing in Project A. The cash flows and NPV are as follows.

	$
Year 0	(150,000)
Year 1 - 5	45,000
NPV at cost of capital of 9%	25,050

What is the sensitivity of the investment decision to a change in the annual net cash inflow?

A   0.30%
B   14.3%
C   16.7%
D   30.0%   (2 marks)

3   **What does 'primary market' refer to?**

A   The biggest stock market in an economy
B   The market for new finance being obtained by businesses
C   The market for trading existing financial instruments
D   The most senior market in an economy.   (2 marks)

4   The following information relates to PWT Co.

Current ratio:	2.0
Receivables days:	60 days
Annual (360 days) turnover:	$3.6 million
Gross margin:	25%
Inventory turnover:	18 times
Payables days:	90 days

What is PWT's positive cash balance?

A $427,500
B $350,000
C $150,000
D $600,000   (2 marks)

5   TW Co needs to purchase raw supplies of 2,000 kgs of material M each year. There is a standing charge of $10 per order. Purchase price is $5 per kg, and it costs TW 10% of purchase price to store one unit for a year.

What is the annual inventory related cost at the economic order quantity to the nearest $10?

A $10,140
B $10,200
C $10,210
D $140   (2 marks)

6   AG Co has recently decided to adopt an increasingly aggressive working capital finance policy.

Which of the following best describes what this means for AG Co?

A   Reducing credit periods for customers and inventory holding periods.
B   Chasing unpaid debts more vigorously.
C   Financing working capital with a higher proportion of short- term finance.
D   Financing fluctuating working capital levels with long term finance.   **(2 marks)**

7   Sarah is self-employed and putting a quote together for installing a customer's kitchen – a skilled job. It will require 200 hours of skilled labour. 100 hours is available from her current employees who are paid $20 an hour for a guaranteed 40-hour week. They are currently between assignments. Sarah could provide the remaining time herself. Alternatively she could hire in labour at $30 an hour to free her time up to install her own kitchen at home, saving herself the $2,800 it would cost to pay someone else to install her own kitchen.

What is the relevant cost of labour to include in the quotation?

A $4,800
B $3,000
C $2,800
D $5,000   **(2 marks)**

8   TW Co is considering submitting a proposal for work to a new customer. TW Co estimates the work will generate costs of $20,000 per annum each year for 5 years. TW Co has a weighted average cost of capital of 10% and pays corporation tax at a rate of 30%.

What is the minimum tender price they should include in their proposal, receivable at the end of the project, that will leave shareholder wealth unaffected?

A $122,109
B $85,476
C $53,074
D $75,820   **(2 marks)**

9   A project requires an initial outlay of $100,000 and will generate net cash inflows of $40,000 per annum.

At a cost of capital of 10%, what is the adjusted payback period to the nearest month?

A   2 years 6 months
B   3 years
C   2 years 10 months
D   3 years 2 months   **(2 marks)**

10   ACB Co is appraising a project with an initial investment of $1 million that will generate net cash inflows after tax of $150,000 per annum indefinitely. ACB Co estimates its cost of capital to be 12%.

What is ACBs percentage sensitivity to their estimate of a 12% cost of capital?

A   3%
B   15%
C   25%
D   20%   **(2 marks)**

11 Which of the following statements about capital rationing are correct?

1 A capital expenditure budget is evidence of a soft capital constraint.

2 Whether projects are divisible or indivisible, the investment plan should seek to maximise net present value per $ invested.

A 1 only is correct
B 2 only is correct
C Neither is correct
D Both are correct   (2 marks)

12 In Islamic finance, which of the following is false?

A Mudaraba – profits are shared according to a pre-agreed contract. Dividends as such are not paid.

B Sukuk – The 'lender' maintains ownership of the underlying asset and shares in the risks/rewards of ownership.

C Murabaha – a pre agreed mark-up is agreed for the convenience of credit.

D Charging interest on murabaha is only acceptable provided all parties agree.   (2 marks)

13 Which of the following is not an advantage of withholding a dividend as a source of finance?

A Retained profits are a free source of finance
B Investment plans need less justification
C Issue costs are lower
D It is quick   (2 marks)

14 The following relates to ZAR Co.

	$000
Ordinary share capital	30
$1 5% Preference shares	50
Reserves	100
Long term loan note	120

Shares are currently quoted at $3 per $1 nominal. Preference shares are quoted at nominal value, and the loan note at 85%.

What is financial gearing (prior charge capital / equity) using market values?

A 169%
B 125%
C 137%
D 67%   (2 marks)

15 RZS Co has recently paid a dividend of 34c per share. 4 years ago the dividend was 12c a share. There was a 1:1 bonus issue of shares 2 years ago. Current share price is $5 a share.

What is the cost of equity capital for RZS Co?

A 38.5%
B 16.4%
C 17.9%
D 6.8%   (2 marks)

16   DFE Co's gearing is slightly above the industry average, so when seeking finance for a new project DFE Co opts for equity finance.

The capital structure theory they appear to subscribe to is:

A   Traditional view
B   Modigliani-Miller (no tax)
C   Modigliani-Miller (with tax)
D   Residual view

(2 marks)

17   **Which of the following is least directly relevant to the discounted cash flow valuation of a business?**

A   Forecast synergies
B   Realisable value of operating assets
C   Cost of equity to appraise the investment
D   Value of surplus assets

(2 marks)

18   The Board of MNO Co appoint a Media Liaison officer as they believe the timing and method of public announcements is important in managing the value of MNO shares.

How efficient does the Board believe the markets to be?

A   Completely inefficient
B   Weak form efficient
C   Semi-strong form efficient
D   Strong form efficient

(2 marks)

19   The US$/European € spot rate is quoted currently at 1.9612 – 1.9618 $/€. The 3 month forward rate is quoted at $0.0012 – 0.0006 premium in Europe. A US company is expecting to receive €2.5 million in three months time and would like to hedge this using a forward contract.

What will be the US$ receipt in 3 months time?

A $1,274,730
B $1,273,950
C $1270,123
D $1,275,510

(2 marks)

20   **Which of the following could cause the interest yield curve to steepen?**

1   Increased uncertainty about the future
2   heightened expectations of an increase in interest rates
3   the expectation that interest rate decreases will happen earlier than previously thought.

A   1 and 2 only
B   1,2 and 3
C   2 and 3 only
D   1 only

(2 marks)
(Total = 40 marks)

Section B

1   TGA Co, a multinational company, has annual credit sales of $5·4 million and related cost of sales is $2·16 million. Financial information relating to TGA Co is as follows:

	$'000	$'000
Inventory	473.4	
Trade receivables	1,331.5	1,804.90
Trade payables	177.5	
Overdraft	1,326.6	1,504.10
Net working capital		300.8

TGA Co plans to change working capital policy in order to improve its profitability. This policy change will not affect the current levels of credit sales, cost of sales or net working capital. As a result of the policy change, the following working capital ratio values are expected:

Inventory days	50 days
Trade receivables days	62 days
Trade payable days	45 days

Assume there are 365 days in each year.

Required

(a)   **For the change in working capital policy, calculate the change in the operating cycle, the effect on the current ratio and the finance cost saving. Comment on your findings.   (6 marks)**

(b)   **Discuss the key elements of a trade receivables management policy.   (4 marks)**

(Total = 10 marks)

2   TGA Co's sales are exported to a European country and are invoiced in euros.

TGA Co expects to receive €500,000 from export sales at the end of three months. A forward rate of €1·687 per $1 has been offered by the company's bank and the spot rate is €1·675 per $1.

Other relevant financial information is as follows:

Short-term dollar borrowing rate   5% per year

Short-term dollar deposit rate   4% per year

TGA Co can borrow short term in the euro at 9% per year

Assume there are 365 days in each year.

Required

(a)   **Calculate the dollar income from a forward market hedge and a money market hedge, and indicate which hedge would be financially preferred by TGA Co.   (4 marks)**

(b)   **Explain the different types of foreign currency risk faced by a multinational company.   (6 marks)**

(Total = 10 marks)

3   Dartig Co is a stock-market listed company that manufactures consumer products and it is planning to expand its existing business. The investment cost of $5 million will be met by a 1 for 4 rights issue. The current share price of Dartig Co is $2.50 per share and the rights issue price will be at a 20% discount to this. The finance director of Dartig Co expects that the expansion of existing business will allow the average growth rate of earnings per share over the last four years to be maintained into the foreseeable future.

The earnings per share and dividends paid by Dartig over the last four years are as follows:

	20X3	20X4	20X5	20X6	20X7
Earnings per share (cents)	27.7	29.0	29.0	30.2	32.4
Dividend per share (cents)	12.8	13.5	13.5	14.5	15.0

Dartig Co has a cost of equity of 10%. The price/earnings ratio of Dartig Co has been approximately constant in recent years. Ignore issue costs.

Required

(a) Calculate the theoretical ex rights price per share prior to investing in the proposed business expansion.
(3 marks)

(b) Calculate the expected share price following the proposed business expansion using the price/earnings ratio method.
(3 marks)

(c) Discuss whether the proposed business expansion is an acceptable use of the finance raised by the rights issue, and evaluate the expected effect on the wealth of the shareholders of Dartig Co.
(4 marks)

(Total = 10 marks)

4   HDW Co is a listed company which plans to meet increased demand for its products by buying new machinery costing $5 million. The machinery would last for four years, at the end of which it would be replaced. The scrap value of the machinery is expected to be 5% of the initial cost. Tax allowable depreciation would be available on the cost of the machinery on a 25% reducing balance basis, with a balancing allowance or charge claimed in the final year of operation.

This investment will increase production capacity by 9,000 units per year and all of these units are expected to be sold as they are produced. Relevant financial information in current price terms is as follows:

		Forecast inflation
Selling price	$650 per unit	4·0% per year
Variable cost	$250 per unit	5·5% per year
Incremental fixed costs	$250,000 per unit	5·0% per year

In addition to the initial cost of the new machinery, initial investment in working capital of $500,000 will be required. Investment in working capital will be subject to the general rate of inflation, which is expected to be 4·7% per year.

HDW Co pays tax on profits at the rate of 20% per year, one year in arrears. The company has a nominal (money terms) after-tax cost of capital of 12% per year.

Required

(a) Calculate the net present value of the planned purchase of the new machinery using a nominal (money terms) approach and comment on its financial acceptability.   (11 marks)

(b) Discuss the difference between a nominal (money terms) approach and a real terms approach to calculating net present value.
(4 marks)

(Total = 15 marks)

5   AMH Co wishes to calculate its current cost of capital for use as a discount rate in investment appraisal. The following financial information relates to AMH Co:

Financial position statement extracts as at 31 December 2012 ($'000)

Equity

Ordinary shares (nominal value 50 cents)	4,000	
Reserves	18,000	22,000
Long-term liabilities		
4% Preference shares (nominal value $1)	3,000	
7% Bonds redeemable after six years	3,000	
Long-term bank loan	1,000	7,000
		29,000

The ordinary shares of AMH Co have an ex div market value of $4·70 per share and an ordinary dividend of 36·3 cents per share has just been paid. Historic dividend payments have been as follows:

Year	2008	2009	2010	2011
Dividends per share (cents)	30.9	32.2	33.6	35.0

The preference shares of AMH Co are not redeemable and have an ex div market value of 40 cents per share. The 7% bonds are redeemable at a 5% premium to their nominal value of $100 per bond and have an ex interest market value of $104·50 per bond. The bank loan has a variable interest rate that has averaged 4% per year in recent years.

AMH Co pays profit tax at an annual rate of 30% per year.

Required

(a) Calculate the market value weighted average cost of capital of AMH Co.   (10 marks)

(b) Discuss why the cost of equity is greater than the cost of debt.   (5 marks)

(Total = 15 marks)

Answers

DO NOT TURN THIS PAGE UNTIL YOU HAVE
COMPLETED THE MOCK EXAM

A PLAN OF ATTACK

We've already established that you've been told to do it 101 times, so it is of course superfluous to tell you for the 102nd time to **take a good look at the paper before diving in to answer questions.** You are going to remember aren't you; good!

Which order to do the questions

As a general rule work through Section A first. During reading time you should then decide the **order** in which to attempt the questions in Section B. You will probably have decided which question looks the easiest and started with that one. Answer plans will help you to decide how to approach each question.

The next step

You're probably thinking that you don't know where to begin or you could answer all of the questions in two hours!

Option 1 (Oh dear)

If you are challenged by this paper, do the **questions in the order of how well you think you can answer them.**

*   **Section A** is a good place to start – plenty of short questions to ease you into the paper. Then move on to Section B:

*   **Question 1** is half numbers. There are some easy calculations to warm up with in part (a). Do a detailed answer plan for part (b) to help you get started.

*   **Question 2** has some reasonably tricky numbers to start with, but part (a) is only worth 4 marks – leave plenty of time for the relatively straightforward discussion in part (b)

*   **Question 3** is a valuations question, – show all your workings and don't panic! Part (a)(i) is straightforward.

*   **Question 4** requires you to calculate NPV, with inflation. Don't get swamped by inflation – show clear workings and lay your thinking on the page like a road map for the marker.

*   **Question 5** Asks you to calculate WACC for 10 marks, then discuss why the cost of equity is larger than the cost of debt. There are plenty of easy marks in the calculations provided you break it down into its component parts – deal with one source of finance at a time.

Option 2 (This one's definitely easier)

Are you **sure** it is? If you are then that's encouraging but don't forget to do answer plans to make sure you don't miss the point of the questions.

*   Don't just do a brain dump of everything you know in **Question 2 (b).** Make sure you interpret the mark allocation carefully to help you assess the volume you need to write.

*   Time management is going to be important in **Question 3** as there are a lot of calculations to get through.

*   Work through **Question 4** slowly and carefully making sure you answer each part fully and accurately.

Once more for the road

You must **allocate your time** according to the marks for the question in total, and for the parts of the questions. And you must also **follow the requirements exactly.**

Finished with fifteen minutes to spare?

Looks like you slipped up on the time allocation. However if you have, make sure you don't waste the last few minutes; go back to **any parts of questions that you didn't finish** because you ran out of time.

BPP LEARNING MEDIA

Forget about it!

Forget about what? Excellent, you already have.

Section A

1 **A** Total shareholder return = $\dfrac{\text{Dividend} + \text{increase in share price}}{\text{Opening share price}}$

$$= \frac{15 + (315 - 250)}{250}$$

$$= 0.32 = 32\%$$

Syllabus area A3

2 **B** Sensitivity of NPV $= \dfrac{\text{NPV of project}}{\text{PV of net cash inflow}} \times 100\%$

NPV of \$45,000 for 5 years at cost of capital

$= \$45,000 \times 3.890 = \$175,050$

Sensitivity $= \dfrac{25,050}{175,050} \times 100\% = 14.3\%$

Syllabus area D3b

3 **B** The term refers to capital market where new securities are issued and sold to investors. The secondary market is where existing financial instruments are traded between investors.

Syllabus area B2c

4 **D** Receivables = (60/360) × \$3.6 million = \$600,000.

If gross margin = 25% then cost of sales = \$3.6million × 75% = \$2.7 million

then payables = (90/360) × \$2.7m = \$675,000

and inventory = (\$2.7m /18) = \$150,000

Current ratio = (Receivables + inventory + cash) / payables = 2.0

= (\$600,000 + \$150,000 + cash) / \$675,000 = 2

so (\$750,000 + cash) = (2 × \$675,000) = \$1,350,000

Cash = \$1,350,000 − \$750,000 = \$600,000

Syllabus area C2f

5 **A** EOQ = $\sqrt{[(2 \times C_o \times D) / C_h]}$ = $\sqrt{[(2 \times \$10 \times 2,000)/(10\% \times \$5)]}$ = 283 units

Total cost = purchase cost + order costs + holding costs

= (2,000 × \$5) + [(2,000/283) × \$10] + [(283/2) × (\$5 × 10%)]

= \$10,000 + \$70.67 + \$70.75 = 10,141.42

= \$10,140 to the nearest \$10

Syllabus area C2c

6 **C** 'A' refers to an increasingly aggressive working capital **investment** policy.

'B' would probably reduce the receivables period, which is reducing the amount of money tied up in working capital, but is not changing the working capital **finance** policy.

'C' is by definition an increasingly aggressive working capital finance policy. Short term finance is relatively inexpensive (low risk from the lender's perspective) but risky for the borrower (renewal risk – it may not be renewed next time; and rate risk – interest rates can vary when renewed).

'D' describes a more conservative financing policy – more long term finance being used to finance working capital.

Syllabus area C3b

7   C   The 100 hours from the current workers has a relevant cost of zero – the work can be absorbed at no extra cost.

Sarah's time – if she hires in labour to enable her to install her own kitchen this will cost her $30 \times 100 = \$3,000$. A better alternative would be to pay someone else \$2,800 to install her own kitchen, so she can save this \$3,000 by working on the customer's installation herself. This way she would be overall \$200 better off.

The relevant cost of labour to include in the quote is therefore \$2,800.

Syllabus area D1a

8   A   Net present value of the after tax costs = ($20,000 \times (1 - 30\%)) \times AF_{1-5}10\% = \$14000 \times 3.791$ (tables) = \$53,074.

The tender price is receivable at the **end** of the contact hence would be $\$53,074 \times (1.1)^5 = \$85,476$.

However, TW Co pays tax so \$85,476 is the value of the after tax tender price. The pre-tax gross tender price to go into the proposal would be $\$85,476 / (1 - 30\%) = \$122,109$.

Syllabus area D1e

9   B

Time	Cashflow	Discount factor	Present value	Cumulative
	$	10%	$	PV $
0	(100,000)	1	(100,000)	(100,000)
1	40,000	0.909	36,360	(63,640)
2	40,000	0.826	33,040	(30,600)
3	40,000	0.751	30,040	(560)
4	40,000	0.683	27,320	26,760

Adjusted Payback period = 3 years + [(560/27,320) × 12] months = 3 years to the nearest month.

Syllabus area D3d

10   C   The decision will change should the cost of capital change sufficiently to force Net Present Value to equal zero. This will occur at the IRR.

(150,000/IRR) – 1,000,000 = 0   i.e. the NPV will be zero at the IRR.

150,000/IRR =1,000,000.

IRR = 150,000/1,000,000 = 0.15 = 15%.

The current estimated cost of capital is 12%, hence sensitivity = (15 – 12)/12 = 25% sensitivity.

Syllabus area D3b

11   A   A soft capital constraint is internally imposed. A capital expenditure budget is an internal limit of capital investment hence it is evidence of a soft capital constraint.

The investment plan should seek to maximise net present value overall, not per dollar invested. This latter might suggest only investing in the project with the highest profitability index. Other projects may have a lower profitability index, but this does not mean they should be rejected if there is sufficient capital available to invest in them also.

Syllabus area D4c

12 D Charging interest is forbidden under Sharia'a law.

Syllabus area E1d

13 A Although free to raise, using retained earnings as a source of finance (by withholding a dividend) is not free to use – it is equity finance and requires the cost of equity to be generated as a return.

B is true – other forms of finance require up-front justification to be considered by potential investors before funds are made available for investment.

C is true – there are no issue costs.

D is true – as the funds are already on hand, availability is essentially instant.

Syllabus area E1e

14 A Preference shares are part of prior charge capital and preference shareholders receive a relatively fixed return, and as they cannot vote are not strictly business owners.

Market value of shares = $30,000 × ($3/$1) = $90,000   Note: market value also includes reserves.

Market value of preference shares = nominal value = $50,000

Market value of loan note = $120,000 × (85/100) = $102,000

Gearing = ($50,000 + $102,000) / $90,000 = 169%

Syllabus area E3d

15 B The bonus issue would have halved dividend per share, so the comparable dividend from 4 years ago is 12c × 2 = 24c a share to ascertain growth.

Average annual growth rate: $24(1+g)^4 = 34$

$$(1+g)^4 = (34/24)$$

$$g = [\sqrt[4]{(34/24)}] - 1 = .09 \text{ or } 9\%$$

$$r_e = \frac{D_0(1+g)+g}{P_0}$$

$$= \frac{34(1.09)}{500} + 0.09$$

$$= 16.4\%$$

Syllabus area E2a

16 A The traditional view assumes there is an optimal balance between debt and equity (there is a 'U' shaped weighted average cost of capital (WACC) curve) hence choosing finance to aim for the optimum suggests the traditional view is adopted.

Modigliani-Miller (no tax) concludes the WACC is unaffected by the finance decision hence the choice of debt compared to equity is irrelevant.

Modigliani-Miller (with tax) concludes that due to the tax benefits of paying interest, as much finance as possible should be in the form of debt as increasing gearing will reduce the WACC. Hence equity would never be chosen.

Residual view / theory is not directly relevant to the capital structure decision. This term more directly relates to dividend policy.

Syllabus area E4a&b

17 B   The realisable value of operating assets is less relevant as this valuation technique is primarily involved in valuing the income of a going concern, hence values for the statement of financial position assets used to generate that income are not immediately relevant.

The value of surplus assets would be relevant however as they are likely to be sold off immediately - they will create an immediate income without affecting forecast operational flows.

Syllabus area E2c

18 C   Share price in a semi-strong form market reflects all publicly available information, but not privately held information. Thus the majority of share price reaction occurs to and around public announcements.

Syllabus area F4a

19 D   The correct spot rate to use (the worst one for the US company) is 1.9612 as they will receive fewest US$ using this rate.

The correct premium to deduct from this is the $0.0012 – left hand side – hence the forward rate =

1.9612 – 0.0012 = $1.96 /€.

Hence the US co will receive €2.5m / 1.96 = $1,275,510.

Syllabus area G3a

20 A   Statement 1: Increased uncertainty will increase the preference for liquidity, and will increase required yields into the future.

Statement 2: If the markets feel interest rates are going to rise, the required return on longer dated bonds will increase in line with these expectations.

Statement 3 is false: this will lead to the curve flattening.

Syllabus area G2c

SECTION B

Question 1

Marking scheme

			Marks
(a)	Current inventory, receivable and payables days	1	
	Current operating cycle	0.5	
	Revised operating cycle	0.5	
	Reduction in operating cycle	0.5	
	Current ratio	0.5	
	Revised inventory, receivables and payables days	1	
	Revised overdraft	0.5	
	Revised current ratio	0.5	
	Finance cost saving	0.5	
	Comment on findings	1	
		Maximum	6
(b)	Discussion of credit analysis	1-2	
	Discussion of credit control	1-2	
	Discussion of receivables collection	1-2	
		Maximum	4
			10

(a) (i) Current operating cycle

Current inventory days = 473.4/2,160 × 365 = 80 days

Current trade receivables days = 1,331.5/5,400 × 365 = 90 days

Current trade payables days = 177.5/2,160 × 365 = 30 days

Current operating cycle = 80 + 90 − 30 = 140 days

Operating cycle after changes

50 + 62 − 45 = 67 days

Change in operating cycle = 140 − 67 = 73 days

(ii)   The present current ratio = 1,804.9/1,504.1 = 1.20 times

Net working capital is currently $300,800

Revised working capital levels (in $'000)

Revised inventory = 2,160 × 50/365 = $295.9

Revised trade receivables = 5,400 × 62/365 = $917.3

Revised trade payables = 2,160 × 45/365 = $266.3

Revised overdraft = 295.9 + 917.3 − 266.3 − 300.8 = $646.1

Current assets = 295.9 + 917.3 = $1,212.9

Current liabilities = 266.3 + 646.1 = $912.4

Revised current ratio = 1,212.9/912.4 = 1.33 times

The current ratio increases from 1.20 to 1.33 times (an 11% increase)

(iii)   The reduction in the overdraft is 1,326.6 − 646.1 = $680.6.

At a short-term borrowing rate of 5% this is an annual saving of $34,000.

(b)   The factors that should be considered are an analysis of credit, the credit control policy and collection of amounts owing.

Analysis of credit

Finding a level of credit that can be offered involves finding a balance between enticing credit customers, which comes at a cost to the business and refusing opportunities to make sales.

Creditworthiness is an important area to consider, the risk of the customer defaulting must be balanced against the profitability from sales to that customer.

A company should use the following information when assessing creditworthiness of its customers. New customers should provide two references, one from a bank and one trade reference. Publicly available information from published accounts and other sources such as credit reference agencies may be considered. Previous experience of the individual customer should also be taken into account.

The company could devise their own credit rating system based on the customer's characteristics. This process depends on having good quality information to make creditworthiness decisions on.

Credit control policy

Customer's payment records and the aged receivables analysis should be reviewed on a regular basis to see if customers are acting within the agreed credit terms.

Regular contact should be made with customers either through statements, letters or telephone calls to ensure that they are aware of the debt and when payment is likely to be received. Regular contact with customers who are in financial difficulty is necessary to assess going concern issues and to work out whether extended credit terms will be beneficial.

Collecting amounts owing

The overall debt collection policy should be that the costs of collecting the debt do not exceed the benefits of the collection.

Procedures for pursuing overdue debt must be established and followed by credit control staff. Initiating legal proceedings or the use of a debt collection agency should only be considered as a last resort as this is likely to antagonise customers and may end important trade relationships.

Question 2

Marking scheme

			Marks
(a)	Income from forward market hedge	1	
	Income from money market hedge	2	
	Indication of financially preferred hedge	1	
			4
(b)	Transaction risk	2	
	Translation risk	2	
	Economic risk	2	
			6
			10

(a) **Forward market hedge**

Receipt from forward contract = €500,000/1.687 = $296,384

Money market hedge

3-month euro borrowing rate = 9% × 3/12 = 2.25%

3-month dollar deposit rate = 4% × 3/12 = 1%

Borrow euros now	500,000/1.0225 = €488,998
Convert to $ now	488,998/1.675 = $291,939
$ after investing	$291,939 × 1.01 = $294,858

The receipt for the forward contract is higher by $1,526 and so is preferable for TGA Co.

(b) **Transaction risk**

This is the risk of adverse exchange rate movements occurring in the course of **normal international trading transactions**. This arises when the prices of imports or exports are fixed in foreign currency terms and there is movement in the exchange rate between the date when the price is agreed and the date when the cash is paid or received in settlement.

Transaction risk therefore affects cash flows so companies often choose to **hedge** or protect themselves against transaction risk.

Translation risk

This is the risk that the organisation will make exchange losses when the accounting results of its foreign branches or subsidiaries are **translated** into the home currency. Translation losses can result, for example, from restating the book value of a foreign subsidiary's assets at the exchange rate on the statement of financial position date.

Translation risk does not affect cash flows so does not **directly** affect shareholder wealth. However, **investors** may be influenced by the changing values of assets and liabilities so a company may choose to hedge translation risk through, for example **matching the currency of assets and liabilities**. For example an asset denominated in euros would be financed by a euro loan.

Economic risk

This refers to the effect of exchange rate movements on the **international competitiveness** of a company. For example, a UK company might use raw materials which are priced in US dollars, but export its products mainly within the EU. A depreciation of sterling against the dollar or an appreciation of sterling against other EU currencies will both erode the competitiveness of the company. Economic exposure can be difficult to avoid, although **diversification of the supplier and customer base** across different countries will reduce this kind of exposure to risk.

Question 3

Text references. Rights issues are covered in Chapter 12, business valuation in Chapter 17.

Top tips. You need to recognise the need to calculate the growth rate of dividends in this question which you can then use in part (b). If this is too tricky, state a suitable figure and carry on with the calculations. Make sure you write suitably detailed points in the discussion parts and don't just focus on the calculations.

Easy marks. There are easy marks available for the calculations in part (a).

Examiner's comments. In part (a) many candidates gained full marks for their calculations. Weaker answers made errors as regards the form of the issue (it was 1 for 4, not 4 for 1), or thought the theoretical ex rights price was the rights issue price, or calculated the value of the rights. In part (b) a number of candidates were not able to calculate the price/earnings ratio by dividing the current share price by the current EPS. Calculating the EPS after the expansion by multiplying the current EPS by the average historic EPS growth rate was also a problem for some candidates, who were unable to calculate average historic growth rate, or who applied the growth rate to the average EPS rather than the current EPS. Some students were also unfamiliar with the P/E valuation method, even though this is discussed in the study texts.

Better answers in part (c) looked to compare the theoretical rights price per share (the share price before the rights issue funds were invested) with the share price after the investment had taken place (for example the share price calculated in part (b)), or to compare the return from the investment (for example, total shareholder return, which is the sum of capital gain and divided yield) with the cost of equity.

			Marks
(a)	Rights issue price	1	
	Theoretical ex-rights price per share	2	
			3
(b)	Existing P/E ratio	1	
	Revised EPS	1	
	Share price using P/E method	1	
			3
(c)	Discussion of share price comparisons	2-3	
	Calculation of capital gain and comment	1-2	
		Maximum	4
			10

(a)   Rights issue price = $2.50 × 80% = $2.00 per share

Theoretical ex-rights price

	$
4 shares @ $2.50	10.00
1 share @ $2.00	2.00
5	12.00

Theoretical ex-rights price (TERP) = 12.00/5 = **$2.40**

(b)   Average growth rate of earnings per share:

$$1 + g = \sqrt[4]{\frac{32.4}{27.7}}$$

$1 + g = 1.03996$

$g = 4\%$

EPS following expansion = 32.4 × 1.04 = 33.7 cents per share

Current P/E ratio = 250/32.4 = 7·7 times

Share price following expansion = $0.337×7.7 = **$2.60**

(c)   A company will only be able to raise finance if investors think the **returns** they can expect are satisfactory in view of the **risks** they are taking. The proposed business expansion will be an acceptable use of the rights issue funds if it **increases shareholder wealth**.

This can be measured by looking at the effect on the **share price.** The current share price is $2.50 and the future share price predicted by the P/E method is $2.60. This indicates that shareholder wealth would increase. However, the capital gain is actually larger than this as shareholders will obtain new shares at a discount, resulting in a theoretical ex-rights price of $2.40. The **capital gain for shareholders** is therefore $2.60 − $2.40 = 20 cents per share.

Alternatively, we can consider the effect on **total shareholder wealth**. The rights issue involves 2.5 million shares ($5m/$2 per share). There were therefore 10 million shares (2.5 × 4) before the investment and Dartig was worth $25m (10m × $2.50). After the investment, Dartig is worth $27.5m (12.5m × $2.60 − $5m) which is a **capital gain** of $2.5m.

If investors believe that the expansion will enable the business to grow even further, the capital gain could be even greater. If, however, investors do not share the company's confidence in the future, the share price could fall.

Question 4

Marking scheme

		Marks
(a)	Inflated selling price per box	0.5
	Sales income	0.5
	Inflated total variable cost	0.5
	Inflated incremental fixed costs	0.5
	Tax liability	1
	Tax allowable depn, years 1 to 3	1
	Balancing allowance, year 4	1
	Tax allowable depn tax benefits, years 1 to 4	1
	Timing of tax liabilities and benefits	0.5
	Incremental working capital investment	1
	Scrap value	0.5
	Discount at 12%	1
	Calculated value for NPV net present value	1
	Comment on financial acceptability	1
		11
(b)	Discussion of nominal terms approach	1-3
	Discussion of real terms approach	1-3
	Maximum	4
		15

(a) Present value of cash flows

Year	0 $'000	1 $'000	2 $'000	3 $'000	4 $'000	5 $'000
Sales revenue (W1)		6,084	6,327	6,580	7,034	
Variable costs (W2)		(2734)	(2504)	(2,642)	(2,787)	
Fixed costs*		(263)	(276)	(289)	(304)	
Taxable cash flow		3,447	3,547	3,649	3,753	
Tax liabilities			(689)	(709)	(730)	(751)
CA tax benefits(W3)			250	188	141	372
Capital cost/Scrap	(5000)				250	
Working capital (W4)	(500)	(24)	(25)	(26)	(27)	
After-tax cash flow		3,423	3,083	3,102	3,387	(379)
Discount at 12%	1	0.893	0.797	0.712	0.636	0.567
Present values	(5500)	3,057	2,457	2,209	2,154	(215)
NPV	**4,162**					

This project has a positive NPV which indicates it should be undertaken.

*Fixed costs are inflated by 5% year on year.

Workings

1   *Sales revenue*

Year	1	2	3	4
Selling price ($/unit)	676.00	703.04	731.16	760.41
Sales (units/year)	9,000	9,000	9,000	9,000
Total sales revenue ($'000)	6,084	6,327	6,580	6,844

2   *Variable costs*

Year	1	2	3	4
Variable cost ($/unit)	263.75	278.26	293.56	309.71
Sales (units/year)	9,000	9,000	9,000	9,000
Variable cost ($'000)	2,374	2,504	2,642	2,787

3   *Capital allowance*

Year		Capital allowance $'000	Tax effect (20%) $'000
1	5,000 × 0.25	1,250	250
2	1,250 × 0.75	937.5	188
3	937.5 × 0.75	703.1	141
4	5,000 – 1,250 – 937.5 – 703.1 – 250	1,859.4	372

4   *Working capital*

Year	0	1	2	3	4
Total working capital	500	523.50	548.11	573.87	600.84
Incremental (nearest $'000)	500	24	25	26	27

Note the incremental figure is taken from the increase in each year and then rounded as appropriate. It would also be acceptable to look at the overall increase requires and decide that year 2, for example, would also be 24.

Working capital is not refunded at the end of this project as the machine will be replaced, so it is assumed that this working capital investment will continue.

(b)   **Money terms and real terms**

A nominal (or money) terms approach to investment appraisal, uses a **nominal cost of capital** to discount the **nominal cash flows** associated with the project. Nominal cash flows are obtained, by using forecast inflation rates and current price levels or estimates. Different cash flows may be inflated at different rates. Sometimes this is referred to as **specific inflation**.

A real terms approach to investment appraisal, uses a **real cost of capital** to discount the **real cash flows** associated with the project. Real cash flows can be obtained be deflating the nominal cash flows by the general rate of inflation, or by using the current price level or estimate. The real discount rate can be found by using the **Fisher equation**:

$(1 + i) = (1 + r)(1 + h)$

Where h   =   rate of inflation

r   =   real rate of interest

i   =   nominal (money) rate of interest

Whichever approach is used, the net present value will be the same because nominal cash flows and the nominal cost of capital are both discounted by the general rate of inflation to obtain real cash flows and the real cost of capital.

Question 5

Marking scheme

			Marks
(a)	Calculation of historic dividend growth rate	1	
	Calculation of cost of equity using DGM	2	
	Calculation of cost of preference shares	1	
	Calculation of after-tax interest payment on bond	1	
	Setting up linear interpolation calculation	1	
	Calculation of after-tax cost of debt of bond	1	
	Calculation of after-tax cost of debt of bank loan	1	
	Calculation of market values	1	
	Calculation of WACC	1	
			10
(b)	Relationship between risk and return	1-2	
	Creditor hierarchy and related discussion	3-4	
	Maximum		5
			15

(a) **Cost of equity**

Using geometric growth

$$g = \sqrt[4]{\frac{36.3}{30.9}} - 1 = 0.041 \text{ or } 4.1\%$$

The dividend growth model then gives

$$k_e = 0.041 + \frac{(36.3 \times 1.041)}{470} = 0.121 \text{ or } 12.1\%$$

Cost of preference shares

$$k_p = 4/40 = 0.1 \text{ or } 10\%$$

Cost of debt – bonds

The post-tax interest payment = $7 \times 0.7 = \$4.9$ per bond.

Time	Cash flow $	Discount factor (5%)	Present value $	Discount factor (4%)	Present value $
0	(104.50)	1	(104.50)	1	(104.50)
1-6	4.90	5.076	24.87	5.242	25.69
6	105.00	0.746	78.33	0.790	82.95
			(1.30)		4.14

Post-tax cost of debt = $4 + [4.14/(4.14 + 1.30)] \times (5 - 4) = 4.76 = 4.8\%$

Cost of debt – bank loan

Post-tax cost of interest = $4\% \times 0.7 = 2.8\%$

Market values

		$'000
Equity	(4m / 0.5) × 4.7	37,600
Preference shares	3m × 0.4	1,200
Bonds	3m × 104.5/100	3,135
Bank loan	Use book value	1,000
		42,935

WACC

$$\frac{(12.1\% \times 37,600) + (10\% \times 1,200) + (4.8\% \times 3,135) + (2.8\% \times 1,000)}{42,935} = 11.3\%$$

One of the assumptions behind the capital asset pricing model (CAPM) is that investors hold well diversified portfolios and that unsystematic risk has been diversified away. As a result, AMH Co would only be concerned with **systematic risk** when using the CAPM to calculate a project-specific discount rate.

The CAPM can be used where the business risk of a project is different to the business risk of the existing operations. To use this method, a **proxy company** (or proxy companies) should be found which have a **similar business risk** to that of the investment project. The equity beta of the proxy company (or companies) reflects the business risk of the proxy company's business operations and also the financial risk of the company's capital structure.

Since AMH Co is only interest in the business risk, the proxy company beta should be ungeared to **remove the effect of the capital structure**. The creates an asset (or ungeared) beta which represents only business risk. If several proxy companies have been identified an **average asset beta** can be used to take account of small differences in business operations.

The asset beta can then be **regeared** for the capital structure of AMH Co, to take into account its **financial risk** so the regeared beta will take into account the business and the financial risk. Both ungearing and regearing is done using the weighted average beta formula.

The project specific equity beta calculated for AMH Co can then be used to calculate a **project specific cost of equity** using the CAPM. This project specific cost of equity can then be used to calculate a project-specific weighted average cost of capital, using the capital funding structure for the project, which could be used for investment appraisal of the project.

(b) The cost of equity is the **return required by shareholders** from their investment in the company. The cost of debt is the return required by debt holders from their investment. The **risk-return principle** is that for higher levels of risk there should be higher returns. When the risk of a company increases, the shareholders will require a higher return and the cost of equity increases.

The creditor hierarchy in the event of a liquidation determines the level of risk of a company's creditors. Any debt finance has to be paid off before equity shareholders will receive any cash. This means that the **risk faced by shareholders is greater** than the risk faced by debt holders and therefore the cost of equity is higher than the cost of debt.

A further point here is that debt interest has to be paid before any dividends can be paid to ordinary shareholders. This again shows that the **risk faced by ordinary shareholders is higher** than that faced by holders of debt as the payment of interest means there is less cash available for dividends.

ACCA

Paper F9

Financial Management

Mock Examination 2

Question Paper	
Time allowed	
Reading and Planning Writing	**15 minutes** **3 hours**
ALL questions are compulsory and MUST be attempted	
During reading and planning time only the question paper may be annotated	

DO NOT OPEN THIS PAPER UNTIL YOU ARE READY TO START UNDER EXAMINATION CONDITIONS

Section A

Answer ALL questions

1 A school changes its stationery suppliers to save money, and increases class sizes. As a result the latest set of exam results are lower than previous years.

How has the school performed in terms of the value for money framework?

A   Well on economy and efficiency, but at the cost of effectiveness
B   Well on efficiency, but not well with economy or effectiveness
C   Well on efficiency and elasticity, badly on effectiveness
D   Well on effectiveness and economy, but badly on efficiency.   **(2 marks)**

2 The government in a country is following an expansionary fiscal policy.

How might this affect many businesses?

A   Higher taxes, less government contracts being offered, less subsidies, lower demand.
B   Lower interest rates, increased availability of credit from banks, higher demand.
C   Lower taxes, increased government subsidies and contracts being offered, higher demand.
D   Higher interest rates, less availability of credit from banks, lower demand.   **(2 marks)**

3 **Which of the following money market instruments would be classed as 'discount' instruments as opposed to 'interest bearing'?**

1   Commercial paper
2   Treasury bills
3   Certificate of Deposit
4   Bankers acceptance

A   1 and 2 only
B   1, 3 and 4 only
C   2,3 and 4 only
D   1,2 and 4 only   **(2 marks)**

4 The following information is relevant to ABC Co:

Receivables days: 56 days

Inventory turnover: 10 times

Payables days: 45 days

Days per year: 360 days

ABC implements an inventory holding policy that reduces inventory days by 6.

What is the new length of the working capital cycle?

A   143 days
B   53 days
C   41 days
D   131 days   **(2 marks)**

5   NMW Co is considering offering a 2% early settlement discount to its customers. Currently sales are $10 million and customers take 60 days to pay. NMW Co estimates half the customers will take up the discount and pay cash. NMW is currently financing working capital using an overdraft on which it pays a 10% charge. Assume 365 days in a year.

What will be the effect of implementing the policy?

A   Benefit of $17,808
B   Cost of $17,808
C   Benefit of $82,192
D   Benefit of $182,192   (2 marks)

6   FMB Co uses the Miller-Orr model to help manage its cash balances. It has calculated the standard deviation of daily cash flows is $1,200. The cost of buying / selling securities is $25 per transaction, and the daily interest rate is 0.03%. It decides to set a minimum balance of $5,000.

What is the spread, upper limit and return point?

	Spread	Upper Limit	Return point
A	$13,444	$18,444	$11,148
B	$1,265	$6,265	$5,422
C	$2,896	$7,896	$5,965
D	$273	$5,273	$5,091

(2 marks)

7   QWE Co is appraising a new 5-year project that will generate net cash inflows of $50,000 for an initial investment in machinery of $250,000. The machinery has an estimated scrap value of $100,000.

What is the return on capital employed (ROCE) for the project (using the average investment method)?

A   26.7%
B   11.4%
C   8%
D   142.9%   (2 marks)

8   ASD Co has appraised 4 mutually exclusive projects using 4 different investment appraisal techniques:

	Return on capital employed (%)	Payback period (years)	Net present value ($'000)	Internal rate of return (%)
Project 1	15	2	20	20
Project 2	12	3	24	15
Project 3	10	1.5	6	17
Project 4	11	4	10	35

Which should ASD Co invest in?

A   Project 1
B   Project 2
C   Project 3
D   Project 4   (2 marks)

9   A project is estimated to have an initial outflow of $100,000 followed by 10 years of operational net cash inflows of $20,000. Inflation is currently assumed to be zero.

What would be the impact of the net present value ('NPV') of the project if the inflation assumption was changed to be uniformly 4% per annum?

A   NPV would increase
B   NPV would decrease
C   No impact
D   Cannot say   (2 marks)

10 Which of the following statements is false regarding simulations?

- **A** They can consider several variables changing simultaneously.
- **B** They have a clear decision rule.
- **C** They give a better understanding of risk.
- **D** They describe a range and probability of possible outcomes. (2 marks)

11 A games emporium has one space for a new slot machine. Machine A lasts for 4 years and has a net present value of $10,000. Machine B last for 6 years and has a net present value of $12,800. The emporium has a cost of capital of 10%, and intends to indefinitely replace the machine with an identical model going forwards.

Which machine should the games emporium select and why?

- **A** Machine B as it has the highest net present value.
- **B** Machine A as the average net present value per year is higher.
- **C** Machine A as it offers the highest equivalent annual benefit.
- **D** Machine B as it offers the highest equivalent annual benefit. (2 marks)

12 MH Co has a 7% convertible loan note in issue, currently priced at $125. It is convertible at any time over the next 5 years into 25 ordinary shares. The share price is currently $4.10.

How much is the conversion premium?

- **A** $22.50
- **B** $2.50
- **C** $32.5
- **D** $102.5 (2 marks)

13 A company follows a policy of only paying a dividend after it has reserved sufficient funds for new investment.

What is this type of dividend policy is known as?

- **A** Constant payout ratio
- **B** Constant growth
- **C** Pecking order
- **D** Residual (2 marks)

14 Which of the following best describes financial risk when it comes to the gearing decision?

- **A** No less interest is paid in bad years, and no more in good years – it is a fixed cost so increased gearing makes returns to shareholders more volatile.

- **B** More new gearing means existing lenders are less likely to receive a settlement upon winding up.

- **C** High gearing will increase the cost of capital due to financial distress.

- **D** There is an increased possibility of cash flow/liquidity issues with higher gearing. (2 marks)

15 Company A's shares have a higher Beta factor than Company B's.

Which of the following is true about Company A?

- **A** Total risk is higher than Company B
- **B** It is exposed to more systematic risk factors than Company B
- **C** Its shares are under priced
- **D** It is exposed to higher levels of systematic risk than Company B. (2 marks)

16 Which of the following is true in relation to Modigliani-Miller (with tax)?

- **A** The cost of equity line is flat.
- **B** The weighted average cost of capital line is flat.
- **C** The cost of equity line is upward sloping.
- **D** The cost of debt line is downward sloping. (2 marks)

17 The following information relates to a business.

Debt collection period	5 weeks
Raw material inventory holding period	1 week
Suppliers' credit period	3 weeks
Production period	1 week
Finished goods inventory holding period	4 weeks

What is the working capital cycle of the business ?

A   3 weeks
B   4 weeks
C   8 weeks
D   14 weeks

(2 marks)

18 The following relates to a profit warning announcement by HGF Co:

30 September   Discussion and agreement at Board Level that profits for the year are likely to fall short of expectations.

4 October   announcement of the expected shortfall at a press conference.

Share price fell 40% on 2 October.

What does this imply about the efficiency of the capital markets?

A   A weak form efficient market
B   A semi-strong form efficient market
C   A strong form efficient market
D   Complete inefficiency in the market

(2 marks)

19 The US \$/€ spot exchange rate is \$1.4000: €1 +/- 1.2c. Interest rates In the US are currently 5%, whereas they are 2% in Europe. A US company buys €5 million of supplies from Europe, with settlement due in 12 months time. The transaction is unhedged.

What will be the expected dollar cost?

A   \$7,060,000
B   \$7,267,500
C   \$6,858,500
D   \$7,144,000

(2 marks)

20 What type of option would a borrower use to hedge against interest rate rises and when would it be abandoned?

A   Put option, abandon when rates rise
B   Put option, abandon when rates fall
C   Call option, abandon when rates rise
D   Call option, abandon when rates fall

(2 marks)
(Total = 40 marks)

Section B

Answer ALL questions

1   Plot Co sells Product P with sales occurring evenly throughout the year.

Product P

The annual demand for Product P is 300,000 units and an order for new inventory is placed each month. Each order costs $267 to place. The cost of holding Product P in inventory is 10 cents per unit per year. Buffer inventory equal to 40% of one month's sales is maintained.

Other information

Plot Co finances working capital with short-term finance costing 5% per year. Assume that there are 365 days in each year.

Required

(a)   **Calculate the following values for Product P:**

    (i)   **The total cost of the current ordering policy;**   **(2 marks)**

    (ii)   **The total cost of an ordering policy using the economic order quantity and the net cost or saving of introducing an ordering policy using this economic order quantity;**

                                                                  (3 marks)

(b)   **Identify the objectives of working capital management and discuss the central role of working capital management in financial management.**

                                                                  (5 marks)

                                                       (Total = 10 marks)

2   Spot Co is considering how to finance the acquisition of a machine costing $750,000 with an operating life of five years. There are two financing options.

Option 1

The machine could be leased for an annual lease payment of $155,000 per year, payable at the start of each year.

Option 2

The machine could be bought for $750,000 using a bank loan charging interest at an annual rate of 7% per year. At the end of five years, the machine would have a scrap value of 10% of the purchase price. If the machine is bought, maintenance costs of $20,000 per year would be incurred.

Taxation must be ignored.

Required

(a)   **Evaluate whether Spot Co should use leasing or borrowing as a source of finance, explaining the evaluation method which you use.**   **(7 marks)**

(b)   **Discuss the attractions of leasing as a source of both short-term and long-term finance.**

                                                               (3 marks)

                                                          (Total = 10 marks)

3   ABC Co is considering options for long-term finance. ABC Co is considering loans of varying maturity, and potentially some Islamic financial instruments.

Required

(a)   **In Islamic finance, explain briefly the concept of riba (interest) and how returns are made by Islamic financial instruments.** **(5 marks)**

(b)   **Discuss briefly the reasons why interest rates may differ between loans of different maturity.** **(5 marks)**

(Total = 10 marks)

4   Darn Co has undertaken market research at a cost of $200,000 in order to forecast the future cash flows of an investment project with an expected life of four years, as follows:

Year	1	2	3	4
Sales revenue	1,250	2,570	6,890	4,530
Sales (units/year)	500	1,000	2,500	1,750

These forecast cash flows are before taking account of general inflation of 4.7% per year. The capital cost of the investment project, payable at the start of the first year, will be $2,000,000. The investment project will have zero scrap value at the end of the fourth year. The level of working capital investment at the start of each year is expected to be 10% of the sales revenue in that year.

Tax allowable depreciation would be available on the capital cost of the investment project on a 25% reducing balance basis. Darn Co pays tax on profits at an annual rate of 30% per year, with tax being paid one year in arrears. Darn Co has a nominal (money terms) after-tax cost of capital of 12% per year.

Required

(a)   **Calculate the net present value of the investment project in nominal terms and comment on its financial acceptability.** **(10 marks)**

(b)   **Discuss the problems faced when undertaking investment appraisal in the following areas and comment on how these problems can be overcome:**

   (i)   **assets with replacement cycles of different lengths;**
   (ii)   **an investment project has several internal rates of return;** **(5 marks)**

(Total = 15 marks)

5   Card Co has in issue 8 million shares with an ex dividend market value of $7.16 per share. A dividend of 62 cents per share for 20X3 has just been paid. The pattern of recent dividends is as follows:

Year	20X0	20X1	20X2	20X3
Dividends per share (cents)	55.1	57.9	59.1	62.0

Card Co also has in issue 8.5% bonds redeemable in five years' time with a total nominal value of $5 million. The market value of each $100 bond is $103.42. Redemption will be at nominal value.

Card Co is planning to invest a significant amount of money into a joint venture in a new business area. It has identified a proxy company with a similar business risk to the joint venture. The proxy company has an equity beta of 1.038 and is financed 75% by equity and 25% by debt, on a market value basis.

The current risk-free rate of return is 4% and the average equity risk premium is 5%. Card Co pays profit tax at a rate of 30% per year and has an equity beta of 1.6.

Required

(a)   Calculate the cost of equity of Card Co using the dividend growth model.   (2 marks)

(b)   Calculate the weighted average after-tax cost of capital of Card Co using a cost of equity of 12%.
                                                                                          (4 marks)

(c)   Calculate a project-specific cost of equity for Card Co for the planned joint venture.   (3 marks)

(d)   Discuss whether changing the capital structure of a company can lead to a reduction in its cost of capital and hence to an increase in the value of the company.   (6 marks)

(Total = 15 marks)

Answers

DO NOT TURN THIS PAGE UNTIL YOU HAVE
COMPLETED THE MOCK EXAM

A PLAN OF ATTACK

We've already established that you've been told to do it 102 times, so it is of course superfluous to tell you for the 103rd time to **take a good look at the paper before diving in to answer questions.** You are going to remember aren't you?

Which order to do the questions

As a general rule work through Section A first. During reading time you should then decide the **order** in which to attempt the questions in Section B. You will probably have decided which question looks the easiest and started with that one. Answer plans will help you to decide how to approach each question.

The next step

You're probably thinking that you don't know where to begin or you could answer all of the questions in two hours!

Option 1 (Oh dear)

If you are challenged by this paper, do the questions in the order of how well you think you can answer them.

- **Section A** is a good place to start – plenty of short questions to settle you in. Then move on to Section B:

- **Question 1** is half numbers. There are some easy calculations to warm up with in part (a). Do a detailed answer plan for part (b) to help you get started.

- **Question 2** has some reasonably tricky numbers to start with on leasing, but get your workings down and you should pick some sufficient marks.

- **Question 3** is purely discursive. Plan your answer out first with reference to the mark allocation – decide on the points you'll make and the order you'll make them in before you start,

- **Question 4** requires you to calculate NPV, with inflation. Don't get swamped by inflation – show clear workings and lay your thinking on the page like a road map for the marker.

- **Question 5** Asks you to calculate WACC and then a project specific cost of capital (degearing and regearing betas). Although the numbers on this latter part are tricky, there are 6 marks to finish that are reasonably generic – make sure you leave enough time to mop them up!

Option 2 (This one's definitely easier)

Are you **sure** it is? If you are then that's encouraging but don't forget to do answer plans to make sure you don't miss the point of the questions.

- Don't just do a brain dump of everything you know in **Question 3.** Make sure you interpret the mark allocation carefully to help you assess the volume you need to write.

- Time management is going to be important in **Questions 4 and 5** as there are a lot of calculations to get through.

Once more for the road

You must **allocate your time** according to the marks for the question in total, and for the parts of the questions. And you must also **follow the requirements exactly.**

Finished with fifteen minutes to spare?

Looks like you slipped up on the time allocation. However if you have, make sure you don't waste the last few minutes; go back to **any parts of questions that you didn't finish** because you ran out of time.

Forget about it!

Forget about what? Excellent, you already have.

Section A

1   **A**   Economy is the cost of inputs hence saving money by switching suppliers is good performance in this regard.

Efficiency is the volume of output per unit of input – in this example increased class sizes means increased efficiency as more children are receiving an education per teacher/classroom.

Effectiveness is the quality of outputs. In this case, exam results have reduced hence the education 'produced' is less effective than previously.

Syllabus area A4b

2   **C**   Statement A describes a contractionary fiscal policy.

Statement B describes an expansionary monetary policy.

Statement C is correct: fiscal policy refers to the balance of taxation and government spending. In an effort to boost demand, the government would reduce taxes and increase government spending, net injecting demand into the economy.

Statement D describes a contractionary monetary policy.

Syllabus area B1c

3   **D**   Commercial paper, treasury bills and bankers acceptances do not pay interest. They are issued at a discount and redeemed at a higher value. A certificate of deposit does earn and pay interest however.

Syllabus area B3c

4   **C**   Current inventory days = 365/10 = 36 days. After new policy: 36 – 6 = 30 days.

Length of the working capital cycle = receivables days + inventory days – payables days

= 56 + 30 – 45 = 41 days.

Syllabus area C3a

5   **B**   Current receivables = $10 million × (60 / 365) = $1,643,835.

Overdraft interest charge per annum relating to current receivables = $1,643,835 × 10% = $164,383.50 pa

Interest saved when half customers pay cash = 0.5 × $164,383.50 = $82,191.75 pa

Annual cost of the discount = 0.5 × $10 million × 2% = $100,000.

Net cost of offering the early settlement discount = $100,000 – $82,191.75 = $17,808.25 cost pa

Syllabus area C2d

6   **A**   The spread

$$= 3\left[\frac{\frac{3}{4} \times \text{transaction cost} \times \text{variance of cash flows}}{\text{interest rate}}\right]^3$$

= 3[(0.75 × $25 × (1200)^2)/0.0003)]$^{(1/3)}$ =$13,444

Upper limit = lower limit + spread = $5,000 + $13,444 = $18,444

Return point = lower limit + ((1/3) × spread) = $5,000+ (4481/3) = $11,148

Syllabus area C2f

7   B   ROCE = Average annual accounting profits / Average investment

Average annual accounting profits   = (Total cash inflows − total depreciation) / 5

$$= [(5 \times \$50,000) - (250,000 - 100,000)] / 5$$

$$= \$20,000 \text{ pa}$$

Average investment = ($250,000 + $100,000) / 2 = $175,000

ROCE = $20,000 / 175,000 = 0.114 = 11.4% pa

Syllabus area D1e

8   B   Project 2 should be chosen as it has the highest net present value and will therefore add most to shareholder wealth should it be accepted.

Syllabus area D1g

9   C   An increase in inflation to 4% would both increase the net cash inflows and increase the cost of capital (the discount rate). These two should cancel each other out exactly, leaving no net effect on the net present value of the project.

Syllabus area D2a

10   B   The output of a simulation is likely to be a spread/range of possible outcomes and usually a probability distribution associated with those outcomes. It is not an 'optimising' technique ie the output of a simulation is designed to better inform the decision maker, but there is no clear 'invest / don't invest' decision rule to apply. It does consider many variable changing together and present a range of possible outcomes with associated probabilities so statements A, C and D are all true.

Syllabus area D3d

11   C   The machines have unequal lives and will be replaced with identical machines indefinitely hence the choice should be made based on equivalent annual benefit (EAB).

EAB Machine A = $10,000 / AF_{1-4}10% = $10,000 / 3.170 = $3,155 pa

EAB Machine B = $12,200 / AF_{1-6}10% = $12,800 / 4.355 = $2,939 pa

Therefore Machine A should be chosen as it offers the highest equivalent annual benefit.

Syllabus area D4b

12   A   The conversion premium compares the current loan note price with the value should it be converted ie $125 − (25 × $4.10) = $22.50.

Syllabus area E1b

13   D   A constant pay-out ratio assumes a consistent percentage of earnings is distributed by way of a dividend.

A constant growth policy assumes that, regardless of earnings, dividends grow by a predictable percentage.

Pecking order is not a dividend policy. It refers to a priority list for sources of finance.

The policy described is known as a residual policy – only funds available after budgeting for capital expenditure are distributed by way of a dividend.

Syllabus area E1e

14   A   Although B,C and D may be true, but they do not describe financial risk as such. By definition financial risk is the increases variability in dividends the shareholders suffer as a result of increased gearing.

Syllabus area E4

15 **D** Statement A is not necessarily correct. Beta factors only measure systematic risk, not total risk (which also includes specific/unsystematic risk).

Statement B is incorrect. Companies with different Beta factors may face the same systematic risk factors, only to a differing degree.

Statement C is incorrect. This (assumed) temporary mispricing is unlikely to affect the Beta factor overall.

Statement D is correct. Beta factors measure the level of systematic risk associated with a share.

Syllabus area E2a

16 **C** In all theories of capital structure the cost of equity line is upward sloping – there is an increased required rate of return from shareholders as gearing increases. This is due to increases levels of income variability ie financial risk.

Syllabus area E4b

17 **C** 5 + 1 – 3 + 1 + 4 = 8 weeks.

Syllabus area C2a

18 **C** Only a strong form efficient market reflects privately held information. The announcement made public on 4 October was reflected in share price two days earlier on 2 October (possibly due to insider dealing) meaning at that point privately held information was reflected in share price.

Syllabus area E4a

19 **B** The relevant spot rate currently for a US company seeking to buy € is $1.4000 + $0.012 = $1.412 (as this will cost most $).

Using interest rate parity, In 1 year's time this rate should move to $1.412 × (1.05/1.02) = $1.4535/€.

The expected $ cost will therefore be €5m × 1.4535 = $7,267,500.

Syllabus area G2b

20 **B** **B**orrowers **P**urchase a **P**ut – remember 'BPP' – the publisher of this Study Text!

It will be exercised when rates rise to effectively cap the net interest rate paid. Conversely, it will be allowed to lapse when rates fall so the borrower can benefit from the fall in the spot interest rate. There is a premium to pay for this flexibility.

Syllabus area E4b

Section B – Question 1

Marking scheme

				Marks
(a)	(i)	Current ordering cost	0.5	
		Buffer inventory	0.5	
		Average inventory	0.5	
		Holding cost	0.5	
				2
	(ii)	Economic order quantity	0.5	
		EOQ order cost	1	
		Holding cost	0.5	
		Total cost	0.5	
		Saving from EOQ ordering policy	0.5	3
(b)		Objectives of working capital management	2-3	
		Role of working capital management	2-3	
			Maximum	5
				10

(a) (i) **Cost of current ordering policy**

Total cost = order costs + holding costs.

Ordering cost = 12 × 267 = $3,204 per year   Note: One order per month

Monthly order = monthly demand = 300,000/12 = 25,000 units

Buffer inventory = 25,000 × 0.4 = 10,000 units

Average inventory excluding buffer inventory = 25,000/2 = 12,500 units

Average inventory including buffer inventory = 12,500 + 10,000 = 22,500 units Holding cost = 22,500 × 0.1 = $2,250 per year

Total cost = 3,204 + 2,250 = $5,454 per year

(ii) **Cost of ordering policy using economic order quantity (EOQ)**

$EOQ = \sqrt{(2 \times C_o \times D)/C_h}$

$EOQ = \sqrt{(2 \times 267 \times 300{,}000)/0.10} = 40{,}025$ per order

Number of orders per year = 300,000/40,025 = 7.5 orders per year

Order cost = 7.5 × 267 = $2,003

Average inventory excluding buffer inventory = 40,025/2 = 20,012 units

Average inventory including buffer inventory = 20,012 + 10,000 = 30,012 units

Holding cost = 30,000 × 0.1 = $3,001 per year

Total cost = $2,003 + $3,001 = $5,004 per year

Saving from introducing EOQ ordering policy = 5,454 − 5,004 = $450 per year

(b) The objectives of working capital management are usually taken to be profitability and liquidity. The two objectives are naturally in conflict as less liquid investments tend to be more profitable. The investor is compensated for the lack of liquidity.

In terms of working capital investment (the amount of money tied up in working capital) organisations can have a conservative (high level of investment) or aggressive (low level of investment) approach. The former is likely to be low risk but expensive, the latter the opposite. In terms of working capital finance, organisations can have a conservative (mainly long-term finance) or aggressive (mainly short-term finance) approach. The former is likely to be low risk but expensive, the latter more risky but cheaper (as short-term finance is low risk from the investors perspective.)

Organisations therefore need to decide where to strike a balance between these two objectives.

Cash is the lifeblood of a business, hence managing the level and finance of cash and near-cash assets is central to financial management. Poor financial management of working capital can lead to cash flow difficulties or even the failure of a business. Astute working capital management can also create profits/minimise costs, which adds to the wealth of shareholders ultimately – a key objective in the vast majority of businesses.

Question 2

Text reference. Lease v buy is covered in Chapter 11.

Top tips. Don't forget to explain the method you're using. This is required by the question and discussion always scores highly in this paper.

Easy marks. Show your workings in part (a) and don't dwell too long on them. You'll pick up some marks but the easier marks are going for the explanation in part (a), and some of the more obvious points in part (b).

Marking scheme

			Marks
(a)	Timing of lease payments	0.5	
	PV of cost of leasing	0.5	
	PV of maintenance cost	1	
	PV of salvage value	0.5	
	PV of cost of borrowing	0.5	
	Evaluation of financing choice	1	
	Explanation and evaluation of financing method	3	
			7
(b)	Attractions of leasing as short-term finance source	1-2	
	Attractions of leasing as long-term finance source	1-2	
	Maximum		3
			10

(a) **Cost of leasing**

The lease payments should be discounted using the cost of borrowing of Spot Co. Since taxation must be ignored, the before-tax cost of borrowing must be used. The 7% interest rate of the bank loan can be used here.

The five lease payments will begin at year 0 and the last lease payment will be at the start of year 5, ie at the end of year 4. The appropriate annuity factor to use will therefore be 4.387 ($1.000 + 3.387$).

Lease payment are in advance (T_0-T_4) so the Present value = $155,000 \times (1+AF_{1-4}7\%)$

(Note: 7% is the cost of borrowing.)

$= 155,000 \times (1 + 3.387) = \$679,985$ cost.

Cost of borrowing and buying

Year	Cash flow	$	7% Discount factor	Present value
0	Purchase	(750,000)	1.000	(750,000)
1–5	Maintenance	(20,000)	4.100	(82,000)
5	Scrap value	75,000	0.713	53,475
				$(778,525) cost

The cheaper source of financing is leasing, since the present value of the cost of leasing is $98,540 less than the present value of the cost of borrowing.

(b) Operating leases can act as a source of short-term finance, while finance leases can act as a source of long-term finance.

Operating lease

Operating leases, being relatively short term, will protect against the risk of obsolescence as old machinery can be returned in the relatively near future. In addition, the lessor may provide technical assistance that otherwise would be relatively expensive.

Finance lease

Finance leases may be a legitimate source of finance when conventional loans are not possible, for example if the company has little to offer in the way of security. Since ownership of the leased asset technically remains with the lessor it can be retrieved if rental payments are not forthcoming.

Question 3

Text reference. Islamic finance is covered in Chapter 12. The yield term is covered in Chapter 20.

Top tips. As it is wholly discursive, this question needs some careful planning. Think of the points you will write and the order you'll write them in before starting your final answer. Also, make sure your answer mirrors the structure of the question. For example, your answer to (a) should start by explaining riba in its own paragraph, the remainder being answered in separate paragraphs underneath.

Easy marks. Provided you've learned and understood the Islamic finance section of the syllabus, part (a) should be relatively straightforward.

Marking scheme

			Marks
(a)	Explanation of interest (riba)	2-3	
	Explanation of returns on Islamic financial instruments	2-3	
		Maximum	5
(b)	Liquidity preference theory	1-2	
	Expectations theory	1-2	
	Market segmentation theory	1-2	
	Fiscal policy	1-2	
		Maximum	5
			10

(a) Interest (riba) is a fixed amount payable for the use of finance, irrespective of the performance of the investment. Riba is strictly forbidden under Sharia'a law. It is seen as detrimental to the borrower if their investment underperforms, and detrimental to the lender if the investment performs exceptionally well.

As a general principle in Islamic finance, risks in report of ownership are shared between both the provider of the finance and the party who purchases the underlying asset. For example, with sukuk (bonds), certificates are issued to the lender and both share the risks and rewards of ownership of that asset.

In a musharaka contract, profits and losses are shared in proportions agreed upfront. Dividends as such are not paid.

(b) The term structure of interest rates can be seen with reference to the yield curve, which compares periodic rate of return with the term of debt. The yield curve is a general upward slope, indicating that longer-term debt commands a higher interest rate. There are several reasons put forward to explain this.

Liquidity preference theory

Investors prefer to have cash now, and require increasing amounts of compensation for money tied up for longer. Hence, a lender who is prepared to part with their money for a long period of time will only do so if compensated by receiving a higher rate of interest. In addition to this convenience point, the distant future is inherently more risky than the near future as it is less certain, also helping to explain why longer-term debt commands a higher rate of interest.

Expectations theory

Expectations of future interest rate rises are built into the yield curve. If expectations change such that the markets on average believe any interest rates rise is imminent, this will be reflected by an increased rate of return required on longer term debt. The curve will slope upwards more steeply.

Market segmentation theory

At times the yield curve is discontinuous, or 'kinked.' One possible explanation for this is that fundamentally different types of investors invest in short-term loans, compared to long-term loans. Their differing risk/return profile is reflected as a change in the shape of the curve at certain terms.

Fiscal policy

The government may use short-term interest rates to manage demand in an economy. This activity may affect short-term interest rates more than long-term if the markets believe the government policy to be relatively temporary in nature.

Question 4

Text reference. Net present value calculations with inflation are covered in Chapters 8 and 9.

Top tips. Watch your time carefully on part (a). Start with the easy numbers and work your way up to the harder numbers always keeping an eye on the clock. Don't let the inflation aspect of this calculation drag you down.

Easy marks. Don't forget to conclude in part (a), it's the easiest mark in the question! Part (b) is a fairly straightforward discussion on limitations of investment appraisal in certain circumstances and approaches that can solve these problems.

Marking scheme

		Marks
(a)	Inflated sales revenue	1
	Inflated costs	1
	Tax liability	1
	Tax allowable depreciation, years 1 to 3	1
	Balancing allowance, year 4	0.5
	Tax allowable depreciation tax benefits	1
	Timing of tax liabilities and benefits	1
	Incremental working capital investment	1
	Recovery of working capital	0.5
	Market research omitted as sunk cost	0.5
	Calculation of nominal terms NPV	1
	Comment on financial acceptability	0.5
		10

(b) Discussion of asset replacement decisions   2-3

Discussion of projects with several IRRs   2-3

5

15

(a) As the requirement states calculations are to be performed in nominal terms, cash flows need to be stated in their future amounts (ie inflated if necessary) and discounted at the nominal rate – the nominal rate also includes inflation.

$'000	0	1	2	3	4	5
Net cash inflow before corporation tax (working 1)		785.25	1,721.05	5,038.54	3,340.65	
Tax in net cash inflow @ 30% 1 year in arrears			(235.58)	(516.32)	(1,511.56)	(1,002.20)
Benefit of tax allowable depn (working 2)			150	112.5	84.38	253.13
Investment	(2,000)					
Working capital (working 3)	(130.88)	(150.86)*	(509.06)	246.43	544.36	
Net cash flow	(2130.88)	634.39	1,126.41	4,881.15	2,457.83	(749.07)
12% Discount factor	1	0.893	0.797	0.712	0.636	0.567
Present value	(2130.88)	566.51	897.75	3,475.38	1,563.18	(424.72)

Net present value = $\sum$ Present values = 3,947.22

ie Positive $3,947,220 therefore the project is financially acceptable as accepting it should increase shareholder wealth.

Workings

1 *Inflated net cash inflows*

	1	2	3	4
Sales revenue	1,250	2,570	6,890	4,530
Less Costs	(500)	(1,000)	(2,500)	(1,750)
Net cash inflow in real terms	750	1,570	4,390	2,780
Inflation factor	× 1.047	× $(1.047)^2$	× $(1.047)^3$	× $(1.047)^4$
Net cash flow in nominal terms	785.25	1,721.05	5,038.54	3,340.65

2 *Tax allowable depreciation*

		Tax saved @30%	Timing
Initial cost	2,000		
1st year TAD 25%	(500)	150	T_1
TWDV end year 1	1,500		
2nd year TAD 25%	(375)	112.5	T_2
TWDV end year 2	1,125		
3rd year TAD 25%	(281.25)	84.38	T_3
TWDV end year 3	843.75		
Disposal	(0)		
Balancing allowance	843.75	253.13	T_4

3 *Working capital*

	0	1	2	3	4
Sales revenue (real terms)		1,250	2,570	6,890	4,530
Inflation factor		× 1.047	× $(1.047)^2$	× $(1.047)^3$	× $(1.047)^4$
Sales revenue (nominal terms)		1,308.75	2,817.26	7,907.87	5,443.58
Working capital (10%)		130.88	281.73	790.88	544.36
Increments (= cash flow) in place at start of year	(130.88)	(150.86)*	(509.06)	246.43	544.36

*for example, 281.73 – 130.88 = 150.86

(b)   (i)   The NPV method does not assess when or how frequently an asset should be replaced. The annual equivalent cost method addresses this issue. The annual equivalent cost is the present value of cost over one replacement cycle divided by the cumulative present value factor for the number of years in the cycle. The optimum replacement period is the period with the lowest equivalent annual cost.

      (ii) Investment projects with non-conventional cash flows can have more than one internal rate of return. Decision makers need to be aware of this to avoid making the wrong decision. The use of NPV can remove this issue as the NPV method deals with non-conventional cash flows. This is a reason why NPV is considered to be superior to the IRR method.

Question 5

Text reference. The cost of capital is covered in Chapter 15. Project specific cost of capital and capital structure theories are covered in Chapter 16.

Top tips. There are several small requirements leading up to part (d). Don't allow yourself to spend too long on any one requirement in case you miss out on the relatively easy marks later on.

Easy marks. Part (d) is a standard question not particularly related to the scenario. There are easy marks to be had here, just make sure you don't run out of time before you get to part (d).

Marking scheme

			Marks
(a)	Calculation of historic dividend growth rate	1	
	Calculation of cost of equity using DGM	1	
			2
(b)	After tax interest payment	0.5	
	Setting up linear interpolation calculation	0.5	
	Calculation of after-tax cost of debt	1	
	Calculation of market value of equity	0.5	
	Calculation of market value of debt	0.5	
	Calculation of WACC	1	
			4
(c)	Ungearing proxy company equity beta	1	
	Regearing asset beta	1	
	Project-specific cost of equity using CAPM	1	
			3
(d)	Traditional view of capital structure	1-2	
	Miller and Modigliani views of capital structure	2-3	
	Market imperfections view of capital structure	1-2	
	Other relevant discussion	1-2	
	Maximum		6
			15

(a)   Cost of equity of Card Co using DGM

Average annual growth rate: $55.1 (1 + g)^3 = 62.0$

$g = \sqrt[3]{(62.0/55.1)} - 1 = 0.04$ or 4%

$Ke = [d_0(1 + g) / P_0] + g = [(62 \times 1.04)/716] + 0.04 = 0.13$ or 13%

(b) WACC of Card Co

The annual after-tax interest payment is $8.5 \times (1 - 0.3) = \$5.95$ per bond

Using linear interpolation:

Year	Cash flow	$	5% DF	PV ($)	6% DF	PV ($)
0	Market price	(103.42)	1.000	(103.42)	1.000	(103.42)
1–5	Interest	5.95	4.329	25.76	4.212	25.06
5	Redemption	100	0.784	78.40	0.747	74.70
				0.74		(3.66)

After-tax cost of debt $= 5 + [((6 - 5) \times 0.74)/(0.74 + 3.66)] = 5 + 0.17 = 5.17\%$

Market values

	$'000
Equity: 8m × 7.16 =	57,280
Bonds: 5m × 103.42/100 =	5,171
Total value of Card Co	62,451

WACC calculation

WACC of Card Co =

$$WACC = \left[\frac{V_e}{V_e + V_d}\right] k_e + \left[\frac{V_d}{V_e + V_d}\right] k_d$$

$[57,280/62,451]12\% + [5,171/62,451]5.17\% = 11.4\%$

(c) First, the proxy company equity beta must be ungeared:

$$\text{ß}a = \text{ß}_e \times \frac{V_e}{(V_e + V_d (1 - t))}$$

$= 1.038 \times (0.75/[0.75 + (0.25 \times 0.7)])$

$= 0.842$

The asset beta must then be regeared to reflect the financial risk of Card

$$\text{ß}a = \text{ß}_e \times \frac{V_e}{(V_e + V_d (1 - t))} = 0.842$$

$= \text{ß}e \times ((0.75/[0.75 + (0.25 \times 0.7)]) = 0.895$

Project-specific cost of equity (using CAPM formula) $= Rf + \text{ß}(E(rm) - Rf) = 4\% + (0.895 \times 5\%) = 8.5\%$

(d) As the weighted average cost of capital (WACC) is the discount rate that can be applied to the cash flows of a business, the net present value of those cash flows is maximised when the WACC is minimised.

The traditional view states that at moderate levels of gearing, increased amounts of relatively cheap debt reduces the cost of capital. However, with extremely high levels of borrowing, financial distress increases the cost of capital. The traditional view concludes that there is an optimum – a balance to be struck between debt and equity. Taking this view, a business with a low level of gearing should reduce its cost of capital if it gears up. Conversely if a business is highly geared, it can reduce its cost of capital by reducing its gearing level towards the optimum. Unfortunately the traditional view does not give any formulae that can be used to assist in this process.

Modigliani-Miller (MM) initially showed that if no tax is assumed, the capital structure of the business does not affect the WACC. This is because total payments to investors are not affected by the proportions of interest versus dividends paid. In such circumstances therefore, the value of the company is not affected by its capital structure.

MM went on to show that if interest is tax-deductible, tax is saved by paying interest as opposed to dividends hence the total returns to investors increases as relatively more interest is paid and less dividends.

In these circumstances, increasing gearing should always lead to a reduction in the cost of capital, hence gearing up will increase the value of the company.

On balance, MM assume a perfect world and make some limiting assumptions. In reality, the traditional view of moderate levels of gearing adding value (provided it is not excessive) is probably more realistic.

ACCA

Paper F9

Financial Management

Mock Examination 3

Question Paper	
Time allowed	
Reading and Planning Writing	**15 minutes** **3 hours**
ALL questions are compulsory and MUST be attempted	
During reading and planning time only the question paper may be annotated	

DO NOT OPEN THIS PAPER UNTIL YOU ARE READY TO START UNDER EXAMINATION CONDITIONS

Section A

1   **In relation to hedging interest rate risk, which of the following statements is correct?**

   A   The flexible nature of interest rate futures means that they can always be matched with a specific interest rate exposure

   B   Interest rate options carry an obligation to the holder to complete the contract at maturity

   C   Forward rate agreements are the interest rate equivalent of forward exchange contracts

   D   Matching is where a balance is maintained between fixed rate and floating rate debt   **(2 marks)**

2   The home currency of ACB Co is the dollar ($) and it trades with a company in a foreign country whose home currency is the Dinar. The following information is available:

	Home country	Foreign country
Spot rate	20.00 Dinar per $	
Interest rate	3% per year	7% per year
Inflation rate	2% per year	5% per year

   What is the six-month forward exchange rate?

   A   20.39 Dinar per $
   B   20.30 Dinar per $
   C   20.59 Dinar per $
   D   20.78 Dinar per $ **(2 marks)**

3   The following financial information relates to an investment project:

	$000
Present value of sales revenue	50,025
Present value of variable costs	25,475
Present value of contribution	24,550
Present value of fixed costs	18,250
Present value of operating income	6,300
Initial investment	5,000
Net present value	1,300

   What is the sensitivity of the net present value of the investment project to a change in sales volume?

   A   7.1%
   B   2.6%
   C   5.1%
   D   5.3%   **(2 marks)**

4   TKQ Co has just paid a dividend of 21c per share and its share price is $3·50 per share. One year ago its share price was $3·10 per share.

   Working to one decimal place, what is the total shareholder return over the period?

   A   17.4%
   B   18.2%
   C   18.9%
   D   19.7%   **(2 marks)**

5   Gurdip plots the historic movements of share prices and uses this analysis to make her investment decisions.

   To what extent does Gurdip believe capital markets to be efficient?

   A   Not efficient at all
   B   Weak form efficient
   C   Semi-strong form efficient
   D   Strong form efficient   **(2 marks)**

6   **Which of the following statements concerning capital structure theory is correct?**

    A   In the traditional view, there is a linear relationship between the cost of equity and financial risk

    B   Modigliani and Miller said that, in the absence of tax, the cost of equity would remain constant

    C   Pecking order theory indicates that preference shares are preferred to convertible debt as a source of finance

    D   Business risk is assumed to be constant   **(2 marks)**

7   **What is the impact of a fall in a country's exchange rate?**

    1   Exports will be given a stimulus
    2   The rate of domestic inflation will rise

    A   1 only
    B   2 only
    C   Both 1 and 2
    D   Neither 1 nor 2   **(2 marks)**

8   **Which of the following actions is LEAST likely to increase shareholder wealth?**

    A   The average cost of capital is decreased by a recent financing decision
    B   The financial rewards of directors are linked to increasing earnings per share
    C   The board of directors decides to invest in a project with a positive net present value
    D   The annual report declares full compliance with the corporate governance code   **(2 marks)**

9   Value for money is an important objective for not-for-profit organisations.

    Which action is LEAST consistent with increasing value for money?

    A   Using a cheaper source of goods without decreasing the quality of not-for-profit organisation services

    B   Searching for ways to diversify the finances of the not-for-profit organisation

    C   Decreasing waste in the provision of a service by the not-for-profit organisation

    D   Focusing on meeting the objectives of the not-for-profit organisation   **(2 marks)**

10   **Which of the following statements are features of money market instruments?**

    1   A negotiable security can be sold before maturity
    2   The yield on commercial paper is usually lower than that on treasury bills
    3   Discount instruments trade at less than face value

    A   2 only
    B   1 and 3 only
    C   2 and 3 only
    D   1, 2 and 3   **(2 marks)**

11   The following are extracts from the statement of profit or loss of CQB Co:

	$000
Sales income	60,000
Cost of sales	50,000
Profit before interest and tax	10,000
Interest	4,000
Profit before tax	6,000
Tax	4,500
Profit after tax	1,500

60% of the cost of sales is variable costs.

What is the operational gearing of CQB Co?

A 5.0 times
B 2.0 times
C 0.5 times
D 3.0 times   (2 marks)

12 The management of XYZ Co has annual credit sales of $20 million and accounts receivable of $4 million. Working capital is financed by an overdraft at 12% interest per year. Assume 365 days in a year.

What is the annual finance cost saving if the management reduces the collection period to 60 days?

A $85,479
B $394,521
C $78,904
D $68,384   (2 marks)

13 **Which of the following statements concerning financial management are correct?**

1 It is concerned with investment decisions, financing decisions and dividend decisions
2 It is concerned with financial planning and financial control
3 It considers the management of risk

A 1 and 2 only
B 1 and 3 only
C 2 and 3 only
D 1, 2 and 3   (2 marks)

14 SKV Co has paid the following dividends per share in recent years:

Year	2013	2012	2011	2010
Dividend (cents per share)	36.0	33.8	32.8	31.1

The dividend for 2013 has just been paid and SKV Co has a cost of equity of 12%.

Using the geometric average historical dividend growth rate and the dividend growth model, what is the market price of SKV Co shares to the nearest cent on an ex dividend basis?

A $4.67
B $5.14
C $5.40
D $6.97   (2 marks)

15 'There is a risk that the value of our foreign currency-denominated assets and liabilities will change when we prepare our accounts.'

To which risk does the above statement refer?

A Translation risk
B Economic risk
C Transaction risk
D Interest rate risk   (2 marks)

16 The following information has been calculated for A Co:

Trade receivables collection period	52 days
Raw material inventory turnover period	42 days
Work in progress inventory turnover period	30 days
Trade payables payment period	66 days
Finished goods inventory turnover period	45 days

What is the length of the working capital cycle?

A   103 days
B   131 days
C   235 days
D   31 days   **(2 marks)**

17   **Which of the following is/are usually seen as benefits of financial intermediation?**

1   Interest rate fixing
2   Risk pooling
3   Maturity transformation

A   1 only
B   1 and 3 only
C   2 and 3 only
D   1, 2 and 3   **(2 marks)**

18   **Which of the following statements concerning working capital management are correct?**

1   The twin objectives of working capital management are profitability and liquidity
2   A conservative approach to working capital investment will increase profitability
3   Working capital management is a key factor in a company's long-term success

A   1 and 2 only
B   1 and 3 only
C   2 and 3 only
D   1, 2 and 3   **(2 marks)**

19   Luke Co has 8% convertible loan notes in issue which are redeemable in five years' time at their nominal value of $100 per loan note. Alternatively, each loan note could be converted after five years into 70 equity shares with a nominal value of $1 each.

The equity shares of Luke Co are currently trading at $1·25 per share and this share price is expected to grow by 4% per year. The before-tax cost of debt of Luke Co is 10% and the after-tax cost of debt of Luke Co is 7%.

What is the current market value of each loan note to the nearest dollar?

A $92
B $96
C $104
D $109   **(2 marks)**

20   Governments have a number of economic targets as part of their monetary policy.

Which of the following targets relate predominantly to monetary policy?

1   Increasing tax revenue
2   Controlling the growth in the size of the money supply
3   Reducing public expenditure
4   Keeping interest rates low

A   1 only
B   1 and 3
C   2 and 4 only
D   2, 3 and 4   **(2 marks)**
                                                      (Total = 40 marks)

Section B

1   Cat Co places monthly orders with a supplier for 10,000 components which are used in its manufacturing processes. Annual demand is 120,000 components. The current terms are payment in full within 90 days, which Cat Co meets, and the cost per component is $7·50. The cost of ordering is $200 per order, while the cost of holding components in inventory is $1·00 per component per year.

The supplier has offered a discount of 3·6% on orders of 30,000 or more components. If the bulk purchase discount is taken, the cost of holding components in inventory would increase to $2·20 per component per year due to the need for a larger storage facility.

Required:

(a)   **Discuss briefly the factors which influence the formulation of working capital policy.   (6 marks)**

(b)   **Calculate if Cat Co will benefit financially by accepting the offer of the bulk purchase discount.**

(4 marks)

(Total = 10 marks)

2   GWW Co is a listed company which is seen as a potential target for acquisition by financial analysts. The value of the company has therefore been a matter of public debate in recent weeks and the following financial information is available:

Year	2012	2011	2010	2009
Profit after tax ($m)	10.1	9.7	8.9	8.5

Statement of financial position information for 2012

	£m	£m
Non-current assets		91.0
Current assets		
Inventory	3.8	
Trade receivables	4.5	8.3
Total assets		99.3
Equity finance		
Ordinary shares	20.0	
Reserves	47.2	67.2
Non-current liabilities		
8% bonds		25.0
Current liabilities		7.1
Total liabilities		99.3

The shares of GWW Co have a nominal (par) value of 50c per share and a market value of $4.00 per share. The business sector of GWW Co has an average price/earnings ratio of 17 times.

The expected net realisable values of the non-current assets and the inventory are $86.0m and $4.2m, respectively. In the event of liquidation, only 80% of the trade receivables are expected to be collectible.

Required

(a)   **Calculate the value of GWW Co using the following methods:**

(i)   **market capitalisation (equity market value);**
(ii)   **net asset value (liquidation basis); and**
(iii)   **price/earnings ratio method using the business sector average price/earnings ratio.**

Note: The total marks will be split equally between each part.   **(6 marks)**

(b)   **Discuss briefly the advantages and disadvantages of using the dividend growth model to value the shares of GWW Co.**   **(4 marks)**

(Total = 10 marks)

3 ZPS Co, whose home currency is the dollar, took out a fixed-interest peso bank loan several years ago when peso interest rates were relatively cheap compared to dollar interest rates. Economic difficulties have now increased peso interest rates while dollar interest rates have remained relatively stable. ZPS Co must pay interest of 5,000,000 pesos in six months' time. The following information is available.

Spot rate: 12·500–12·582 pesos per $

Six-month forward rate: 12·805–12·889 pesos per $

Interest rates which can be used by ZPS Co:

	Borrow	Deposit
Peso interest rates	10.0% per year	7.5% per year
Dollar interest rates:	4.5% per year	3.5 per year

Required

(a) Explain briefly the relationships between:

    (i)   exchange rates and interest rates;

    (ii)   exchange rates and inflation rates.

    Note: The total marks will be split equally between each part.   **(4 marks)**

(b) Calculate whether a forward market hedge or a money market hedge should be used to hedge the interest payment of 5 million pesos in six months' time. Assume that ZPS Co would need to borrow any cash it uses in hedging exchange rate risk.   **(6 marks)**

                                                                (Total = 10 marks)

4 PV Co is evaluating an investment proposal to manufacture Product W33, which has performed well in test marketing trials conducted recently by the company's research and development division. The following information relating to this investment proposal has now been prepared:

Initial investment	$2 million
Selling price (current price terms)	$20 per unit
Expected selling price inflation	3% per year
Variable operating costs (current price terms)	$8 per unit
Fixed operating costs (current price terms)	$170,000 per year
Expected operating cost inflation	4% per year

The research and development division has prepared the following demand forecast as a result of its test marketing trials. The forecast reflects expected technological change and its effect on the anticipated life-cycle of Product W33.

Year	1	2	3	4
Demand (units)	60,000	70,000	120,000	45,000

It is expected that all units of Product W33 produced will be sold, in line with the company's policy of keeping no inventory of finished goods. No terminal value or machinery scrap value is expected at the end of four years, when production of Product W33 is planned to end. For investment appraisal purposes, PV Co uses a nominal (money) discount rate of 10% per year and a target return on capital employed of 30% per year. Ignore taxation.

Required

(a) Calculate the following values for the investment proposal:

    (i)   net present value;   **(5 marks)**

    (ii)   internal rate of return, and;   **(3 marks)**

    (iii)   return on capital employed (accounting rate of return) based on average investment.

                                                                  (3 marks)

(b) Discuss briefly your findings in each section of (a) above and advise whether the investment proposal is financially acceptable.   **(4 marks)**

                                                                  (Total = 15 marks)

5   DD Co has a dividend payout ratio of 40% and has maintained this payout ratio for several years. The current dividend per share of the company is 50c per share and it expects that its next dividend per share, payable in one year's time, will be 52c per share.

The capital structure of the company is as follows:

	£m	£m
Equity		
Ordinary shares (par value $1 per share)	25	
Reserves	35	
		60
Debt		
Bond A (par value $100)	20	
Bond B (par value $100)	10	
		30
		90

Bond A will be redeemed at par in ten years' time and pays annual interest of 9%. The cost of debt of this bond is 9.83% per year. The current ex interest market price of the bond is $95·08.

Bond B will be redeemed at par in four years' time and pays annual interest of 8%. The cost of debt of this bond is 7.82% per year. The current ex interest market price of the bond is $102.01. DD Co has a cost of equity of 12.4%. Ignore taxation.

Required

(a)   Calculate the following values for DD Co:

    (i)   ex dividend share price, using the dividend growth model;   **(3 marks)**

    (ii)   capital gearing (debt divided by debt plus equity) using market values; and   **(2 marks)**

    (iii)   market value weighted average cost of capital.   **(2 marks)**

(b)   Discuss whether a change in dividend policy will affect the share price of DD Co.   **(8 marks)**

                                                        (Total = 15 marks)

Answers

DO NOT TURN THIS PAGE UNTIL YOU HAVE
COMPLETED THE MOCK EXAM

A PLAN OF ATTACK

We've already established that you've been told to do it 103 times, so it is of course superfluous to tell you for the 104th time to **take a good look at the paper before diving in to answer questions.** You are going to remember aren't you?

Which order to do the questions

As a general rule work through Section A first. During reading time you should then decide the **order** in which to attempt the questions in Section B. You will probably have decided which question looks the easiest and started with that one. Answer plans will help you to decide how to approach each question.

The next step

You're probably thinking that you don't know where to begin or you could answer all of the questions in two hours!

Option 1 (Oh dear)

If you are challenged by this paper, do the questions in the order of how well you think you can answer them.

- **Section A** is a good place to start – plenty of short questions to settle you in. Then move on to Section B:

- **Question 1** is half numbers. There are some easy calculations to warm up with in part (a). Do a detailed answer plan for part (b) to help you get started.

- **Question 2** has some reasonably tricky numbers to start with on leasing, but get your workings down and you should pick some sufficient marks.

- **Question 3** is purely discursive. Plan your answer out first with reference to the mark allocation – decide on the points you'll make and the order you'll make them in before you start,

- **Question 4** requires you to calculate NPV, with inflation. Don't get swamped by inflation – show clear workings and lay your thinking on the page like a road map for the marker.

- **Question 5** Asks you to calculate WACC and then a project specific cost of capital (degearing and regearing betas). Although the numbers on this latter part are tricky, there are 6 marks to finish that are reasonably generic – make sure you leave enough time to mop them up!

Option 2 (This one's definitely easier)

Are you **sure** it is? If you are then that's encouraging but don't forget to do answer plans to make sure you don't miss the point of the questions.

- Don't just do a brain dump of everything you know in **Question 1 part (a).** Make sure you interpret the mark allocation carefully to help you assess the volume you need to write.

- Time management is going to be important in **Questions 4 and 5** (4 in particular) as there are a lot of calculations to get through.

Once more for the road

You must **allocate your time** according to the marks for the question in total, and for the parts of the questions. And you must also **follow the requirements exactly.**

Finished with fifteen minutes to spare?

Looks like you slipped up on the time allocation. However if you have, make sure you don't waste the last few minutes; go back to **any parts of questions that you didn't finish** because you ran out of time.

Forget about it!

Forget about what? Excellent, you already have.

Section A

1   C   Statement A is incorrect: Although futures are flexible with timing, they are for standardised amounts which may therefore not match the size of hedge needed exactly.

Statement B is incorrect: Options afford the holder the right but not the obligation to exercise an option. They can be allowed to lapse. In the case of exchange traded options they can also be sold on mid-term.

Statement C is correct: A forward rate agreement ('FRA') creates an obligation for a 'top-up' payment or receipt. In the case of a loan, when the FRA payment it is added to the underlying loan interest payment, the net interest payment is fixed at the FRA rate.

Statement D is incorrect: The statement refers to smoothing (a mix of fixed and floating rates to make effective interest rates less variable.) Matching – generally employed by banks – refers to matching interest rates on asset to the interest rate on liabilities.

Syllabus area G4b

2   A   Forward rates are calculated by using interest rate parity:

$F_0 = S_0 \times \dfrac{(1+i_c)}{(1+i_b)}$ The six month forward is required but annual interest rates are given so they must be halved.

= 20 × (1.035/1.015)

= 20.39 Dinar to the $

Syllabus area G2b

3   D   Sales volume affects contribution (i.e. both revenue and variable cost). A sensitivity calculation states how far in percentage terms contribution can fall before NPV (currently $1,300) reaches zero. The present value of contribution is currently $24,550, so this could afford to drop by $1,300/$24,550, or 5.3%.

Syllabus area D3b

4   D   Total return to shareholders is a combination of income and capital gain. The capital gain over the period is $3.50 – $3.10 = 40c a share. Dividends were 21c so total return was (40 + 21) = 61c. As a percentage of the opening share price ('what return has been generated with the money tied up from the start of the period') = 61/310 = 19.7%

Syllabus area A3d

5   A   In a weak form efficient market, all investors are aware of previous share price movements. This means patterns will not reliably repeat (for example if all investors predict a price fall at the same time, they will all wait to buy shares, meaning the price does not fall as trading stops). The fact that Gurdip believes she can spot and trade reliably based on historical patterns suggests she does not consider the markets to be even weak-form efficient.

Syllabus area F4a

6   D   Statement A is incorrect: A linear relationship between the cost of equity and financial risk suggest the cost of equity line to be straight. In the tradition view it curves upwards – financial risk is assumed to be more acute per unit increase in gearing at higher gearing levels.

Statement B is incorrect: In Modigliani-Miller (no tax) the Weighted Average Cost of Capital line is flat, not the cost of equity line. The latter is upwards sloping reflecting financial risk.

Statement C is incorrect: Pecking order theory would suggest convertible debt is preferable to preference shares, perhaps because interest on convertible debt is tax deductible.

Statement D is correct: Business risk is generated by the projects invested in, not where the finance comes from. As the projects are unaffected by the source of their finance, business risk is therefore unaffected by the capital structure decision.

Syllabus area E4a&b

7   C   A fall in a country's exchange rate (for example if in America to US $ exchange rate fell from $2: 1€ to $3: 1€ means $ revenue for a given level of exports will increase. A fall in the exchange rate will make imports more expensive. Given imports may include raw materials, this pushes local prices up – inflation.

Syllabus area B1b

8   B   Options A,C and D are all likely to increase shareholder wealth. A lower cost of capital will increase the net present value ('NPV') of projects in the business, increasing the business' value. Taking on positive NPV projects adds to business value and therefore shareholder wealth. Similarly, complying with corporate governance codes is likely to be met with a reduced cost of equity as shareholders feel risk is reduced if there business if being well managed. A lower cost of equity will again increase the NPV of the business and add to shareholder wealth.

However, linking rewards to earnings per share may not increase wealth – this is a short term measure, whereas wealth is a long term value proposition. This may encourage short-termism which could actually be damaging to long term value (for example, cancelling training to save money or reducing research and development expenditure). In addition, if directors' bonuses increase as a result, there will be less cash available for distribution to shareholders. Although not guaranteed to damage shareholder wealth, it is the least likely to create it.

Syllabus area D1e

9   B   Value for money is concerned with measuring a combination of economy, efficiency and effectiveness.

Statement A concerns economy: the cost of inputs

Statement B concerns efficiency: the ratio of inputs to outputs. Minimising waste is consistent with increasing efficiency.

Statement C concerns effectiveness: the quality of outputs. Focussing on meeting objectives is measuring output quality.

Statement D is less directly concerned with economy, efficiency, or effectiveness.

Syllabus area A4b

10   B   Statement 1 is correct: the term negotiable means it can be sold on before maturity.

Statement 2 is incorrect: commercial paper (short term corporate debt) is generally less risk than treasury bills (short term government debt) hence commercial paper commands a higher yield (return).

Statement 3 is correct: By definition a discount instrument does not provide a return by way of additional interest, rather they are issued at a discount and redeemed at par – the difference representing the return.

Syllabus area B3c

11   D   Operational Gearing refers to the proportion of costs that are fixed. One approach to measuring this is to calculate Contribution / profit before interest and tax ('PBIT'). Contribution only contains variable cost, whereas PBIT is after both variable and fixed cost. A higher ratio indicates a higher proportion of fixed costs.

In this case, cost of sales = $50,000 of which 60% is variable cost = ($50,000 × 60%) = $30,000.

Hence contribution = Sales – Variable cost = $60,000 – $30,000 = $30,000

Operational gearing = $30,000/$10,000 = 3 times.

Syllabus area E3d

12 A If the credit period is reduced to 60 days, receivables will become (30/365) × $20 million = $3,287,671.

This is ($4 million – $3,287,671=) $712,329 lower than before, saving interest of 12% × $712,329 = $85,479 p.a.

This interest is saved as lower receivables implies more money (lower overdraft) in the bank.

Syllabus area C2d

13 D Financial management concerns the management of cash flow and wealth generation. This encompasses Investment, financial and dividend decisions ('financial strategy'), financial planning and control and risk management. The latter is safeguarding future cash flows, and lower risk should result in a lower cost of capital, increasing the value of the business for the shareholders.

Syllabus area A1a

14 C The 31.1c dividend grew into 36.0c in 3 years. Assuming a constant per annum growth rate:

$31.1(1+g)^3$ $=$ 36

$(1+g)^3$ $=$ $(36/31.1)$

g $=$ $\sqrt[3]{(36/31.1)} - 1$

$=$ 0.05 or 5%

P_0 $=$ $\dfrac{d_0(1+g)}{(r_e - g)}$ From formula sheet

$=$ $\dfrac{36(1.05)}{(0.12 - 0.05)}$

$=$ $540 = \$5.40$

Syllabus area F2c

15 A Statement A is correct: by definition translation risk is the risk that movements in the spot exchange rate will create profits or losses upon re-translation of foreign denominate assets/liabilities at a reporting point.

Statement B is incorrect – economic risk is the long-run risk to the Net Present Value of an overseas operation as a result of long-term exchange rate movement trends.

Statement C is incorrect: transaction risk relates to cash – the risk that domestic cash flow is different from expected due to movements in the spot exchange rate between the point of commitment (sale/purchase overseas generally) and settlement (customer / supplier payment).

Statement D is incorrect: interest rate risk is not directly relevant to foreign exchange risk.

Syllabus area G1a

16 A The length of the working capital cycle is the difference in time between cash being paid to suppliers for raw materials and cash being received from customers.

It is calculated as Receivables days + inventory days – payables days. In this case inventory has been analysed into component parts hence : 52 + 42 + 30 + 45 – 66 = 103 days

Syllabus area C3a

17 C Risk pooling is seen as a benefit. Banks for example have many borrowers and many lenders. If one borrower fails this risk is spread over many lenders, meaning the risk to any one lender is drastically reduced.

Maturity transformation is seen as a benefit. Many short term deposits can be transformed into long term loans as short term deposits are placed and removed at different times, so there is a 'stock' of cash in the system at any one time that can be lent for the long term.

Interest rate fixing is not usually seen as a benefit of financial intermediation.

Syllabus area B2b

18   B   Statement 1 is correct - Sufficient working capital should be maintained to ensure bills can be paid on time, however working capital (receivables, inventory, payables) do not earn a return as such, so excessive working capital is undesirable – spare cash for example should be temporarily placed to earn a return (provided risk is low).

Statement 2 is incorrect – A conservative approach to working capital investment implies aiming to keep relatively high levels of working capital. The reason for this is generally to reduce risk (less risk of inventory shortages, give customers plenty of time to pay, pay supplier cash) but it is expensive – it is money tied up not directly earning a return – hence will decrease profitability, not increase it.

Statement 3 is correct – too much or too little working capital leads to poor business performance. Too much reduces profitability, too little is risky. Hence managing it to an appropriate level is important for a business if it is to be successful.

Syllabus area C1b

19   B   The conversion value is $100 cash or 70 shares, whichever is worth more (as conversion is at the investor's option). The share price on conversion is predicted to be $1.25 \times (1.04)^5 = 1.52, hence if converted the shares would be worth $70 \times $1.52 = 106.40. As this is more than the cash alternative ($100) investors would choose to convert, hence the conversion value = $106.40.

The investor pays market price, and they receive the pre tax interest hence the pre tax cost of debt is used to value the loan note:

Time		Cash flow ($)	Discount factor 10%	Present value ($)
1-5	Interest	$8\% \times $100 = 8	3.791	30.33
5	Redemption proceeds	$106.4	0.621	66.07
				96.40

$96.40 = $96 to the nearest $

Syllabus area F3a

20   C   Statements 1 and 3 refer to fiscal policy – the balance of taxation and government expenditure.

Statements 2 and 4 refer to monetary policy: control of the money supply and interest rates.

Syllabus area B1b

Section B – Question 1

Marking scheme

		Marks
(a)	Nature of the business	1-2
	Operating cycle	1-2
	Terms of trade	1-2
	Risk appetite	1-2
	Other relevant factors	1-2
		Max 6
(b)	Inventory cost under current ordering policy	1
	Revised holding and ordering costs	1
	Inventory cost if discount is taken	1
	Benefit if bulk purchase discount taken	1
		4
		10

(a) There are many factors which influence the formulation of working capital policy including:

The nature of the business: Service businesses for example don't require large amount of physical inventory so need less working capital. A supermarket does not generally sell on credit so will not have any receivables.

The length of the operating cycle: For example, a manufacturing company with a long production cycle (whisky distilling for example) will naturally need more working capital as it has to fund more inventory.

The terms of trade: Periods of credit tend to be fairly standardised around industry segments and are a basis for competition. For example, if the industry standard customer credit in an industry is 30 day terms, offering less may lose business, offering more may gain business.

Risk appetite: A risk-seeking business will aim for low levels of working capital (known as an 'aggressive' policy). This results in less money tied up in working capital, hence the business is more profitable as finance costs are reduced. However, chasing debts too vigorously may lose custom, under-stocking risks unsatisfied customers or disrupted production and taking excessive periods of credit from suppliers may mean supplier goodwill is lost and supply disruptions may occur. There is a balance to strike.

Similarly a risk-seeking business may aim to finance working capital more with short-term finance than long-term (again, known as an 'aggressive' policy), such as bank overdrafts, short term loans and supplier credit. Again, this is profitable (short term finance is cheaper than long term as it is low risk from the lender's perspective) but is riskier than long-term as short-term finance is renewed more frequently – it may be refused when seeking to renew and new terms/rates may be applied.

The reverse approach would apply for a risk-averse business.

(b)   **Current cost**

= purchase cost + order cost + holding cost

Purchase cost = 120,000 units × $7.50 = $900,000 pa

Order costs = number of orders × fixed order cost = (120,000/10,000) × $200 = $2,400 pa

Holding cost = average inventory level × cost per unit per year = (10,000/2) × $1 = $5,000.

Total current cost = $900,000 + $2,400 + $5,000 = $907,400

To gain the discount, the company must **order 30,000 units** at which point the cost will be:

= purchase cost + order cost + holding cost

Purchase cost = 120,000 units × $7.50 × (1 – 3.6%) = $867,600 pa

Order costs = number of orders × fixed order cost = (120,000/30,000) × $200 = $800 pa

Holding cost = average inventory level × cost per unit per year = (30,000/2) × $2.20 = $33,000.

Total current cost = $867,600 + $800 + $33,000 = $901,400.

Thus by ordering 30,000 at a time, Cat Co are ($907,400 – $901,400 =) $6,000 per annum better off.

Question 2

Text references. Valuations are covered in Chapter 17.

Top tips. Interpret the mark allocation for part (b) carefully – 4 marks, 2 for advantages, 2 for disadvantages. Assume a mark per point. Decide on the points you'll make and spend 30 seconds thinking here – you want your BEST 4 points not the FIRST 4 points you think of.

Easy marks. There are easy marks for calculations in part (a) – just don't spend too much time on each one as they are only worth 2 marks per valuation!

Marking scheme

		Marks
(a)	Market capitalisation	2
	Calculation of Net Asset value (liquidation basis)	2
	Calculation of price/earnings ratio basis	2
		6
(b)	Advantages of using the dividend growth model	2
	Disadvantages of using the dividend growth model	2
		4
		10

(a)   (i)   **Value of the shares**

$20 million on the balance sheet, each share has a nominal value of $0.50 (given) hence ($20m/$0.5=) 40m shares.

Market value of all shares = 40m × $4 per share (given) = **$160 million** (=market capitalisation of the shares)

(ii)   **Net asset value (liquidation basis)**

Note: 'liquidation basis' means net realisable value. If the company was 'liquidated' i.e. broken up and sold, what would be realised?

	$ million
Balance sheet value of equity:	67.2
Deduct book value of non-current assets	(91.0)
Add net realisable of non-current assets	86
Deduct book value of inventory	(3.8)
Add net realisable value of inventory	4.2
Deduct uncollectible receivables (20% × 4.5 =)	(0.9)
Net assets value (liquidation value)	**61.7**

(iii) **Price/earnings valuation**

Latest earnings = $10.1million

Sector P/E = 17   (Note: no adjustment required for lack of marketability of the target company shares as the target is listed.)

Valuation = $10.1m × 17 = **$171.7 million**

(b) **Advantages**

Values a minority holding: Although GWW Co are looking to acquire a controlling stake, there is no reason why current shareholders should accept less than the dividend growth valuation. They currently receive dividends and would continue to do so. It may form a 'floor' in an acceptable price range for negotiations.

Income based: If GWW is being purchased as a going concern, the dividend growth valuation, being income based, is consistent with this. A purchaser is likely to be buying a future income stream.

Disadvantages

Based on estimates of the future: the calculation assumes for example that historical dividend growth will continue into the future. This may well not be the case.

Assumes constant growth rate: the dividend growth rate is assumed not a vary going forwards. This is unlikely to be the case as experience shows dividend growth rates are likely to vary from period to period.

Question 3

Text references. Purchasing power parity, interest rate parity and foreign exchange hedging are covered in Chapter 19.

Top tips. Be brief in part (a) – only 2 marks are available for each sub part. In part (b), calculate the outcomes of the 2 hedging techniques separately and compare the results at the same point in time.

Easy marks. Don't get bogged down in the money market hedge calculation in part (b). Start with the forward market hedge first – the numbers are easier – and work your way up to the harder numbers.

| Marking scheme |

		Marks
(a) Explanation of interest rate parity	2	
Explanation of purchasing power parity	2	
		4
(b) Dollar cost of forward market hedge	1	
Calculation of six month interest rates	1	
Use of correct spot rate	1	
Dollar cost of money market hedge	2	
Comparison of cost of hedges	1	
		6
		10

(a) **(i)** **Relationship between exchange rates and interest rates**

This relationship is explained by Interest Rate Parity (IRP). The forward exchange rate (in itself an unbiased estimate of the future spot rate) is calculated by taking the current spot rate and adjusting it for differences in interest rates in the 2 countries:

$$F_0 = S_0 \times \frac{(1+i_c)}{(1+i_b)}$$

Where F_0 is the forward rate (c:b), S_0 is the spot rate (c:b), i_c is the interest rate in country c, i_b is the interest rate in country b. Essentially if interest rates are higher in country c, this will weaken c's currency cancelling out the differences in interest rates between 2 locations.

(ii) **Relationship between exchange rates and inflation rates**

This relationship is explained by Purchasing Power Parity (PPP). An unbiased estimate of the future spot is calculated by taking the current spot rate and adjusting it for differences in inflation rates in the 2 countries:

$$S_1 = S_0 \times \frac{(1+h_c)}{(1+h_b)}$$

Where S_1 is the spot rate in 1 period's time (c:b), S_0 is the current spot rate (c:b), h_c is the inflation rate in country c for the period, h_b is the inflation rate in country b for the period. PPP is based on 'the law of one price' – with efficient capital markets the same goods should cost the same in different locations. If inflation is higher in country c, this creates an incentive for foreigners to sell there (and subsequently sell 'c' currency) thus weakening the currency. This cancels out the difference in inflation rates.

(b) **Forward hedge**

ZPS CO needs to pay 5 million Pesos in 6 months time. They will receive the 'worst' forward rate – from the bank ie it will cost the most $, hence forward rate = 12.805 pesos/$. In 6 months the payment will be

5m pesos /12.805 = $390,472.

Money market hedge

ZPS Co would pay Pesos immediately, leave on deposit in pesos and pay the 5 million pesos in 6 months' time using this deposit.

The Peso deposit rate is 7.5% pa = (7.5/2) = 3.75% for 6 months.

The amount to put on deposit today would need to be 5,000,000 (1 + 3.75%) = 4,819,277 pesos. This will accrue 3.75% interest over the 6 months and grow into the 5 million pesos needed in 6 months time.

To translate $ into 4,819,277 pesos today would cost 4,819,277/12.5 = $385,542 today (the 12.5 pesos/$ is the 'worst' rate for ZPS Co as it will cost the most $ to buy, hence this is the rate the bank would offer). Assuming this money is borrowed today for the 6 months until the 5 million is paid, this will accrue interest charges at a rate of 4.5% per annum, or (4.5/2=) 2.25% for the six months. The $ amount in 6 months would therefore be: $385, 542 × 1.0225 = $394,217.

The forward hedge is marginally cheaper than the forward hedge, saving ($394,217 – $390,472) $3,745.

Question 4

Text references. Net present value and internal rate of return are covered in Chapters 8 and 9. Return on capital employed is covered in Chapter 7.

Top tips. Lots of students let inflation drag them down in NPV calculations. Make a decision on how you're going to deal with it up-front, and stick to that. Once you've calculated the nominal cash flows, these numbers can be re-used to calculate the Internal rate of return and return on capital employed.

Easy marks. Part (b) contains some easy marks for basic interpretation of your answers in part (a). Remember this paper is 'method marked' so if you get the numbers wrong in part (a), provided you interpret YOUR answers appropriately in part (b), you'll get the credit.

				Marks
(a)	(i)	Inflated income	2	
		Inflated operating costs	2	
		Net present value	1	
				5
	(ii)	Internal rate of return	3	
	(iii)	Return on Capital Employed	3	
(b)		Discussion of investment appraisal findings	3	
		Advice on acceptability of project	1	
				4
				15

(a) **(i)** As inflation rates differ for revenue and cost, nominal cash flows (ie including inflation) need to be calculated and discounted at the nominal rate (also including inflation).

		0	1	2	3	4
Revenue	W1		1,236,000	1,485,400	2,622,000	1,012,950
Variable Cost	W2		(499,200)	(605,500)	(1,080,000)	(421,200)
Fixed cost	W3		(176,800)	(183,872)	(183,872)	(198,876)
Investment		(2,000,000)				
Net cash flow		(2,000,000)	560,000	696,028	1,350,773	392,874
10% discount factor (tables)		1	0.909	0.826	0.751	0.683
Present value		(2,000,000)	509,040	574,919	1,014,430	268,333

Net present value = total of the present value line = $366,722 positive.

(W1) Revenue

$	1	2	3	4
Price (Current terms) ($)	20	20	20	20
Inflation factor	× (1.03)	× (1.03)^2	× (1.03)^3	× (1.03)^4
Inflated price ($)	= 20.60	= 21.22	= 21.85	= 22.51
× Volume (units)	60,000	70,000	120,000	45,000
= Nominal sales ($)	1,236,000	1,485,400	2,622,000	1,012,950

(W2) Variable cost

$	1	2	3	4
Unit cost (current terms) ($)	8	8	8	8
Inflation factor	× (1.04)	× (1.04)^2	× (1.04)^3	× (1.04)^4
Inflated price	= 8.32	= 8.65	= 9.00	= 9.36
× Volume (units)	60,000	70,000	120,000	45,000
= Nominal variable cost ($)	499,200	605,500	1,080,000	421,200

(W3)   Fixed cost

$	1	2	3	4
Fixed cost (current terms) ($)	170,000	170,000	170,000	170,000
× Inflation factor	× (1.04)	× (1.04)^2	× (1.04)^3	× (1.04)^4
= Nominal fixed cost ($)	176,800	183,872	183,872	198,876

(ii)   Internal rate of return.

Net present value (NPV) at 10% = $366,722.

NPV at 20%:

	0	1	2	3	4
Net cash flow (see above)	(2,000,000)	560,000	696,028	1,350,773	392,874
20% discount factor (tables)	1	0.833	0.694	0.579	0.482
Present value	(2,000,000)	466,480	483,043	782,098	189,365

NPV 20% = total of present values = $(79,014) negative.

$$IRR = a + \frac{NPV_a}{(NPV_a - NPV_b)} (b\text{-}a) = 10\% + [(366,722/(366,722 + 79,014)](20 - 10) = \textbf{18.2\%}$$

(iii)   Return on capital employed

$$ROCE = \frac{\text{Average annual accounting profits}}{\text{Average investment}}$$

Average annual accounting profits= total accounting profits / 4

Total accounting profits = total net operating cash inflow – depreciation = (560,000 + 696,028 + 1,350,773 + 392,874) – (2,000,000 – 0) = $999,675

Average annual accounting profit = $999,675/4 = $249,919.

Average investment = (initial cost + scrap) / 2 = ($2,000,000 + 0) / 2 = $1,000,000

ROCE = $249,919/$1,000,000 = 25%

(b)   **NPV:** NPV is positive which suggests the proposal should be accepted on the basis that to do so will increase shareholder wealth.

Internal rate of return: the internal rate of return of 18.2% is in excess of the cost of capital of 10%. This suggests that the proposal should be accepted as the rate of return on the project exceeds the cost of its finance.

Return on capital employed: the return on capital employed of 25% is less than the target rate of 30%. This suggests that the proposal should be rejected as it falls short of the hurdle rate.

Conclusion: On the assumption that the objective behind the decision of whether or not to invest is to maximise shareholder wealth, the project should be accepted. This is on the basis that the NPV is positive. As NPV is a direct measure of the impact that the project is expected to have an shareholder wealth, the NPV calculation gives a direct and unambiguous answer.

Question 5

Marking scheme

			Marks
(a)	(i)	Dividend growth rate	1
		Share price using dividend growth model	2
			3
	(ii)	Capital gearing	2
	(iii)	Weighted average cost of capital	2
(b)		Dividend irrelevance	4
		Dividend relevance	4
			8
			15

(a) (i) **Ex-div share price, using the formula from the formula sheet:**

$$P_0 = \frac{D_0(1+g)}{(r_e - g)}$$

D_0 = latest dividend

g = average annual growth rate

r_e = cost of equity

D_0 = $0.50 (given)

r_e =12.4% (given)

g, using dividend growth model. The 50c dividend is set to grow to 52c in 1 year, a growth of 2/50 = 4%

$P_0 = (\$0.50 \times 1.04) / (0.124 - 0.04) = \$6.19$

(ii) **Gearing using market values**

= MV Debt / (MV Debt + MV Equity)

MV Debt= total value of Bond A plus total value of bond B

= [$20m x (95.08/100)] + [$10m × (102.01/100) = $29.217million.

MV Equity = number of shares × $6.19 (from (i) above) = ($25m/$1) × $6.19 = $154.75m

Gearing = $29.217m / ($29.217m + $154.75m) = 15.9%

(iii) Weighted average cost of capital (WACC)

Source	Cost (%)	Market Value ($m)	Cost x Market Value
Bond A	9.83	19.016	186.92728
Bond B	7.82	10.201	79.77182
Equity	12.4	154.75	1,918.9
		183.967	2,185.5991

WACC = 2,185.5991 / 183.967 = 11.88%

OR using the formula from the formula sheet:

$$WACC = \left[\frac{V_e}{V_e + V_d}\right]k_e + \left[\frac{V_d}{V_e + V_d}\right]k_d$$

but with 3 terms as 3 sources of finance:

WACC = (154.75/183.967)12.4% + (19.016/183.967)9.83% + (10.201/183.967)7.82% = **11.88%**

(b) Modigliani-Miller (MM) dividend irrelevance theory

MM demonstrated that if certain assumptions hold true, the pattern of dividends and changing that pattern should have little or no effect on the value of the organisation.

Their assumptions:

- Perfect information - with perfect (strong form) capital markets there will be no information content in the dividend announcement. In other words, the dividend announcement is not price sensitive information. It will not be telling the investors anything that they didn't know already.

- No taxes – with no taxes there is no taxation reason why investors should prefer dividends (income) to capital gains.

- No transaction costs – with no transaction costs shareholders can costlessly switch between income and capital gains. For example, if dividend policy changes to increased retention and a particular shareholder prefers that the cash was paid out as the dividend, the retention will lead to capital growth in the price of the share and the shareholder can sell off a proportion of their portfolio to 'manufacture' a dividend. There is therefore no liquidity preference reason why changing dividend policy should affect share price.

The importance of dividend policy

However, in the real world:

- Capital markets are semi-strong – announcing a dividend is the creation of publicly available information. If the announcement is different from investor expectations, this is likely to have an effect on share price. This is known as the signalling effect.

- Taxes exist – investors have preferences the tax reasons for either income or capital gains. Switching from one to the other is therefore likely to cause some to sell their shares, and potentially for others to buy more. In other words, due to tax reasons a change in dividend policy is likely to affect share price.

- Transaction costs exist – brokerage fees and other transaction costs mean that it is not costless for investors to switch between incoming capital gains. These costs represent friction in the capital markets and so changing dividend policy is likely to affect share price.

Any change in the status quo is likely to upset some shareholders and cause them to sell shares. The fact that investors like the current policy is known as the clientele effect.

In practice therefore, changes in dividend policy need to be carefully considered as it is highly likely to have an impact on share price. DD Co would be well advised to speak to the investing community openly and transparently to both assess their views and ensure they are fully informed of the reasoning behind the change in policy before the policy change takes effect.

ACCA examiner's answers:
Specimen paper

Section A

1   C

2   A

Using interest rate parity, six-month forward rate = $20.00 \times (1.07/1.03)^{0.5}$ = 20.39 Dinar per \$
Alternatively, $20 \times (1.035/1.015)$ = 20.39 Dinar per \$

3   D

The sensitivity to a change in sales volume = $100 \times 1,300/24,550$ = 5.3%

4   D

Total shareholder return = $100 \times [(350 - 310) + 21]/310$ = 19.7%

5   A

6   D

7   C

8   B

9   B

10   B

11   D

Contribution = $60,000,000 - (50,000,000 \times 0.6)$ = \$30,000,000
Operational gearing = Contribution/PBIT = \$30m/\$10m = 3.0 times

12   A

The current collection period is $4/20 \times 365$ = 73 days
Therefore a reduction to 60 days would be a reduction of 13 days
Hence $13/365 \times \$20m$ = \$712,329
Finance cost saving = $\$712,329 \times 0.12$ = \$85,479

13   D

14   C

The geometric average dividend growth rate is $(36.0/31.1)^{1/3} - 1$ = 5%
The ex div share price = $(36.0 \times 1.05)/(0.12 - 0.05)$ = \$5.40

15   A

16 A

The length of the operating cycle is 52 + 42 + 30 − 66 + 45 = 103 days

17 C

18 B

19 B

Using a conversion value after five years of $106·40 ($1·25 x 1·04^5 x 70) and the before-tax cost of debt of 10%, we have (8 x 3·791) + (106·40 x 0·621) = $96·40 or $96. Conversion is preferred in five years' time as it offers a higher value than the redemption value of $100.

20 C

Section B

1   (a)   Working capital policies can cover the level of investment in current assets, the way in which current assets are financed, and the procedures to follow in managing elements of working capital such as inventory, trade receivables, cash and trade payables. The twin objectives of working capital management are liquidity and profitability, and working capital policies support the achievement of these objectives. There are several factors which influence the formulation of working capital policies as follows:

Nature of the business
The nature of the business influences the formulation of working capital policy because it influences the size of the elements of working capital. A manufacturing company, for example, may have high levels of inventory and trade receivables, a service company may have low levels of inventory and high levels of trade receivables, and a supermarket chain may have high levels of inventory and low levels of trade receivables.

The operating cycle
The length of the operating cycle, together with the desired level of investment in current assets, will determine the amount of working capital finance needed. Working capital policies will therefore be formulated so as to optimise as much as possible the length of the operating cycle and its components, which are the inventory conversion period, the receivables conversion period and payables deferral period.

Terms of trade
Since a company must compete with other companies to be successful, a key factor in the formulation of working capital policy will be the terms of trade offered by competitors. The terms of trade must be comparable with those of competitors and the level of receivables will be determined by the credit period offered and the average credit period taken by customers.

Risk appetite of company
A risk-averse company will tend to operate with higher levels of inventory and receivables than a company which is more risk-seeking.

Similarly, a risk-averse company will seek to use long-term finance for permanent current assets and some of its fluctuating current assets (conservative policy), while a more risk-seeking company will seek to use short-term finance for fluctuating current assets as well as for a portion of the permanent current assets of the company (an aggressive policy).

(b)   Bulk purchase discount

Current number of orders = 120,000/10,000 = 12 orders
Current ordering cost = 12 x 200 = $2,400 per year
Current holding cost = (10,000/2) x 1 = $5,000 per year
Annual cost of components = $900,000 per year
Inventory cost under current policy = 900,000 + 2,400 + 5,000 = $907,400 per year

To gain the bulk purchase discount, the order size must increase to 30,000 components.

The number of orders will decrease to 120,000/30,000 = 4 orders per year
The revised ordering cost will be 4 x 200 = $800 per year
The revised holding cost will be (30,000/2) x 2·2 = $33,000 per year
The annual cost of components will be 120,000 x 7·50 x 0·964 = $867,600 per year
Inventory cost using discount = 867,600 + 800 + 33,000 = $901,400 per year

Cat Co will benefit financially if it takes the bulk discount offered by the supplier, as it saves $6,000 per year in inventory costs or 0·66% of current inventory costs.

2 (a) (i) Market capitalisation of GWW Co

Value of ordinary shares in statement of financial position = $20·0 million
Nominal (par) value of ordinary shares = 50 cents
Number of ordinary shares of company = 20m/0·5 = 40 million shares
Ordinary share price = $4·00 per share
Market capitalisation = 40m x 4 = $160 million

(ii) Net asset value (liquidation basis)

Current net asset value (NAV) = 91·0m + 8·3m – 7·1m – 25·0m = $67·2 million

Decrease in value of non-current assets on liquidation = 86·0m – 91·0m = $5 million
Increase in value of inventory on liquidation = 4·2m – 3·8m = $0·4 million
Decrease in value of trade receivables = 4·5m x 0·2 = $0·9 million

NAV (liquidation basis) = 67·2m – 5m + 0·4m – 0·9m = $61·7 million

(iii) Price/earnings ratio value

Historic earnings of GWW Co = $10·1 million
Average price/earnings ratio of GWW Co business sector = 17 times
Price/earnings ratio value of GWW Co = 17 x 10·1m = $171·7 million

(**Tutorial note:** *Price/earnings ratio calculation using forecast earnings would receive full credit*)

(b) The dividend growth model values the shares of GWW Co as the present value of the future dividends expected by its shareholders. The input variables for the valuation model are the cost of equity, the future dividend growth rate and the current dividend per share (or next year's dividend per share).

One advantage of the dividend growth model is that its input variables are well-known and understandable. Dividend information is published regularly in the financial media and discussed by financial analysts. Many companies now provide information in their annual report on the cost of equity.

For shareholders, another advantage of the dividend growth model is that it gives an estimate of the wealth they would lose if they sold their shares now and hence the model estimates the minimum price at which they might be persuaded to sell their shares. This can be useful information for both sellers and buyers.

One disadvantage of the dividend growth model, however, is that the cost of equity and the dividend growth rate are future values and so cannot be known with any certainty. Forecasts of future dividend growth rates are often based on historical dividend trends, but there is no guarantee that the future will repeat the past.

Another disadvantage is that although experience shows that dividends per share do not grow smoothly, this is assumed by the dividend growth model. The future dividend growth rate is assumed to be constant in perpetuity, which is an idealised state of affairs.

3 (a) Movements in exchange rates can be related to changes in interest rates and to changes in inflation rates. The relationship between exchange rates and interest rates is called interest rate parity, while the relationship between exchange rates and inflation rates is called purchasing power parity.

Interest rate parity holds that the relationship between the spot exchange rate and the forward exchange rate between two currencies can be linked to the relative nominal interest rates of the two countries. The forward rate can be found by multiplying the spot rate by the ratio of the interest rates of the two countries. The currency of the country with the higher nominal interest rate will be forecast to weaken against the currency of the country with the lower nominal interest rate. Both the spot rate and the forward rate are available in the current foreign exchange market, and the forward rate can be guaranteed by using a forward contract.

Purchasing power parity holds that the current spot exchange rate and the future spot exchange rate between two currencies can be linked to the relative inflation rates of the two countries. The future spot rate is the spot rate which occurs at the end of a given period of time. The currency of the country with the higher inflation rate will be forecast to weaken against the currency of the country with the lower inflation rate. Purchasing power parity is based on the law of one price, which suggests that, in equilibrium, identical goods should sell for the same price in different countries, allowing for the exchange rate. Purchasing power parity holds in the longer term rather than the shorter term and so is often used to provide long-term forecasts of exchange rate movements, for example, for use in investment appraisal.

(b) The costs of the two exchange rate hedges need to be compared at the same point in time, e.g. in six months' time.

Forward market hedge
Interest payment = 5,000,000 pesos
Six-month forward rate for buying pesos = 12·805 pesos per $
Dollar cost of peso interest using forward market = 5,000,000/12·805 = $390,472

Money market hedge

ZPS Co has a 5 million peso liability in six months and so needs to create a 5 million peso asset at the same point in time. The six-month peso deposit rate is 7·5%/2 = 3·75%. The quantity of pesos to be deposited now is therefore 5,000,000/1·0375 = 4,819,277 pesos.

The quantity of dollars needed to purchase these pesos is 4,819,277/12·500 = $385,542 and ZPS Co would borrow this quantity of dollars now. The six-month dollar borrowing rate = 4·5%/2 = 2·25% and so in six months' time the debt will be 385,542 x 1·0225 = $394,217. This is the dollar cost of the peso interest using a money market hedge.

Comparing the $390,472 cost of the forward market hedge with the $394,217 cost using a money market hedge, it is clear that the forward market should be used to hedge the peso interest payment as it is cheaper by $3,745.

(Tutorial note: *Geometric mean interest rates would receive full credit*)

4 (a) (i) Calculation of NPV

Year	0	1	2	3	4
	$	$	$	$	$
Investment	(2,000,000)				
Income		1,236,000	1,485,400	2,622,000	1,012,950
Operating costs		676,000	789,372	1,271,227	620,076
Net cash flow	(2,000,000)	560,000	696,028	1,350,773	392,874
Discount at 10%	1·000	0·909	0·826	0·751	0·683
Present values	(2,000,000)	509,040	574,919	1,014,430	268,333

Net present value: $366,722

Workings

Calculation of income

Year	1	2	3	4
Inflated selling price ($/unit)	20·60	21·22	21·85	22·51
Demand (units/year)	60,000	70,000	120,000	45,000
Income ($/year)	1,236,000	1,485,400	2,622,000	1,012,950

Calculation of operating costs

Year	1	2	3	4
Inflated variable cost ($/unit)	8·32	8·65	9·00	9·36
Demand (units/year)	60,000	70,000	120,000	45,000
Variable costs ($/year)	499,200	605,500	1,080,000	421,200
Inflated fixed costs ($/year)	176,800	183,872	191,227	198,876
Operating costs ($/year)	676,000	789,372	1,271,227	620,076

Alternative calculation of operating costs

Year	1	2	3	4
Variable cost ($/unit)	8	8	8	8
Demand (units/year)	60,000	70,000	120,000	45,000
Variable costs ($/year)	480,000	560,000	960,000	360,000
Fixed costs ($/year)	170,000	170,000	170,000	170,000
Operating costs ($/year)	650,000	730,000	1,130,000	530,000
Inflated costs ($/year)	676,000	789,568	1,271,096	620,025

(ii) Calculation of internal rate of return

Year	0	1	2	3	4
	$	$	$	$	$
Net cash flow	(2,000,000)	560,000	696,028	1,350,773	392,874
Discount at 20%	1·000	0·833	0·694	0·579	0·482
Present values	(2,000,000)	466,480	483,043	782,098	189,365

Net present value ($79,014)

Internal rate of return = 10 + ((20 – 10) x 366,722)/(366,722 + 79,014) = 10 + 8·2 = 18·2%

(iii) Calculation of return on capital employed

Total cash inflow = 560,000 + 696,028 + 1,350,773 + 392,874 = $2,999,675
Total depreciation and initial investment are same, as there is no scrap value.
Total accounting profit = 2,999,675 – 2,000,000 = $999,675
Average annual accounting profit = 999,675/4 = $249,919
Average investment = 2,000,000/2 = $1,000,000
Return on capital employed = 100 x 249,919/1,000,000 = 25%

(b) The investment proposal has a positive net present value (NPV) of $366,722 and is therefore financially acceptable. The results of the other investment appraisal methods do not alter this financial acceptability, as the NPV decision rule will always offer the correct investment advice.

The internal rate of return (IRR) method also recommends accepting the investment proposal, since the IRR of 18·2% is greater than the 10% return required by PV Co. If the advice offered by the IRR method differed from that offered by the NPV method, the advice offered by the NPV method would be preferred.

The calculated return on capital employed of 25% is less than the target return of 30%, but as indicated earlier, the investment proposal is financially acceptable as it has a positive NPV. The reason why PV Co has a target return on capital employed of 30% should be investigated. This may be an out-of-date hurdle rate which has not been updated for changed economic circumstances.

5 **(a)** **(i)** Dividend growth rate = 100 x ((52/50) – 1) = 100 x (1·04 – 1) = 4% per year
Share price using DGM = (50 x 1·04)/(0·124 – 0·04) = 52/0·84 = 619c or $6·19

(ii) Number of ordinary shares = 25 million
Market value of equity = 25m x 6·19 = $154·75 million
Market value of Bond A issue = 20m x 95·08/100 = $19·016m
Market value of Bond B issue = 10m x 102·01/100 = $10·201m
Market value of debt = $29·217m
Market value of capital employed = 154·75m + 29·217m = $183·967m
Capital gearing = 100 x 29·217/183·967 = 15·9%

(iii) WACC = ((12·4 x 154·75) + (9·83 x 19·016) + (7·82 x 10·201))/183·967 = 11·9%

(b) Miller and Modigliani showed that, in a perfect capital market, the value of a company depended on its investment decisions alone, and not on its dividend or financing decisions. In such a market, a change in dividend policy by DD Co would not affect its share price or its market capitalisation. Miller and Modigliani showed that the value of a company was maximised if it invested in all projects with a positive net present value (its optimal investment schedule). The company could pay any level of dividend and if it had insufficient finance, make up the shortfall by issuing new equity. Since investors had perfect information, they were indifferent between dividends and capital gains. Shareholders who were unhappy with the level of dividend declared by a company could gain a 'home-made dividend' by selling some of their shares. This was possible since there are no transaction costs in a perfect capital market.

Against this view are several arguments for a link between dividend policy and share prices. For example, it has been argued that investors prefer certain dividends now rather than uncertain capital gains in the future (the 'bird-in-the-hand' argument).

It has also been argued that real-world capital markets are not perfect, but semi-strong form efficient. Since perfect information is therefore not available, it is possible for information asymmetry to exist between shareholders and the managers of a company. Dividend announcements may give new information to shareholders and as a result, in a semi-strong form efficient market, share prices may change. The size and direction of the share price change will depend on the difference between the dividend announcement and the expectations of shareholders. This is referred to as the 'signalling properties of dividends'.

It has been found that shareholders are attracted to particular companies as a result of being satisfied by their dividend policies. This is referred to as the 'clientele effect'. A company with an established dividend policy is therefore likely to have an established dividend clientele. The existence of this dividend clientele implies that the share price may change if there is a change in the dividend policy of the company, as shareholders sell their shares in order to reinvest in another company with a more satisfactory dividend policy. In a perfect capital market, the existence of dividend clienteles is irrelevant, since substituting one company for another will not incur any transaction costs. Since real-world capital markets are not perfect, however, the existence of dividend clienteles suggests that if DD Co changes its dividend policy, its share price could be affected.

Fundamentals Level – Skills Module, Paper F9
Financial Management

Specimen Exam Marking Scheme

			Marks	Marks

Section A

1–20 Two marks per question — — 40

Section B

			Marks	Marks
1	**(a)**	Nature of the business	1–2	
		Operating cycle	1–2	
		Terms of trade	1–2	
		Risk appetite	1–2	
		Other relevant factors	1–2	
			Maximum	6
	(b)	Inventory cost under current ordering policy	1	
		Revised holding and ordering costs	1	
		Inventory cost if discount is taken	1	
		Benefit if bulk purchase discount taken	1	
				4
				10
2	**(a)**	Market capitalisation	2	
		Calculation of NAV (liquidation basis)	2	
		Calculation of price/earnings ratio value	2	
				6
	(b)	Advantages of using the dividend growth model	2	
		Disadvantages of using the dividend growth model	2	
				4
				10
3	**(a)**	Explanation of interest rate parity	2	
		Explanation of purchasing power parity	2	
				4
	(b)	Dollar cost of forward market hedge	1	
		Calculation of six-month interest rates	1	
		Use of correct spot rate	1	
		Dollar cost of money market hedge	2	
		Comparison of cost of hedges	1	
				6
				10

				Marks	Marks

4 **(a)** **(i)** Inflated income — 2
Inflated operating costs — 2
Net present value — 1
— 5

(ii) Internal rate of return — 3

(iii) Return on capital employed — 3

(b) Discussion of investment appraisal findings — 3
Advice on acceptability of project — 1
— 4
15

5 **(a)** **(i)** Dividend growth rate — 1
Share price using dividend growth model — 2
— 3

(ii) Capital gearing — 2

(iii) Weighted average cost of capital — 2

(b) Dividend irrelevance — 4
Dividend relevance — 4
— 8
15

Mathematical tables

Formulae Sheet

Economic order quantity

$$= \sqrt{\frac{2C_0 D}{C_h}}$$

Miller–Orr Model

Return point = Lower limit + $(\frac{1}{3} \times$ spread$)$

$$\text{Spread} = 3\left[\frac{\frac{3}{4} \times \text{transaction cost} \times \text{variance of cash flows}}{\text{interest rate}}\right]^{\frac{1}{3}}$$

The Capital Asset Pricing Model

$$E\left(r_i\right) = R_f + \beta_i \left(E\left(r_m\right) - R_f\right)$$

The asset beta formula

$$\beta_a = \left[\frac{V_e}{\left(V_e + V_d\left(1-T\right)\right)}\beta_e\right] + \left[\frac{V_d\left(1-T\right)}{\left(V_e + V_d\left(1-T\right)\right)}\beta_d\right]$$

The Growth Model

$$P_0 = \frac{D_0\left(1+g\right)}{\left(r_e - g\right)}$$

Gordon's growth approximation

$$g = br_e$$

The weighted average cost of capital

$$\text{WACC} = \left[\frac{V_e}{V_e + V_d}\right]k_e + \left[\frac{V_d}{V_e + V_d}\right]k_d\left(1-T\right)$$

The Fisher formula

$$\left(1+i\right) = \left(1+r\right)\left(1+h\right)$$

Purchasing power parity and interest rate parity

$$S_1 = S_0 \times \frac{\left(1+h_c\right)}{\left(1+h_b\right)} \qquad F_0 = S_0 \times \frac{\left(1+i_c\right)}{\left(1+i_b\right)}$$

Present Value Table

Present value of 1 i.e. $(1 + r)^{-n}$

Where   r = discount rate
         n = number of periods until payment

Discount rate (r)

Periods (n)	1%	2%	3%	4%	5%	6%	7%	8%	9%	10%	
1	0·990	0·980	0·971	0·962	0·952	0·943	0·935	0·926	0·917	0·909	1
2	0·980	0·961	0·943	0·925	0·907	0·890	0·873	0·857	0·842	0·826	2
3	0·971	0·942	0·915	0·889	0·864	0·840	0·816	0·794	0·772	0·751	3
4	0·961	0·924	0·888	0·855	0·823	0·792	0·763	0·735	0·708	0·683	4
5	0·951	0·906	0·863	0·822	0·784	0·747	0·713	0·681	0·650	0·621	5
6	0·942	0·888	0·837	0·790	0·746	0·705	0·666	0·630	0·596	0·564	6
7	0·933	0·871	0·813	0·760	0·711	0·665	0·623	0·583	0·547	0·513	7
8	0·923	0·853	0·789	0·731	0·677	0·627	0·582	0·540	0·502	0·467	8
9	0·914	0·837	0·766	0·703	0·645	0·592	0·544	0·500	0·460	0·424	9
10	0·905	0·820	0·744	0·676	0·614	0·558	0·508	0·463	0·422	0·386	10
11	0·896	0·804	0·722	0·650	0·585	0·527	0·475	0·429	0·388	0·350	11
12	0·887	0·788	0·701	0·625	0·557	0·497	0·444	0·397	0·356	0·319	12
13	0·879	0·773	0·681	0·601	0·530	0·469	0·415	0·368	0·326	0·290	13
14	0·870	0·758	0·661	0·577	0·505	0·442	0·388	0·340	0·299	0·263	14
15	0·861	0·743	0·642	0·555	0·481	0·417	0·362	0·315	0·275	0·239	15

(n)	11%	12%	13%	14%	15%	16%	17%	18%	19%	20%	
1	0·901	0·893	0·885	0·877	0·870	0·862	0·855	0·847	0·840	0·833	1
2	0·812	0·797	0·783	0·769	0·756	0·743	0·731	0·718	0·706	0·694	2
3	0·731	0·712	0·693	0·675	0·658	0·641	0·624	0·609	0·593	0·579	3
4	0·659	0·636	0·613	0·592	0·572	0·552	0·534	0·516	0·499	0·482	4
5	0·593	0·567	0·543	0·519	0·497	0·476	0·456	0·437	0·419	0·402	5
6	0·535	0·507	0·480	0·456	0·432	0·410	0·390	0·370	0·352	0·335	6
7	0·482	0·452	0·425	0·400	0·376	0·354	0·333	0·314	0·296	0·279	7
8	0·434	0·404	0·376	0·351	0·327	0·305	0·285	0·266	0·249	0·233	8
9	0·391	0·361	0·333	0·308	0·284	0·263	0·243	0·225	0·209	0·194	9
10	0·352	0·322	0·295	0·270	0·247	0·227	0·208	0·191	0·176	0·162	10
11	0·317	0·287	0·261	0·237	0·215	0·195	0·178	0·162	0·148	0·135	11
12	0·286	0·257	0·231	0·208	0·187	0·168	0·152	0·137	0·124	0·112	12
13	0·258	0·229	0·204	0·182	0·163	0·145	0·130	0·116	0·104	0·093	13
14	0·232	0·205	0·181	0·160	0·141	0·125	0·111	0·099	0·088	0·078	14
15	0·209	0·183	0·160	0·140	0·123	0·108	0·095	0·084	0·074	0·065	15

Annuity Table

Present value of an annuity of 1 i.e. $\dfrac{1-(1+r)^{-n}}{r}$

Where   r = discount rate
           n = number of periods

Discount rate (r)

Periods (n)	1%	2%	3%	4%	5%	6%	7%	8%	9%	10%	
1	0·990	0·980	0·971	0·962	0·952	0·943	0·935	0·926	0·917	0·909	1
2	1·970	1·942	1·913	1·886	1·859	1·833	1·808	1·783	1·759	1·736	2
3	2·941	2·884	2·829	2·775	2·723	2·673	2·624	2·577	2·531	2·487	3
4	3·902	3·808	3·717	3·630	3·546	3·465	3·387	3·312	3·240	3·170	4
5	4·853	4·713	4·580	4·452	4·329	4·212	4·100	3·993	3·890	3·791	5
6	5·795	5·601	5·417	5·242	5·076	4·917	4·767	4·623	4·486	4·355	6
7	6·728	6·472	6·230	6·002	5·786	5·582	5·389	5·206	5·033	4·868	7
8	7·652	7·325	7·020	6·733	6·463	6·210	5·971	5·747	5·535	5·335	8
9	8·566	8·162	7·786	7·435	7·108	6·802	6·515	6·247	5·995	5·759	9
10	9·471	8·983	8·530	8·111	7·722	7·360	7·024	6·710	6·418	6·145	10
11	10·37	9·787	9·253	8·760	8·306	7·887	7·499	7·139	6·805	6·495	11
12	11·26	10·58	9·954	9·385	8·863	8·384	7·943	7·536	7·161	6·814	12
13	12·13	11·35	10·63	9·986	9·394	8·853	8·358	7·904	7·487	7·103	13
14	13·00	12·11	11·30	10·56	9·899	9·295	8·745	8·244	7·786	7·367	14
15	13·87	12·85	11·94	11·12	10·38	9·712	9·108	8·559	8·061	7·606	15

(n)	11%	12%	13%	14%	15%	16%	17%	18%	19%	20%	
1	0·901	0·893	0·885	0·877	0·870	0·862	0·855	0·847	0·840	0·833	1
2	1·713	1·690	1·668	1·647	1·626	1·605	1·585	1·566	1·547	1·528	2
3	2·444	2·402	2·361	2·322	2·283	2·246	2·210	2·174	2·140	2·106	3
4	3·102	3·037	2·974	2·914	2·855	2·798	2·743	2·690	2·639	2·589	4
5	3·696	3·605	3·517	3·433	3·352	3·274	3·199	3·127	3·058	2·991	5
6	4·231	4·111	3·998	3·889	3·784	3·685	3·589	3·498	3·410	3·326	6
7	4·712	4·564	4·423	4·288	4·160	4·039	3·922	3·812	3·706	3·605	7
8	5·146	4·968	4·799	4·639	4·487	4·344	4·207	4·078	3·954	3·837	8
9	5·537	5·328	5·132	4·946	4·772	4·607	4·451	4·303	4·163	4·031	9
10	5·889	5·650	5·426	5·216	5·019	4·833	4·659	4·494	4·339	4·192	10
11	6·207	5·938	5·687	5·453	5·234	5·029	4·836	4·656	4·486	4·327	11
12	6·492	6·194	5·918	5·660	5·421	5·197	4·988	4·793	4·611	4·439	12
13	6·750	6·424	6·122	5·842	5·583	5·342	5·118	4·910	4·715	4·533	13
14	6·982	6·628	6·302	6·002	5·724	5·468	5·229	5·008	4·802	4·611	14
15	7·191	6·811	6·462	6·142	5·847	5·575	5·324	5·092	4·876	4·675	15

Mathematical tables

Review Form – Paper F9 Financial Management (06/14)

Name: _____   **Address:** _____

_____

_____

How have you used this Kit?
(Tick one box only)

☐ Home study (book only)

☐ On a course: college _____

☐ With 'correspondence' package

☐ Other _____

Why did you decide to purchase this Kit?
(Tick one box only)

☐ Have used the complementary Study text

☐ Have used other BPP products in the past

☐ Recommendation by friend/colleague

☐ Recommendation by a lecturer at college

☐ Saw advertising

☐ Other _____

During the past six months do you recall seeing/receiving any of the following?
(Tick as many boxes as are relevant)

☐ Our advertisement in *Student Accountant*

☐ Our advertisement in *Pass*

☐ Our advertisement in *PQ*

☐ Our brochure with a letter through the post

☐ Our website www.bpp.com

Which (if any) aspects of our advertising do you find useful?
(Tick as many boxes as are relevant)

☐ Prices and publication dates of new editions

☐ Information on product content

☐ Facility to order books off-the-page

☐ None of the above

Which BPP products have you used?

Text	☐	Passcards	☐	Home Study Package	☐
Kit	☑	i-Pass	☐		

Your ratings, comments and suggestions would be appreciated on the following areas.

	Very useful	Useful	Not useful
Passing F9			
Questions			
Top Tips etc in answers			
Content and structure of answers			
Mock exam answers			

Overall opinion of this Kit	Excellent ☐		Good ☐		Adequate ☐		Poor ☐

Do you intend to continue using BPP products?	Yes ☐		No ☐	

The BPP author of this edition can be e-mailed at: heatherfreer@bpp.com

Please return this form to: Pippa Riley, ACCA Range Manager, BPP Learning Media Ltd, FREEPOST, London, W12 8AA

Review Form (continued)

TELL US WHAT YOU THINK

Please note any further comments and suggestions/errors below.